How To...

AUDIO ACCESS INCLUDED

Record at Home on a Budget

By Chad Johnson

To access audio visit:
www.halleonard.com/mylibrary

Enter Code
1834-2394-8539-3943

ISBN 978-1-4803-9813-9

HAL•LEONARD®
CORPORATION

7777 W. BLUEMOUND RD. P.O. BOX 13819 MILWAUKEE, WI 53213

In Australia Contact:
Hal Leonard Australia Pty. Ltd.
4 Lentara Court
Cheltenham, Victoria, 3192 Australia
Email: ausadmin@halleonard.com.au

Visit Hal Leonard Online at
www.halleonard.com

CONTENTS

4   About the Author

5   Dedication and Acknowledgments

6   Introduction

8   How to Use This Book

9   About the Recordings

10   **Chapter 1: Basic Equipment Checklist**

28   **Chapter 2: Choosing Your Space and How to Treat It**

39   **Chapter 3: Wish-List Equipment**

49   **Chapter 4: Recording Primer and Terminology**

68   **Chapter 5: Anatomy of a Software-Based DAW**

78   **Chapter 6: Anatomy of a Standalone Recorder**

85   **Chapter 7: Getting Your Feet Wet—Recording Your First Song**

112   **Chapter 8: Recording Guitars**

147   **Chapter 9: Recording Bass Guitar**

161   **Chapter 10: Recording Keyboards and Other Virtual Instruments**

172   **Chapter 11: Drum Samples and Loops**

189   **Chapter 12: Recording Vocals**

197   **Chapter 13: Effects and Processing**

220   **Chapter 14: Mobile Devices—Today's Portable Studio**

226   **Chapter 15: Editing**

246   **Chapter 16: The Mixing Process**

264   Final Thoughts

265   Appendix:
         The DIY Corner
         Recording Index

ABOUT THE AUTHOR

Chad Johnson is a freelance author, editor, and musician. For Hal Leonard Corporation, he's authored over 65 instructional books covering a variety of instruments and topics, including *Guitarist's Guide to Scales Over Chords*, *The Hal Leonard Acoustic Guitar Method*, *Pentatonic Scales for the Guitar: The Essential Guide*, *Ukulele Aerobics*, *Radiohead Guitar Signature Licks*, *Teach Yourself to Play Bass Guitar*, *Bass for Kids*, *Play Like Eric Clapton*, and *Bass Fretboard Workbook*. He's a featured instructor on the DVD *200 Country Guitar Licks* (also published by Hal Leonard) and has toured and performed throughout the East Coast in various bands, sharing the stage with members of Lynyrd Skynyrd, the Allman Brothers Band, and others. He works as a session guitarist, composer/songwriter, and recording engineer when not authoring or editing, and his latest band, Sun City, recently released their self-titled debut album, which can be purchased at www.suncitymusic. bandcamp.com. Chad currently resides in Anna, TX (North Dallas), with his wife and two children. Feel free to contact him at chadjohnsonguitar@ hotmail.com with any questions or comments.

DEDICATION AND ACKNOWLEDGMENTS

This book is dedicated to my beautiful family—my wife, Alli, my son, Lennon Ezra, and my daughter, Leherie Ireland. Y'all are my favorite part of waking up every day and a continuous source of never-ending joy. I'd also like to dedicate the book to Peter McIan, whose excellent book, *The Musician's Guide to Home Recording*, lit a fire in me and gave me the recording bug long ago.

Special thanks go to the following companies for their cooperation and support, which helped make this book a reality: Agile Guitars, Alvarez Guitars, Applied Acoustics Systems, Breedlove Guitars, CAD Audio, Danelectro, dbx Professional Audio, DigiTech, Dunlop Manufacturing, the ESP Guitar Company, Gallien-Krueger, Garritan, Höfner, Hotone Audio, Ibanez Guitars, IK Multimedia, KAT Percussion, Kustom, MXL Microphones, Orange Amplification, Peavey Electronics, Primacoustic Acoustic Solutions, Radial Engineering, Seventh Circle Audio, Shure, Snark Tuners, Steinberg, Sterling Audio, Sterling by Music Man, Tascam, TC Electronic, Toontrack, Tannoy, VHT Amplification, VOX, and Waves.

Very special thanks to everyone at Hal Leonard for their fine efforts in turning this humble manuscript into the professional product that you hold in your hands (or view from a screen).

INTRODUCTION

Welcome to *How to Record at Home on a Budget*. With this book, I aim to demonstrate that you don't need to spend thousands of dollars to make great-sounding recordings from the comfort of your own home. The advantages afforded to the home recordist today are truly astounding and have leveled the playing field between pro and amateur like never before. With the right know-how and determination, you can produce amazing results on affordable gear that's within nearly everyone's reach.

There have certainly been many books geared toward home recording over the years, and I've read plenty. But there's always been one thing that I've felt was lacking: specificity. In other words, they provided lots of good general knowledge, but I was always left wondering things like, "Well, how would this sound with *my setup*?" Even though these books talked about home studios, many of them still mentioned top-of-the-line gear consistently, such as Neumman mics, Apogee converters, Avalon or Neve mic preamps, etc. I always thought, "Well, can I really get great sounds from my gear?" I don't know about a lot of other people, but I certainly can't afford much of that type of gear. So I wanted this book to be for "the rest of us" who have to make do with what we can.

In this book, I aim for total gear transparency. In other words, you're going to know exactly *every piece of gear* that was used to create every single recording in the book. From the guitars, basses, amps or keyboards to the preamps, compressors, processors, and interfaces, the entire signal chain will be made known for every track. But why do this when it's unlikely that any reader will possess the exact same signal chain as I do? I've thought a lot about that, and I can certainly see the logic behind that question. I'm sure that's why most books treat the topic with generalizations as opposed to getting specific. But my question in response to that is, "Why not?" Sure, no one probably has the *exact* same gear as I do, but many people will likely have some of it. Or they may have a piece of equipment in the same price range, so they can get a rough idea for comparative purposes. In my mind, getting specific about the gear can only help, because:

- It doesn't change the fact that the generalized information still applies

- It will likely help someone determine what kind of quality they can expect from their similarly priced gear

Of course, the phrase "on a budget" means different things to different people. Some people may think a $200 microphone is terribly cheap, while others may think it's very expensive. Therefore, I'll have to define what I mean when I use the term as it applies to this book. First of all, I'll say this: no piece of equipment used in this book cost over $500, and the vast majority cost much less. There are no $2,000 compressors or $3,000 mics being used. Most of the guitars and basses range from $150 to $300, as do the amplifiers. The virtual instruments generally range from $70 to $150, and the interface I used throughout the book cost $150. Since the topic of recording music often includes such a vast array of gear, there are many specific products mentioned in this book, but that's only because I've covered a wide range of styles and applications. The typical person won't need most of the gear mentioned because much of it won't apply to their specific situation.

Before moving forward, I'd like to say just a few more things in regard to the goal of this book and your expectations from it:

- The #1 rule of recording is this: garbage in, garbage out. It should be understood that, in order for a recording to be effective, the performances that are recorded need to be of a high caliber.

- I'm going to assume that you're a beginner or intermediate recordist wanting to learn how to record the most common instruments used in popular music, including vocals, guitars, bass, and keyboards. The recording of drumsets is not covered in this book, as they are by far the most difficult instruments to record well at home, and the topic would be beyond the scope of this book. However, the use of drum loops, samples, and virtual drums is discussed in detail.

- I won't get too bogged down in technical details in this book. We're going to focus on the things you need to know in order to get good sounds from your system. There's certainly plenty more knowledge to be had with regard to the inner workings of things (how microphones do what they do, the digital recording/conversion process, etc.), but the pursuit of that will be left up to your discretion, as I simply did not have the space in this book to delve into such topics.

- As should be understood by now, the world of computers is a highly volatile one, and therefore any specifics mentioned in this book concerning computer software or hardware are likely to become outdated before too long. That's the nature of the beast, however, and, since I don't have the benefit of a crystal ball, the best I can hope to do is combat this with updates and revisions in possible future editions of the book.

- I'm just going to say this once: One of the most important things you can do to help you achieve good sounds—with any piece of gear or software—is to **read the manual**. (Okay…I may say that again later, as well.)

- Recordings, and music in general, are subjective arts. Sometimes one man's genius is another man's rubbish. This may or may not have to do with the skill of the recordist, musician, composer, etc. It could just be that a certain song or recording rubs someone the wrong way. You can't please everyone with your music or recordings, so you may as well try to please yourself. (The exception to this, of course, is if you're recording a client; then you should try to please them, too.)

Now that that's out of the way, let's get down to it and have some fun.

HOW TO USE THIS BOOK

This book is more of a reference than a method. I'd certainly encourage everyone, regardless of their experience level, to read it cover to cover—just in case there's something new in there for them—but it will no doubt eventually serve as more of a reference in the long run. There's a lot of ground to cover in the world of recording, and I tried my best to distill it down to its essence, but this book still turned out to be longer than I'd planned.

If you're brand new to recording, you should absolutely start at the beginning and read it thoroughly. In fact, the complete beginner will likely not want to read it cover to cover at first, because he'll likely need to try out some of the earlier techniques and concepts before he'll begin to understand some of those found later in the book. The book begins with a good bit of groundwork before we "hit record," and if most of this is old hat to you, feel free to skip ahead a bit. (I'd still suggest at least skimming through to make sure nothing new leaps out at you.)

Most of the instrument chapters are designed to be self-contained, but if and when a certain idea or concept borrows from that of another chapter, you'll be directed to the appropriate page or section. Also, there may be slight redundancy within these chapters as a result of this self-contained concept, but it never hurts to have something reiterated a few times!

ABOUT THE RECORDINGS

All of the recordings in this book were done in my home studio, which resides in a two-story house that was in no way constructed with the slightest regard for acoustics. I've done a good amount to improve this situation in my control room and "live room" (a.k.a. my children's play room), and this type of work is covered in Chapter 2. But just to be clear: this is a home studio through and through!

Here are some specifics:

- Every track (with the exception of those recorded to the Tascam DP-24 standalone recorder) was recorded with a Steinberg UR22 audio/MIDI interface.

- My computer is an HP Compaq 8000 with an Intel Core 2 Duo 3.16 GHz processor. It has 8GB of RAM, a 1 TB hard drive, and is running Windows 7 Professional.

- I used Dunlop picks, strings, and capos, SoundRunner by MXL guitar cables, and Marshall XLR microphone cables for all the recordings in this book.

- There were a few items used on some recordings that weren't mentioned specifically in the book but are disclosed in the Recording Index. This is because they're no longer available, save for the used market, and therefore I couldn't give exact pricing info. (None of them are remotely close to the $500 ceiling, however.)

I had a lot of fun creating these recordings, and I hope you find them enjoyable and inspiring, as well!

Note: All songs and examples in this book are owned by the author and therefore cannot be recreated without author's express consent.

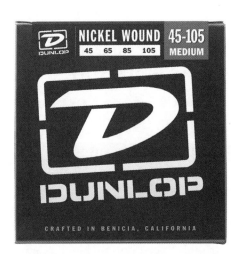

CHAPTER 1

BASIC EQUIPMENT CHECKLIST

So you're ready to start recording at home, but you have no idea where to begin. A cursory glance through a retail catalog will likely give you option anxiety and leave you more confused than you were at first. That's what this chapter is for. We're going to break down the home studio into its essential ingredients and look at each piece, its function, and its importance in the overall scheme. By the end of the chapter, you'll begin to realize that you don't need to spend mega bucks these days to generate awesome sounds. **Note:** We won't include instruments (guitar, bass, etc.) in this list, as it's expected that you'll supply those (if you want to record them).

There are two large basic categories into which the vast majority of home recordists fall: the computer-based system and the standalone recorder. Although technically both are considered a "DAW"—which stands for *digital audio workstation*—most people nowadays think of a computer (software)-based system when they hear the term DAW. But each system has its advantages, which is why we'll be looking at both in this book (although we will spend more time on the computer-based system). **Note:** If you're a total beginner, you may be confused by some of the terms mentioned here. If so, don't worry; just keep reading. Your questions will no doubt soon be answered. If you're still in the dark about something at the end of this chapter, refer to Chapter 4.

COMPUTER-BASED SYSTEM

Let's start with the system that's completely transformed the way we record music in the modern era: the computer-based system. Just as word processing software has made typewriters all but obsolete, the computer-based recording system has driven the analog cassette studios and their big-brother reel-to-reel tape recorders to their knees. There are still users of these systems out there, but to say that they're in the minority is a colossal understatement. In fact, at the time of this writing, there are no more cassette-based multi-track recorders in production, and the few reel-to-reel recorders still available are prohibitively expensive, especially to the home recordist. (It should be noted that, in professional studios, reel-to-reels still do see a significant amount of action as implemented in a hybrid system.)

Item 1: The Computer

It's obvious, of course, but it's not quite as obvious as you may think. While many computers are up to the task of recording audio—at least in some capacity—it's common to use a computer dedicated solely to music production above all else. This is because, in a nutshell, recording music is a CPU-intensive process, and the leaner and cleaner your machine is, the more smoothly things will run. It's not that you can't do it on a system that you also use for other things; it's just usually more prone to trouble. So if you've been meaning to upgrade your home computer for a while but just haven't gotten around to it, now you have a good excuse. Except…you shouldn't upgrade your home computer; you should use the new, more powerful system for the music recording and stick with the old clunker for surfing the net and making cat memes!

One big thing to consider is whether you want a laptop or desktop system. Both have advantages and disadvantages, so you'll need to identify your needs and make an informed decision. Obviously, if you need your system to be portable, then a laptop is your only option (unless you want to use a tablet or other mobile device exclusively, which we'll talk about in Chapter 14). However, desktop systems will usually offer more in terms of flexibility (ports, etc.) and room to grow, so if you're wanting a more robust system, that's certainly something to consider.

Apple MacBook Pro
Courtesy of Apple

Dell OptiPlex 7020 Small Form Factor
Courtesy of Dell, Inc.

The Question on Everybody's Lips: Mac or PC?

Of course you have to wonder about this. Just as with any other computer-based art form, you have the diehard fans of each seriously camped out in their respective corners. However, most people will tell you that it really doesn't matter. Both are used in countless studios—both home and professional—with equally stunning results. So it really comes down to a matter of preference. You most likely have a platform preference already, and that often makes the decision for many. You simply stick with what's comfortable.

By and large, the majority of software is available for both systems. However, the software is normally *not* cross-platform in this regard, and you usually won't be able to dump the files from your PC-based DAW system onto a flash drive, head over to your friend's house and his Mac system, and start working away without a glitch. Each system has its own ways of dealing with audio files, virtual instruments/effects, etc., so once you pick a camp, just know that you'll be working with it exclusively for the most part. Also keep in mind that Macs are more expensive. However, they also maintain their resell value much more, generally speaking.

With regard to recording audio, it's simple: more is more. The faster your processor, the more RAM you have, and the bigger the hard drive (and faster its speed), the better. However, this isn't to say you've got to blow $2K on a brand new system that has every bell and whistle under the sun. Remember that people have been recording audio on computers since back when RAM was measured in megabytes. Of course, the continual upgrading of software and hardware means that those systems won't do much good these days.

So let's take a look at what I would say are the *minimum* performance requirements you'd want to look for in a machine used specifically for recording audio today:

Windows-based System
- Intel Pentium dual core, 2.5GHz
- Windows 7
- 4GB RAM
- 500 GB hard drive, 7200 RPM

Mac-based System
- Intel Core 2 Duo, 2.4GHz
- OS X (latest)
- 4GB RAM
- 500 GB hard drive, 5400 RPM

Realize that when I say "minimum requirements," this isn't in the way that software companies like to use that term when trying to sell their products. These are the requirements that will still work well for several years to come, assuming you keep the machine well-maintained and as lean as can be. You could make music with much less power than this (and many people do), but if you're just getting into the game, this will give you a system that still has a bit of growing left in it.

That said, of course, more is more! So, if you can swing it, move up to the Intel Core i5 or i7 processor, 3GHz or faster, 8+GB of RAM, and a 1+TB hard drive. At the time of this writing, you can get a new such desktop system (minus the monitor) from HP for about $650 and a comparable MacBook Pro (laptop) from Apple for about $1,100. And, of course, used computers are always one of the biggest bargains around. The massive demand for "new, newer, newest!" means that many extremely capable systems quickly get sold for a fraction of their original price only a few years later. You can really cash in on this when selecting your system if you just make sure it meets all your requirements.

A Word on Ports

Things are shifting a bit in the world of ports. For a while, it was neatly divided into three camps: PCI, USB (1.0 and 2.0), and FireWire. Although PCI cards are the fastest and are extremely reliable, they've been nudged out of the race by the convenience of USB and FireWire devices. While nearly all PCs (in both desktop and laptop format) still come with USB ports (most are 2.0 now), until recently only Macs were available with FireWire. You could add a FireWire card to a PC desktop via a PCIe slot, but doing the same to a PC laptop was sketchy and often problematic when recording audio.

However, FireWire ports are officially on the way out, as Apple has replaced them with the Thunderbolt port, which is incompatible, and PC makers all but abandoned them as standard features long ago. (Apple does offer a Thunderbolt-to-FireWire adapter, but it has its limitations and has been problematic for some.) For some reason, manufacturers of A/I (audio interface, see Item 2) devices are a little slow to react to this trend, and many FireWire devices are still available, although they're outnumbered 4-to-1 by USB (most 2.0) devices. At the time of this writing, only a handful of Thunderbolt A/I devices are on the market, but that's likely to rise soon. USB 3.0 is gaining ground in other realms now, as well, but A/I manufacturers haven't taken the bait yet.

So, to summarize, if you're just starting out now, USB 2.0 is a safe bet. If you want to use a FireWire device, you'll either need to buy a used Mac or add a FireWire card to a PC desktop machine. (You can try adding one to a PC laptop, but it's risky. Be sure to do your research!) If you want to anticipate the future, you could shell out some pretty big bucks for a Thunderbolt device (the cheapest I could find at the time of this writing is a Zoom TAC-2 for $400) for use on a Mac.

Another option is to buy a used PCI card, such as the M-Audio Audiophile 2496 (2 in/2 out) or Delta 1010LT (8 in/8 out). Both of these are supported on Windows 7, but they don't show Windows 8 support, so their days are likely numbered, as well. (However, you have to remember that just about any piece of equipment falls into this category, in varying degrees, when it comes to computers.) I still use a PCI card on one of my machines, and it works flawlessly.

Item 2: The Audio Interface (A/I)

The audio interface is the device that turns your analog signal (from a guitar, microphone, keyboard, etc.) into a digital one so that the computer can work with it. It then turns it back into an analog signal so that it can be played back over the speakers. As such, it features A/D (analog to digital) and D/A (digital to analog) converters for this purpose. You don't need to know exactly how this process works in order to use them, so don't worry too much about it. You just need a decent interface that performs well and contains the features you require. There are several issues to consider when choosing your interface; let's look at the most important.

Number of Analog Inputs: How many tracks do you want to record at once? This is probably the most important thing you need to think about, because it's not something you can overcome by upgrading anything. You'll have to buy a new interface if you need more inputs. For most home recordists who do everything themselves, two inputs will work just fine. In fact, one input is often all you really need, but two inputs offers you the ability to use two mics on an acoustic guitar (a common practice) or to record an acoustic/vocal performance with one mic for each, for example.

If you need to record several sources at once, though, and you want to have individual control over the tracks, then you'll need more inputs than that. Interfaces are normally available with an even number of inputs. Two is most common, but you'll find four, six, and eight in the affordable range as well. (The aforementioned Delta 1010LT 8-in/8-out PCI card sells used for around $100 at the time of this writing.)

Number of Analog Outputs: If you're planning on doing everything "in the box"—i.e., using plug-ins for all your effects and mixing everything entirely within your DAW software—then you'll only really need two outputs (left and right for the stereo mix). But if you want to integrate any outboard effects processing during the mixing process, or you want to be able to generate a separate headphone mix, you'll need more than two outputs. (You could still use outboard processors while tracking if you have only two outputs; this is called "printing an effect," and we'll look at that idea later in the book.) Interfaces usually either come with only two outputs, or their outputs match their inputs, although there are certainly exceptions.

Mic Preamps, XLR Inputs, and Phantom Power: Most microphones use "balanced" XLR cables, which contain three connectors. These are sometimes referred to simply as "mic cables."

XLR "mic cable"

Microphones produce a very low output on their own and therefore need a *preamp* in order for their signal to be increased to a useable level. Many interfaces contain one or more XLR inputs with a built-in preamp, allowing you to plug the microphone directly into it. Whereas dynamic microphones don't need any power to operate, condenser microphones do require additional current. This is sometimes supplied by an external power supply that comes with the mic (or a battery inside the mic), but most often it's supplied through the cable via *phantom power*. Be sure to check and see if your interface features phantom power. If it doesn't, you can purchase an external phantom power supply for around $20 or $30 per channel (a one-channel phantom power supply can power one condenser mic at a time).

MIDI Inputs/Outputs: Many interfaces contain MIDI in and out jacks, which allow you to plug in your MIDI controllers directly to send and receive MIDI data. If your interface doesn't have MIDI jacks, you can easily get a USB-powered MIDI interface for around $40 new.

Computer Connection: As mentioned earlier, you'll find USB 1.0, USB 2.0, and FireWire devices mostly. Be sure you select one that's compatible with your computer system.

Direct Monitoring: This is a feature that allows you to overcome the *latency* issue that's a part of every computer-based recording system. It allows you to monitor the incoming signal directly after the input instead of waiting for it to make the trip through the computer. It's a very nice feature if your system is not efficient enough to work smoothly with a low enough latency setting.

Other features include digital inputs and outputs, which are handy if you're working with digital signals from other gear, and a headphone output, which is handy, as well.

All of the recordings made in this book on a computer-based DAW were done with a Steinberg UR22 interface.

Steinberg UR22 audio/MIDI interface

The Steinberg UR22 is a two-channel USB audio/MIDI interface with a maximum 192 kHz sample rate and 24-bit resolution. It comes in a handsome, rugged, desktop design and contains just enough features to make it flexible but nothing to make it overcomplicated, including:

- Combination XLR/1/4-inch jacks for channels 1 and 2 on the front
- 1/4-inch output jacks, MIDI in/out, and USB jack on rear
- Switchable phantom power
- Zero-latency monitoring
- Hi-Z input switch on channel 2 for direct instrument input
- Separate phones and output level knobs
- Input/DAW mix knob that allows you to select your monitoring source (input signal or DAW mix)

Also included with the UR22 is Cubase AI, an extremely powerful recording suite with more than enough flexibility for just about any recording project you'll dream up. The unit features two Class A D-PRE mic preamps from Yamaha, which deliver clean, pristine quality, and peak LEDs for each channel, as well as a phantom power LED indicator. The UR22 is built like a tank and was up and running on my system (Windows 7) in no time at all, with zero issues. It sounds great, contains usable features, and for the price, can't be beat, in my opinion.

Every track in this book, with the exception of those recorded to the Tascam DP-24 standalone recorder, was recorded with this interface.

Street price: $150

Item 3: MIDI Controller

Although these border on being instruments (and I said I wasn't going to list instruments), I feel they're a bit unique in that they're incapable of producing any sound on their own. They have to be *controlling* something else that can make sound. *MIDI* (musical instrument digital interface) is to recording what a word processor is to writing. A MIDI signal is not audio; it's simply data that tells a digital instrument what to play. Grossly simplified, it's a series of instructions, such as, "play this C note at this time, hold it for this long, and release it at this time." These instructions are then sent to a synthesizer, which carries out the instructions and "plays" the data using whichever "sound patch" you desire. That data is then converted from digital form into an analog signal so you can hear it through your speakers.

Just as you can edit text on a word processor or change its font, size, color, etc., you can do the same with MIDI. You can record a part while listening to a keyboard patch. But then, after you've recorded it, you can go in and move a note to a different pitch or a different point (rhythmically) in the measure. You could change the sound patch to a trumpet, upright bass, penny whistle, or anything else for which you have MIDI samples. In this book, the most crucial element for which we'll use MIDI is drums, which we'll cover later. But we'll also use it for keyboard sounds, orchestral sounds, and synthesizer sounds, among others.

A *MIDI controller* is simply the name for a device we use to input MIDI data. The most common is the MIDI keyboard controller, which usually resembles a plain-looking electronic keyboard—although they can feature a good amount of bells and whistles, too.

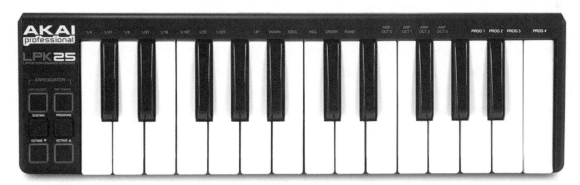

Akai LPK 25 keyboard controller

By the way, just about any keyboard (with built-in sounds) these days will usually feature a MIDI out jack, which means that it can be used as a MIDI keyboard controller, as well.

Item 4: Microphones

If you want to record vocals, you'll need a microphone, and you'll probably really want to use them for recording acoustic (and possibly electric) guitars, as well, not to mention a slew of other instruments from time to time, including bass, piano, auxiliary percussion, your child's first words, etc. Microphones come in two main categories with regard to the home recordist: dynamic and condenser. A third type, the ribbon mic, is also occasionally used. We'll take a look at all three at some point in this book.

A *dynamic* mic is more rugged in construction and is therefore used a great deal in live situations, where lead singers are apt to swing it around by the cable (which is hopefully securely attached!). They're more likely to survive a fall unscathed. They're not as detailed in the treble frequencies as a condenser, but they can generally handle higher volume levels without distorting, which makes them good choices for loud guitar amps, drums, etc. They're also commonly used for louder, more aggressive vocals at times.

Shure SM57

Shure SM7B

Shure is a popular manufacturer of dynamic microphones (as well as condensers), with two commonly employed in the studio being the SM57 and SM7B. I used both of these microphones while making the recordings in this book.

The SM57 dates back to the mid-1960s and has since become one of the most ubiquitous microphones of any kind. It's used in countless live performances—you'd be hard-pressed to attend a concert anywhere at which at least one wasn't being used—and studio recordings every day and has been for decades. It features a frequency response of 40 Hz to 15 kHz and is a studio staple on snare drums and electric guitar amps, among other things.

The origins of the SM7B date back to 1976 with the SM7, and it's been a mainstay in radio/broadcast application since, as well as musical recording and performance. The SM7B uses the same Unidyne III cartridge as found in the SM57, but the diaphragm in the SM7B is slightly different and has been optimized for greater low end response. The SM7B includes a larger windscreen than previous versions and is better at rejecting hum, among other small differences, but it performs the same, sonically. Its frequency response ranges from 50 Hz to 20 kHz.

The SM7B is legendary in home recording circles as one of the best bangs for the buck around, usable on dozens of applications, including vocals, acoustic guitar, electric guitar amps, kick drums, and bass amps. Its sound quality rivals microphones that cost five or ten times as much, and you can hardly read a bad word about it on the internet. If you're still not convinced, consider the fact that engineer Bruce Swedien used the SM7 to record most of Michael Jackson's vocals for the album *Thriller*—the best-selling album *of all time*—not to mention many of his other hits throughout his career.

A *condenser* mic comes in two main categories: *large diaphragm* and *small diaphragm*. As you may have guessed, the large diaphragm (LDC) is physically larger. It's the prototypical mic you see in photos when someone's singing in a studio. It's featured on most vocals, but it's also used on guitars, percussion, piano, and other instruments. LDCs are *side-address* microphones, which means you sing (or aim the sound source) into the side of the microphone. Small diaphragm mics are usually short and kind of stubby—much like a cigar—and are usually *top-address* (sometimes called *end-address*) like most dynamic mics, meaning you sing or play into the top (or end) of the mic. They're often used on instruments with a lot of high-end content, such as acoustic guitar, cymbals, or piano. These are often used when miking an instrument in stereo, such as a piano or a drum kit. If you intend to do this, it's really nice to have two identical mics for this purpose, as it will generally result in a more accurate stereo image of the instrument.

Condenser microphones use a more delicate mechanism than dynamics do. As such, they're easier to damage and should be handled with great care. They're also generally more expensive than dynamics, but that trend has changed a lot in the past 15 years. There are now many LDC microphones available under the $200 or $150 mark that would serve the home recordist extremely well.

Sterling Audio ST55 large diaphragm condenser microphone

Sterling Audio ST31 small diaphragm condenser microphone

The Sterling Audio ST55 is a cardioid pattern large diaphragm condenser mic with a one-inch brass capsule and an ultra-thin 3-micron gold-evaporated Mylar diaphragm. It features a high-pass filter (located at 75Hz), a -10 dB pad, and an attractive black nickel-plated brass body complimented by a stainless steel head and grill. With a 20 Hz to 18 kHz response, it excels on vocals, acoustic guitar, piano, and auxiliary percussion. One additional feature of this mic is the use of a Disc Resonator (a small, secondary brass diaphragm), which is attached to the center of the capsule. This helps to smooth out some of the harsher artifacts in the 10-12kHz range usually associated with lower-priced condensers.

The ST31 is a small diaphragm condenser mic with a 3/4-inch diameter, 6-micron gold-evaporated Mylar diaphragm. It's an end-address mic, which means you aim the end at the source, as opposed to most LDCs. It shares the same aesthetics as the ST55, only in a smaller package, and features a frequency response of 20 Hz to 18 kHz. The ST31 does a beautiful job on most stringed acoustic instruments, such as acoustic guitar, mandolin, etc., as well as piano, drum overheads, and auxiliary percussion.

Street price: ST55 – $140, ST31 – $70

A *ribbon* mic uses yet another method for capturing sound, and it's generally the most delicate mechanism of all. They're the least common type of mic found in the home studio, but only because most people don't really know much about them. Although they were the most common type of mics found in the early part of the 20th century (circa 1920 to 1950), their popularity dwindled with the rise of dynamic and condenser mics. They've remained in service at pro studios for certain applications, but their price made them a pipe dream for the home recordist. However, several affordable models have become available as of late, and if you have a few extra bucks to spare, they can certainly make a valuable addition to your mic locker. They're commonly used on brass and strings, but they can also sound great on electric guitars and other instruments, too. You have to be wary of the volume level, as the ribbon inside the microphone is very sensitive and can therefore be damaged with excessive SPL (sound pressure levels). They're not as airy-sounding as a condenser microphone, but they usually capture more high detail frequency than a dynamic. You really need to hear them to form your own opinion.

CAD D82 ribbon microphone

Copyright CAD Audio, used with permission.

The CAD D82 ribbon mic represents a new take on an old design. The thought of a ribbon mic being taken out on the road for use on guitar amps in a live setting would have once been considered the stuff of fairy tales, as the high SPL and wear and tear of live performances would have been too much to handle for the delicacies of a ribbon. But, working from the ground up, the engineers at CAD have created just such a product with the D82.

Though the frequency response of the D82 is listed at 30 Hz to 20 kHz, it's one of the darker mics I've used. Having said that, it's extremely sensitive to slight changes in orientation and distance, allowing you to coax well-balanced tones from just about any source with a little patience. The figure-eight pattern also proves very useful when you want to avoid bleed from another nearby source, as the sound rejection from the sides of the mic is extremely effective.

The D82 is specifically designed for use on electric guitar amps, and it certainly shines in this regard. But I also had good experiences with it on acoustic guitar, and I'm certain it could perform admirably on other sources, as well, with the right placement. Its durability is also a big plus, as you don't have to worry about being quite so delicate with it. (Of course, you don't want to throw it around or anything.)

Street price: $140

Polar Patterns

Microphones are also placed in different classes by way of their *polar patterns*. This refers to the directions in which they're most sensitive to sound. There are three basic categories: *cardioid, figure eight*, and *omnidirectional*.

A cardioid mic will pick up sound in the front and to the sides, but not from the back of the microphone. The name "cardioid" refers to the way that the pattern resembles a heart when seen from above. One variation on this is *hyper cardioid*, which simply rejects more sound from the back than cardioid. Most LDC mics are cardioid, although some of them have switchable patterns, including figure eight and/or omnidirectional. The most common application for a cardioid mic is vocals.

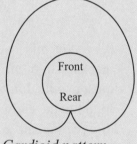

Cardioid pattern

A figure-eight pattern, as its name implies, will pick up sound from the front and back equally, but it will reject sound from the sides of the mic. All ribbon microphones feature this pattern. Figure-eight patterns are useful for when you want to record two singers at once onto the same track, since they can each stand on opposite sides of the mic. They can also be used at times to generate a little more separation because of the fact that they greatly reject sound from the sides. So, if you're recording an acoustic guitar and vocal simultaneously, for example, and you want to mic each source independently, you can often arrange the ribbon mic so that its front (or rear) is facing its source but its side is facing the other source (and therefore rejecting it).

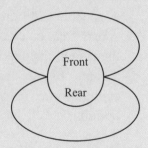

Figure-eight Pattern

An omnidirectional microphone will pick up sound equally from all sides. They're used often for ambient recordings—if you just want to pick up the sound of the room with several people gathered in a circle performing live, for example. The results of this will vary with the "sound" of the room, however. We'll talk more about this later.

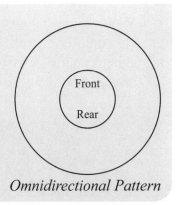

Omnidirectional Pattern

Item 5: Software

Next we have software, which includes a few types. Most software programs will fit into one of the following categories:

- The DAW program, which can also be called sequencer, recording, or production software

- Effect plugins (such as reverb, compression, or EQ)

- Virtual instruments (MIDI-controlled sounds such as piano, strings, or drums)

- Loops & Samples (short audio files that can be looped to form a drumbeat or added to your own tracks as you please)

- Samplers (a program you can use to record and/or manipulate samples of your own)

We'll discuss software in much greater detail in Chapter 5.

Item 6: Headphones and Studio Monitors (Speakers)

If you're going to be using a microphone at all, you're going to need headphones in order to hear the backing tracks while you record vocals/guitar/piano/etc. on top of them. But even if you record everything direct and can therefore always monitor with speakers (we'll talk more about the subject of monitoring in Chapter 4), you'll still want a pair of decent headphones. This will allow you to hear how your mixes are translating to them, which is very important nowadays considering the sheer number of people who listen to music predominantly on mobile devices. Ideally, you'll want a pair of headphones that are designed for studio use—not recreational listening—as they'll typically provide a more accurate representation of the sounds you've recorded.

Studio monitors (speakers) are another important part in obtaining a well-balanced mix. Whereas stereo speakers are designed to make music sound more pleasant by accentuating certain frequencies and deemphasizing others, studio monitors are designed to give a much flatter frequency response—in other words, they color the sound less. This helps you create a mix that will translate better to the many different speakers (and headphones) on which people will eventually hear your music. If you mix with standard stereo speakers, you'll usually end up with something that sounds great on your system but probably pretty lousy on someone else's. This is a bit simplistic, but studio monitors level the playing field a bit more so that it ends up sounding really good on everyone's system (more or less), instead of just really awesome on only one person's (yours).

Sennheiser HD 280 Pro headphones

Monitors come in two flavors: *active* (powered) or *passive* (non-powered). Powered monitors require no amplifier to work because they have one built into them. You can plug them straight into your system's output. Passive monitors require a power amp to work. You would plug your system's outputs into the power amp and then run speaker wire from the amp to the monitors.

Tannoy Reveal 502 active monitor

The Tannoy Reveal 502 monitors feature a five-inch high-efficiency woofer, a one-inch, soft-dome, "poke resistant" tweeter, and an accurately tuned, front-firing bass port engineered to deliver optimal low-frequency response even with near-wall placement. On the back are balanced (XLR) and unbalanced (1/4-inch) inputs, an Aux section with an 1/8-inch input for MP3 players and an 1/8-inch "monitor link" jack for connecting the other speaker when using this function (1/8-inch cable included!), a volume knob, and a three-position EQ selector switch (normal, hi boost, hi cut). Each monitor features a 75-watt Bi-Amp module, an active crossover filter for exceptional clarity, and a frequency response of 49 Hz to 43 kHz.

These monitors have received rave reviews, and I can only concur with the consensus. I used these monitors exclusively for the recordings in this book, and I couldn't be happier with them. The sound is clean, detailed, and deep; they're compact, lightweight, and durable; and they're quite attractive to boot. The aux input is incredibly convenient when you want to reference your tracks against your favorite recordings, which is always a useful strategy.

Street price: $180 each

Having said that, it's a fact that you're likely the only one that will be listening to *your mixes* in *your control room* on *your speakers*. Everyone else will be using headphones, stereo speakers, etc. So it's a good idea to have some cheap boombox or desktop computer speakers available to reference from time to time, as well. Most professional mixing engineers, including Chris Lord-Alge and Michael Brauer, to name but a few, employ this principle and are constantly referencing the cheap little speakers to make sure they're on the right track.

Item 7: Cables, Stands, and Miscellaneous Items

All this equipment has to connect in some fashion, so you'll need several different types of cables. Here are the most common types:

XLR Mic Cables

These are the three-conductor cables mentioned earlier under Item 2 (the A/I). You'll most often use these to connect your mic to the preamp or interface, although you may also use them to connect your studio monitors, as well as other equipment. Marshall XLR cables were used exclusively for the recordings in this book.

1/4-inch Instrument Cables

This is your basic guitar cord. It's also known sometimes as a TS (tip-sleeve) cable, which means it has two conductors: hot (the signal, which is found on the tip of the plug) and ground (which is found on the "sleeve" of the plug—the opposite side of the black band from the tip). These are typically used in the studio as longer cables (10 feet or more, for plugging in guitars, keyboards, and such) and as shorter "patch cables" (anywhere from six inches to three feet) for connecting rackmount gear, guitar pedals, etc.

SoundRunner by MXL guitar cables were used exclusively for the recordings in this book.

Speaker Cables

These are 1/4-inch cables that are used to connect a guitar or bass amp to the speaker cabinet. Although they look just like a standard guitar cord (and use the TS format), they're quite different inside. They will usually say "speaker cable" or something similar along the outside of the cable. It's not a good idea to use a standard guitar cord for this purpose, as it's possible to damage the speakers. At the very least, it won't sound as good.

These should not be confused with the cables used to connect your studio monitors, which will typically be a normal TS instrument cable, a TRS cable, or an XLR cable (possibly an RCA cable).

RCA Cables

These are the two-conductor cables that are normally paired together in a red/white or red/black configuration. Some equipment makes use of RCA jacks, while others use 1/4-inch or XLR jacks. You can also use RCA-to-1/4-inch adapters (or vice versa) if necessary.

RCA cable and adapter

USB Cables

You'll most likely end up using standard USB cables, as well as specialized ones that will usually come with a piece of gear.

USB cable with one "A" end and one "B" end

1/4-inch TRS Cables

These look like guitar cables, but they're actually three-conductor cables. You can tell them apart from a normal (TS) guitar cable by the extra band on the end of the plug. "TRS" stands for "tip-ring-sleeve." The "ring" carries the extra signal. These provide a "balanced" signal—like an XLR cable—in a 1/4-inch package. You likely won't use these as often, but you may have a need for them at times.

Insert Cables

These are most often found in the 1/4-inch format, but they can appear in other forms, as well. An insert cable has one plug on one end and two on the other. The single end will be the TRS type, while the other two ends will be the TS type. One of the dual ends will "send" a signal somewhere, while the other will "return" it. They're used to "insert" another piece of gear into the signal path.

Insert cables

Stands

Then there are stands, including microphone stands (and mic clips), guitar/ bass stands, and keyboard stands (although, if it's small enough, such as many MIDI controllers, you can fit in on a desk), among others. With regard to mic stands, a *boom mic stand* is especially useful in the studio, as it will allow you access to many more spots than a standard vertical mic stand will.

Boom mic stand

Miscellaneous Items

Under the miscellaneous umbrella, you have many little things. Most of these will just be collected as you need them. Among the numerous items on this list, some of the most common are:

- Power strips/surge protectors
- Picks
- Tuner
- Metronome
- Adapters (They come in all types: male XLR to female 1/4-inch, female XLR to male 1/4-inch, female RCA to male TS, male RCA to female TS, etc. You'll no doubt pick these up as you find the need for them, eventually ending up with a whole shoebox full of them.)
- Cable ties
- Capos
- Flash drive
- Flashlight
- Electrical tape

That just about wraps it up for the basics. It may seem like a lot, but let's do a quick review. Basically, we've got:

- Computer
- Audio interface
- MIDI controller
- Microphone(s)
- Software
- Headphones/Speakers
- Cables/Stands

BUT DO I REALLY NEED...?

It should be mentioned that, even though this is a basic equipment checklist, there are some of you for whom one or more of these items may be optional. For example, if you plan to record nothing but acoustic guitar and vocals, then you don't really need a MIDI controller or any virtual instrument software. Or maybe you absolutely only plan to record instrumental electronic music for the foreseeable future. If that's the case, then you don't need to spend your money on a microphone right now. This list applies to most people but certainly not all. So, if you can't find a use for something on the list, feel free to skip it for now (even though I have a sneaking suspicion that the day may come when you'll need it!).

STANDALONE RECORDER SYSTEM

If you'd prefer to go the standalone recorder route, your list will change a bit, but it will still have many things in common with the computer-based system. Standalone recorders are popular with people who like a more "hands on" approach—they like turning knobs and moving faders instead of moving/clicking a mouse. They're also generally more portable than a computer-based system—certainly more portable than a desktop computer-based system. Laptops can seem portable, as well, but you still have the A/I to worry about (and the cables to and from it). As per the recording quality, many standalone systems are fully capable of pro results. So let's check out the bare minimum you'll need for this approach.

Item 1: The Recorder

Standalone recorders typically come in 4-, 8-, 12-, 16-, 24-, and 32-track formats; in other words, there's one built for your needs. Whereas they once typically recorded to an internal hard disk, nowadays most use some type of removable media, such as SD or SDHC cards. Most include an onboard mixer with faders and knobs and some type of graphic display, which can range from a simple text-only display to a full-color LCD screen of 3.5 inches or more. Many will include one or more XLR inputs with phantom power and/or a dedicated D/I (direct injection) input for guitars or basses. Nowadays, most recorders feature a good selection of built-in effects (including reverb, compression, delay, and amp simulation), and some even feature a built-in drum machine. Another useful common feature is MIDI input and output, which we'll talk more about in Chapter 6.

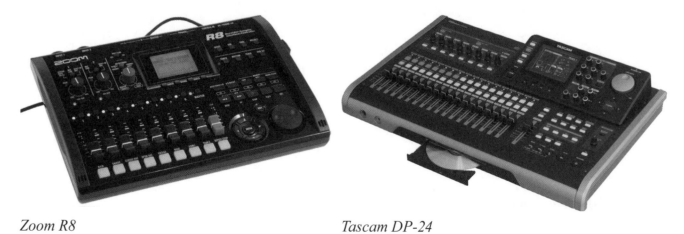

Zoom R8   Tascam DP-24

Item 2: Microphones

The same needs apply here as in the computer-based system.

Item 3: Headphones and Studio Monitors (Speakers)

The same needs apply here as in the computer-based system.

Item 4: Drums/Other Sounds Solution

This is where the two systems can possibly diverge a bit. If you want to completely avoid a computer altogether, then you'll need to supply your drum sounds and other sounds (keyboards, strings, etc.) via hardware options. This could be a keyboard workstation that will have all of that built in. It could be a drum machine along with a MIDI keyboard controller and hardware sound module. Or it could be any combination thereof. Nowadays, especially with the increasing power of mobile devices, more options exist in this regard than ever before. Here are just a few possible solutions:

- Drum Machine and Keyboard with Built-in Sounds

- Keyboard workstation

- MIDI keyboard controller paired with a computer (modest laptop or desktop) and standalone virtual instrument (drums and others) software

- MIDI keyboard controller paired with a mobile device and virtual instrument apps

Zoom RT-223 drum/bass machine

Korg Kross keyboard workstation

Okay, so a keyboard workstation is most certainly an instrument, so I'm breaking my rule. However, unless you want to record live drums, which is not easy (or cheap) and is therefore not covered in this book, you have to get your drum sounds from somewhere. And that usually means a standalone drum machine or a keyboard workstation. Some of the keyboard workstations can get pretty pricey—they start around $500 or so—but when you figure everything they include, it's really a pretty good bargain. For example, if you figured the price of a modest laptop, MIDI controller, and virtual instrument software, you'd probably end up saving a bit with the lower-end workstations (unless you went with freeware for the software), which combines all of those functions into one package. While the laptop route may offer more flexibility, the workstation is an all-in-one solution, which often means more reliable (you can't discount Murphy's Law when it comes to recording!)—not to mention more easily transported.

Item 5: Cables, Stands, and Miscellaneous Items

The same needs apply here as in the computer-based system.

PROS AND CONS

Now that we've looked at the basic needs of each type of system, let's look at the pros and cons of each. If you've not yet decided on a system, this could help you do so.

Computer-based System

Pros

- **Powerful:** The editing capabilities alone are simply staggering when compared to the days of old.

- **Versatile:** With the advent of plugins (effects and virtual instruments), there's almost no limit to the sounds you can generate.

- **Flexible:** DAW software can often be customized to best suit your preferences, and software can be added, upgraded, etc. as you please.

- **Industry standard:** Since it's the wave of the future (and has been for a good while), learning to use a computer-based system is a nice, marketable skill to have.

Cons

- **Portability:** A desktop system is decidedly un-portable, whereas a laptop fares much better in this regard. It may be smaller than some standalones, but it still involves more pieces, cables, etc.

- **Option anxiety:** Some people find the infinite options available to be a bit paralyzing. For example, it's easy to burn through hours and hours trying out various plugins looking for just the right sound/effect/etc. In other words, it's easy to get distracted and forget about the focus: the music. The same can be said for editing. It's easy to get tunnel vision and start moving every single note so that everything is perfectly aligned, which can end up sucking a good bit of the human element out of a performance. We'll talk more about this in Chapter 15.

- **User Interface:** "Mixing with a mouse" isn't exactly the most satisfying endeavor to many people. A lot of older folks, who were recording back in the days when dino-tape-machines ruled the earth, prefer the hands-on feel of moving faders, twisting knobs, etc. There are some workarounds in this regard, which we'll examine a bit later in the book. Some of the younger kids, who never knew the old ways, however, don't seem to mind the mouse as much.

- **Reliability:** When you combine all the different software, hardware, drivers, etc., you're using, there's always a possibility you'll find two that don't want to play nice with each other. It can almost always be resolved, but sometimes it can take a while, and it's always frustrating when it happens.

Standalone System

Pros

- **Portability:** You've got your recorder, mic preamps (audio interface), and mixer all in one box. You still can't beat the standalone when it comes to taking it with you.

- **Hands-on interface:** Being able to simply twist a knob instead of having to navigate a menu with a mouse is a very nice feature. While some of the smaller standalone recorders may also rely on a few sub-menus to reach certain functions, many people still prefer doing this by pushing buttons instead of dragging the mouse.

- **Limitations:** This may sound counterintuitive, but the same people who battle with option anxiety while using a computer system often enjoy the limitations of the standalone system. You have a limited number of tracks, built-in effects (although you can add outboard effects as well, which we'll look at later), etc., so there's no "endless" experimentation. In other words, you're forced to make decisions and move ahead.

- **Latency:** There's virtually no latency involved with a standalone recorder (technically, there is a tiny bit, but it's negligible), so that's one less thing you have to worry about.

Cons

- **Expandability:** There's usually not much (if any) upgrading ability, so if you want something more, chances are you'll need to buy another unit.

- **Editing capacity:** Although the editing has come a long way on the standalone machines, it still seems incredibly cumbersome compared to the computer-based system. This includes not only the process but also the display.

- **Limitations:** Yes, this is in both lists. Some people really don't like to feel limited, and they want to be able to try out as many sounds and record as many tracks as they want. For those people, the CPU is the way to go.

If you haven't yet chosen a recording system, think long and hard about these lists and try to imagine yourself using each system. (This will be even more effective if you read—or at least scan—even further into the book before deciding.) You'll more than likely discover that one method suits you better. Both are capable of generating excellent-sounding recordings when paired with good skills and musicianship, so the choice will really be one of personal preference.

CHAPTER 2
CHOOSING YOUR SPACE AND HOW TO TREAT IT

If you're really new to recording, and your head's still reeling a bit from the barrage of equipment listed in the first chapter, don't fret. We'll look much more closely at all of it in the coming chapters with regard to use, function, etc. So now that you have a general picture of what kind of gear you're going to be using, let's have a look at where you'll be using it. This chapter is all about choosing where your studio will be located and how to make the most out of that space.

For some of you, there may not be a choice. It may be, by default, your 11x8-foot bedroom or nothing. Or possibly you have a finished (or somewhat finished) basement that's yours for the taking—or a converted garage. No matter which room you set up shop in, they will most likely all have one thing in common: they were not designed for listening to music, unfortunately, much less recording it. Most bedrooms, for example, are rectangular in shape. A rectangle has parallel sides, and that's bad when it comes to listening to music. The reasoning for this is beyond the scope of this book. It has to do with waves being able to bounce back and forth in a straight line (for the most part) between the walls, which results in certain frequencies building up and others not. In short, this means that the sound you're hearing through your speakers is not very accurate.

A Pro Studio Is More Than Just Pro Equipment and Atmosphere!

Professional studios have rooms constructed specifically with acoustics in mind from the ground up. This often means, among other things, they avoid parallel walls (the ceiling will often be sloped as well). If a studio is built into an existing structure, then the rooms are often "tuned" (with the use of diffusers, absorbers, and other acoustic manipulative devices) with the aid of a professional acoustical engineer. For the vast majority of us home recordists, this is not a luxury we can afford (it's not cheap!). If, however, you have the opportunity to construct your own home studio—whether it be renovating an existing home or building a separate structure on your acreage—then you'll definitely want to thoroughly research the topic with books/videos/etc. that are dedicated to the topic of studio construction. Some of the many fine books in this regard include *Sound Studio Construction on a Budget* by F. Alton Everest, *Acoustic Design for the Home Studio* by Mitch Gallagher, *Home Recording Studio: Build It Like the Pros* by Rod Gervais, and *Master Handbook of Acoustics* by F. Alton Everest. And if you're not the DIY type (or even if you are and have the budget for it), you would certainly benefit from consulting with an acoustical engineer on the construction.

If at all possible, you really want to avoid a room that's perfectly square-shaped. A rectangle-shaped room is considerably better. (The absolutely worst shape for a room would be a perfect cube, but that would be extremely rare.) The good news is that we can go a long way to make these bedrooms or basements fairly decent in terms of recording and mixing music. Is it going to rival a fully professional, "spare no expense" studio designed from the ground up? No, of course not. But the truth is that it doesn't need to. For our purposes, it just needs to be pretty good, and we can get there—without spending a fortune either.

One Room or Two? (or Three?)

Many home studios exist entirely within the confines of one room. By this I mean that the music is not only recorded there but it's also mixed. In this case, the "control room" (the room with the monitors, mixing desk, etc.) is also the "studio" or "recording room." Others have a dedicated control room (perhaps a bedroom) with another room serving as the "studio." This may be an adjoining living room or den, perhaps. Some people get really ambitious and even install a window between these two rooms. (If you're considering doing this, please research the process with a book devoted to studio design, as it's not as simple as plopping in a double-pane exterior window and calling it a day.) Others may even convert a large adjoining closet into a makeshift vocal booth. This is something that's practical on a temporary basis, too, as we'll see later.

However, no room is off limits when it comes to the recording (except the cube!). You will, of course, want your control room to be well established, but feel free to try out many different rooms for recording if you're feeling adventurous. You may find that the study, with wooden floors, lots of bookshelves to diffuse the sound a bit, and a higher ceiling, sounds nice for recording solo acoustic guitar. Or maybe the large, tiled bathroom has a cool slap-back echo to it that works well for electric guitars (or whatever). The list of fully professional albums that were recorded in a house (in whole or in part) is not a terribly short one and includes *Business as Usual* by Men at Work, *Exile on Main St.* by the Rolling Stones, *OK Computer* by Radiohead, *The Downward Spiral* by Nine Inch Nails, *Wasting Light* by the Foo Fighters, *Boston* by Boston, and *For Emma, Forever Ago* by Bon Iver, among many others. Granted, many of these (not all!) featured professional equipment, engineers, and producers, but the point is that they were recorded in houses—not professionally designed studios. In the case of *Wasting Light*, it was not only recorded in Dave Grohl's home studio (the drums were tracked in his garage), but it was also mixed there, as well!

Perhaps the big daddy of all home-recorded album stories is Bruce Springsteen's *Nebraska*. Bruce was doing nothing more (or so he thought) at the time than recording demos at home on his newly acquired Tascam 144 Portastudio four-track *cassette* recorder. However, after trying to recreate the songs in a professional studio and failing, Bruce succumbed to his runaway "demo-itis" (the act of falling in love with the "magic" and "vibe" of a demo recording), pulled the mixdown cassette from his back pocket (which was *mixed* on a normal, everyday boombox cassette recorder!), and submitted it to the label. Now, granted, the sound of *Nebraska* is on the "lo-fi" side; it certainly doesn't sound like most professionally recorded albums. However, the bottom line is that an album that was recorded in a totally untreated bedroom on a cassette four-track and mixed onto a standard boom box hit #3 on the *Billboard* 200 and went platinum—and that's a fact. "Well," you may say, "Bruce's reputation had a lot to do with that. People were willing to listen past the production because they knew Bruce was a top-notch songwriter." And there's probably truth to that. But it's also true that "home recording equipment" has grown by leaps and bounds since those days, and it's capable of delivering astounding sound quality when paired with know-how, good musicianship, and care. The divider between "pro" and "home" equipment is constantly getting fainter with every passing year.

BASIC LAYOUT: CONTROL ROOM

We'll look at separate recording rooms (should you so choose) in a bit, but let's start with the control room. There are several basic layout features that are common to nearly every control room, including symmetry, listening position, and acoustic treatment. Let's take a look at those now.

Monitor Placement

You want to place your monitors along the short wall in a rectangular room, and they should ideally be several feet from the wall. They should be set at ear height (when you're sitting) and pointing toward you. As such, they're normally placed on stands or on top of a desk. They should be symmetrical with regard to their distance to the side (long) walls. Below are several different typically shaped rooms and the (approximate) ideal monitor placement and listening position.

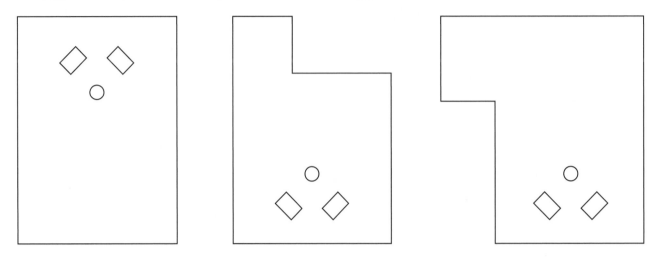

The monitors should form an equilateral triangle with your head as you sit in the listening position. This is referred to as *near-field monitoring*, and while it's not how the pros always do it (although they almost always do have a near-field setup for reference), it's usually the best we can do in a bedroom-type control room. The idea is to be physically close to the monitors so that the sound of the "room" is minimized when listening to the speakers. (We'll talk more about this later.) The sides of this equilateral triangle will usually be between three and four feet, depending on your setup.

Specifically, your ideal listening position will usually be at 38% of the length of the long walls. In other words, if your room was 10x8, you'd want to be facing an eight-foot wall, with your head approximately 3.8 feet from it and directly centered between the long (10-foot) walls.

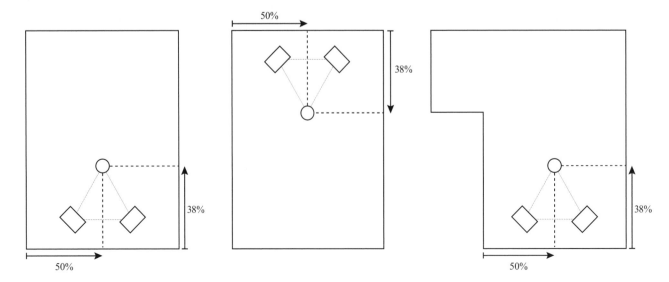

You may feel as though you don't want to give up that much room behind your speakers, especially if you're also going to be sleeping in this room, etc. The reason that this number is a standard is that it places you in a certain spot that's fairly devoid of nulls or peaks with regard to frequency buildup. However, it's not a rule; it's only a convention. Feel free to try other spots if you'd like, as well. One benefit to having space behind your desk is that it allows you walking room back there, which is always nice when you need to check for a loose connection, hook up a new piece of gear, etc.

Author's control room. Though it's difficult to tell from this photo, the speakers are actually three feet from the rear wall.

Phantom Image

Once you get your monitors positioned, you can check for proper stereo imaging by playing a mono signal (such as a single guitar or vocal track) and panning it to the center. The signal should appear to be coming from directly between the speakers. This is the so-called "phantom image" and is one of the fun phenomena of stereo sound. You can try slowly panning the signal to hard left and all the way to hard right to follow it from speaker to speaker. This is also a nice way to test your monitors. The signal should be the same volume when panned hard left as it is hard right.

Quieting the Noise

Computers can tend to get a little noisy at times, so it should also be mentioned that, if using a desktop computer, you should try to place the machine a good distance away from your listening position if possible. Some computers have louder fans/hard drives than others, and these noises can become a bit of a nuisance when you're listening to quieter tracks and/or when you're recording with a microphone in the room. Pro studios solve this issue by keeping all the noisy equipment in a separate room, but that's not always an option for the home recordist (although, if you're single, it's probably not out of the question). An adjoining closet is an option, assuming you allow for some ventilation to prevent the machine from overheating.

One option is to upgrade the fans in your machine(s) (if they're still consumer-grade). This will lower the noise significantly. Some people also treat the case with weather stripping at the seams to help prevent leakage and/or ringing or rattling. If, after these options, the noise is still a real issue, you can try placing it in a nearby closet and running a few extension USB cables, etc. if necessary for the mouse, keyboard, monitor, A/I, etc. Make sure there's adequate ventilation so that it doesn't overheat.

Alternatively, some people choose to place the machine inside a specially designed enclosure. There are several companies that make these, including Acoustiproducts and Custom Consoles, but they can get pretty pricey.

However, before you go to all these lengths, make sure that it's a problem in the first place. Fortunately, I've never had to mess with much of this, as the fan in my computer is relatively quiet. I actually have two computers in my control room because it also doubles as my office (which is where I'm writing this book right now!). The "office" computer is a little noisier than my music computer (not much), but my music machine is quiet enough; I just have it placed on the floor several feet away and aim it so that the noisiest side is facing the wall opposite of where I'm located if/when I record in this room. I turn off the office machine if I'm using a mic, and I'm good to go.

Other Noise Culprits

Aside from the computer, there are several other leading contributors to noise in the studio. Here are some of the most common:

- **Air conditioner/heater:** This is a big one, and it's by far the biggest thorn in my side. (Living in Texas, the idea of going without AC in the summer is like someone in Minnesota going without heat in the winter.) First of all, removing the vent from the ceiling will *significantly* cut down the noise in your room. In fact, if the main AC unit in my house wasn't located right on the other side of my office wall, this tweak alone would make my room quiet enough for recording even fingerpicked acoustic guitar. One issue with this is that the air won't be deflected and will blast straight out. If you happen to be seated anywhere near the vent, this can bit uncomfortably chilly when it's running. There's also the problem of it blowing papers off a desk that's directly underneath it, as is the case in my office. I solved this by building a little makeshift deflecting wooden panel that prevents it from blasting me with air.

If, after removing a vent, you're exposed to blasts of air, you can add a simple deflective panel using a sheet of plywood and some angled brackets.

- **Clocks:** This is especially true of a cheap, plastic $8 special. They'll usually tick loud enough to be picked up by a condenser. The easiest way to deal with this is to avoid those types of clocks—i.e., use a digital one—or simply move it to another room or cover it with a blanket during recording.

- **Cars, pets, and other domestic disturbances:** Unfortunately, there's not a whole lot you can do if sound is leaking in through a window from the outside world. Aside from filling the window and blocking it off (you can research online how to do this in a non-permanent fashion if you'd like), you may just have to try to schedule your session at the quietest times. Of course, this all depends on your location. Fortunately, I don't have much of a problem in this regard; my neighbor has a dog that's kept outside often, but the only time he really barks a lot is usually when I go into my back yard to take out the trash. Also, my control room is located in a room farthest from the street, so car noise isn't an issue either.

- **Refrigerators and other household appliances:** If your studio is located in a den next to the kitchen, the fridge may very well be loud enough to creep into the mics. Many of my vocal takes throughout the years (in various home studios) have begun with "Remember the fridge!" After ruining an entire fridge worth of groceries once because you forgot to turn it back on, you don't want to do that again. So if you must turn it off while recording, do what's necessary to remind yourself about it! Other appliances that you'll most likely need to work around can include dishwashers, washers and dryers, etc. Always listen to a newly recorded track on headphones, as this will reveal the noise floor much more dramatically than with speakers.

- **Weather:** A heavy rain will almost certainly be audible, so unless you're recording a cranked guitar amp or something similar, you may have to wait it out. However, if you have mics set up ready to go and it starts thundering, don't miss your chance to open your window briefly and record a bit of it! It's a very cool sound.

Acoustic Treatment

This is a big one. If you've done much recording at home and have been baffled by the fact that, although your mixes may sound nice on your system, they sound terrible when you listen elsewhere, you've no doubt dealt firsthand with the problems of bedroom mixing. As I mentioned earlier, houses are not designed with mixing in mind, so we've got the odds stacked against us from the beginning. By far the most neglected puzzle piece in terms of getting pro sounds from a home studio lies in acoustic treatment. That bears repeating: *the lack of acoustic treatment is by far the most common problem in home studios.* So, what do we mean by acoustic treatment? Well, there are two main types: soundproofing and sound treatment.

Soundproofing involves keeping sounds from getting into or out of a room. This is not easy to do, and it can also be fairly expensive and very labor-intensive to do it well. The short story is that it's not something that a home recordist will deal with unless they're planning on renovating their home or building from scratch. Basement studios generally have a head start with this, as the fact that the room is entombed in earth will greatly help to prevent noise from entering through the walls. But the ceiling will still leak sounds from the rooms above, not to mention particularly loud sounds (lawn mowers, motorcycles, etc.) entering the house from outside. So the best we can usually do with regard to this problem is try to record during quiet times around your neighborhood and don't disturb the peace by recording your Marshall stack on 11 at 3:00 A.M. With regard to the last point, it's a very good idea to have someone walk outside around your home to get a sense of the sound level while you're playing instruments (bass, electric guitar, etc.) at the level you'd like them to be for recording. This can let you know if you'll need to worry about this type of thing.

Sound treatment deals with the way sound reacts within a certain room. We don't want sound waves to bounce back and forth between parallel walls or bounce endlessly around the room, because this will greatly affect the frequencies we hear while we're mixing/recording. If we can't accurately hear what's going on, we're likely to make ill-informed decisions come mix-time. This is why, although our song may sound great when we're listening in our room in our mixing chair, it will sound completely different in your car or at your friend's house. It's because we mixed it while hearing the inaccurate representation caused by our rectangular room. This is where acoustic treatment comes in. There are two main categories we'll discuss: absorption and diffusion.

Absorption deals with absorbing sound waves. This helps to prevent them from bouncing all over the room. Ideally, we'd like to hear only the sound coming from the speakers straight to our ears. In an untreated room, however, this is not what's happening at all. You'll hear the sound from the speakers but also every other possible reflective point, as well. In other words, the sound will travel from the speakers and bounce off each wall and the ceiling before reaching you. We use absorption mostly in the control room, because we want to create a *reflection-free zone* for the listening position. (It's not totally reflection-free, but we can seriously tame the *early reflections*, which are by far the most troublesome.)

Diffusion deals with scattering, or breaking up, sound waves, which helps avoid standing waves and resonant frequencies (the buildup of certain frequencies due to the natural resonance of the room, which is determined by its size, shape, and physical properties). We generally use diffusion a bit more in the "live" or "recording room" (if you have a two-room setup), because we're usually trying to create a room with a natural, even-sounding decay in that instance. This is why you'll often see funny-shaped structures hanging from the ceiling or walls in a musical theater. These are most often diffusers of some sort.

Take into account that these are generalizations and that, since almost every room (live or control room) is slightly different, we can employ different strategies if necessary to provide the most effective treatment. That said, there are some tried-and-true methods for typical situations. So let's look at those.

Absorption

So we've already determined what we don't want: the sound bouncing off all the walls before it reaches our ears. So what we'll do is place absorbers at these reflective points to help stop the sound from bouncing off the wall to our head. Again, this is usually at 10 main points: two spots (one for each speaker) on each wall and two on the ceiling. For our purposes, we'll treat these as four larger spots on the wall and one larger one on the ceiling (large enough to account for both speakers).

Here's where these five spots would be located in a typical bedroom-style control room:

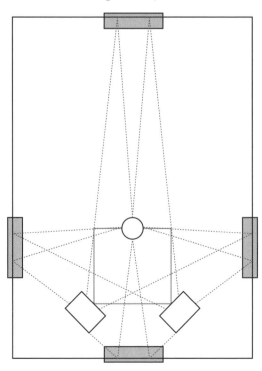

We can place absorptive panels (or some furniture) at these spots to block (most of) the sound from bouncing back to our ears. These panels can be made of various materials, including acoustic foam, rigid fiberglass, or mineral wool, among others. Soft, fluffy furniture, such as a sofa or futon, can also provide some absorption, as well. Generally speaking, the denser the material, the better it will be at absorbing lower frequencies. Whereas a one-inch sheet of foam may do a passable job at controlling the high frequencies, it's not terribly effective in the mid range and hardly effective at all in the lower mids or bass. Materials that are known for absorbing fairly well throughout the frequency spectrum are known as *broadband absorbers*, and rigid fiberglass and mineral wool are two such materials.

A two-inch thick panel of a broadband absorptive material is usually adequate for each of these reflective points. It's recommended that you mount them a few inches away from the wall, as the space between the rear of the panel and the wall will aid in lower-frequency absorption. The ceiling panel (or "cloud" as it's commonly called) should also hang down several inches or more from the ceiling. For the side wall reflective points, I'd recommend at least a 2x2-feet (two inches deep) panel. Make sure to position them accurately so that you're adequately covering the reflective point on the wall. For the ceiling and front/rear walls, I'd recommend a wider panel of 3x2 or (better) 4x2 feet (two inches deep).

There are numerous companies that sell these types of panels (and numerous ones that sell acoustic foam, as well), including Primacoustic, Auralex, RealTraps, and GIK Acoustics, to name a few. Unfortunately, they can get pricey pretty quickly. The foam starts off fairly affordable. However, you get what you pay for, and the affordable foam pieces aren't terribly effective at the lower frequencies. You can expect to pay anywhere from $60 to $300 or more for a broadband panel measuring 48x24x2 inches. When you start to add that up (not to mention the shipping charges if you're not near a company), it can quickly turn into an expensive venture. And that's not even including bass traps, which we'll look at next.

This is the reason that I suggest that, if you have to DIY *anything*, acoustic treatment is the area to do it. You can easily save yourself *hundreds* or *thousands* of dollars by doing the work yourself, and you can end up with a perfectly decent-sounding control room. And to be honest, I think it's kind of fun! Once you have the materials in hand (see Appendix for information on this), you can easily knock out five panels over a weekend if you hunker down. And you can make them look pretty nice, as well (not to mention you can tailor them to match your studio).

Bass Traps

Unfortunately, the early reflections aren't the only thing we have to tame in the control room. Bass response is also a big problem in the home studio control room. This can really mess with your monitoring experience and result in poor mixing decisions. Enter the *bass trap*. The purpose of a bass trap, which we place in the corners of the room, is to absorb the extra bass frequencies that build up.

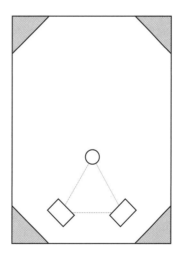

Again, you can buy ready-made traps, but they are quite expensive—much more so than the absorptive panels. You could easily pay over $3K, $4K, or $5K in bass traps alone if you buy quality ones. Lucky for us, though, you can make pretty decent ones for a fraction of that. It's actually done the same way as the panels; it's just that instead of two inches thick, bass traps should be at least four inches thick. Ideally they should span from floor to ceiling, but anything and everything helps. If you have access to a bunch of old, thick blankets, piling them up in the corner will be a lot better than nothing. The less budget you have, the more creative you'll need to get. However, if you follow the advice in the Appendix, you can build four decent, full-size bass traps for around $100–$120. How's that for frugal?

What About the Door?

If your control room is in a bedroom, there's a very good chance that the entry door will be in one of the four corners. If that's the case, what do you do about that bass trap? That's a good question. There are several possibilities:

1. **You don't have a bass trap in that corner:** This is the least desirable option.

2. **You rig up some sort of apparatus, allowing the trap to slide into place as the door is closed and retreat behind the door when the door is opened:** This is the most impressive option, but it's the most difficult.

3. **You have a temporary bass trap that can easily be moved into place when you need it:** This is the most practical option.

I use the third method. It works great as long as you work out some system whereby you make sure no one will come barging in without knocking. Otherwise, you could end up with a crashing bass trap on your hands!

DIY bass traps in author's control room.

TIPS FOR A LIVE ROOM

If you'd like to be able to record several people at once, you may not be able to fit them into your control room—or comfortably, at least. In this situation, you may want to use an adjacent den or living room as your "live room." In this room, we usually want it to sound fairly balanced throughout the room, meaning that we want some reflections, but we want them to be scattered.

Ideal Rooms

The ideal room for this type of thing is a fairly large space—say 20x30 feet or greater—with hard floors and a high, sloped ceiling. You sometimes see this type of room in the ground-level living area of a two-story house. Of course, unless you live alone, the chances of you making use of this type of room for recording exclusively are pretty slim. (But it may be roomy enough to just temporarily move a few pieces of furniture out of the way when the need arises.) If the walls are filled with bookshelves, dressers, entertainment centers, sofas, etc., you may just end up with a pretty nice-sounding room on your hands naturally. Filled bookshelves make very decent diffusers, as do anything with curved or jagged surfaces. If you have access to this type of space, try making some recordings in it and see how it sounds. You can use close mics and also "room mics" to pick up some of the ambience of the room and blend it to taste. (We'll talk much more about this idea in later chapters.)

Other Possibilities for Live Rooms

If you don't have access to a room like the one described, welcome to the club. It's certainly not the norm for most of us. But that doesn't mean we're out of luck. My "live room" is an upstairs loft/den that's adjacent to my control room. It has laminate floors and is not a perfect rectangle—it has a few nooks and crannies—but the basic area measures around 13x25 feet, with standard eight-foot ceilings. It doubles as a play room for my children. (Such is often the way of the home studio.) But with a bit of treatment, it serves as a nice-sounding room when I want a little ambience.

I'd say that the dimensions of my live room are on the smaller side of what would be acceptable for a "live room." Once you get much smaller, you're not really going to be able to get much more than early reflections. This can add a bit of realism to some instruments, but it's not really going to generate any reverb. Let's take a look at some typical treatment for a live room.

Bass Traps

Even though we do want ambience in a live room, we'll still most likely want to use bass traps in the corners. You can experiment with the amount to see if you can get away with less, but you'll most likely want to do the same as in the control room.

Diffusion

What you want to try to do is avoid parallel surfaces whenever possible. In this regard, if you place a diffuser on one wall, then it's not parallel with the opposing wall. So you don't need to have diffusers opposite each other. As mentioned, there are several objects found within the home that can make good diffusers, and a filled bookshelf is one of them. There are several types of diffusers available commercially, ranging in price from affordable ($3 per square foot) to quite expensive ($75 per square foot or more), and they vary greatly in design. They all aim to do basically the same thing, which is to scatter, or diffuse, the sound waves.

A typical use in a live room may be to place them at certain spots along one wall with possibly some absorptive panels along the opposite wall. If you have a high ceiling, you'd probably want to hang some diffusers from it, as well—especially if it's flat. But even if it's vaulted and comes to a single point in the middle, you'll benefit greatly from adding some diffusers at the intersection of the two slopes.

Absorption

Aside from the scattering of panels along two of the walls perhaps, you'll most likely want to use absorptive panels in your live room if your ceiling is the standard height of eight feet (or close to it). This is simply too short to produce useable reflections. Therefore, it's best to hang two-inch-thick panels—much like the "cloud" in the control room—covering most of the ceiling and therefore making it "acoustically invisible," so to speak. In fact, a low, absorptive ceiling is not all that different from a very high, diffusive ceiling when it comes to the sound. It may seem counter-intuitive, but covering the ceiling (you don't have to cover every single square inch) with absorptive panels can actually make the room *sound* bigger than it really is.

Author's live room with absorptive ceiling panels.

Other Concerns for the Live Room

There are some other concerns in a live room besides the acoustics; these are the more logistical ones, like getting cables and headphones out there, etc. You could just run the mic cables (and headphone extension cables if necessary) under the door as needed, but if you'd like to have more of a permanent setup, here are some tips:

- **Mount a snake to the wall and send it through a small hole in the wall (assuming the live room is adjacent to the control room):** You can make the hole look halfway nice by simply adding a wooden border around it.

- **Add a headphone amp on a shelf near the snake and run the cable to the control room:** If you have the ability and/or need to generate different mixes for numerous performers, you can have several line mixers (with four or six channels, for example) with headphone jacks, so that each person can tailor the mix as they see fit; drums could be mono on channel 1, bass on 2, etc. (More on this later in the book.)

- **Run some RCA cables out to a simple stereo system in the live room that can be used as a basic playback system or a talkback system:** This can be an inexpensive old boombox even, as it's not meant for critical listening.

You can get as fancy as you'd like with this type of thing. You'll have to evaluate your particular needs and go from there.

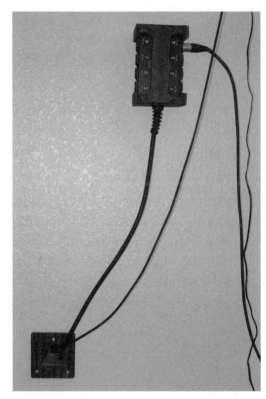

Custom-mounted snake and cable hole connecting author's live room and control room.

Live End/Dead End

If you have a decent-sized control room—say, 20 feet or longer—another option is a live end/dead end arrangement. In this scenario, you'd set up one end of the room as a typical control room, creating a reflective-free zone for the listening position. But on the opposite end, you could add diffusers, a hard floor (a 4x4 or 4x8 sheet of plywood can work on a temporary basis), and absorptive panels on the ceiling to create a live end to the room. Granted, this won't really be generating any reverb, but it will generate some nice ambience, which is especially nice when recording acoustic instruments.

Other aspects of studio treatment include creating a vocal/isolation booth—either permanent or temporary—and we'll look specifically at that idea in Chapter 12.

CHAPTER 3
WISH-LIST EQUIPMENT

Beyond the basics listed in Chapter 1, there are still plenty of other pieces of gear you could add to your arsenal if you so desired or needed. In this chapter, we'll take a look at the most common of those. The choice of whether or not you implement any of these will depend on several things, including:

- Your budget

- How you want to you use your studio

- Your preferences on workflow

- Your patience when it comes to learning new things

- What you started on

Even though it may seem that most people record the same way—in that most people use a DAW program on their computer—there are a huge number of ways that people get from A to B. You'd actually be hard-pressed to find several people who use the same collection of gear (and I'm talking function of the gear—not the same brand)—much less use it the same way. So you may want to come back to this chapter after you've gotten your feet wet and discovered what you like, hate, lack, or lust for in the world of home studio gear. I'm not going to make a separate list for the computer system vs. the standalone system, because so many of these are common to both, but there will be a few items that would be redundant or unnecessary on one system or the other.

ITEM 1: OUTBOARD (HARDWARE) SIGNAL PROCESSORS

In this category I'm including any type of hardware processor, such as rackmountable reverb units, delays, multi-effects, compressors, and equalizers. It could also apply to guitar effect pedals or even tape machines (for an echo effect) if you really wanted to get serious. When plugin effects and built-in effects (on a standalone recorder) are so prevalent, why would you ever want or need hardware versions? Well, there are several reasons people use them. Among the most common are:

- **You already have them:** Some people may have processors left over from an older, non-digital system. They most likely know these units well and know how to coax good sounds out of them, so why not use them?

- **You prefer the sound:** You'll hear endless debate about this topic. Many will make somewhat outrageous claims like, "Even the most expensive plugin will pale in comparison to even a modest hardware unit." Clearly this is not a common statement, but it demonstrates the polarization that can develop in the recording world. This is notoriously an issue when it comes to compression. Many people swear by hardware compressors and claim that software ones "just aren't the same at all." The bottom line is that, if you like what something does, then use it! If not, then don't. It's really that simple.

- **You prefer the feel or interface:** Lots of people just prefer working with hardware; they like turning knobs and pushing buttons instead of moving the mouse. These are generally people that started recording in the analog world and migrated to a digital setup, but you'll occasionally find youngsters like this, too.

- **Your CPU isn't the most powerful and has trouble running a lot of plugs:** Certain plugins are memory hogs and can really tax your system. However, using external hardware won't do that because it's just a matter of routing—not computing power.

- **They can increase flexibility in a standalone system:** Although many standalone recorders feature built-in effects, it's certainly not the seemingly endless cornucopia of sonic sweetening that's possible with a DAW. You may have two stereo processors at your disposal or possibly just one. But many standalones will have external effects sends (one or two, usually), which means you can add another processor or two via your outboard gear.

- **You hate staring at that empty equipment rack:** An empty rack is a sad thing. Plus, if it's filled with gear, it makes your mixing desk heavier and therefore more stable.

(Okay, so the last one isn't a good reason.) Again, it really comes down to personal preference. You can certainly make a great recording using nothing but plugins, and you can also do the same using nothing but hardware processors. By combining them, you get the best of both worlds. Commonly used devices in the home studio include reverbs/multi-effects by Lexicon (although they can get a little pricey, they do have more affordable models, as well), TC Electronic, and Yamaha; compressors by ART, Joemeek, and DBX; and equalizers by dbx, Peavey, Presonus, and others.

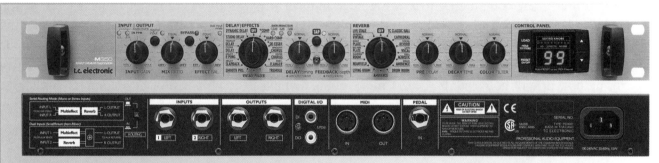

TC Electronic M350 Multi-effects Processor

Copyright TC Electronic, used with permission.

The TC Electronic M350 is a one-space rackmountable, dual-engine multi-effects processor with an extremely user-friendly design. It features 15 high-quality reverbs and 15 additional effects (including compression, several delays, chorusing, flanging, phasing, tremolo, and de-essing), with all parameters quickly accessible via multi-function knobs for highly intuitive operation. Dialing in sounds is quick and painless with the M350, yet it features enough flexibility to tailor the sounds to suit your needs. On the rear panel are 1/4-inch inputs and outputs, SPDIF digital I/O jacks, MIDI in and out jacks, and a 1/4-inch pedal input for remote control of certain parameters.

There are 256 factory presets on board and an additional 99 user-assignable presets that are accessible via up/down buttons. The reverbs on this unit are quite stunning and well worth the price tag alone. I really enjoy the simple, user-friendly layout and design, as it allows you to get right down to it and set up some nice patches right away. Even if the 15 additional effects weren't any good, the unit would still be relevant by virtue of the verbs alone, but the fact is that they sound great, as well!

Street price: $185

ITEM 2: PATCH BAY

If you end up getting several different pieces of outboard gear, a *patch bay* can certainly make your life easier. A patch bay is a rackmountable unit that's filled with nothing but jacks on the front and the back—usually 16, 24, or 32 pairs (top and bottom rows) on the front panel and corresponding ones on the back panel. Simply put, they allow you to bring all your gear's input and output jacks to a common place (the patch bay), so that you don't need to get behind your gear every time you want to connect your processor (reverb, EQ, etc.) to a different place.

For example, let's say you wanted to run your mic through an external preamp and then through an outboard compressor instead of just straight into the interface. On the patch bay, you simply run a short cable from, say, the "preamp out" jack to the "compressor input" jack and then one from the "compressor out" jack to the "interface input" jack. Most patch bays used by home studios feature TS jacks (1/4-inch) on the front and back panels, although you will occasionally find RCA jacks on the back panel (rarely on the front panel, though).

dbx PB-48 Patch Bay

Normalled, Half-Normalled, and De-normalled (Straight-Through)

Patch bays can be configured a few different ways, depending on your needs. However, regardless of their configuration, it's standard practice that the top row of jacks is used for device outputs, and the bottom row is used for device inputs. This will make a bit more sense once we look at how they work.

De-Normalled Mode

In *de-normalled* mode (sometimes referred to as "straight-through" mode), the top channel 1 jack on the back leads straight through to the top channel 1 jack on the front only. This is the easiest routing to understand, but it's actually not the most commonly used.

De-normalled (side view)

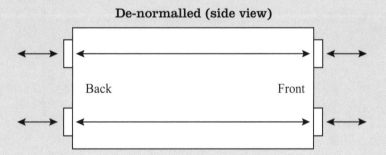

Normalled Mode

Normalled mode is the most commonly used in a patch bay. This is because it saves cables and the act of patching. In normalled mode, the signal enters the back top row jack and heads to the front jack, just as with the straight-through mode. However, as long as nothing is plugged into that top row jack on the front, the signal will continue down to the bottom row on its own and head back out the bottom row jack on the back.

Normalled (side view)

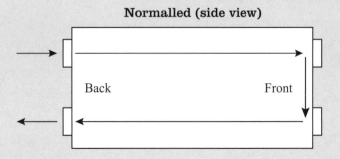

Why would we want this? Well, it allows you to set up routing for things you "normally" do. For example, let's say you normally plug your mic into your preamp's input and then plug your preamp's output into your A/I's channel 1 input. You *could* accomplish this in de-normalled mode by doing the following:

- Run a cable from the output of your preamp into the top jack of channel 1, for example, on the rear of the patch bay.

- Run a cable from the input of channel 1 on your A/I to the bottom jack of channel 1 on the rear of the patch bay.

- Run a patch cable from the top jack of channel 1 on the front panel of the patch bay to the bottom jack of channel 1 on the front panel of the patch bay.

This scenario would look like this:

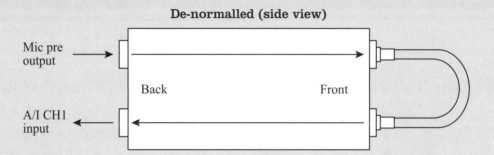

However, with the normalled mode, the patch cable on the front is not even necessary. The patch bay makes the connection for you internally.

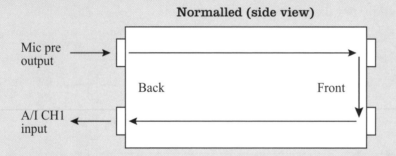

You'll find that, by setting up the patch bay with your "normal" way of working, the normalled mode will be incredibly convenient.

Okay, so what happens when you want to route the mic preamp into channel 2 of your A/I instead of channel 1? Glad you asked. At this point, we'll have to break the normal. The way in which the bay allows us to break the normal determines whether we have a normalled connection or a half-normalled connection.

Breaking the Normal: Normalled Mode

In normalled mode, if we plug something into the top jack on the front panel, then the patch bay breaks the connection between the top and bottom jacks. In other words, it acts the same as straight-through mode.

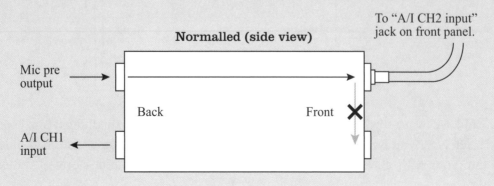

Breaking the Normal: Half-Normalled Mode

In half-normalled mode, when we plug a cable into the top row jack on the front panel, the connection to the bottom row jack isn't broken. The signal is split and appears at both the front-panel top jack and the rear-panel bottom jack.

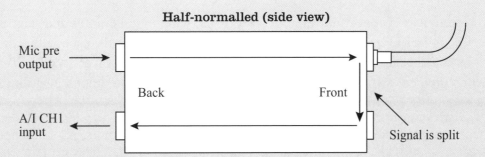

Half-normalled (side view)

As mentioned, normalled mode is by far the most common mode, but you may find uses for the other modes, as well. A patch bay can be hard-wired one way for all channels, it can have removable channels so they can be configured individually as needed, or they can have a switch for each channel that configures its mode.

ITEM 3: EXTERNAL MIC PREAMPS OR CHANNEL STRIPS

Another extremely common piece of outboard gear is the external mic preamp or channel strip. What's the difference? Well, a channel strip is simply a mic preamp (or "pre") with a bunch of extra goodies built in, such as a compressor/limiter, equalizer, de-esser, exciter, etc. or any combination thereof. Mic pres (including the ones in the audio interface, if it has them) can all sound noticeably different, and many people like to have several for the purpose of flexibility. Some may sound very clean and pristine, while others impart their own unique character to the sound. Professional studios will often have a dozen or more different mic preamps from which to choose, and we certainly don't need to go that far. But having one or two in addition to your A/I pres can add a lot of flexibility to your rig.

dbx 286s Channel Strip

The dbx 286s Channel Strip combines several useful tools in one concise, rackmountable package, including:

- Mic preamp with gain meter and clip indicator, phantom power, and an 80 Hz high-pass filter

- Overeasy compressor with gain reduction meter, drive, and density controls

- De-esser with threshold and frequency settings

- Enhancer with LF and HF detail settings

- Expander/Gate with threshold and ration settings

The 286s is a lifesaver when you need a lot of tone-shaping tools in one package. The preamp sounds great, and the compression is quick and easy to dial in thanks to its stripped-down interface. The enhancer is a nice addition and can add a different dimension to your sound when needed, and the de-esser is always a good tool to have when you're dealing with harsh high frequencies.

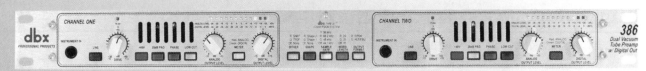

dbx 386 Dual Vacuum Tube Preamplifier with Digital Output

The dbx 386 is a two-channel tube microphone preamp with digital outputs and selectable sample rate (96, 88.2, 48, or 44.1 kHz). The front panel features duplicate channels, each with a drive (gain) knob, 1/4-inch instrument jack with activating "line" switch, phantom power switch, 20 dB pad switch, phase switch, low cut switch (75 Hz), and analog and digital output knobs. A peak input LED and a 12-segment output LED meter help to ensure accurate level-setting.

On the back, each channel has its own XLR balanced inputs and outputs, 1/4-inch inputs and outputs, and TRS insert jack. There's also BNC word clock input/output, a coaxial S/PDIF digital out, and an XLR AES/EBU digital out. The frequency response is 10 Hz to 75 kHz, and the unit uses two 12AU7 tubes. The Type IV conversion system features options for setting dither, shape, sample rate, word length, and output format.

The sound of the 386 is warm and detailed. I really enjoy the way it treats acoustic guitar, bass, and vocals, but it also functions as an excellent DI box for both bass and guitar when using the instrument input. The option to run either analog or digital outs makes it incredibly flexible, as well—not to mention its sleek appearance makes it an attractive addition to any rack. Considering you're getting two fantastic-sounding independent preamps makes it well worth the money.

Street price: 286s – $200, 386 – $500

One of the main things that separates a professional studio—aside from the acoustics of the building, which is certainly a big factor—is that a pro studio often has a lot of redundancy. In other words, they need to be able to record a lot of tracks at once, and this means they need to have a lot of channels of great equipment. One advantage of a home recordist is that we often don't need to do that. Many home recordists record one track at a time (or two at most), which means that we don't need to spend the extra money on dozens of channels of great gear. In this regard, many will put together one or two channels of nice gear rather than many channels of mediocre gear. This idea, of course, will depend on your personal situation and needs, but it's certainly something to consider when you're putting together your rig.

ITEM 4: ADDITIONAL MICS

Lots of mics sound significantly different, which means they're useful for different things. One mic may excel when used on your acoustic guitar, for example, but it might not sound that great on your voice, etc. So the more mics you have, the more options you have. This isn't to say that you need a mic locker with 40 or 50 different mics in it (which isn't uncommon in pro studios), but at least one decent LDC (large-diaphragm condenser), one SDC (small-diaphragm condenser), and one dynamic would be a nice start if you can swing it. After you feel (if ever) that you've outgrown those, you can start thinking about expanding your collection. An identical pair of SDCs, for example, is especially nice for recording something in stereo.

ITEM 5: ADDITIONAL MIDI CONTROLLERS

Another common MIDI controller is the percussion pad-type, which is most often used for programming drum parts (or playing drum samples in a live setting). All of the drum parts for the recordings in this book were done so with the KAT Multipad percussion controller (see sidebar). Although you can "play" the drum parts on your keyboard, it's much more intuitive, and therefore more effective (in my opinion), to do so on a percussion controller. You can generally control dynamics better, and you're able to think more like a drummer in general, which usually translates (even if you're not a drummer) into a better-feeling drum track. We'll talk more about this in Chapter 11.

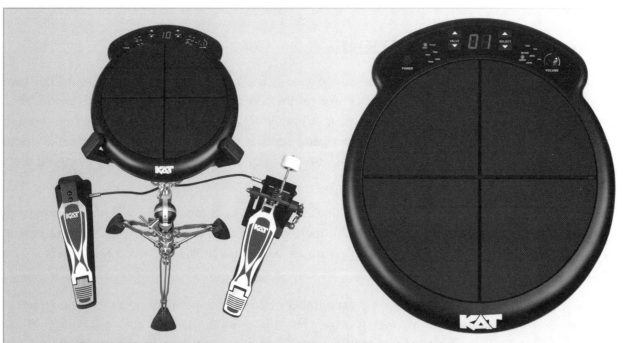

KAT KTMP1 Multipad Drum & Percussion Pad Sound Module
Copyright KAT Percussion, used with permission.

The KAT KTMP1 Multipad is a four-pad percussion MIDI controller and sound module that allows you to control MIDI drum sounds with authentic drumming feel. It features 50 built-in drum sounds which can be used for practice, performance, or recording virtually anywhere, and the MIDI out and/or USB jacks allow you to use it to control any virtual instrument. The MIDI note of each pad is easily assignable (from 00 to 99), as is the sensitivity range, level, reverb amount, panning, and tuning.

The unit also features input jacks for expansion pedals, including the KT-HC1 hi-hat controller pedal and the KT-KP1 kick drum trigger (kick pedal sold separately). Making use of these allows for precise control of kick, hat, and three other sounds from a standard drumset (such as snare, tom, and crash) all at once. For recording, this means you can lay down the basic beats (say, kick, snare, and hat) in one pass and then quickly reassign a few pads to come back and overdub some fills (toms, ride, and crash).

Street price: KTMP1– $120, KT-HC1 – $50, KT-KP1 – $80

Other types of MIDI controllers include:

- **Pedal controllers:** simulate the bass pedals on an organ

- **Pad controllers:** contain many smaller pads (usually 16 or more) and often knobs/faders, allowing you to access a large amount of samples and effects

- **Wind controller:** allows control of MIDI wind instruments, such as saxophone, clarinet, etc., with a familiar-feeling interface

- **Miscellaneous/expression controllers:** various types of controllers that allow you to manipulate sound in different ways, including pads on which you can "draw" with your fingers to control pitch, timbre, etc., and light-sensitive controllers that respond to your movement

Note that just about any of these controllers can be configured to play any MIDI instrument. In other words, a wind controller can be used to plays sounds other than wind instruments. You could use it to play piano sounds, drum sounds, etc. It's just that it's easier to generate more realistic wind instrument sounds by playing a MIDI controller that mimics the real instrument. This is the same reason that MIDI keyboard controllers work best for pianos, and drumpad controllers work best for playing MIDI drum sounds.

ITEM 6: EXTERNAL MIXER

This is mostly applicable to a computer-based system, as most standalone recorders have their own faders and knobs, etc. Many home recordists mix "in the box" when using a DAW. This means that, regardless of how many inputs they have on their A/I, they only use two outputs for listening through their speakers. They do things like pan the tracks and adjust volume all within the DAW on a virtual mixer. It looks like a real mixer, except you push up the faders and twist the knobs by dragging them with your mouse.

However, if you have a lot of outputs on your interface (say, eight or more), and you like the hands-on feel of real faders, etc., you can route individual tracks to individual outputs on your A/I. From there, they can be fed into individual channels on your mixer, and you can use the mixer's channels—with all its real faders and knobs—to mix with.

I must reiterate here, again, that there are a great number of ways of implementing a mixer into a setup. The above example pertained to an analog mixer, but digital mixers are another possibility. These will often contain built-in effects and generally some level of automation, or at least the possibility to save different mixer "scenes" for easy recall. Some digital mixers act as audio interfaces, as well, which could then replace the need for a separate A/I. (This also plays into Item 7—see below.) Other uses for a small (say, four- to eight-channel) mixer may include allowing yourself to listen to several different sources (your CPU stereo mix or an aux input such as an iPod) through the same speakers and/or hearing your CPU mix through different sets of speakers (your nice studio monitors and your cheap computer speakers, for example) for reference. In the home recording world, there are literally hundreds of ways to skin a cat. You'll just need to find the way that works best for you. After reading this book, you'll most likely have a pretty good idea of whether or not you'll want to include a mixer in your setup.

ITEM 7: CONTROL SURFACE

A *control surface* is a nice way to bridge the power of the software DAW to the analog feel of a mixer. Most of them work via USB connection, and they allow you to control the features of your software DAW program with actual knobs, faders, and buttons. They range in complexity from fairly basic models, which may include some channel faders (possibly with mute/solo buttons) and transport controls (record, play, etc.), to incredibly sophisticated models with enough buttons and gadgets to just about negate the need for your mouse altogether. Obviously, the prices vary greatly with the included features.

Many of them will come from the factory already configured to work with a particular DAW program, but most of them can be configured to work with just about any. There's often a bit of a learning curve with this type of thing, however, so you may have to do a few online searches here and there to get everything running smoothly. It's well worth the effort, though, if you desire the more traditional feel of a mixer (as I certainly do!). They can usually be configured any way you want them to, with each knob, fader, or button assigned to control whichever DAW parameter you'd like.

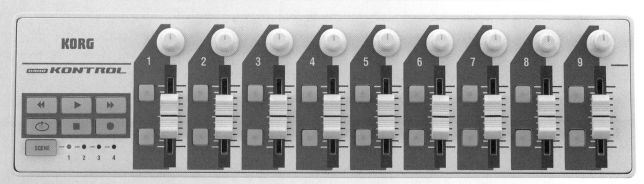

Korg nanoKontrol   Copyright Korg, used with permission.

The Korg nanoKontrol is a compact USB MIDI controller for your DAW. With transport controls (play, record, FF, RW, stop, and loop) and nine channels, each featuring one fader, one knob, and two buttons, you can easily set it up to control level, pan, solo, and mute functions for nine tracks in your DAW. But that's not all. The unit has four different "scenes," with each one independently assignable, which means you can actually control 36 tracks when using all four scenes.

I got this thing up and running in Reaper with no trouble using this setup. I added blank tracks 10, 20, and 30 to the project, since this would make scene 1 control tracks 1-9, scene 2 control tracks 11-19, etc. This just made it more intuitive to me, since the "1s" and "2s," etc. would line up for each scene. If you're not a big fan of using the mouse (and I'm not), this will make your work much more enjoyable. It's so much nicer, in my opinion, to move a real fader instead of clicking and dragging a virtual one.

However, the functionality hardly stops there. This thing is completely programmable and customizable. You can assign any button/knob/fader to control virtually any function on your DAW. For example, I rarely use more than 15 tracks or so when recording (I know many people use way more than that, but I usually don't), so scenes 3 and 4 were basically wasted on my nanoKontrol. Therefore, I created another key map (you can create as many as you'd like) designed for 18-track operation that took advantage of these unused controllers. I assigned the top row of buttons in scenes 3 and 4 as track arming for tracks 1–18, respectively, and assigned the bottom row of buttons to access functions like displaying the current track's effects window, scrolling through tracks, naming tracks, and adding markers. The knobs were assigned to effect send level, etc.

The end result is that my mouse usage has diminished *tremendously*, which is something I love. And since these are so reasonably priced, if you really did need all 36 tracks for a project, you could easily add another nanoKontrol, using the first for 36-track operation of level, pan, solo, and mute, and dedicating the other one to handle all the other commands and functions you'd like to control mouse-free.

The nanoKontrol has since been updated with the nanoKontrol2, which has made a few minor changes. One of the nine channels has been forfeited in favor of a more robust transport set, which includes marker set, next marker, and previous marker. There's also track forward and backward buttons for selecting different tracks. In addition to this, each channel now also features a third button, which is set to track arm by default. Again, though, all of these are completely assignable to any function you'd like. At this price, there's no reason that anyone has to mix entirely with the mouse anymore if they don't want to!

Street price: $60

Again, the line is often blurred between digital mixers, control surfaces, and audio interface. Some products that are described as "digital mixers" can sometimes actually act as all three. Granted, these are generally more expensive—typically $1,500 or more new—but for a powerful all-in-one solution, they're nice if you have the budget. The PreSonus StudioLive 16.0.2 Digital Mixing System, for example, can act as a standard analog/digital mixer for live work (with great built-in effects) or a digital mixer/firewire audio interface for the studio, allowing you to record up to 16 channels simultaneously and playback 16 individual tracks. It's not truly a control surface in that it won't allow you to assign any button or fader to control different DAW features, but it will allow you to mix 16 tracks from your DAW with an analog feel and use its built-in effects if you'd like.

SUMMARY

Again, I'd suggest that, if you don't already have your recording equipment, you wait until after reading the entire book before making your decision. There are so many different ways to configure your studio that you don't need to be stuck with something you don't like. If you're just a bit patient and do a little research up front, you'll be better prepared to find something that will work for you.

CHAPTER 4
RECORDING PRIMER AND TERMINOLOGY

Before we get too deep into the details of the tools we'll be using, let's look at a brief overview of the recording process and the terminology used to discuss it. Although every artist/producer/engineer is different, and no two will most likely do everything the same, there are some general, larger areas of the process that are fairly standard, and so we'll start there. You may well be familiar with many of these terms. If so, feel free to skim through for ones that are new to you.

The home recording process can usually be divided into four basic categories: *initial tracking*, *overdubs*, *editing*, and *mixing*. Again, this is very general, and there are some areas that we've left out—most notably, pre-production and mastering. *Pre-production* deals with anything you need to do before the song is ready to be recorded, including arrangements and rehearsals. *Mastering* deals with polishing a mix of an individual song or a group of songs (album or EP) to make them ready for commercial airplay (should that be a possibility).

The mastering process involves a number of tools, such as multi-band compression, equalization, limiting, and stereo enhancement (among others), and it also helps ensure that all the tracks of an album sound like a cohesive unit. While many home recordists will try their hand at mixing their own music, it's fairly common to send your album to a professional mastering engineer if you're serious about the music (i.e., you want to sell it or possibly use it to shop for a record deal). It's hard to distill the mastering process down into a paragraph, but some terms that are generally used to describe a mastered song are "louder," "punchier," "bigger," and "more sparkle," among others. In short, it helps a good mix sound more "professional," for lack of a better term.

Of course, there are no rules when it comes to home recording. And even the four basic categories may not apply to everyone. If you're the type that only records a live, one-take performance (such as a singer/songwriter playing guitar and singing at the same time), then you won't need to do any overdubs, and you may not need to do any edits. If you're wanting a perfect, pristine production, however, with nary a note out of place, you may spend a good amount of time editing. And you may want to try your hand at mastering your own stuff. What the pros usually offer is some very expensive gear, a very nice room/set of monitors, and lots of experience. But even the pros had to start somewhere, right? There's certainly no harm in practicing anyway, and there are lots of available plugins geared toward mastering. You can always pay to have a song mastered if you're really serious about making it sound the best it can. But if you just plan on sharing music with your friends or maybe just selling a few CDs at some shows, you may want to see what you can come up with.

INITIAL TRACKING

The initial tracking usually involves laying down the rhythm instruments—most often the drums and bass, and possibly a rhythm guitar and/or keyboards. Since we're not dealing with recording live drums in this book, this step will also involve drum programming (though you could argue to place that in pre-production). When people do record live drums, they'll often record the bass and guitars/ keys at the same time for several reasons:

- Even though the drummer may be playing to a click, it's much easier for him to get into the music if he has others playing the song with him.

- The other instruments will generally feed off the drummer's energy, as well.

- Time is money in the studio, and if you can knock out some bass and rhythm guitar while you're doing the drums, all the better.

However, the main reason is that it generally results in a better "vibe." When you're playing to programmed drums, of course, the vibe is not going to change from take to take, but if you have two people available to record (a bassist and a guitarist, for example), you should try recording at the same time, assuming you have the means to do so. There's always some form of communication when two people play music together—including in the studio—and it usually makes a difference in the recorded product. If you're the sole musician, however, then you'll have to generate all the vibe by yourself. Try some candles or lava lamps to create mood lighting.

So let's take a look at some of the terms you'll come across, with regard to the initial tracking stage, that may not be completely self-explanatory to the beginning recordist. This will be the biggest list of the bunch, as many of these will also apply to the other three stages.

Project/Song

This is simply the title of the song file or project file you're working on with your DAW or standalone recorder. Within it, you can make many types of settings that will be specific to that song, including:

- Time signature
- Tempo
- Sample rate
- Bit depth

Things like time signature and tempo will affect the click track and playback speed of MIDI instruments, whereas the bit depth and sample rate will affect recording quality and file size.

Track

A *track* was easier to explain in the analog days, because it corresponded to a physical space on the tape. If it was an eight-track machine, then the tape's width was (basically) divided into eight equal parts corresponding to each track, and the record/playback heads featured individual sections for each one. So basically, a track corresponds to one recorded performance that you can manipulate via volume, panning, EQ, etc. without altering the rest of the tracks.

In a typical small production, for instance, you may:

1. Record a guitar on track 1

2. Record another guitar on track 2

3. Record a lead vocal on track 3

4. Record a harmony vocal on track 4

Since each instrument is on its own separate track, you can then mix them however you want—i.e., the first guitar can be loud while the second one is soft.

Tracking

This is simply a term for recording instruments on tracks. "Honey, tomorrow we'll be tracking the guitars, so take an extra long lunch (but bring me something back)."

Arm/Disarm

Arming a track means that you've put it into record-ready mode. When a track is armed, and you press record, that track will begin recording. When you don't want to record on a track anymore, you *disarm* it.

Click

The *click* (or *click track*) is a metronome sound that allows performers to play in time. If you're going to be adding MIDI instruments or performing any edits at some point in the song, it's incredibly useful to record with a click. If not, it's not completely necessary, but it never hurts to get some practice playing with a metronome. "I need either more click or less acoustic in my headphones please!"

Take

A *take* is an attempted recording of a part. Each time you try to record a guitar solo, for example, it's a new take. Or each time the band tries to lay down the basic tracks together, that's a take. "We're rolling. This is take 58. Maybe we should have rehearsed a bit more?"

Basic Tracks or Bed Tracks

The *basic tracks* or *bed tracks* refer to the song's foundation, usually including the drums, bass, and rhythm guitars/keyboards. As previously mentioned, these are often recorded all at once in pro studios to achieve a certain vibe and to give the tracks life and excitement.

Mic (Miking, Mic'ing)

The term "mic" can either be the short form of the noun "microphone" or it can be a verb meaning "to set up a microphone for recording a sound source." Regardless of whether it's spelled "miking" or "mic'ing," the meaning is the same. "Not now, mom! I'm in the middle of miking my acoustic guitar."

Off-Axis

This refers to the relationship between a sound source and a mic. When a mic is not pointed directly at a speaker or instrument—and instead is angled—it's said to be *off-axis*. The same can be said for a singer singing into a mic. When singing from anywhere other than right in front of the mic, they are said to be off-axis.

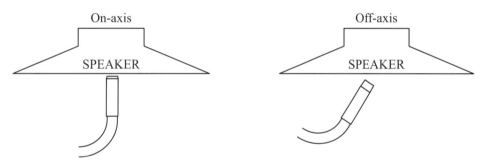

Bleed (Leakage)

This is a term used to describe when the sound of one instrument is also being picked up by a microphone that's meant to record a separate instrument. If, for example, you're recording drums and bass together in the same room, the sound from the bass amp will likely *bleed* into the drum mics unless you do something to prevent it. This means that, later on, anything you do to those drum tracks (EQ, etc.) will also affect a portion of the bass, because it was partly present on those tracks, as well as its own track. (Coincidentally, in this scenario, the drums may very well bleed into the bass mic, too.)

Usually whenever a group of musicians perform together in the same room for a recording, there is going to be some amount of bleed. Among the many factors that affect the severity of it include the volume of the instruments, the type of mics being used (an omni-directional condenser mic will certainly pick up more than a cardioid dynamic mic), and the size/shape of the room(s) and placement of the instruments/mics within it. The goal (when bleed is undesirable) is to reduce it to an effect where it's basically negligible.

Sometimes the "messier" sound of many instruments bleeding through is desired for the quality it produces. This is something about which you should make a decision before you start tracking, though, because, as with printing effects (see "Recording Wet/Printing Effects"), once the bleed is on a track, you can't remove it.

Gobo

A *gobo* is a moveable absorption panel that's generally used to isolate performers and/or cut down on ambient reflections. For example, if you want to record two guitar players playing together in the same room and reduce the amount of bleed between the tracks, you can place gobos between them to help absorb much of the sound.

Gobos come in various shapes and sizes, and many of them are very affordable. Ones that are meant to isolate a single guitar cabinet can be quite small but effective, while others, meant to isolate drum sets and more, can stand eight feet or taller. You can also make your own gobos relatively easily. This idea is covered in the Appendix.

The CAD Acousti-Shield AS16 is a mountable enclosure designed to provide separation and prevent track bleed in recording or live applications. It's made from high-quality, 16-gauge perforated metal and features 30mm density micro cell acoustic foam that reduces reflections and other interference. With a switchable mount, it can either be used with a short stand for electric guitar/bass amps or a standard mic stand for acoustic guitars or other similar applications.

For having such a small spatial footprint, the AS16 makes quite an audible difference. I was quite surprised by the added detail and presence it lent to both electric and acoustic guitar tracks. It also features the ability to house both pencil condenser mics and dynamic mics by way of a removable extra rubber ring that fits into the mic hole. It seems quite durable, as well, and I would have no reservations about using it in a live setting.

Street price: $55

CAD Acousti-Shield AS16
Copyright CAD Audio, used with permission.

Live/Dead

These terms refer to the acoustics (sound properties) of a certain space. A *live* space is one in which there are many echoes and/or much reverb. Garages, gyms, large bathrooms, etc., are generally live. A *dead* space has very few reflections. This would include carpeted rooms with lots of thick curtains and soft, plush furniture or a child's room with a large collection of stuffed animals.

A-B

When you *A-B* something, you compare one sound to another. This can be the sound of two different microphones, two different guitars, two different mic positions, etc. It's often useful when miking up an instrument for the first time. You can record quick samples with two different mics and then A-B them to see which one sounds best.

Phones (Cans)

These are both short (or slang) for headphones. "Which pair of cans do you want?"

Channel

This is often confused with track. Again, this was easier when dealing with tape, because you could say (roughly) that a track pertained to the tape, whereas a channel pertained to the mixer. But now the line is blurred a bit more. However, the gist is that a *channel* does not contain any audio. It's simply a signal path through which the audio can pass. If you have a two-channel interface, for example, that means you can record up to two channels of audio at the same time. You don't have to record to two tracks, though. You could, for example, plug your guitar into channel 1 and a vocal mic into channel 2, but you could send both of those channels to track 1 in your DAW and record them onto a single track. (You wouldn't normally do this, because once you do that, you're not able to have individual control over them anymore. Since they're on the same track, whenever you turn it up, both the guitar and vocal will move together.)

So a channel simply refers to a signal path. A standalone recorder can help make this concept clear, because the faders can represent either a channel (when recording) or a track (when playing back). For example, if you're recording a vocal to track 1 on a standalone recorder, you don't have to plug your mic into *channel 1*. You can plug it into channel 2 or 3 or whatever and then send that signal (through the unit's internal mixer) to *track 1*.

One analogy is to think of a series of adjacent homes on your street in which the garages represent the tracks (on the tape or hard drive), the cars represent the audio signal, and the roads through your neighborhood represent the channels. Four different cars (audio signals) could drive down the same main street (channel 1) to get to the homes and park-in garages (tracks) 1, 2, 3, and 4, respectively, *if they went one after the other*. But they wouldn't be able to do that at the same time because the road (channel) is only big enough for one car (signal) at a time. This is the equivalent of recording a song by yourself one track a time, using the same channel on your interface but sending it to a different track in your DAW each time.

But if two cars took two different roads (channels 1 and 2), they could both arrive at garages 1 and 2 at the same time. This is because the cars (signals) aren't driving on the same road (channel). This is the equivalent of two people playing at the same time, each into their own channel and then onto their own track.

Routing

This term is often used when discussing channels and tracks. It refers to where an audio signal is sent. When you plug a mic into channel 1 of your recorder, you can then *route* it to any track you want. In this case, the words "route" and "send" are interchangeable. "Are you routing the guitar to track 5? I'd prefer track 7, because that's my lucky number."

Assigning

This is basically synonymous with routing. In the above scenario, you could also say that channel 1 is *assigned* to track 1. "Channel 1 is assigned to track 4, and channel 2 is assigned to track…um…I forgot. Just look at it, for Pete's sake! You're closer than I am!"

Signal Path

The *signal path* is a term describing the electronic route the signal takes within one piece of equipment (mixer, for example) or several pieces of equipment.

Signal Chain

The *signal chain* is a list of each piece of equipment, in series, through which the signal passes en route to the recorder (DAW). This can also refer to the virtual path inside a DAW. "The weakest link in my signal chain is my compressor, so I'd really like a new one."

Submixing

Again, this greatly has to do with channels. If you only have the ability to record two tracks at once (which could be because your interface has only two channels or your standalone recorder only allows two tracks at once), but you want to record more audio signals (instruments) than that simultaneously, you'll have to *submix*. A simple *mic mixer* can make this idea fairly clear.

Nady RMX 6 Mic/Line Mixer

A mic mixer (which is just a basic form of a *mixer*) is a device that allows you to plug in several different mics (usually four or more) and then mix those signals to one or two outputs. The most basic type will mix it to one output. For example, let's say you want to record your acoustic band with everyone playing together at once.

- You mic the acoustic guitar with mic A and plug it into channel 1 on the mixer

- You mic the washboard with mic B and plug it into channel 2 on the mixer

- You mic the thumb piano with mic C and plug it into channel 3 on the mixer

- You mic the second thumb piano with mic D and plug it into channel 4 on the mixer (and it's not easy to find two good thumb piano players)

Then you run a cable from the mic mixer's output to the recorder or interface. The mic mixer will then allow you to control the individual level of each mic to make sure that the second thumb piano isn't drowning out the washboard, for example. Once you have the levels set the way you want, you can record all four instruments onto one track. Congratulations, you just submixed!

The above procedure will result in a monophonic recording because you only recorded to one track. If you want a stereo recording (which is almost universally preferred these days), you'd need a stereo mic mixer, which means it will have two outputs. That means you can not only control the volume of each mic, but you can also control how much of the signal goes to each output. And that brings us to…

Panning

The subject of *panning* deals with the stereo field. You can pan an instrument to appear only in the left speaker (known as *hard left*), only in the right speaker (*hard right*), or anywhere in between. Panning is almost always controlled with a knob, and when it's placed in the 12:00 position, the signal will appear directly between the speakers. If you turn it to the 10:00 position, for example, it'll appear mostly in the left speaker, but a little in the right, etc.

In the example above, each channel of a stereo mic mixer would not only have a volume knob/slider, but also a pan knob. So you could decide how loud you want the second thumb piano *and* where you'd like to position it within the stereo field. You'd set each channel up how you want it. Maybe you want the guitar down the middle, so you'd pan it at 12:00 on the mic mixer. You want the washboard hard left, so you'd pan it all the way left on the mic mixer. And you want the two thumb pianos hard right, so you'd pan them all the way to the right on the mic mixer. Then you'd run a cable from the left output of the mic mixer to channel 1 of your interface and assign that to track 1, for example. And you'd run a cable from the right output of the mic mixer to channel 2 of your interface and assign that to track 2. Then you'd record the performance to both tracks 1 and 2. When you play back those tracks on your recorder or DAW, however, you need to pan track 1 hard left and pan track 2 hard right in order to achieve the desired result.

Console/Board/Desk/Mixer

All of these terms refer to a *mixing board* (or *mixer*), which was a must-have in the days of analog recording (although it was usually combined with the recorder when it came to portable 4-track cassette studios). The most basic type is a simple mic mixer (see "Submixing"), but more complicated ones are/were generally used for recording.

The function of a mixer is to take in several distinct audio signals, mix them together in various ways, and send them out various outputs. In the days of analog, the individual tracks were recorded onto a tape machine, or ATR (analog tape recorder). An eight-track machine, for example, allowed you to record onto eight separate tracks. The outputs for each track of the tape machine were connected to a separate input on the mixer, which allowed you to control how loud each track would be and pan it wherever you wanted within the stereo spectrum (assuming it was a stereo mixer, which most were). Early digital tape-based systems, like ADAT, worked this way, as well, although they could also make use of digital outputs instead of the analog outputs. Of course, most mixers allowed for much more control than that, including EQ, the ability to add effects, etc. For a long time, though, the only real "effect" that was present on a mixer was EQ. Any type of reverb, delay, or chorusing would all be handled with external processors, which were housed in an equipment rack. This is all still very common in larger and professional studios today, where a hybrid analog/digital system may be used, but in a typical home studio today, you may find no mixer at all, since all of the same functionality can essentially be handled within the DAW software.

Insert

When you *insert* something, this usually means placing a piece of equipment in series with the signal. For example, if you want to apply compression to a vocal, the entire vocal signal will usually pass through the compressor and come out the other end effected. The word can also be used as a noun. An *insert jack* (or *point,* if speaking virtually) is a way to add something into the signal chain in series. On a mixer or preamp, they're usually in the form or a 1/4-inch TRS ("tip-ring-sleeve") jack, which conducts two signals. Using a special insert cable—a Y cable with one TRS plug and two TS ("tip-sleeve," or standard instrument cable) plugs—the signal will leave the mixer/preamp, travel through the "send" cable into the device (like a compressor). It will then leave the output of the device and travel back to the mixer via the "return" cable and continue on down the signal path.

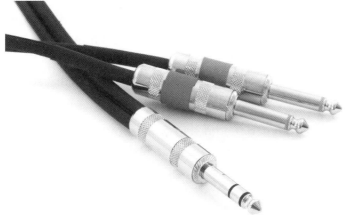

Insert cables:
Note the two rings on one plug (TRS) and the one ring on the other two plugs (TS).

Meter

A *meter* shows a graphic representation of signal level. In the old days, VU meters (with the needles that bounced left and right) were mostly used, but now you usually see LED peak-style (vertical bars that rise and fall) meters on standalone recorders or virtual peak meters on a DAW. Several plugins, however, feature virtual VU meters merely for the aesthetic quality.

Monitor

The word "monitor" has a few different meanings when it comes to audio recording. As a noun, *monitor* refers to your control room speakers, as well as your computer screen. When you *monitor* (verb) something, you listen to it. As an adjective, a *monitor mix* is one that's usually meant for listening as opposed to what's being sent to the final two-track stereo recorder. You'll hear some people use monitor mix the same way as cue mix (see below), or they can be referring to the mix that's running through the control room monitors.

Cue Mix (Foldback Mix)

Cue mix refers to a mix of the instruments separate from what's being heard by the engineer in the control room. It's most commonly used for the performer(s) in the studio room. A pro studio will have the ability to generate different cue mixes for several different performers simultaneously. For example, if the guitar player wants to hear more drums and less piano, but the bassist wants to hear more bass (go figure) and no guitar, the engineer can do this while listening to his own preferred mix in the control room.

This requires numerous outputs on your A/I, however: one for each separately generated mono mix, or two for each separately generated stereo mix. For example, if you had eight outputs on your A/I, you (the engineer) could be listening to a stereo mix on outputs 1 and 2, the guitarist could have his own mix on 3 and 4, the bassist could have his own on 5 and 6, and the drummer could have his own on 7 and 8. If you used mono cue mixes, you could have your stereo mix in the control room plus six other separate mixes for various performers.

Main Mix

The main mix is the final destination for most signals. It's represented by two main (left and right) meters that indicate the signal level that will be "printed" to the final stereo file upon rendering (see "Mixing" section). In digital recording, you don't ever want the main mix to clip (go above 0 dB), as this results in an unpleasant, unmusical distortion. If your interface only has two outputs, the main mix will be sent through those (left side through channel 1 and right through channel 2 by default). If you have additional outputs, you can set up cue mixes to send through them, as described above.

Headphone Amp

A *headphone amp* is a device that allows you to listen to music with several sets of headphones simultaneously, each with their own independent volume. The most basic incarnation is one in which one stereo signal comes in (usually a 1/4-inch headphone jack) and several (usually four at least) go out to independent 1/4-inch headphone jacks. This only allows various listeners to adjust the overall volume of their headphones.

Another type of headphone amp is commonly used when it comes to the cue mix (see above). In this type, several signals come in, and each one goes out its own headphone jack with adjustable volume (and often other functions, such as EQ). This way, you can send a stereo cue mix from outputs 3 and 4 of your interface to channel A (stereo) on your headphone amp. A separate stereo cue mix could be sent from outputs 5 and 6 of your interface to channel B (stereo) of your headphone amp. This way, the drummer, for example, can have his own personal mix on channel A, and the acoustic guitarist can have his own mix on channel B. Then they can control their own headphone volume from the headphone amp in the studio while you (the engineer) control your own mix and volume through your monitors in the control room.

Art Headamp6 Pro Headphone Amplifier

Wet/Dry

A signal (such as a guitar) is said to be *wet* when it has effects, such as reverb, delay, tremolo, and phasing, applied to it. (Some people use the term "wet" when talking about reverb only.) If a signal has no effects applied to it, it's said to be *dry*. Many people choose to track (record) most signals dry and add the desired effects later during the mixing process, as this allows control over how much reverb, delay, etc. you'd like to add to the track.

Recording "Wet"/Printing Effects

Sometimes an effect is integral to the sound of an instrument or particular performance to such an extent that it's difficult to record without it. One example is a guitar part that uses a timed delay effect. This is a common trick in which a guitarist picks eighth notes with the delay set to a dotted eighth rhythm. This causes the delayed notes to fall in between the picked notes, creating a 16th-note phrase (U2's The Edge is famous for this). In this instance, the delay effect is usually present while the track is being recorded. This is called recording "wet" or *printing the effect*.

There are other reasons for printing effects, as well. Let's say you're working on a standalone recorder with two built-in effects processors, and you know you want to use one of them as a plate reverb for several instruments and the other as a delay for the lead vocal. That will eat up all your internal effects at mixdown. If you have one auxiliary send, you could add another effect, such as tremolo, to an electric piano track with an external effects processor, but that would be it. Let's say that, in addition to all this, you really want a spring reverb effect applied to the guitar track. Your only option in this case is to print that effect to the track as you're recording it. Once this is done, that effect processor (whether it's one of the built-in ones or the external one) will be freed up for use on something else.

The biggest drawback to printing effects is that you're stuck with it. If you later discover that you applied too much reverb to the guitar track, there's nothing you can do about it—aside from re-recording it with less reverb. And this is assuming that the track is still on its own and hasn't been combined with anything else—which brings us to track-bouncing, something we'll discuss in a bit.

Timbre

Timbre is somewhat analogous to tone. It's the quality of a sound that allows us to distinguish between, say, a piano and a clarinet even when they're playing the same exact note.

Direct Box (D.I. Box)

A *direct box* allows you to plug in a high-impedance audio signal, such as that from a guitar's output jack, into a low-impedance input on an interface or a mixer. Without running through a direct box, the signal from a guitar or bass is much too weak and will result in an inferior tone. Nowadays, many interfaces and standalone recorders have 1/4-inch inputs specifically designed for guitar/bass input, which is the equivalent of running through a direct box. The advantage of a dedicated direct box is that it can also be used in a live situation.

The Radial SB-1 is a high-performance active DI box that easily fits inside a guitar case. It features a 1/4-inch input jack with a thru-feed jack for a tuner and/or amp. A -15 dB pad allows you to use the box with even the loudest instrument, and a phase reverse switch can help with feedback removal in a live acoustic guitar setting. The unit converts the signal to balanced, low-impedance level and features an XLR output jack for plugging into a mixer or interface. Since the unit runs on phantom power, there's no need for batteries.

Radial StageBug SB-1 Active DI

The SB-1 provides a full, rich tone when recording bass or guitar direct, ensuring that you're hearing the most well-rounded tone possible from your instrument. It also doubles as a great tool when playing acoustic live—win-win!

Street price: $70

Trim

This is usually a knob on a mixer channel or interface channel that determines the input level into the channel. For example, if you're plugging your guitar into a dedicated guitar/bass input on your interface, you would play your guitar and adjust the trim on your interface to get a good record level into your DAW. The track fader on the DAW will be used to determine how loud the playback of that track is.

Fader

A *fader* is a sliding *potentiometer* ("pot," or variable resistor) that's moved up and down to control the level of its corresponding track. A DAW has *virtual faders* that you move by dragging the mouse or with an external control surface.

Distorting/Overloading/Clipping

This refers to when a signal is being recorded at too high a volume, and it's distorting the input. On analog tape systems, a small bit of overloading was often used purposefully to get a more saturated, compressed sound on certain instruments—drums, for example. In the digital domain, however, clipping does not produce the same effect and is therefore avoided at all costs during tracking.

Note that there are several places this distorting/clipping can occur. If, for example, you like the distorted sound you get when you run your bass through an external mic preamp with the gain cranked, you can still record that signal at a useable level in your DAW by turning the output level of your mic preamp down and/or the input level of your interface down. However, you never want the input level on your DAW track to be clipping when you record.

Attenuate

This is simply a fancy word meaning to reduce the level of a signal—i.e., to turn down.

Pad

This is a feature found on many mixers and interfaces. It's usually a switch that, when engaged, attenuates the signal by a preset amount. It's particularly useful when recording sources that are exceptionally loud, such as a cranked amp or a bass drum. If you have the input level turned all the way down but you're still overloading the channel's input, you can press the *pad* button to lower the signal to a usable level.

Phantom Power

This is a DC voltage that's necessary to power most condenser mics. Many interfaces and standalone recorders come equipped with at least one or two channels of phantom power. If yours doesn't, you can always buy external phantom power supplies.

Phase Cancellation/"Out of Phase"

Though they sound full and rich on their own, two signals are said to be *out of phase* when their combined sound results in a thin, weak tone. This is the result of their two waves working against each other—one's crest is mostly occurring during the other's trough. You may run into this phenomenon when using multiple mics for the same source, such as when miking an acoustic guitar with two mics. If both mics sound fine when soloed, but the sound turns weak and anemic when the mics are combined, you could have a phasing problem.

There are several possible remedies for this. Options 1 and 2 are necessary if you're combining the sounds of both mics onto one track, because you won't be able to alter the phase relationship after they've been combined. Options 3 and 4 are additional ways to deal with the problem if you're recording each mic to its own track.

1. Slightly move one of the mics so that it's a different distance from the source. This could even be less than an inch.

2. If your interface or mic preamp (whichever you're using) has a "phase inversion" switch, try pressing that. This will turn the signal's wave around by 180 degrees.

3. Your DAW will likely have a phase inversion switch on each track, as well, so you can reverse the phase of one of them this way.

4. Finally, you can also zoom in on the waveforms after recording and slightly nudge one of them. You should be able to see whether a phase problem exists, because, though the waveforms will be similar, one will most likely dip while the other rises.

If you were to take two identical tracks and adjust (nudge) one of them so that they were exactly 180 degrees out of phase, the signals would cancel each other completely, and you would hear nothing at all!

Mute

To *mute* a channel means to silence it. Sometimes you may be hearing a noise/buzz when you have several mics going at once. By muting the channels one by one, you can track down which one is causing the issue. Muting is also used during mixdown when you're wanting to concentrate on a certain group of instruments instead of listening to all of the tracks at once.

Solo

Similar to muting, but kind of the opposite, *soloing* a track effectively mutes all other tracks so you hear only the soloed track. This is also a common way to track down a buzz or refine an instrument's sound during a mix.

Transport

On a tape recorder, this refers to the collection of buttons (play, record, etc.) that control the tape motor. On digital recording equipment, it refers to the same collection of buttons (on a standalone recorder) or virtual buttons (on a software DAW).

Scratch Vocal

Sometimes when a band records the basic tracks together, the singer also records a *scratch vocal*: a temporary vocal track that acts as a placeholder until the real vocal is recorded. This can also be overdubbed after the rhythm tracks have been recorded. This serves two purposes: In the first instance, it can help the band feel the music better and/or keep track of their place within the form. And in both instances, it helps to prevent further overdubs from conflicting with the vocal, which is usually considered the focal point of a recording (in a typical pop, rock, or country song, for example).

Scratch Guitars/Keys/Etc.

Along the line of the scratch vocal, sometimes scratch versions of other instruments are recorded during the basic tracks with the intent on spending more time on the tone and performance later on.

OVERDUBS

After the initial tracks are done, the *overdubs* usually come next. If the basic tracks can be thought of as the foundation of a house, the overdubs would constitute the walls, floors, and ceilings. Overdubs usually consist of tracks added one at a time, although they can also include several instruments playing together. A brass section or string section would be a good example of this. Overdubs are not the final touches we'll put on a song, but they make up a good portion of what's being heard. If you're a one-man operation, and you're recording a full-band pop song arrangement, you'll spend a good amount of time on overdubs.

Rough Mix

A *rough mix* is a quick, decent-sounding mix of the instruments recorded thus far so you can play along with them while you overdub new tracks.

Punch-In/Out

A *punch-in* (or "punch") is the act of recording only a part of a track instead of recording the entire track from beginning to end. If, for example, you have a keyboard part that's only featured in the song's intro and outro, you'd most likely record the intro part, stop, and then punch in at the beginning of the outro, rather that waiting through the entire track. Another common use for a punch is fixing a mistake. If you like your guitar solo, but you hit one bum note, you can punch in just long enough to play a new (better) lick there and then punch out. In the early days of tape recording, you had to manually punch in and out. And if you punched in too early (or punched out too late) and accidentally erased a keeper portion of the take, then you were out of luck and had to re-record it. Eventually, even tape recorders developed auto punch-in/out, which allowed you to specify the exact locations on the tape for the in and out points, removing the scary possibility of erasing over something by accident. Nowadays, of course, all aspects of the punches can be automated, including…

Pre-Roll and Post-Roll

The *pre-roll* is the amount of "runway" you get before punching in. Let's say you're in auto-punch mode and have your punch-in point set at the beginning of the chorus and your punch-out point set at the end of measure 2 of the chorus. If you have your pre-roll and post-roll set at five seconds and press record, it will start playing from five seconds before the chorus. It will then automatically punch you in at the chorus (whether you play anything or not), punch you out at the end of measure 2, and then stop five seconds after that.

You can also set up your pre-roll and post-roll points using measures and beats (this will only be accurate, though, if you record to a click). So you could have it start playing one measure before the punch and stop one measure after the punch. The pre-roll length is normally the more important of the two, because you could simply just stop it on your own after the punch out. But the post-roll length becomes important as well when you're using *loop mode*. You could set up loop points at the pre-roll and post-roll points, which would allow you to punch in the lick as many times as necessary until you nail it. In other words, you'd press record, and it would:

- play from the pre-roll point

- punch in at the punch-in point

- punch out at the punch-out point

- play until the post-roll point

- then go back to the pre-roll point and start all over

Pop Filter

A *pop filter* is a device mounted to a microphone that prevents certain syllables from causing a "pop" in a vocal track. Letters like "p" and "b," especially, produce a burst of air when sung (or spoken), and this burst can temporarily disrupt the diaphragm in a microphone, creating an unwanted "pop" sound.

Proximity Effect

Proximity effect is the interesting increase in bass frequencies as you get nearer to a microphone when singing. This is something that you really need to hear in order to fully understand, but it can lead to a muddy-sounding vocal if not kept in check. Generally speaking, eight inches or so from a condenser mic is a good place to start if you want to avoid it altogether. The closer you get, the more low end will start to creep in. In fact, this is why the voices of so many deejays sound deeper on the radio than in person; they often exploit the proximity effect to add a sense of weight to their voice.

Vocal Booth

A *vocal booth* is generally an enclosed area that's been treated acoustically to sound dead (few reflections). This allows the vocal to sound present (or "up front") in the mix. Usually, any ambience that's added to a vocal track (reverb, delay, etc.) is done artificially after the fact with effects processors, as this allows you to be very specific with the amount and type. If you record a vocal wet (say, in a bathroom), then you're stuck with that ambience on the track. If that's the sound you want, though, go for it!

There are also "portable vocal booths" of varying sizes and complexity. Some of these are quite expensive and basically constitute a temporary room, while the more affordable options can consist of a semi-circle frame with absorptive foam mounted to a mic stand. You can also check out the Appendix for some DIY options.

Bouncing Tracks

Track-bouncing was much more common in the days of tape, when tracks were limited by the machine on which you were working. If you had an eight-track machine, for example, but you wanted to record more tracks than that, you'd have to bounce some tracks to make room for others. Here's how it would typically work. Let's say you record a song with the following track layout:

- Tracks 1–2: Stereo drum machine
- Track 3: Bass
- Track 4: Rhythm guitar
- Track 5: Lead guitar
- Track 6: Acoustic guitar
- Track 7: Piano
- Track 8: Synth lead line

At this point, you've used all your tracks, but you still have a lead vocal and harmony vocal to record. What do you do? Well, since you've filled up all your tracks, your only option is an *external bounce*. This is essentially a pre-mix. You'd send the eight tracks to a stereo recorder—it could be a DAT, a two-track reel-to-reel, or even a cassette recorder back in the day—mixing them as if it were a finished product down to a stereo recording (two tracks). You could then record these two tracks back onto tracks 1 and 2 on a fresh portion of tape on your tape machine (thereby keeping the original eight tracks intact in case you needed to start from the bounce again). In doing so, you'd then have tracks 3–8 free to add your vocals and even more parts if your heart desired.

Another option is an *internal bounce*. With this idea, you'd record, say, your drums, bass and rhythm guitar on tracks 1–4. You could then perform a pre-mix of just those four tracks, recording them to a stereo pair of tracks on the same tape machine—say, tracks 7 and 8. Then you'd have drums, bass, and rhythm guitar on tracks 7 and 8, and you could then fill up tracks 1–4 with other instruments.

The big drawback to bouncing tracks is that you lose flexibility. Once you combine the drums, bass, and rhythm guitar, as in the above scenario, you lose the ability to bring up the level of the rhythm guitar without also bringing up the bass and drums. If you try to EQ the bass, you'll also be EQing the guitar and drums, etc. Because of this, it requires a great deal of planning and forethought. You couldn't just start tracking and worry about it later the way you can today with an essentially unlimited number of tracks. In order for the Beatles to record *Sgt. Pepper's Lonely Hearts Club Band* on a four-track recorder, they had to carefully plan and execute several bounces along the way. It was even more critical with tape machines because of the fact that they can add hiss with each bounce.

If you're using an eight-track standalone digital recorder, you may very well need to bounce tracks, as well. The good news is that you don't have to worry about added hiss building up, but you will need to think ahead to make sure that your pre-mixes (bounces) are leaving room for the other elements you've yet to record. To this end, standalone recorders also benefit from…

Virtual Tracks

Virtual tracks are featured on most standalone recorders these days, and they allow you to store alternate takes for each track. A typical standalone recorder may feature 16 tracks, each with 16 virtual tracks. This means that you can record up to 16 times on track 1 and keep every single take. When you play back the song, however, you can only listen to one of those virtual tracks at a time. Many people will use this function to piece together the perfect guitar solo, for example. You could record eight guitar solos on track 1 using virtual tracks 1–8. Then you could choose the best bits from each, cutting and pasting them to virtual track 9 to form the final complete take (see "Comping Takes" in the Editing section, page 237).

Also, when bouncing tracks, the virtual tracks allow you to keep the original tracks intact in case you need to revert to them at some point later. For example, if you record on tracks 1–8 (virtual track 1) and bounce those over to tracks 15–16 (virtual track 1), you can move the original tracks 1–8 to virtual track 16, for example, thereby keeping them safe, before you begin recording new material on tracks 1–8 again using another virtual track.

EDITING

Editing usually refers to the manipulation of tracks mostly with regard to time and pitch. This is really where digital music production trumps analog in every way. It's the equivalent of using an old-school typewriter and correction fluid versus a word processing program. You can literally do on a computer with a few mouse clicks what could take you hours or more with the traditional splicing methods of the analog world. That's not to say that splicing tape is not an art and a joy of its own to many people; it's just that, if you want to engage in the analog versus digital debate (and many still do), you should really just leave editing out of the discussion if you're on the analog side (unless, of course, you're arguing that splicing tape is more fun than clicking the mouse—that's a subjective opinion and therefore can't be proven or disproved!).

After all the tracks and overdubs are recorded, many people will sit back and listen to the song as a whole, paying special attention to the performances with regard to accuracy in timing, intensity, pitch, etc. If the bass player really rushed the first note of the chorus, it's a simple matter on a digital system to move that note so that it's in time. You can also rearrange the song at this point. If you decide, for example, that the song should start right on the verse instead of the intro, you can do that.

It should be mentioned that editing can sometimes occur before all the overdubs are complete. For example, you may choose to edit a bass track before even starting the overdubs. However, in the spirit of workflow, it's often done all at once, after all the tracking has been completed. Whatever works best for you is the important thing.

Waveform Display

Each track is represented in your DAW graphically by a *waveform display*. This is a horizontal beam that shows what the audio wave looks like. When editing, you can zoom in on these when necessary to perform precise edits.

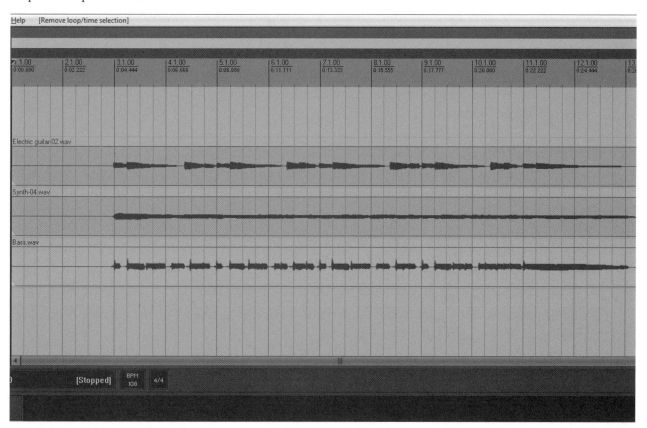

Waveform display in Reaper

Edit Point

An *edit point* is simply the precise spot along the timeline at which an edit is going to be performed. "The cut will start at this point."

Split (Cut)

When you *split* an audio file, you cut it into two separate files, which can then be manipulated individually. If you wanted to move one ill-timed bass note, you would split it before the note starts and after the note ends. You could then move that one forward or backward along the timeline so that it's on the proper beat.

Trim

Trimming a file refers to lengthening or shortening the beginning or end of it. If, after splitting the aforementioned bass note, the end of the edited note spills over onto the beginning of the next note, you can trim the end of the edited note so that it ends right before the next note.

Copy/Cut/Paste/Move

These terms are analogous to those of a word processor. If you want, you can select a part of the guitar track (the verse riff, for example), copy or cut it, and then paste it to another location or to a completely different track.

Glue/Join

When you *glue* two files together, they become one single file and can therefore be manipulated as such. This is kind of the opposite of split.

Comp

Short for composite, a *comp* is a complete track that's been assembled from several other individual tracks. A very common practice with vocals, for example, is to record, say, four complete takes of the vocal. Then you go back and pick the best lines from each take, comping together the final vocal take. This can be done all on the same track or with a new track for each take. When you record a new take over an old one on the same track, the old take is still accessible; it's not deleted (unless you specifically set up your system to behave this way). Depending on how you have your DAW setup, this may or may not be visible.

Import/Export

Occasionally you'll want to *import* other audio files into your song. For example, you may use this function with drum loops. You can also *export* a track, section of a track, or section of the song to another file (an mp3, for example).

Grid

A *grid* is a system of light vertical lines that help make it clear where you are within your song. You can set the grid so that it shows only measures, beats, eighth notes, etc. Or you can arrange it via time. It's kind of like a piece of graph paper under your waveform display. For the purpose of editing, it's very helpful when aligning certain tracks.

Snapping

Snapping is a function that works with the grid. You can enable snapping so that, when you drag an audio file, it will "snap" to the nearest beat, eighth note, etc.—whatever you have it set for. When doing larger scale edits, such as the form of the song, this is invaluable.

Quantizing

A common term when using MIDI instruments, *quantizing* refers to the rhythmic correction of a note's timing. If you record a MIDI drum pattern, for example, and the hi-hat pattern is rushing or dragging a bit, you can quantize those notes (assuming you're recording to the click) so that they will snap to the nearest rhythmic point of your choosing. If you quantize to eighth notes, for example, then each hi-hat will snap either forward or backward to the nearest eighth note and line up in perfect time.

Of course, if you're wanting the drum track to sound at all human, you most likely won't want things lining up to be metronomically perfect. This is why you can also specify the percentage of quantization.

Instead of every hi-hat note moving all the way to the nearest eighth note, you can tell them to move only 50 percent of the way—or 85 percent, or whatever. This way, you can leave as much or as little of your human performance in as you'd like.

Undo/Redo

This is something that you'll most likely use during the tracking phases, as well, but it just strikes me more as an edit function, so I put it here. Again, this is analogous to the word processor function. If you make an edit (say, move a note) and don't like it, just click *undo*, and it's back to the way it was. *Redo* will re-perform the edit. Most DAW programs have a ridiculous amount of undo levels, so you can pretty much undo your whole life if you'd like.

Fade In/Fade Out/Crossfade

You can easily *fade in* or *fade out* a file, and you have complete control over the duration of the fade and the envelope (shape of the fade—i.e., if it will it fade quickly at first and then take a long time to finish or vice versa). Also, if you have two files that are overlapping, you can *crossfade* them if you'd like, so that the first one will begin to fade out while the second one begins to fade in.

Crop

The term *crop* refers to the choosing of a specific take when you've recorded several takes on one track. If you have four different vocal takes on one track, for example, and you decide you like take 3 during the verse, you can crop to that take, and it will become the chosen take to play from then on. The other takes will no longer be shown, but they will not be deleted, and you can still access them later if you so choose.

Time-Stretch

Stretching a file usually refers to the act of lengthening or shortening it while changing its speed, as well. For example, if you have a guitar lick that normally lasts five seconds, you can stretch it so that it lasts five and a half seconds. The pitch will remain the same (although you could change that in a setting), but the phrase would sound as if it were played slower. Minor adjustments of this kind are negligible and can't really be detected, but if you drastically stretch a phrase, it more often than not will sound unnatural. For example, guitarists and vocalists often add vibrato to their notes. When you time-stretch these types of audio files, the vibrato will start to sound more unnatural the further you stretch the file.

One of the most common uses for stretching is drum loops. If you have a drum loop (typically a stereo track of a one- or two-bar drum pattern that you import into your project) that was recorded at 96 beats per minute, but your song is 94 beats per minute, you can stretch the drum loop a bit so that it will line up with the tempo of your song. You can then copy it and paste it as many times as you'd like. For this reason, most drum loops will contain the tempo in their file name. Again, the further from the original tempo you move, the more unnatural it will begin to sound.

Keyboard Shortcuts

A *keyboard shortcut* is fairly self-explanatory. The most common functions in a DAW can typically be accessed with a keyboard shortcut so you don't have to click the mouse for everything. In many DAW programs, you can customize these yourself and assign your own shortcuts for virtually any function.

Non-Destructive

This refers to the fact that none of these edits you make need to be permanent. It's not like cutting a piece of magnetic tape that would need to be spliced. Nor do you need to worry about accidentally recording over something, since you can just undo it. Anything you record is saved on the hard drive as a file and can always be accessed at a later time, unless you deliberately go in and delete the file.

MIXING

"In the Box"

This refers to something that's happening within the confines of the DAW software and not using any external signal processing. For example, if someone mixes a song entirely *in the box*, it means that they use only the virtual mixer of their DAW software and only software plugins for their effects.

Equalization (EQ)

Equalization is the shaping of a sound by boosting or cutting certain frequencies within it. Most stereos (home, car, mp3 player, etc.) have some type of rudimentary EQ built into them in the form of bass and treble settings, if nothing else. The EQs available to the home recordist are usually much more specific than that and allow much more precise tailoring of a sound. The frequency range is generally divided into four basic areas: bass, low mid range, high mid range, and treble. If an electric guitar is sounding too shrill, for example, you may try cutting a frequency within the upper mid range. If a keyboard sound is too muddy, you might try cutting some low mids.

There are many different kinds of equalizers, but the most common in the home studio are graphic, sweepable, and parametric. A parametric EQ is the most precise, as it allows the most control. We'll talk more about EQs later. It should be mentioned that EQ can certainly be implemented during the tracking phases, as well. (After all, the bass, mid, and treble knobs on a guitar or bass amp are EQ knobs, as well.) Mixers and channel strips usually have some on-board EQ, and some people choose to make use of them while recording a track. Generally speaking, however, most choose to wait until mixdown to apply EQ because, just like printing effects, once you record a signal with the EQ added, it's a permanent part of the track.

FX

This is simply a shorthand way to write "effects," and it refers to any kind of audio effect, such as reverb or delay. Again, you may be using FX during the tracking phases, as well, but many people also choose to record everything completely dry and add all FX during the mix.

Effects (FX) Send/Effects Loop

An *effects send* is a signal path in which a portion (anywhere from 0 to 100 percent) of a signal, such as a keyboard track, is split from the main mix, sent through an effect (or series of effects) and then returned to the main mix to be blended with the original signal. Technically, an *effects loop* consists of an effects send and an *effects return*, but the term effects send is sometimes used in the place of effects loop. This is the most common way that effects are applied to tracks during mixdown, because you can decide exactly how much of the effect (reverb, delay, etc.) you want to add to the signal.

Effects Chain

This is similar to signal chain, but it's only referring to a series of effects through which a signal is passing. An *effects chain* may involve anywhere from two different effects up to...however much your CPU can handle.

Series and Parallel

These recording terms refer to the way in which signals can pass through various stages. In a *series* path, one signal passes completely through a stage and then comes out the other end, continuing on. A perfect example of this is a typical guitar effect pedal. The cord (carrying the guitar's signal) runs from the guitar, into the pedal where it's processed, and then it goes out of the pedal to carry on (to another pedal, possibly, or the amp).

In a *parallel* path, one signal is split into two. One side of it continues on, but the other side runs through an additional stage before being combined (mixed) again with the original signal. An example of this type of path is a typical effects loop (see page 76).

Automation

Back in the old days, if you wanted a track's volume to swell up or down during mixdown, you had to move the fader yourself (or get someone to help you while you took care of other things). If you wanted the guitar to cut out during the verse, you had to mute the track. Nowadays, virtually any aspect of a mixdown can be controlled automatically. *Automation* refers to the idea of the program making automatic mixing adjustments for you as the song plays. For example, you can write (or draw) automation envelopes that control things like a track's volume and panning. You can save these envelopes and turn them on or off at any time. So, if you still want to mix old school, and you have an external mixer or control surface with which to do it, you can. If you want to program the entire mix to be automated, you can. Or you can do anything in between—have the computer automate the volumes of your tracks while you control the muting if you'd like. Whatever floats your boat is pretty much possible!

Rendering

When you render something in your DAW, you turn it into a playable file on its own. For example, if you have a MIDI track on your DAW, you're only able to hear the instrument because it's running through some kind of sound generator, such as a VSTi (virtual instrument). But the MIDI file itself doesn't contain any audio data. However, if you render the MIDI track, you'll create an audio file (most commonly a WAV file, but it can be many different file types) of the way it sounds, and that file can be played through your media player, burned to DVD, etc. You can also render a guitar track that has a bunch of plugins applied to it, such as an amp simulator, a compressor, EQ, etc. All of those plugins eat up CPU power, and by rendering the track, you create a new file with all of those effects "printed" to it. The original guitar track with all the plugins can then be muted, thereby freeing up more CPU power again.

Another common use of rendering refers to creating the final mix of your song. In this respect, you can simply think of render as another word for "mix." When you're ready to print your final stereo mix of your song, you'll render it to a stereo file, using various settings that you'll specify (file type, bit depth, etc.). This will be the song file that you send to your friends to play on their stereos and mobile devices.

CHAPTER 5

ANATOMY OF A SOFTWARE-BASED DAW

In this chapter, we'll examine the aspects of the software-based DAW so you can get acquainted with its basic functionality. While every program is slightly different, and there's always a learning curve when moving to a new system, the basic operating procedure from one to the next is the same; they just may have slightly different names for the processes. So let's start by looking at the key elements involved.

INPUTS AND OUTPUTS

The audio signals enter and exit your system through your audio interface, which can be one of many different types and include many different features. See page 13 for details on audio interfaces.

DAW PROGRAM/SEQUENCER/RECORDER

The most commonly used music production program, and the industry standard, as it were, is Pro Tools. In 1989, it was the first DAW program available (then called Sound Tools) and, once it became Pro Tools in 1991, it quickly caught on within the recording industry. For years, it was a proprietary system; in order to run the software, you had to use a DigiDesign (the makers of Pro Tools) interface. However, after Avid acquired DigiDesign, the software eventually became hardware independent (in 2010), meaning that you can now use it with any interface.

Aside from Pro Tools, there are a number of extremely popular DAW programs, including GarageBand, Digital Performer, Sonar, Reason, Cubase, Nuendo, Reaper, Logic Pro, Ableton Live, and FL Studio. They range in price from around $60 (for Reaper) to almost $1,000 (or perhaps more). It's important to remember, though, that none of them sound different in and of themselves. They may come with different virtual instruments and effects plugins that will sound different (although many people use third party software for these things anyway), but the "sound" of the guitar you record has much more to do with the signal chain (the microphone, the mic preamp, interface, etc.) than the DAW software. You can think of them kind of like an internet browser. You may prefer one over the other because you like the layout, or it does certain things faster than others, etc. But you're still surfing the same internet.

Most people expect to see Pro Tools or Logic in a pro studio, but when it comes to home recording, the majority of people select a DAW program by what feels best to them—what's intuitive and what makes sense. Some people make use of several, but many stick to one because there's a steep learning curve involved with most of them, as they're usually very powerful programs with dozens and dozens of pull-down menus filled with seemingly innumerable functions.

It should be mentioned that oftentimes a piece of hardware will come bundled with a piece of software. And this is usually the case with interfaces and DAW programs. This may often be a "lite" version of the flagship program, but it will certainly be more than up to the task of recording quality music—especially for a newcomer. The Steinberg UR22 interface that I used for the recordings in this book, for example, comes with Cubase AI, which is a leaner version of the standard Cubase program. These "lite" versions may feature a limit on the number of tracks you can record (although it will still usually allow 24, 32, or 48 audio tracks, which should be more than enough), and won't have as many effect plugins. However, they're more than capable of getting you started, and if nothing else, they'll help you determine what you may like or dislike about the way a certain DAW program operates, which will help you choose another one should you feel the need to make a change.

EFFECT PLUGINS

Another extremely common type of software is that of effect *plugins*. These are basically "virtual" versions of all the effects that used to only be available in rackmount or pedal format, such as reverb, delay, EQ, and compression. (We'll look much more closely at effects in Chapter 13.) There are also MIDI effects, which are meant to process MIDI files by transposing them, arpeggiating, etc. Many DAW programs come with numerous effects, but you can also buy them independently one at a time, filling up your "virtual rack" as necessary. The prices for these effects can range from nothing ("freeware") to thousands, but there are a number of awesome-sounding products under the $200 mark. Many of the freeware programs can sound great in the right circumstance, as well. Don't let the (lack of a) price tag fool you; you should always listen for yourself! However, some freeware plugins can also be unstable, causing your DAW to crash. If this ever happens, you should remove the plugin from your machine to avoid further instances of instability.

T-RackS Classic Compressor
Copyright IK Multimedia, used with permission.

IK Multimedia's T-RackS Classic Compressor models the classic analog compressors of the past and can be used to add extra punch and girth to your tracks or mixes. It's very usable on numerous sources, and includes presets for such applications as acoustic guitar, bass, kick, snare, drum bus, mix bus, and electric guitar. These make excellent starting points from which you can tweak the parameters as necessary for your specific needs. The controls are intuitive and very easy to get a hang of, and the VU-style gain reduction meter is a nice aid in determining proper release times when you're starting out.

I really love the sound of this plugin on drum buses and acoustic guitar, among other things. It adds punch and thickness without muddiness or loss of high-end detail. It's an incredibly versatile compressor, and I've had a hard time finding something it didn't do well!

Street price: $50

Mac OS vs. Windows—Again!

Although the vast majority of effect plugins (and virtual instruments—see below) are available in both Mac and PC formats, the files are often not compatible. In other words, whereas most PC plugins come in a VST format, most Mac plugins come in an AU format. This is a simplification, because it's really more reliant on the DAW program, but certain DAW programs will only run on one or the other (Mac or PC). Here's a brief summary of the most common plugin formats and compatibility:

- **VST (Virtual Studio Technology):** Windows and Mac OS

- **AU (Audio Units):** Mac OS

- **RTAS (Real Time Audio Suite):** Windows and Mac OS

- **DirectX:** Windows

- **DSSI:** Windows, Mac OS, Linux

- **LADSPA:** Windows, Mac OS, Linux

- **LV2:** Linux

It should be noted, though, that even though a program may be offered in VST format for both Mac and Windows, you'll need to download the specific version associated with your platform.

Generally speaking, you'll have a folder in which all your plugins are kept. There will be a setting in your DAW that allows you to specify this location. Whenever your DAW boots up, it will check this folder and load all the plugins, making them available for you to use. Some plugins are very CPU-intensive, meaning they'll hog much of your computing power. If you try to run too many of these types of plugins simultaneously, your system can become sluggish, and the audio can become glitchy. It may even fail to play back at all. Most DAW programs will have a performance meter that allows you to see the percentage of CPU that's busy. You'll also be able to see which programs are using the most memory. There are ways around this, however, and we'll talk more about that in Chapter 16.

VIRTUAL INSTRUMENT PLUGINS

This is where the MIDI controller comes in. There are a myriad of virtual instruments, controlled via MIDI, that mimic the sound of just about any type of instrument you can imagine—from the human voice to a saxophone to a theramin to an upright bass and anything in between. Probably the most common one is drums, as we've been emulating drum sounds in one form or another since 1959. As with effect plugins, virtual instruments are generally kept in the same folder and are available in various formats for Mac and PC platforms. Be sure to check the compatibility before you make a purchase.

A Walk Down Virtual Instrument Lane

Originally meant to accompany organs, the first "drum machines" simply allowed you to select from several preset drum patterns. You often had virtually no control on these types of machines other than tempo and volume, if that, but they served their purpose. The first real programmable drum machines arrived in the early 1970s, allowing users to create their own unique drum patterns by various methods. These early machines used synthesis to generate drum sounds—white noise to simulate a snare, for example—and didn't sound terribly realistic as such, but they had their own charm for sure.

In 1980, the drum machine took a huge step forward with the Linn LM-1 Drum Computer. This was the first machine to use digitally sampled drum sounds (actual recordings of a drum hit that are triggered by a button), and it retailed for $4,995 (and this was in 1980!). It's heard on a huge selection of 1980s pop songs, including hits by Devo, The Human League, Gary Numan, and Prince, who used it extensively. Another drum machine released in 1980 was the synthesis-based Roland TR-808 Rhythm Composer. Although it didn't have a huge impact at the time (as sampling drum machines were becoming in vogue), it has since gone on to become one of the most famously used and coveted drum machines of all. It's been a staple in the hip-hop and R&B genres for decades, and its iconic bass drum and snare tones can be heard on countless hits, as can those of its successor, the TR-909 (introduced in 1983). Both of these instruments can still be found used, where they fetch a pretty penny if in good shape. As an alternative, however, Roland has recently released the TR-8 Rhythm Performer, which essentially combines the 808 and 909 into one unit, at a price of $499.

Roland TR-808 Rhythm Composer
Copyright Roland, used with permission.

With the advent of MIDI technology, standalone drum machines have waned in popularity since the late 1990s, slowly being replaced by MIDI-controlled samplers (which allow you to record and playback various pre-made samples or those of your own creation), sound modules, and eventually software plugins. Ironically, there are now many plugins designed to emulate the sounds of famous drum machines (which were originally designed to emulate the sounds of real drums). As such, they've become instruments in their own right.

Other common examples of this are the Chamberlin and Mellotron. Henry Chamberlin invented his namesake device in 1949—a keyboard-like instrument that played sampled instrument sounds. Each key featured a tape-playing device underneath it, which was activated by pressing the key. The tape contained a real recording of a specific instrument (violin, for instance), and while the key was held, the tape would spool along the playback head, sounding the note. The tapes were short in length and could therefore only last about eight seconds long. In the early 1960s, Bill Franson, who was hired by Chamberlin as a salesman, headed for England via boat carrying two Chamberlin 600 models with him. Upon arriving, he removed the Chamberlin name badges and sought out a company who could manufacture the machines, claiming they were his design. He slightly refined the design, re-named it the Mellotron Mark 1, and began selling them in the U.K. Eventually, Chamberlin discovered this and forced a legal settlement with Streetly Electronics (the name of the company producing the Mellotrons). They decided that Mellotrons would only be sold in England (and Chamberlin would receive royalty payments on them) and Chamberlins would only be sold in America.

Both sold fairly well through the 1960s and early part of the 1970s (though the Mellotron always outsold the Chamberlin), but they soon fell prey to the growing popularity of synthesizers. Since then, both have become prized vintage instruments, although the Mellotron is much more widely known due to its use by bands such as the Beatles, King Crimson, Genesis, and later by bands such as Oasis and Radiohead. Now there are many plugins that emulate the sound of the Mellotron and some based on the Chamberlin, as well. Again we have instruments designed to emulate instruments that were designed to emulate instruments.

DAW LAYOUT

Now that we've got a broad picture of what's going on within the DAW program, let's see how it ticks. There are several different sections of the screen where various features exist and functions are performed. Again, each program may be slightly different, so these areas may have different names, but many of them are roughly the same, with only slight variation. It should be mentioned also that you can often customize the layout of your program to your liking. I highly recommend looking into this as you get more familiar with your system, as it can greatly speed up your workflow. Let's dissect the typical DAW screen layout.

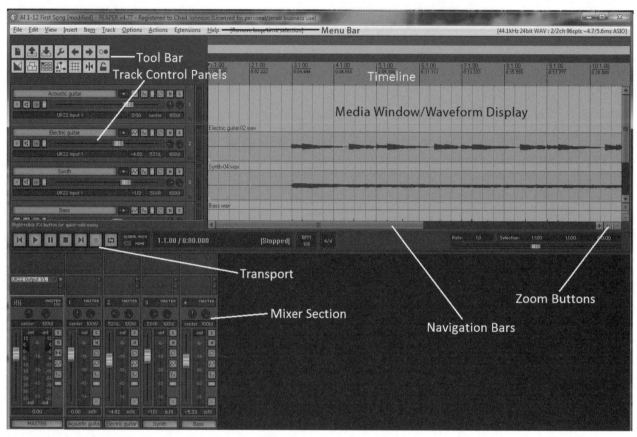

Typical screen layout in Reaper

Menu Bar

Just as with a word processor, you'll normally have a *menu bar* along top that will include multiple pull-down menus. Larger, general functions, such as opening/saving/creating a new project will be accessible here, as well as editing functions, track functions, viewing options, tempo settings, etc.

Tool Bar

Underneath the menu bar is often a *tool bar*, which generally consists of graphic icon shortcuts of the most commonly used menu items. This can usually be customized to include the functions you'd like.

Track Control Panels

These areas give you various controls over each track in your project, allowing you to name each track, arm/disarm them for recording, change the monitoring status, flip the phase, adjust the volume/pan, and add plugins.

Main Window/Waveform Display/Media Window

This window goes by several different names, but it's easy to spot because it's normally the focal point of any DAW. It displays the waveforms of the audio tracks and the MIDI data for any MIDI tracks. It's the part of the screen you'll most often use for editing, since most operations involve manipulating one or more of these waveforms (splitting, cutting, moving, trimming, copying, pasting, etc.). You can also usually import audio/MIDI files by dragging and dropping them onto this window.

Zoom Buttons and Navigation Bars

These will appear along the side and bottom of the media window and allow for zooming in vertically/ horizontally or scrolling through your project along its length. All of these functions can also be controlled by various mouse movements or command (shortcut) keys.

Timeline

The *timeline* runs along the top of the media window and lets you know where you are within your project. You can set it to display measures and beats, minutes and seconds, or both.

Transport

The *transport* is the collection of buttons such as play, record, etc. that mimic their functions on old tape machine recorders. By default, it normally appears below the track control panels or media window, but you can often move it around to any spot on the screen if you'd like.

Mixer

Generally placed along the bottom of the screen, the *mixer* is just that: a virtual mixer that resembles its real-life counterpart. Each vertical track channel (vertically separated) usually allows the same control as that in the track control panel, and each will typically display the level meter, as well. The main mix channel is normally found on the far bottom-right or bottom-left corner.

No Way Around the Manual

For those who don't like reading manuals, learning to use a new DAW may not be all that fun. These programs are so powerful and flexible that the manuals can easily run 500 to 1,000 pages or more. Granted, you certainly won't be using most of the features described in a comprehensive manual on a regular basis, but you will no doubt have to crack the manual many times in order to get up and running at first—especially if it's your first time using one. Once you get the basic functionality down in order to do what you need to do, then you can start researching other possibilities—using shortcut keys, etc.—to streamline your process more and tap into some other helpful functions.

TEMPLATES

If you find that you generally end up recording the same group of instruments for each song, you can create a *template* to save time. If, for example, you generally use the same plugin for your drum sounds, use the same setup for your bass track, use the same reverb plugin for your guitar track, and use the same signal chain for your vocal track, you can set all that up and then save it as a template. This is a file that's easily recallable that will get you right back to the same spot immediately. You just start the DAW, load the template, and there you are—all your plugins, levels, panning, etc., are all set the way you saved them.

Templates can come in various formats, as well. You can set up track templates, which will remember everything about one specific track, project templates, which will remember just about everything in the whole project, FX templates, which will remember everything about an effect or effects chain, etc. You may want to set up several templates covering a wide range of recording scenarios: solo acoustic guitar, acoustic guitar and vocals, solo piano (or keyboard), keyboard and vocals, drums/bass/piano jazz trio, electronic setup with a drum machine and four different synths, etc.

Using templates allows you to go from a brand new project to a turn-key setup with one click.

METRONOME (OR CLICK)

As mentioned earlier, the timeline can display minutes/seconds/frames or measures/beats (or both). While the minutes/seconds display is helpful for scoring a movie or commercial, the measures/beats display is more helpful when recording a typical pop song. Every DAW has a metronome or click track that can be turned on or off. After setting the project's tempo, you can record your basic tracks along with this click track so that the measures/beats display will correctly align with your song. This makes navigating your song much easier, not to mention editing. Once the basic tracks are recorded, you'll most likely no longer need the click, because you can just play or sing along to the drums (or whatever constitutes the bed tracks).

The click track is usually completely customizable when it comes to tone, volume (including making beat 1 louder than the others, etc.), and whether it's audible during recording, playback, both, or neither. When you're recording something in which a mic is not involved—such as programming MIDI drums, playing a MIDI synth, or recording your guitar direct—you can have the click as loud as necessary with no worries. If you're recording with a mic that's near you, however—such as with vocals, acoustic guitar, or percussion—you'll need to wear headphones and be wary of the click's volume. If it's too loud in your phones, it can leak into the mic and end up on the track. The use of closed-backed headphones will help here, as they will allow less sound to leak out than open-backed or semi-open ones.

A BRIEF LOOK AT SIGNAL FLOW

The idea of signal flow was a bit easier to grasp in the days of tape because most of the elements (recorder, mixer, etc.) were separate pieces of gear. With a software DAW, however, much of the signal flow is virtual, so you can't trace any physical cables. However, the idea is the same, and that's what we'll look at here. Let's boil the signal flow down to its most basic state:

1. A signal enters the input

2. The signal is sent to the recorder and recorded on the appropriate track

3. The signal is played back from its track on the recorder

4. The signal is possibly manipulated (via EQ and/or effects)

5. The signal arrives at the main mix

This is a bit of an oversimplification of the process, but essentially, that's what's happening. Now let's fill in some of the blanks to see how this works on an actual DAW.

1. A Signal Enters the Input

Let's say this is a microphone recording a voice. You plug the mic into channel 1 of your interface and adjust the trim for good recording level. Create a new track, select channel 1 of your interface as the input device, and arm the track for recording.

2. The Signal Is Sent to the Recorder and Recorded on the Appropriate Track

Since we've assigned our channel 1 interface input to track 1, the signal will then be recorded onto track 1. You can then disarm track 1.

3. The Signal Is Played Back From Its Track on the Recorder

At this point, you'll be monitoring the playback signal from track 1, and it will be displayed on track 1's level meter.

4. The Signal Is Possibly Manipulated (via EQ and/or Effects)

You have the option of EQing the signal or adding effects via plugins. (External hardware effects are also a possibility, which will be covered later in the book.)

5. The Signal Arrives at the Main Mix

After all is said and done, the signal usually reaches its main destination: the main mix. (Signals can also be routed to other destinations, but this just illustrates a typical scenario.)

Now that we have a basic idea of what's going on, let's take a look at some of the other possible stops along the way.

SENDS AND BUSES

After you've recorded a few tracks and gotten your feet wet with adding effects to tracks via plugins, you're eventually going to want to look at using *effects sends* and *buses*. These two terms have a relationship akin to a square and rectangle. In the same way that all squares are rectangles, but not all rectangles are squares, we can say that all effects sends are buses, but not all buses are effects sends. (Note that some people spell "bus" as "buss." They mean the same thing.) But let's look specifically at the idea of effects sends first.

Effects Sends

For this example, let's assume you've just recorded a piano on track 1. You like the sound, but since it was in a carpeted room, the sound is pretty dead, and so you'd like to add a bit of ambience to it. There's more than one way to skin this cat (as is often the case with various functions in a DAW). The seemingly easiest method is to open the FX send on that track and select a reverb plugin that you like. On the reverb's interface, there will usually be a mix knob that allows you to adjust the output anywhere from completely dry (0 percent, or no reverb) to completely wet (100 percent, or only the reverb signal). A typical value may be anywhere from 10 to 40 percent, depending on the reverb's parameters (decay time, room size, etc.) and the type of song it is. And there you have it! You have added reverb to your track, and it sounds great.

This is an example of a series signal path because the piano signal passes completely through the reverb and comes out the other end before carrying on to the main mix.

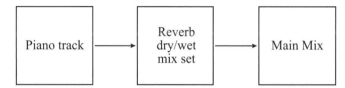

This is a perfectly acceptable way to do this. However, let's say you decide to record two more tracks: an acoustic guitar and a shaker. You decide that you want them to have the same reverb as the piano to create the same musical "space." You could repeat the above procedure for tracks 2 (acoustic) and 3 (shaker), which would result in three tracks, each with their own reverb plugin added.

The problem with this method is that plugins eat CPU resources. Depending on your computer's specs and the particular plugin—some plugins are much more CPU-intensive than others—you could begin to experience glitches if you continue to stack plugin upon plugin. The solution? An effects send!

Here's another way to accomplish the same thing without using nearly as much CPU power. Remove the reverb plugin from each track. Now create a new track (track 4) and name it "reverb bus." Add the reverb plugin to track 4 and set its mix at 100 percent wet. (If there is only a knob labeled "mix," 100 percent wet will be all the way clockwise.) At this point, you'll need to consult the manual of your particular DAW to find out how to create a send on a track. Once you figure out how to do this, create a send for track 1, a send for track 2, and a send for track 3. Their destination should be track 4 ("reverb bus"). For each send, you'll have a send level, which controls how much of the signal you want sent to the reverb. It defaults to 0 dB, which, with the reverb set at 100 percent like we have it, will result in a very wet signal, so you'll most likely want to lower it a bit. If you want more reverb on the guitar than on the piano, simply raise the guitar send level more. You can then use the track 4 fader to control the overall level of the reverb. (Note that some DAWs allow you to create "receives," as well, which is just the opposite way of doing it. Instead of creating a separate send for each of the first three tracks, you would simply create three receives on the reverb track. The end result will be exactly the same.)

This is an example of a parallel signal path because the piano, guitar, and shaker signals are split, sent to the reverb, and then joined again with their dry signals at the main mix.

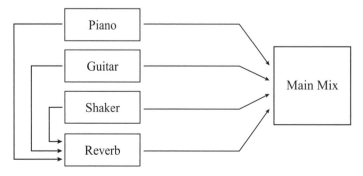

Buses

Again, an effects send is technically a bus, because you're routing several signals to one destination and controlling them all with a single parameter (or stereo pair of parameters). One of the most common buses is the *submix* bus. The idea here is simple: you want to control the volume (a common application) of several tracks with only one fader. Let's say you have three background vocals, and you want to be able to raise or lower their volume as a single unit with one movement. One way is to select all three tracks and then move the fader while performing a particular mouse maneuver (depending on your DAW), but another way is to set up a submix bus.

This is similar to an effects send, but there's one difference. First, you would create a new track and give it a name like "BG vocal bus." You would then create a separate send for each BG vocal track, the same way you did previously for the effects send (see "Effects Sends" section). The difference here is that you don't want the BG vocal signals to split; you only want them to be routed to the send. This is done in different ways, depending on your DAW, but there should be a way within the send setup window to disable the "master send" or "parent send" or something similar. This will prevent any signal from continuing on to the main mix. All three of the BG vocals will take a detour to the BG vocal bus track. You then use the send levels for each of the BG vocal tracks to adjust the mix that's being sent to the bus track. The bus track fader then becomes the overall volume control for all three BG vocals as one unit, and its signal is sent to the main mix.

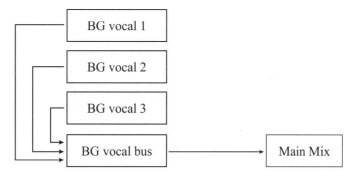

Extra Credit!

If the bus track were a stereo track, you would also be able to specify the panning on the individual BG vocal tracks, too. And if you felt so inclined, you could then process this bus track with compression (a common practice), reverb, etc., which would affect all the BG vocals. You could even send this bus track to a reverb bus track that had been set up for the rest of the instruments, too!

There are plenty of other routing options that are possible within a DAW, but this is a good primer on the most commonly used features. As you learn your particular system, you'll no doubt learn the most effective way to use it for your unique needs.

CHAPTER 6

ANATOMY OF A STANDALONE RECORDER

A standalone recorder's anatomy differs slightly from a DAW's, mainly because there's not as much going on virtually (although there still is plenty more than with the old portastudios of yesteryear). There's definitely more hardware to cover, but there's less in the way of software. (**Note:** Many of the features listed here will directly correlate to those on a DAW, and when this is the case, you'll be referred to the appropriate page in Chapter 5.)

INPUTS AND OUTPUTS

While the outputs are generally located on the back of a standalone recorder, the inputs can be located on the front, face, or the back. The inputs and outputs included can vary greatly from one recorder to the next, but this is usually due to one having less of a certain type (XLR jacks, for example) than another. For our purposes here, we'll take a look at a Tascam DP-24.

With the exception of the headphone jack and remote jack (which allows you to connect a foot pedal for remote control of various transport features), all of the inputs and outputs are located on the rear panel of the DP-24.

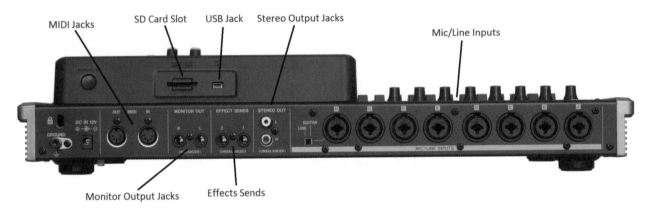

Rear panel of the Tascam DP-24

Mic/Line Inputs

The DP-24 features eight inputs (labeled A–H) that use combination XLR/1/4-inch jacks. This means you can plug either an XLR mic cable or a 1/4-inch guitar cable into them. They all have phantom power available, which is activated in groups of four with switches on the face of the unit. In other words, you can have phantom power present on inputs A–D, on inputs E–H, on all the inputs (A–H), or on none of them. The 1/4-inch jack on input H can be switched between line level (for keyboards, etc.) and a direct input for guitar/bass.

Stereo Out Jacks

These RCA jacks provide a stereo output for the main mix. You could hook these up to your monitors or an external two-track recorder onto which you could record your final mix, such as a DAT machine, two-track reel-to-reel, or a computer DAW. (This is only optional, though, as you can also record your final mix internally within the DP-24.)

Effects Sends

Although the DP-24 does have two internal effects processors, it also features two send jacks on the back, which can be used with external hardware processors. The cable from one of these jacks connects to the input of a processor, and the output(s) of the processor is then connected to an input (or inputs), A–H, which can then be routed to the main bus.

Monitor Out

These jacks output the monitor mix. Normally these cables would be connected to your control room monitors. Alternatively, if you're wanting to generate a headphone mix for performers, you can connect these jacks to a headphone amp and connect the Stereo Out jacks to your monitors.

MIDI In and Out

You can synchronize the DP-24 with external sequencers using these jacks. For example, if you have an external sequencer and sound module, or a keyboard workstation, etc., you can sync them to the DP-24 so that they'll "chase" it and play along with it. Then you just connect cables from the outputs of the sound module (or workstation) to inputs A–H, and their signals will be routed to the main bus without the need to ever record them on the DP-24, thereby saving tracks for other instruments.

USB

This allows for connection to a computer via USB cable. Once connected, you can perform many useful features, including:

- Backing up song data

- Restoring song data

- Exporting stereo master files (mixes) or individual tracks

- Importing audio files from the computer

Nowadays, most standalone recorders will include this feature, and USB is far and away the most popular interface in this regard.

SD Card Slot

(See "Media" section below.)

MEDIA

Standalone recorders can record to various types of media, including internal and external hard drives. However, as of late, most units now record to removable SD cards (or SDHC), which are affordable, reliable, and convenient. This is the method used by the DP-24. They're available in many different configurations, from 1 or 2GB up to 32GB. (**Note:** There are also SDXC cards available, which have much greater capacity [up to 512GB], but the Tascam does not list them as a supported media, nor do any other brands that I'm aware of.)

*Lifetime 32GB
SDHC card*

MIXER SECTION

The mixer section is one reason why many people choose to work with a standalone recorder: you get to move real faders and turn real knobs. In this section, you will normally have a fader for each channel, although not necessarily for every track. Some machines with higher track counts, such as 16, 24, or 32 tracks, will often have several mono channels on the left, which have their own fader, and several stereo channels on the right, each sharing a fader. The Tascam DP-24, for example, has 12 mono channels and six stereo channels (13–14, 15–16, etc.) for a total of 24. This means that tracks 1–12 can each be controlled by their own faders, but tracks 13 and 14 will be controlled by one shared fader. Depending on the particular recorder, sometimes these stereo tracks can be decoupled, and you can control their volumes independently with some fancy button-pushing. (The old Roland VS-series hard disk recorders operated this way.) On many recorders, however, including the DP-24, these tracks are always linked as stereo tracks and are therefore best reserved for recording stereo sources. Of course you'll find a master stereo fader, usually on the bottom-right (or, very rarely, two faders—left and right), which controls the overall volume of the unit.

There will also usually be some combination of buttons for each track, which will often function as mute, solo, record-enable, or select, allowing you to make specific adjustments to that track. For example, on the DP-24, when you press the "select" button for a track, then all of the knobs—pan, EQ, effect send, etc.—will affect that track when adjusted. Some recorders will have a dedicated pan knob for each track and/or a dedicated "reverb" knob, which is basically like an effects send knob.

Tascam DP-24 mixer panel

Level Set/Track Assign

Usually found along the top of the unit's face, you'll have trim knobs, which, just like those found on an audio interface, are used to set the incoming signal level. There will also often be buttons that are used to assign inputs to specific tracks. A common misconception with standalone recorders is that you have to plug into input 1 (or "A" on the DP-24) in order to record to track 1. This isn't true; on most recorders, any input(s) can be routed to any track(s).

EQ and FX Controls

Assuming the recorder has built-in EQ and effects—most do nowadays—there will usually be a collection of knobs and/or buttons with which these functions can be accessed. This is handled in a great deal of different ways on various recorders, so you'll need to consult your manual to see exactly how they operate.

Display Screen

Every recorder will have some type of display screen that you'll use to access its various functions. This can vary greatly, depending on the recorder—from a two-line, text-only monochrome LCD display to a full-color, 3.5-inch (or larger) screen with detailed graphics. Regardless of its size, it will no doubt pale in comparison to a computer monitor, but in fairness, it doesn't need to compare with it, as many of the functions that are displayed on a computer screen (faders, knobs, etc.) are represented in physical form on a standalone recorder.

The display screen will often show the level meters for each track, although these will sometimes be shown as segmented LEDs accompanying the faders. Either method will usually provide adequate level monitoring. Surrounding the display screen are often buttons that allow you to access more general menus or system functions, such as creating, deleting, and naming songs or editing functions, such as copy, paste, and move. Jog wheels or cursor buttons are also common in this area. A word of caution: If you're used to editing on a CPU system, it will likely feel a bit archaic on a standalone. Although you can usually perform just about all of the most important functions on a standalone, it's simply *much* faster on a CPU due to the graphic interface.

Transport Controls

Just like the old tape recorders, these buttons will control the "virtual tape" functions, such as record, play, fast forward, rewind, etc. If the unit includes other features, such as locate markers and auto-punch, the buttons controlling them will usually appear in this area, as well.

Which Standalone Is Right for You?

If you're considering a standalone recorder, there are some things you should keep in mind, as the functionality set is not nearly as standardized as that of most DAW programs, which can all usually do pretty much the same thing, just in slightly different ways. This is not the case with standalones. So here are some things to keep an eye out for when comparison shopping:

Number of tracks that can be recorded at once: Just because it's an eight-track recorder doesn't mean you can record all eight tracks at the same time. It only means that you can *play back* all eight at the same time. In fact, the majority of eight-track recorders on the market can only record two tracks at once. This isn't as drastic as it may sound. Remember, that's also the case with many DAW setups if you're working with an A/I that only has two inputs. The larger the track count, the higher the simultaneous recording count usually becomes. The DP-24, for example, has 24 tracks, and eight can be recorded at the same time.

Built-in effects: While this has become increasingly common as of late, it's not a given. And the amount, variety, and quality of effects included on a recorder vary, as well. For example, does it have amp simulation effects? This may be important to you if you're a guitarist and wanting to keep everything as compact and all-in-one as possible.

Number of effects you can use at a time: Some units will claim to have dozens of effects, but if there's only one processor on board, you'll only be able to use one of them at a time. Some units may have two processors but only allow one type of reverb effect to be used at one time (because reverb is typically data-intensive). There are usually ways around this, such as printing an effect to a track and thereby freeing up the processor for other uses, but they usually result in some sort of compromise.

EQ and/or compression: These two powerful tools can often separate a great mix from a decent one, so they shouldn't be overlooked. However, these are some of the features that are typically compromised or left out altogether in the lower-end models.

XLR inputs and phantom power: This is another one to think about. A typical eight-track recorder will likely only have two inputs (because you can normally only record two tracks at a time) but that doesn't always mean those inputs will be the XLR type with phantom power. Some recorders, such as the Boss Micro BR-80, are really geared toward recording guitar. Even though it's an eight-track recorder with two-track simultaneous recording, it features only one 1/4-inch input and one 1/8-inch input, so if you want to use anything other than its built-in stereo mic, you'll need an external preamp (with phantom power if you want to use a condenser mic). The higher-track machines will often have phantom power and XLR jacks on each input, as is the case with the DP-24.

Built-in CD burner: As the popularity of CDs continues to wane, this becomes less of a factor to many people. But if you do want one, be sure to do your research, as they're not present on many.

Connectivity/Compatibility: Many recorders feature the ability to interface with a computer in some way, whether it be for data backup or importing audio. But others take an extra step and allow the use of the recorder as a control surface for your DAW. This would allow you, for example, to record all your tracks on the standalone on location somewhere and then bring it home, transfer the tracks to your DAW, and mix/edit on the computer with a control surface. It's certainly a nice feature and worth investigating if the idea sounds appealing.

MIDI capability: If you want to use any external sequencers or sound modules, you'll need MIDI capability.

All of these variables fluctuate greatly from one recorder to the next, so it pays to do a little informed research before you pull the trigger on something if you want to be able to grow with it.

TEMPLATES

Similarly to a DAW, standalones often allow you to create templates that can save some time during the setup process. Obviously, things like track count won't be affected, but you can do things like make input/track assignments and EQ/effect settings, which can save some button-pushing. Even if the recorder doesn't offer templates (or "scenes," as they're sometimes called), you can usually at least set up a song (called "Template" if you'd like) with which you can start each time and then save it as something else. Or you may have to copy the template song first and then change the name. The point is, there's normally a way to do it if you're interested.

METRONOME (OR CLICK)

Most standalones will feature an onboard click track, just like a DAW (see page 74 in Chapter 5 for more information).

SIGNAL FLOW

With a few possible exceptions, the signal flow for a standalone recorder is nearly identical to a DAW. (The DAW is, after all, basically a "virtual standalone recorder.") Let's take a look at the same steps as they apply to a standalone recorder.

1. A Signal Enters the Input

Let's say this is a microphone recording a voice. You plug the mic into input 1 of your recorder and adjust the trim for good recording level. Assign the input to track 1, arm the track, and you're ready to record.

2. The Signal Is Sent to the Recorder and Recorded on the Appropriate Track

Since we've assigned our input to track 1, the signal will then be recorded onto track 1. You can then disarm track 1.

3. The Signal Is Played Back From Its Track on the Recorder

At this point, you'll be monitoring the playback signal from track 1, and it will be displayed on track 1's level meter.

4. The Signal Is Possibly Manipulated (via EQ and/or Effects)

You have the option of EQing the signal or adding effects via plugins. External hardware effects are also a possibility if your recorder has effects sends.

5. The Signal Arrives at the Main Mix

After all is said and done, the signal usually reaches its main destination: the main mix. (Signals can also be routed to other destinations, but this just illustrates a typical scenario.)

SENDS AND BUSES

These work similarly to their DAW counterparts, although submix buses aren't typically used nearly as much (if at all) on a standalone recorder.

Effects Sends

As mentioned, most standalone recorders have some type of built-in effects, and these are set up differently, depending on which recorder you have. On the DP-24, for example, there are two types of effects: insert and send. The insert effects (compression, noise gate, de-esser, and exciter) can be used on the inputs (i.e., while you're recording a track), and the send effects (reverb, delay, modulation effects, etc.) can be used on the tracks (i.e. while they're playing back). But this may be handled differently on others. Nevertheless, if built-in effects are included, there will be some type of effect-send configuration with which you can add the same effect to various tracks.

On a standalone recorder, however, you don't need to worry about setting up a send bus the way we discussed for the DAW, because it already is operating that way. You're sending several tracks to the same processor—not adding a separate processor (plugin in the DAW) onto each track (the way we first did for the DAW on page 76).

Buses

Submix buses are certainly not available on many standalone recorders. The DP-24 can somewhat do the equivalent, which it calls "groups." It basically allows you to control the volume of several tracks with one fader (the lowest track number's fader will be the "master"), so after achieving the desirable relative mix between them, you could control four BG vocals on tracks 9–12 with only track 9's fader, for example. But the extensive routing and bus capabilities of the DAW are not available on the standalone recorders of today (although some older machines did allow similar options during their heyday).

A Closer Look at the Tascam DP-24

Considering the fact that I used the DP-24 for all of the standalone recordings in this book—in other words, the recordings made not using the DAW—I thought it would be helpful to know a few more specifics about the unit as you listen to those recordings. This is a 24-track digital recorder with 18 channel faders (12 mono tracks and six stereo tracks), eight mic inputs with phantom power, a dedicated 1/4-inch instrument input, two effects sends, MIDI in/out jacks, monitor and stereo out jacks, headphone jack, USB jack, and remote jack. It records to SD cards for easy storage and at 24-bit/48 kHz resolution for pristine sound.

It features a 3.5-inch color LCD display, built-in effects and dynamic processing, and numerous knobs and buttons for easy tweaking and access of the most commonly adjusted parameters, such as EQ, panning, effects send, solo/mute, etc. A full array of editing functions are included, as well as a built-in CD drive for burning your own copies of your final songs or backing up data. Alternatively, you can use the USB jack to connect to your computer for transfer of tracks (for computer mixing) or data backup. A mastering effect even allows you to add the finishing touches on your mixes and help get them sounding professional.

Considering the quality you get and everything included, the Tascam DP-24 is a steal in my opinion. It truly does contain everything you need to make a pro recording in one box. The build quality is excellent, the faders feel great, and the LCD display is clear and vibrant. Although the editing is a bit tedious when compared to working with a full screen on your computer, it's nevertheless extremely powerful and more than capable of the most common editing tasks and then some. I wouldn't hesitate to recommend this unit to anyone looking for a full-featured standalone recorder that doesn't want to spend an arm and a leg.

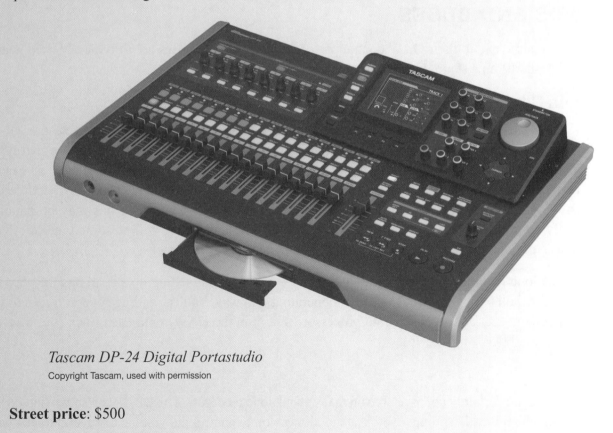

Tascam DP-24 Digital Portastudio
Copyright Tascam, used with permission

Street price: $500

CHAPTER 7
GETTING YOUR FEET WET— RECORDING YOUR FIRST SONG

If you've managed to read the entire book without skipping to this chapter, I commend your sticktoitiveness. I know that some of this stuff isn't exactly like reading a best-selling fiction novel, but what can I say? Recording is a big world, and there's a lot to learn! At any rate, it's time to start putting some sounds down on tape (or hard drive or SD card).

In this chapter, we're going to work through the process of recording our first song to get some hands-on familiarity with the basic operation of a recording studio. For this song, I'll keep it fairly simple, with only four tracks: an acoustic guitar, electric guitar, a synth line, and a bass. The reason for this instrumentation is to cover several different recording processes:

- The **acoustic guitar** will be recorded with a condenser microphone

- The **electric guitar** will be recorded directly using an amp simulator device

- The **synth line** will be recorded using a MIDI controller and an external synth or sound module

- The **bass** will be recorded using the direct out of an amplifier

We'll record the instruments in the order listed above, but feel free to mix it up if you'd like. In subsequent chapters, we'll talk more specifically about recording instruments, vocals, and drum samples. But this chapter is about having fun while learning the ropes of your rig. We're not aiming to make a stellar piece of art here. We are learning to crawl before we can stand, walk, and run. I realize, of course, that many of you may not be able to record each of these instruments (or may not want to!), so feel free make substitutions if you'd like. It would be ideal, though, if they all fell within the above-mentioned categories with respect to the recording process (i.e., a miked track, MIDI track, direct track, etc.), as they're all unique and require different steps. If you can't swing this, do what you can and still follow along, listening to the recordings and pretending when necessary.

Note: In this chapter, I'll include references to both DAW and standalone recorders when necessary. We're purposely avoiding the use of VSTi's, or virtual instruments via plugins, here so that the recording method stays basically the same on either platform. However, beginning in Chapter 8, we'll be dealing exclusively with the DAW world (unless otherwise noted).

On the Level

In the days of analog (tape) recording, tape hiss was always a concern. If you recorded with your levels too low, the hiss from the tape could become very noticeable when you turned up the track to an acceptable level for mixdown. That's not the case with digital recording. The flipside of the coin is that, with digital, the ceiling is the scary part. In digital, 0dB really is a ceiling, and if you exceed that, you can get a very unpleasant, nasty digital distortion. This is completely different than pushing the needles into the red a bit with analog gear. Whereas that practice, at times, can still yield useful results, it doesn't work that way in the digital world.

Therefore, when you're recording digitally, leave yourself plenty of headroom (the space between your signal level and 0dB). Shoot for a level of somewhere between -15 and -18dB to start. You can always bring up the track levels later on, but if you clip (break the 0dB barrier) during a good take, you may ruin it forever.

STEP 1: SYSTEM SETUP

The first step, if you've not already done it, is to make the physical connections of your system. We'll take a look at a basic setup for both DAW and standalone systems here. Yours may differ slightly, depending on your particular situation, but it shouldn't be too far off. If you choose to expand your system at some point with a mixer, control surface, or patch bay, you can still do so at a later time. To be safe, make all these connections with the power off on all components.

DAW System Setup

1. Plug the outputs (or channel 1 and 2 outputs if your interface has more than two) from your interface into your monitors. (If you're not using powered monitors, you would plug the interface outputs into your power amp and then run speaker wires from the power amp to the monitors.) The output plugs on your interface will likely be 1/4-inch or RCA type, and your monitors should have one of those types of inputs available. (Most powered monitors have more than one type of input jack.)

2. Plug your interface into your computer via USB or Firewire cable. Follow the instructions for your interface to get it installed correctly.

3. Plug a pair of headphones into the interface's headphone jack.

There are other connections we'll need to make along the way, but they're specific to the various tracks we're recording, so we'll cover them as needed. Test the system quickly by playing some music (an mp3, m4a, CD, or WAV file) to make sure you can hear it through your speakers. If not, you may need to set your interface as the default sound device of your computer.

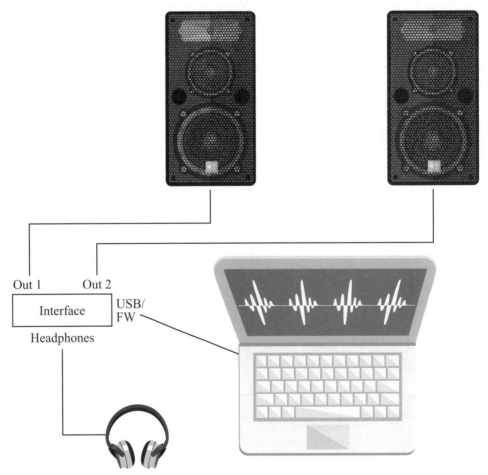

System Sounds and Other Tweaks

If you're using a computer that's specifically dedicated to your recording, then it's best to turn off all system sounds in your operating system, as these can sometimes create glitches in your recording software. It's rare, but it only takes one time to ruin the best vocal take of your life!

There are usually several other tweaks you can make to help improve the performance of a recording-dedicated computer. Unfortunately, it's beyond the scope of this book to cover them, but you can easily read about them online.

Standalone System Setup

1. Plug the monitor outputs (or L/R main outputs) of your recorder into your monitors. (If you're not using powered monitors, you would plug the recorder outputs into your power amp and then run speaker wires from the power amp to the monitors.) The output plugs on your recorder will likely be 1/4-inch or RCA type, and your monitors should have one of those types of inputs available. (Most powered monitors have more than one type of input jack.)

2. Plug the recorder's power cord into the wall.

3. Plug a pair of headphones into the recorder's headphone jack.

There are other connections we'll need to make along the way, but they're specific to the various tracks we're recording, so we'll cover them as needed. Test the system quickly by playing the demo song (if available) on your recorder, consulting the manual if necessary.

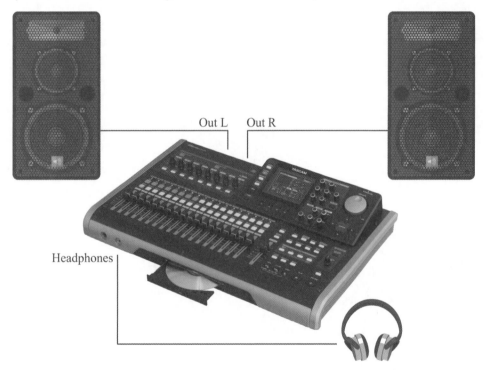

STEP 2: PROJECT SETUP

The first thing we need to do is create a new song (or *project*). This should be fairly self-explanatory, but check your manual if necessary. The first thing you need to do on a DAW system is make sure you know where the files are going to be saved. Consult your manual if necessary. Then we need to make a few decisions: the name of the song, the time signature, and the tempo. For our purposes, we'll call it "First Song," it will be in 4/4, and the tempo will be 100 bpm (beats per minute). Note that, in many DAWs, there will be a way to "tap the tempo" if you're not sure what it should be. In other words, there will usually be a button that you can click with your mouse in the tempo you want, and it will tell you the tempo you're clicking at. Make sure the metronome (or click) is turned on.

Next up on the DAW is to add four tracks. (You don't need to worry about this on a standalone.) Name them as follows (some standalone recorders allow you to name tracks, while others may not):

- Acoustic Guitar
- Electric Guitar
- Synth
- Bass

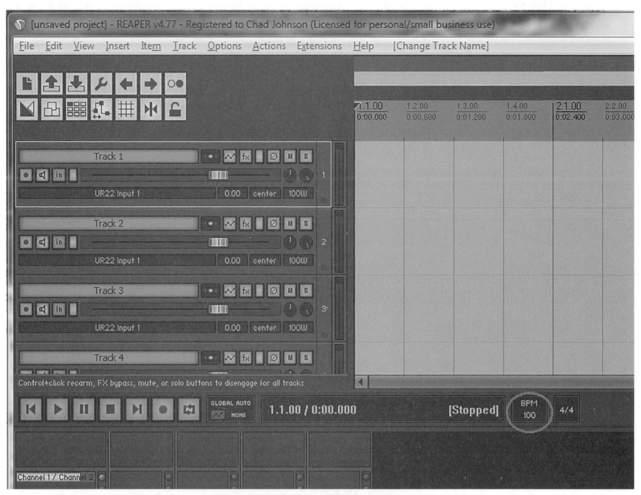

New project in Reaper with a 4/4 time signature, a tempo of 100 bpm, and four tracks added

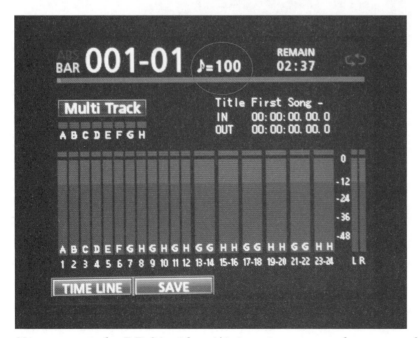

New song on the DP-24 with a 4/4 time signature and a tempo of 100 bpm

Feedback Issues and Speaker Bleed

Pro studios are set up with a separate control room and separate recording rooms. Therefore, when recording with a microphone, the sound from the control room speakers won't bleed into the microphone because they're in different rooms. In a home studio, however, the control room and recording room are sometimes one in the same. If this is the case, there's an issue that comes up when using a mic. You don't want your control room speakers on because:

- At worst, depending on the position, level, and orientation of the microphone, you could get some nasty feedback through the speakers

- At the least, the microphone will pick up the speakers bleeding into the vocal/acoustic/etc. track, which we don't want.

The simplest solution is to simply turn off your monitors (or power amp if using non-powered monitors) while you're recording with a mic. However, this can get a bit tedious, especially if you're doing everything by yourself. Some interfaces, such as the Steinberg UR22, will have a separate headphone level and output level, which allows you to turn the *output* knob down while you have a mic track armed and then turn it back up when the track is disarmed. Other interfaces, though, don't have a separate level for the output jacks and the headphones. In other words, the output knob affects the volume of both the headphones and the signal sent to the output jacks. What to do then? Again, you could turn off your speakers, but there's another way.

The **TC Electronic Level Pilot** is the answer. This little unit is basically a volume control that you can insert between the output of your interface and your monitors so you can have the volume up on your interface to hear your phones if necessary, but you can then turn down your monitors all the way with the Level Pilot. It's *very* well-built (made of aluminum), is totally passive (requires no power), and features a nice six-foot cable that, when extended, can save you a trip back up to the desktop if you're not going too far. Even if your interface does allow for separate phones/monitors level, the Level Pilot allows you the freedom to place the volume control anywhere on your desk that you'd like. It's a must-have for anyone who wants to record in their control room.

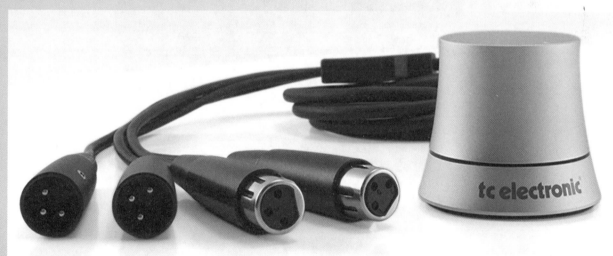

TC Electronic Level Pilot Desktop Volume Control

Street price: $89

STEP 3: RECORDING TRACK 1

Our first track is going to be an acoustic guitar, and we'll record it with a condenser mic. It doesn't matter which kind of condenser mic you're using, as we're just learning the basic idea. I'm using a Sterling Audio ST31 SDC (see photo). You don't need to worry too much about mic placement right now, but a good starting point is pointing toward the neck/body joint about a foot away.

Important Note Regarding Phantom Power!

Never plug your condenser microphone into an interface or preamp while phantom power is on. Always switch off phantom power first, wait five seconds or so, and then plug in the mic. After the mic is connected, you can then switch on phantom power. To unplug the mic, do the reverse: turn off phantom power, wait five seconds, and then unplug the mic.

In summary, you don't want to *connect or disconnect* a condenser mic while phantom power is on, as it can possibly damage your mic!

Before you record anything, you'll want to make sure your instruments are in tune. There are few things worse than recording a great guitar track only to later learn you'd forgotten to tune to a tuner. The guitar could be in tune with itself, but if it's not tuned to A440, then you'll either have to tune every other instrument from there on out to it or re-record the guitar (tuned to A440 of course!). It's a good idea to get in the habit of using the same tuner for all the instruments if possible, as it's usually the most bulletproof way of ensuring everything will gel on the recording. Clip-on tuners, such as the Snark SN-8 (see sidebar), are especially good for this, as they're quick and easy to use.

Snark SN-8 clip-on tuner

The Snark SN-8 is a great little clip-on tuner that, considering its price, delivers astounding results. I have several of them and use them constantly in my studio. The display, which rotates a full 360 degrees, is large, clear, and easy to read, regardless of the lighting. The SN-8 has a quick response time and tremendous accuracy on guitars, bass, mandolin, and any other string instrument on which I've tried it.

To top it off, it has a built-in tap-tempo metronome, and it contains a transpose function for alternate tunings, as well as pitch calibration. For the price, the SN-8 represents one of the best bangs for the buck out there, and you'd be foolish not to have at least one at the ready.

Street price: $14.99

At this point, make sure your speakers are turned down or off to avoid possible feedback issues if you're recording in your control room (see previous sidebar, "Feedback Issues and Speaker Bleed," for other options). After you've placed the mic into position, plug it into channel 1 on your interface (DAW) or the channel 1 (or A) input (standalone) and turn on the phantom power.

Breedlove Pursuit Dreadnought acoustic guitar miked with Sterling Audio ST31 condenser mic. The mic is an end-address (or top-address) mic, which means its top end should be pointed at the sound source.

You'll then need to assign the correct input to track 1. On a DAW, this is usually done by a pull-down menu on the track control panel, but refer to the manual if necessary. On a standalone, there's usually a button you push to enter a track-assign screen, where the assignments can be made. Make sure on the DAW that you have *input monitor* enabled, as this will allow you to hear what you're recording on track 1 as you're recording it. This is usually done with a switch on the track control panel. This is usually the default setting on a standalone, but if not, consult your manual. Now arm the track by placing it in record-enable mode.

Reaper: "First Song" with track 1 assigned and armed for recording

DP-24: "First Song" with track 1 assigned and armed for recording

Turn the input knob (trim knob on a standalone) on channel 1 of your interface up to about the 12:00 position to start. Sit in playing position and strum the guitar a few times, watching the OL (overload) or peak LED indicator on the interface, making sure it doesn't light. Turn the fader on track 1 up to the nominal position (0 dB). If you put on headphones, you should now be able to hear the sound of the mic. Strum the guitar some more and watch the signal on track 1 of the DAW or standalone, making sure that the level doesn't reach above the -15 dB marker on the peaks.

Click Bleed?

When recording with a mic, it's a good idea to check for click bleed before you start recording real takes. This can be done by sitting in playing position and recording with the metronome enabled. Record a few seconds, stop, and then turn off the metronome on the DAW or recorder. Then disarm the track (so you're not hearing the mic anymore) and listen back to what you've recorded. If you can hear the click, then it's too loud in your phones and is bleeding into the mic.

There are three possible remedies:

- Use close-backed headphones if you're not already

- Turn down the volume of the metronome in your DAW or standalone

- Choose an alternate (duller) sound for the click if possible

Try one, two, or all of these things until you're no longer able to hear the click bleeding onto the track but are still able to hear it loudly enough in the phones to play along to. You may need to turn down the track fader so that you'll be hearing less of your guitar through your headphones. Note that this won't affect the level you're recording—only your monitoring level. The only thing that would affect your recording level at this point is the input/trim knob on your interface/standalone (there are other ways to change the input level on a DAW, but we won't need them at this point.)

Once you have a good level on the acoustic guitar and no click bleed (see sidebar), you're ready to record the track. Depending on your DAW's default setting, there may be a *pre-roll* set. This means that, when the click is enabled, once record is pressed, it will count out several beats (often four) before it actually starts recording. (This is less common on standalone recorders, but check your manual.)

Start recording, allow a measure or two of lead-in, and start playing! After you've recorded, you should be able to see the audio file in the media window on the DAW. (Some standalone recorders have an indication of this, and others don't. Consult your manual.) If you mess up, simply undo the recording and try again. Once you have a satisfactory take, you're ready to move on to the next track. Disarm track 1, turn off phantom power on your interface/recorder, wait five or ten seconds, and then unplug the mic cable from the interface/recorder.

Reaper: First track recorded

 1 Track 1 recorded: Acoustic Guitar

STEP 4: OVERDUBBING TRACK 2

Now that you've recorded the guitar, it's time to overdub the electric guitar on track 2. Turn your speakers on (or turn the volume up). We're going to record the electric guitar using an external amp simulation device (amp simulation plugins are an option, as well, and we'll look at those in Chapter 8). This can be a modeling amp with built-in effects and a direct out jack (such as a Peavey VYPYR VIP 1 or Line 6 Spider IV) or a multi-effects pedal or desktop unit with amp simulation capabilities. The Line 6 Pod is a popular desktop model and the DigiTech Element XP, which I used for this track on the recording, is a popular pedal version (see sidebar on the next page for details).

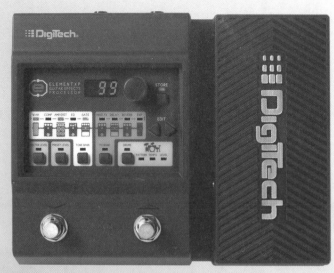

Digitech Element XP effects processor
Copyright DigiTech, used with permission.

DigiTech RP360XP effects processor
Copyright DigiTech, used with permission.

The DigiTech Element XP is a multi-effect guitar pedal that packs serious punch considering its relatively diminutive size. Not only do you get 38 different effect pedals from which to choose, but you also get 12 amps and nine speaker emulations, as well. There's also a built-in drum machine and a headphone jack for private practicing. The expression pedal allows you full control over numerous effects, including volume, wah, and Whammy effects, in real time. There's even an aux-in jack for plugging in your mp3 player so you can jam to your favorite tunes. The interface is quite intuitive, and you'll be dialing up great-sounding patches in no time.

The RP360XP is like the Element's big brother, with more of everything, including 74 effect pedals, 32 amps, and 18 cabinets. It also features an LCD interface that helps with more detailed tweaking of parameters as compared to the Element. A USB port allows direct interface to your computer for storing, editing, and sharing presets (DigiTech's free preset and librarian software makes this a breeze). Additionally, the RP360XP includes 40-second looping capability for spontaneous one-man-band creations.

Both units allow operation as effect only (no amp simulation), which is the preferred method when running through an amp, or amp simulation mode, which makes them a complete direct-recording solution. The sound quality on both units is stunning and completely belies their affordability. When you plug into one of these units, it literally feels like having access to a complete music store.

Street price: Element XP – $99.95, RP360XP – $199.95

Plug your guitar into the input of the device. Run a guitar cable from the direct out of the device (use the left/mono output if there is more than one) to an input on your interface or recorder. (**Note:** If we were going to use the onboard guitar processor of the standalone recorder, we would plug into the high-impedance guitar/bass input. But since the signal coming from our external device will already be at line level, we'll use a normal input, as the signal would likely overload the guitar/bass input.) I'm using an Agile AL-2000 Gold Top guitar with P90 pickups for this recording (see sidebar for details).

Agile AL-2000 Gold Top with P90 pickups

The Agile AL-2000 Gold Top with P90 pickups is basically a copy of a Gibson Les Paul gold top at a fraction of the price. The gold top model was actually the first Les Paul model that Gibson produced in 1952, and it featured P90 pickups, as well. So this is basically a copy of the first Les Paul ever. It features a solid mahogany body with binding, a mahogany neck with rosewood fingerboard, Grover die-cast tuners, two volume and tone controls, and a three-way pickup selector switch. The scale length is 24.7 inches, and it features 22 jumbo frets. Agile guitars are available exclusively through Rondo Music at www.rondomusic.com.

Although I was a bit skeptical at first, considering the low price of this instrument, my skepticism turned to amazement after putting this instrument through its paces. The build quality is extremely nice, it feels very solid (with a weight that feels nearly identical to a Gibson), and it required only a few minor tweaks to get it playing great. As with all P90-equipped guitars, there is a bit of hum when playing with distortion, but you can orientate yourself and face one of two ways to eliminate the majority of that. Once you're playing, this hum is generally completely masked anyway. I initially thought that I may eventually replace the pickups, because I figured they couldn't be that good at this price, but I don't think I'm going to touch the guitar. It sounds perfect the way it is—truly an amazing buy.

Street price: $250

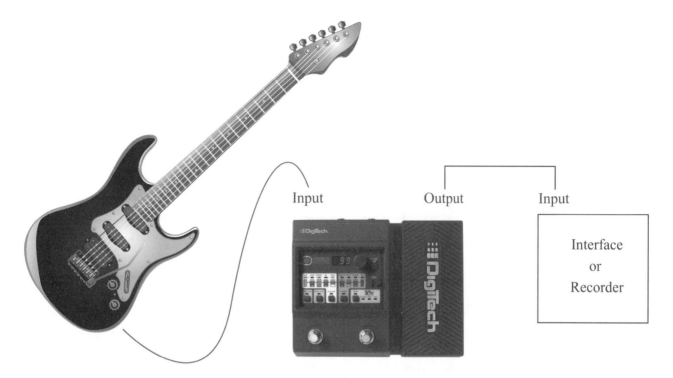

Input   Output   Input

Interface
or
Recorder

Assign the input from the interface/recorder to track 2. Turn up the output level on the amp simulator (DigiTech Element XP in our case), arm track 2 for recording, and enable input monitoring. You should now be able to see the recording level and hear the guitar through your monitors. Select the sound you'd like on the amp simulator and adjust the volume so that you're getting a good level going into the DAW/recorder, with the peaks going no higher than -15 dB to be safe. In my recording, I'm using a fairly clean tone with a phaser effect for the fun of it.

Make sure track 1's fader (acoustic guitar) is turned up and press play. This will allow you to check the level of the acoustic versus the electric. Adjust the mix (i.e., turn track 1 up or down) as necessary until you reach the desired level for each. When you have a good mix, you're ready to record. Rewind back to the beginning of the song and hit record. (If you're going to be starting right at the beginning with the acoustic, take note of how many clicks you allowed before starting the acoustic track.)

Again, if you mess up, hit undo (one of the benefits of digital recording) and try again. Once you're satisfied, disarm track 2, rewind to the top, and give it a listen.

2 Tracks 1 and 2: Acoustic and electric

At this point, you can make the first of many mixing decisions: *panning*. (You could do so after track 1, as well, but when there's only one instrument, there's really no reason to.) Let's try panning the acoustic guitar to the left (about the 9 o'clock position) and the electric guitar to the right (about the 3 o'clock position). This will help make each instrument more distinguishable and easily heard.

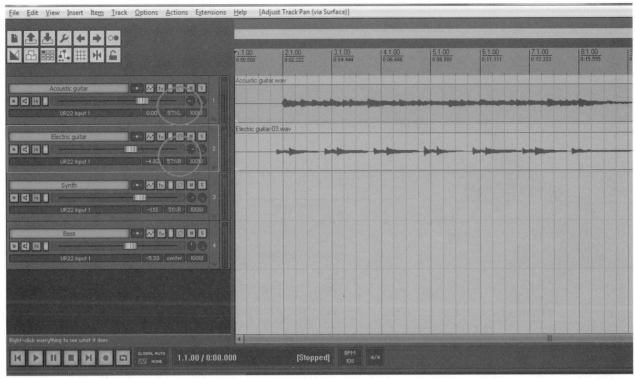

Reaper: "First Song" with tracks 1 and 2 panned L and R

 3 Tracks 1 and 2 panned left and right

STEP 5: OVERDUBBING TRACK 3

Now let's overdub a synth line using an external synth or sound module. In this way, we'll be treating the synth as a normal audio instrument rather than a MIDI track within the DAW. For this, we can just use an external synth with its own onboard sounds. Alternatively, we can use a keyboard MIDI controller to play sounds from a sound module or external analog synth (which often have no keyboard). We'll use the latter method here, controlling a Korg Volca Keys analog synth (see sidebar on the next page for details) with a MIDI keyboard controller.

Korg Volca Keys analog synth
Copyright Korg, used with permission.

The Korg Volca Keys analog synth is one of the coolest little synths to come out in a long time. It's truly amazing how fun this thing is to play with. It's no toy, however; you can craft some killer analog tones from it and tweak them to your heart's content with the onboard knobs. It's not only an incredibly affordable analog synth, it also contains a 16-step sequencer with eight memory locations for storing sequences, built-in delay, and three knob controls each for the VCO, VCF, VFO, and EG. It operates in one of six different modes, including poly (for three-note polyphony), unison, octave, fifth, unison ring, and poly ring, providing enormous flexibility from such a small package. The real-time knob movements can even be stored into your sequence as automation.

The Volca Keys (as well as the Volca Beats and Volca Bass models) seems to me to be an extension of the Monotron of a few years ago. A great-sounding analog synth on its own, the thing that really kept me from using it more than I would have was the small onboard ribbon controller, which was quite difficult to play with any precision. Although the Volca Keys also comes with an onboard ribbon controller, it also comes with what's perhaps my favorite new feature: a MIDI in jack. Now you can control this amazing synth with a full-sized MIDI keyboard controller, which, in my mind, takes it fully out of the realm of novelty and places it squarely in that of a serious musical instrument. In short, I love my Volca Keys!

Street price: $160

Plug a MIDI cable from the MIDI output of the controller to the MIDI input of the sound module (Korg Volca Keys in our case). Then run an audio cable from the output of the sound module to one of the input channels on your interface/recorder.

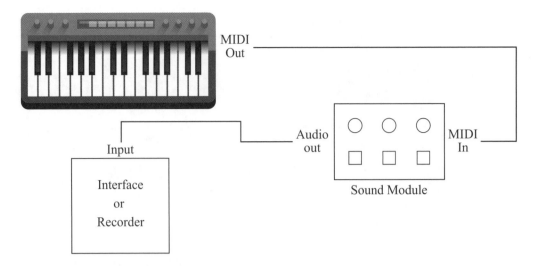

MIDI
Out

Audio
out

MIDI
In

Sound Module

Input

Interface
or
Recorder

Assign the input from the interface/recorder to track 3. Turn up the output level on the synth and play some notes, adjusting the trim on your interface/recorder to get a good level. Arm track 3 for recording, enable input monitoring, and you should now be able to see the recording level and hear the synth through your monitors. Select the sound you'd like on the synth and double-check the level going into the DAW/recorder.

Play back the track and adjust the mix if necessary, making sure you can hear your synth above the guitars. Once you've got it the way you'd like it, rewind back to the top, hit record, and play your heart out. Since the synth is our lead instrument, we're going to leave it panned up the middle.

 4 Tracks 1–3: Acoustic, electric, and synth

STEP 6: OVERDUBBING TRACK 4

Finally, let's overdub some bass to tie it all together. We're going to plug our bass into a bass amp and then run from the direct out into the interface/recorder. This will require a bass amp with a direct out jack (not all of them have this). For this recording, we'll use a Gallien-Krueger MB 112-II bass amp (see sidebar for details).

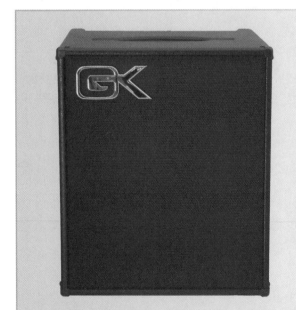

Gallien-Krueger MB 112-II bass combo amp
Copyright Gallien-Krueger, used with permission.

The Gallien-Krueger MB 112-II is a lightweight bass combo amp rated at 200 watts and includes a single 12-inch speaker. Weighing in at only 30 pounds and standing 17 inches tall, you can take it anywhere without worrying about wrenching your back or banging into a doorjamb. It features an XLR direct out jack (switchable between pre and post EQ), a 1/8-inch aux-in jack, headphone jack, and an XLR chain output on the rear that's meant for use with GK powered extension cabinets, allowing you to expand your rig if necessary to play larger venues.

The amp includes a -10 dB pad for use with active basses, a gain knob, and a contour switch for a scooped (low mids and accented treble and bass) sound. There's also a four-band EQ (bass, low mid, high mid, and treble) for increasing sound-shaping. This amp is plenty loud for rehearsals and small gigs (louder than I thought it would be), but I wouldn't play a larger venue without running a DI out or an extension cab, as well. The tone is there, though, for sure. It's a very clean-sounding amp and really puts out just what you put into it: full-bodied, present, and clear.

Street price: $399

Plug your bass into your bass amp and then run a cable from your amp's direct out jack to one of the input channels on your interface/recorder. (Again, use a standard input on the interface/recorder—not a guitar/bass direct input—as the signal will already be line level.)

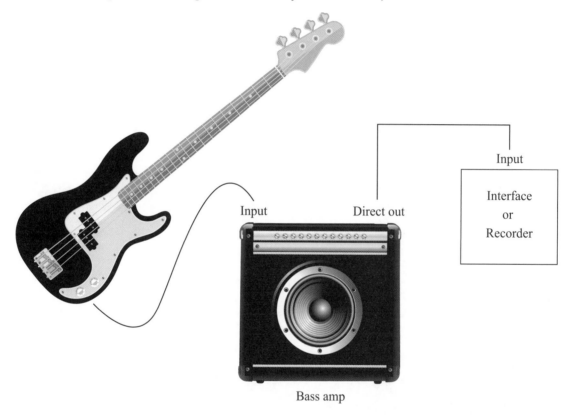

Bass amp

 Assign the input from the interface/recorder to track 4. Play a few notes on your bass, slowly turning up the amp volume and adjusting the trim on the interface/recorder as necessary to avoid overload. Arm track 4, enable input monitoring, and you should be able to hear the bass through your monitors. (**Note**: If the sound from the bass amp's speaker(s) is too loud, you can plug a pair of headphones into the headphone jack [if the amp has one], and that will almost always silence the speaker. If no headphone jack is present, you can either place the amp in a closet and close the door or put it in another room if your cables are long enough.) Double-check the level going into the DAW/recorder.

Play back the track and adjust the mix if necessary, making sure you can hear your bass amidst the other instruments. Once you've gotten it the way you'd like it, rewind back to the top and record the bass. As with the synth, we'll leave the bass panned up the middle. Since bass frequencies are *omnidirectional* (meaning they spread out in all directions rapidly), panning the bass to one side doesn't make as big of a difference as panning a higher-pitched instrument—especially when listening to speakers—so it's a common practice to leave the bass panned up the middle. (It's not a rule, though, so feel free to experiment!)

 5 **Tracks 1–4: Acoustic, electric, synth, and bass**

That's it for the tracking! In case you haven't yet, turn off the metronome and give the track a listen without it.

STEP 7: EDITING

We're going to keep the editing phase very simple here and basically just clean up the tracks. This means getting rid of any extraneous noises at the beginning and ending of the track (or possibly in the middle of a track, too, if you're not playing for a significant length of time). There are several ways to do this on a DAW, but there's usually only one way (that makes the most sense anyway) on a standalone recorder.

DAW Method

This is where you really start to see the power of digital audio—in the editing. In order to clean up the noise at the beginning of track 1 (acoustic guitar), for example, we simply need to select the track item (just by clicking on it usually, but consult the manual if necessary) and placing the cursor at the point just before the audio begins. You can zoom in a bit on the horizontal axis to get a bit more precise if you'd like.

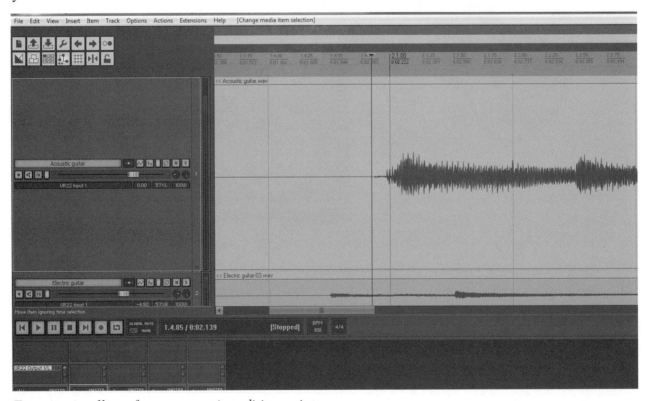

Zooming in allows for more precise editing points.

Snap/Grid Settings

If your DAW is not letting you place the cursor at specific points, and it keeps moving to one beat or the next, it's likely that you have the "snap" option enabled (it may have different names in other DAWs). This is a setting in which the cursor will "snap" like a magnet to the nearest beat (or whichever division you have set). Although this is very helpful in certain instances (such as when dealing with loops or MIDI tracks), it doesn't allow enough precision for cleaning up tracks. So consult your manual to find out how to turn this function off. In Reaper, "Alt+S" (Windows) is the default command key for turning it on or off. You can also toggle it by clicking on the magnet-shaped icon.

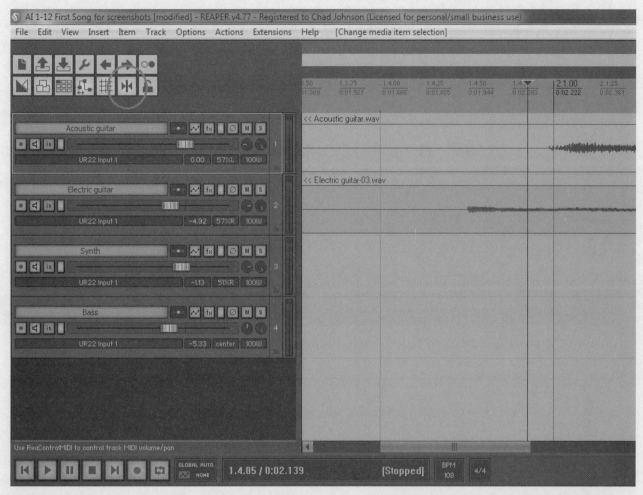

With the "snap" function on, the cursor will always snap to the grid. For more precise editing, turn this feature off.

Once you have the cursor in the right spot (just before the first strum begins), you just need to *split* or *cut* the audio item. In Reaper, "S" is the default command key for this, or you can find the same action listed in a menu. (Consult the manual for your particular DAW.) Once you do this, you'll have two items. Simply select the first item (click on it) and delete it. (The delete key usually does this.)

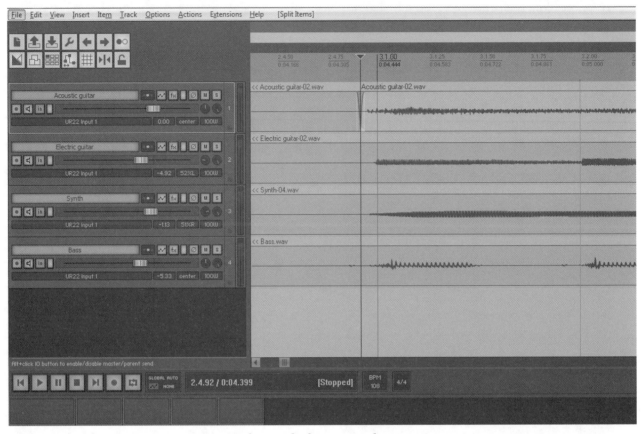

Reaper: Track 1 (acoustic guitar) is split just before strum begins.

Reaper: The first item (with intro noise) is deleted.

To hear the result of what we've done, click the solo button for track 1. This will often have "solo" or "S" on it and can usually be found on the track control panel or in the mixer section. Once you've soloed the acoustic track, it will be the only instrument you hear. Play it from the beginning, and you should hear absolute silence until the first strum—the magic of digital editing!

 6 **Track 1 soloed and trimmed**

Now repeat the same process for each of the other tracks, and you should end up with something like this:

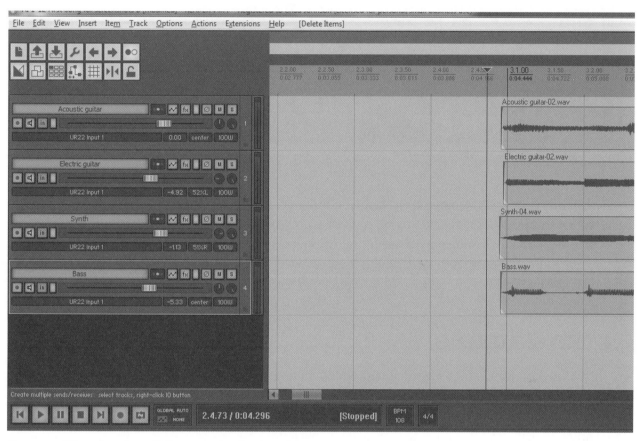

Reaper: Cleaning for all four tracks is complete.

Standalone Recorder Method

You'll most likely have to consult your manual for editing on a standalone recorder, as it's not nearly as intuitive as a DAW at first. Usually, you'll set two edit points on one track and then execute a command such as "erase" or "silence," which will clear the audio within those points. You have to be careful with this, because there will also usually be a similar command called "delete" or "cut," but it will produce a different result: everything behind it will then move forward to meet the first edit point. So be sure to select the proper command for the job.

The DP-24 allows for a timeline display, which lets you see a horizontal representation of the recorded tracks (you could think of this as a low-resolution version of the media window in a DAW). After performing the clean-up of tracks 1–4 on the DP-24, you can see how there is no audio information present at the beginning.

DP-24: Cleaning for all four tracks is complete.

Again, this is only scratching the surface of editing possibilities. For example, you may want to move all of the tracks closer to the beginning so there's not as much blank space at the beginning of the song. While this could be handled by a mastering engineer (or in the mastering stage if you're mastering it yourself), it could easily be done quickly here, as well. We'll look much closer at many more editing topics in Chapter 15.

STEP 8: MIXING

So you've got your tracks recorded and edited, and now it's time to mix them down to a stereo file that can be played in your car, on your mobile device, etc. As with the editing step, we're not going to spend a lot of time on mixing at this stage, because we'll be covering it in depth when we get to Chapter 16. But we'll look at a few basic concepts here.

It should be mentioned that there is no single established method for mixing a song. So the order listed below is by no means the standard; it's what seemed to make the most sense to me for the purpose of our demonstration here.

Panning and Volume Adjustments

Let's first look at panning and volume (or level) adjustments. If you've followed along with me so far, you have the guitars panned out to the side (3:00 and 9:00) and the synth and bass panned up the middle (12:00). Take a moment to move the panning around and experiment with different ideas to see what you think. There are no rules in this regard, so if something strikes your fancy, go with it! Just have fun and try to notice how the sound changes as you move things around.

For example, here are several different mixes at this point with different panning configurations:

 7 Acoustic guitar – middle, Electric guitar – hard right (all the way), Synth – hard left, Bass – middle

8 Acoustic guitar – hard left, Electric guitar – 10:00, Synth – 2:00, Bass – hard right

 9 Acoustic guitar – hard right, Electric guitar – hard right, Synth – hard left, Bass – hard left

When it comes to the levels of the tracks, one thing to be aware of is the level on the master fader. You want to make sure the song never breaches the 0 dB marker, as this would risk digital distortion, which is not a pretty sound. Play the song and watch the master meter. Ideally, you want the peaks to stay around the -6 dB range, as this will give the mastering engineer plenty of room in which to work.

If the peaks are rising much further than that, don't pull the master fader down; it should always be left at 0 dB for most applications. Just pull all the track faders down by the same amount. On a standalone recorder, you can just do this by grabbing all four faders at once and pulling down until the master level gets to where it needs to be. On a DAW, there are two easy ways to do it:

- Select all four tracks (via the mixer or track control panels). This is usually done by holding down control (Windows) or option (Mac) and clicking each one, but refer to your manual. Once you have them all selected, you can pull the fader down for one, and all four will move in sync. Or:

- You can usually enter the exact fader value via the keyboard with most DAWs. On Reaper (Windows), for example, this is done by right-clicking the fader. You can simply lower them all by the same number. If track 1 is set at -2.5 dB, for example, you could subtract 3 from that and set it at -5.5 dB. Then you can subtract 3 dB from each other track, as well.

Adding Effects

After you've got the panning and levels worked out, you may want to add a bit of ambience to the tracks so they don't sound so dry and close. *Reverb* is a very common effect for giving instruments a sense of space and making them feel as though they're situated together. So we're going to use one reverb and add it to all the instruments.

DAW Method

Instead of adding a plugin for each track, we're going to create an effect send and only use one plugin ("Sends and Buses" in Chapter 5, page 83, for an introduction to this idea). You'll likely have to consult your manual to see how these steps are performed in your DAW.

1. Add another track (track 5) and name it "Reverb."

2. Open the effects (plugin) menu and select a reverb effect. For our purposes, I'll use a simple reverb patch that comes with Reaper called ReaVerbate. Leave it set for 100% wet.

3. Now open the "I/O" or "send/receive" window for each track and create a send to track 5 (Reverb).

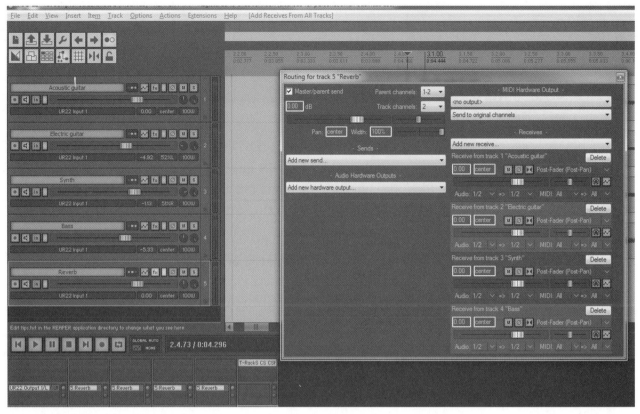

Reaper: All four tracks are being routed to track 5 (Reverb).

If you press play now, you'll most likely hear that all of the tracks are heavily drenched in reverb.

 10 All four tracks very wet with reverb

In order to dial the reverb back a bit, you have two options:

- Turn down track 5's fader. This will lower the level of reverb on all four tracks evenly. Or:
- Turn down the send level of each track until the desired amount of reverb is reached.

We're going to use the second option, because we want to vary the amount of reverb that each track has.

4. Solo track 1 and open up its send/receive window. Play the track and lower the send fader until the desired amount of reverb is reached. Un-solo the track.

5. Repeat this same process for the other three tracks: solo the track, adjust the send level, and un-solo the track.

6. Listen to the song with all four tracks and make final reverb send level adjustments.

Reverb Tips

Again, there are no rules when it comes to effects, but there are some conventions. Here are some that pertain to reverb:

- Bass-frequency instruments, such as a bass guitar or kick drum, generally don't sound as great with a lot of reverb because they tend to become muddy. These instruments usually receive the least amount of reverb of all, if any.
- The less reverb a track has, the more in-your-face it will sound. The more it has, the farther away it will sound.
- You will usually hear more reverb in your headphones than you will through your speakers, so be sure to listen to your mix in both to make sure you're not overdoing it.
- A very basic guide to applying reverb (when you're wanting a fairly natural sound) is to add it until you can clearly hear it and then back it off a bit.

Here's another listen to our mix with a more realistic reverb level for the tracks. The amount ranges from the electric guitar (most) down to the bass (almost none).

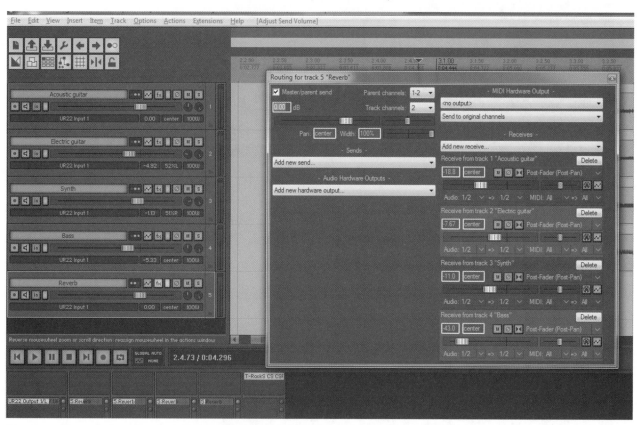

Reaper: Reverb levels after being adjusted.

 11 **Reverb levels adjusted**

Standalone Recorder Method

The process on a standalone recorder is basically the same as with the DAW, but we won't need to add another track to serve as the reverb bus. Most recorders already have one or two effects buses on board for this exact purpose. You'll need to consult your manual to find out how it's done on your particular machine, but I'll show you how it's done on the DP-24.

1. Choose your reverb effect. This is done by pushing the EFFECT button and then pressing F3 (SELECT) repeatedly to choose the effect. Each press of F3 scrolls through the three types of effects: reverb, chorus, and delay. Press F3 until you reach the reverb page.

DP-24: Choosing a reverb.

2. Use the cursor buttons to highlight the Room Type section, and use the jog wheel to select "Plate."

3. Set the Return level at maximum (127).

4. Now press the select button for track 1 (acoustic guitar) and then turn the Send 1 knob clockwise until the desired amount of reverb is heard.

5. Repeat step 4 for each additional track.

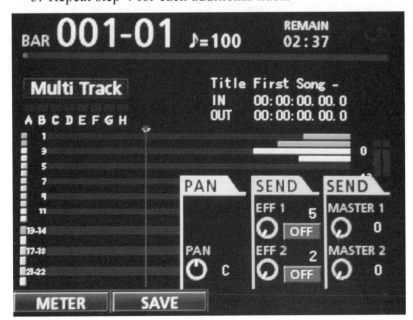

DP-24: Setting reverb send level for track 1.

Here's the sound of our mix with reverb added to all four tracks:

 12 Reverb on all four tracks

Again, this is only a fraction of what's entailed in the mixing process. We didn't get into EQ, compression, or any other effects—not to mention fancier things like automation, etc. We'll take a look at those things and more in Chapter 16.

Congratulations on recording, editing, and mixing your very first song!

CHAPTER 8

RECORDING GUITARS

Is there anyone who doesn't love a great guitar sound? After all, if there's one instrument that's basically *the* sound of rock 'n' roll, it would have to be the guitar. With the numerous options available today, there's never been a better time to get stellar guitar tones out of a home studio. In this chapter, we'll look at this six-string sonic force and discover how to harness its musical goodness.

ELECTRIC GUITARS

The electric guitar is capable of a massive variety of tones—from rip-roaring distortion to sparkling clean and everything in between. It's important to realize that, in order to get the desired sound, it helps to use the proper tools. If you're trying to record super-heavy distorted guitars but you're using a Pignose portable amplifier and a Fender Telecaster, you're likely to be disappointed. On the other hand, that same setup could excel if you wanted to record some Mississippi Delta-style blues guitar.

So the first step is to learn to work with what you have; learn what it does well and work with it. Certainly there are guitars, such as a Gibson Les Paul and Fender Stratocaster (and various guitars similar to them), that can do many things well, just as there are versatile amps. But there are also instruments and amps that are more specialized. So, when it comes to purchasing gear, if you're going to need to cover a wide variety of styles, and you're working on a budget, keep that in mind when choosing your tools. You may not be able to get the absolute best guitar for one style if you also need it to cover other styles just as well. Instead, it would be better to pick one that handled all of the styles pretty well, as this will ultimately be of more use to you. If, of course, you plan on only recording one style of music, then by all means pick the best instrument for that style that you can afford.

First Things First!

Before you record anything, always remember to tune up with a tuner! I can't stress this enough. Just because you tuned to a tuner two days ago doesn't mean you don't have to today. Guitars are not rigid pieces of iron; they're made of wood (most of them anyway), and there's always a chance that tunings can drift slightly with changes in weather, humidity, etc., even with the most expensive guitars. So, before you record the first note, be sure you're tuned to A440 so that you won't have to worry about it later on.

Basic Electric Guitar Types

In the world of electric guitar, there are certain types of sounds you hear over and over again because they simply sound good. They've become iconic and are therefore the basis for the majority of instruments produced today. Again, if you're wanting to cover most of the bases when it comes to guitar recordings in various styles, it's best to own two or three affordable guitars that, together, can do many things, rather than one expensive guitar that does only one thing really well. Of course, that depends on your specific needs.

Let's take a quick look at some guitar archetypes and what they're known for. Then I'll show you some budget-friendly guitars I used on these recordings that are based on these models.

Gibson Les Paul Style

The Gibson Les Paul is a single cutaway guitar traditionally made from a mahogany body with a carved maple top and a mahogany neck with a rosewood fretboard. The earliest model (in 1952) was known as a "Goldtop" and had two *single-coil* P90 pickups, each with its own volume and tone controls. I used an Agile AL-2000 Gold Top guitar on these recordings to mimic this guitar type (see page 96 for more details).

In 1957, Gibson replaced the P90 pickups on the Les Paul with PAF ("patent applied for") *humbucking* pickups, which revolutionized the guitar world. These were originally designed to sound like P90s but without the hum (which plagues most single-coil pickups), but they tend to sound a bit darker with slightly less high mid range. It's this guitar that became *the* sound of hard rock in the late 1960s and through the 1970s. Some of the most notable players in the early days include Eric Clapton (with the Bluesbreakers and Cream) and Jimmy Page (with Led Zeppelin). In the late 1980s, when guitars with whammy bars had become the flavor of the day, Slash (with Guns N' Roses) did much to restore the popularity of the Les Paul, which has continued to this day. For the recordings in this book, I used a Peavey SC-2 for these humbucker-style sounds (see sidebar for more details).

Peavey SC-2

The Peavey SC-2 is a dual-humbucker (alnico), single-cutaway guitar weighing almost nine pounds and featuring a scale length of 24.75 inches. The body is made from basswood, and the neck is made from rock maple and topped with a rosewood fretboard. It features the standard two-volume/two-tone electronic layout and three-way pickup selector. It's available in one of three finishes: Cherryburst, Vintage Tobacco Burst, or Black.

The SC-2 is lighter than most Les Paul-style guitars, which is certainly a welcome difference when it comes to extended playing times. The tones from this guitar are punchy and aggressive when using a distorted tone, and this is where the instrument shines, in my opinion. It cleans up nicely when you roll the volume back, as well, retaining most of the highs thanks to the treble-compensated volume controls, and will even handle clean tones admirably. In my opinion, though, this guitar wants to rock out, and it does that very well.

Street price: $250

Fender Stratocaster Style

The Stratocaster was introduced in 1954 and originally contained a solid ash body, maple neck, and three single-coil pickups; however, they switched to solid alder bodies in 1965, which became the traditionally used wood from then on. The sound of the Strat is generally cleaner, twangier, and brighter than a Les Paul (especially one with humbuckers) and has therefore found favor with lighter rock and country players (although the Fender Telecaster is the reigning king of country guitars), more so than Gibson guitars. Many hard rock players do play Strats, though, and some of the most iconic figures in its history include Buddy Holly, Jimi Hendrix, Eric Clapton (he switched from Gibson guitars to Strats shortly after Cream), David Gilmour, Stevie Ray Vaughan, and Eric Johnson. I used an ESP LTD ST-203 for the Strat-style tones on these recordings (see sidebar for more details).

ESP LTD ST-203

The ESP LTD ST-203 is a Strat-style guitar with a reliced, sunburst finish that looks attractively authentic. It features an alder body, a maple neck, rosewood fretboard with jumbo frets, ESP tuners, a vintage bridge, and three ESP LS-120 single-coil pickups. It comes with a vintage-style vibrato arm that screws into place, allowing you to adjust its stiffness to your liking.

Although the relic job on this guitar is impressive, it would be all for naught if it didn't deliver in the sound department. Thankfully, that's not an issue. The guitar plays and sounds excellent—on par or above the level of many Fenders I've played—and it's become one of my main go-to guitars for numerous applications, including blues, rock, and funk.

Street price: $350

Other Styles

Honorable mentions include the Fender Telecaster, which dominates the country world but is not quite as popular as its Strat sibling in other styles. The "Super Strat," which combined a Strat-type shape with humbucking pickups and a Floyd Rose (or equivalent) whammy bar, became the most popular guitar type in the 1980s. Based on Eddie Van Halen's homemade "Frankenstrat" guitar, it was typified by brands such as Jackson, Kramer, and Ibanez. Super Strats are mostly used today in metal and hard rock. Then there are the semi-hollow and hollowbody guitars, such as the Gibson ES-335 and Rickenbacker 330, which also see a fair bit of action in the rock world, albeit only a fraction when compared to Les Paul- or Strat-style guitars. Check out Epiphone's Dot or Peavey's JF-1 models for great sounding, affordable alternatives in the semi-hollow category.

With all of these established tones in the world of electric guitar, it's always nice to have one "character" guitar—as I call it—which decidedly does *not* sound typical. One of the more common "uncommon" guitars (if that makes sense) is the Danelectro 59 series, which is based on the original 3021 model famously played by Jimmy Page on "Kashmir," among other Zeppelin songs. I used a Danelectro 59M NOS for this purpose on some of the recordings in this book (see sidebar for details). It's a great way to give a track a unique sound when you're looking for something a bit different.

Danelectro 59M NOS in Orange-adelic

The Danelectro 59M NOS is a very unique instrument. Besides its super-cool looks, the first thing you'll notice when you pick up this guitar is how light it is. The Masonite body is chambered, making its weight much closer to that of a semi-hollowbody (like a Gibson ES-335) than a solidbody guitar. It plays great and feels solid, however. The guitar features two lipstick-style single-coil pickups, a three-position selector switch, and combination volume/tone knobs for each pickup.

What makes this a "NOS" version of the normal 59M is that the pickups come from a batch of "found" supplies dating back to approximately 1999. While this doesn't really qualify as "vintage," the company claims that the older pickups possess a slightly different tone than the newer ones, and pretty much all the reviews seem to support this statement. (As I only have the NOS version, I can't personally comment on this.) What I can say is that the guitar sounds great. The sound of the 59M NOS is hard to describe, so it's a good thing the accompanying audio will help me out in that department. The bridge position is thinner than a Strat or Tele, but that's in no way a bad thing; it's just its own thing. It's great for funky parts or country-rock-style licks with cleaner tones, and it has some great bite when overdriven. The middle and neck positions have a chimey quality that's particular well-suited for chording. In short, a "Dano" is inimitable, and you simply need to hear or play one to understand why.

Street price: $349

Now that we have an idea of some common tools for the task at hand, let's get down to the business of recording these guys. There are several options for regarding electric guitars today, and they each have their own advantages and setbacks. But they can all yield terrific-sounding guitar tracks. The decision on which one (or ones) to use will depend on your own specific needs; hopefully, this chapter will enlighten you. For our purposes, we're going to break it down into three main categories:

- Miking an amplifier
- Recording direct with an external amp simulation device
- Recording direct with an amp simulation plugin

Miking an Amplifier

Let's start out with the oldest, most well-established method of them all: miking an amplifier. Not surprisingly, this is often the preferred method for older players who grew up doing this for years before "amp simulation" became a catch phrase. Some of the reasons players prefer this method include:

- **Sound:** Some players simply insist that a digital device can never duplicate the sound of a real tube amp. Others claim that, in a blind listening test, just about anyone can be fooled. While this is a topic of great debate, it doesn't really matter to some people; tube amps will always be the only option.

- **Feel:** This is not often debated, as most people will agree that playing through a cranked tube amp will *feel* different than a modeling amp/device that's simulating the sound but at a lower volume. This is a big issue for some and not so much for others.

- **Practicality:** An amp can be used for a gig, as well as recording in the studio. While it's true that some players do make use of amp simulators (be it self-contained devices or plugins on a laptop), the vast majority of gigging guitar players still use standard amps (tube or solid state) on stage.

- **It's what they know:** Many players that have been using and recording amps for years already know how to get great sounds from their amp, so they simply don't have the desire to learn another way.

Shake, Rattle, and Rock 'n' Roll

One thing you'll want to pay attention to when setting up to record an amp is mechanical noise. This is especially true when recording a loud amp. Make sure nothing is rattling or shaking while the amplifier is making sound. This includes the amp cabinet itself (possibly a loose screw or tube somewhere), anything sitting on top of the amp, or anything on the walls, such as a clock. There are certain resonant frequencies that can cause vibration in everyday objects, and you won't know about them until you crank up the amp and start digging in. But you really don't want to discover the problem after the guitarist has laid down the solo of his life, only to learn that it's unusable because the picture on the wall behind the amp was rattling like a handful of screws falling down the aluminum roof of a tool shed!

With the increasing popularity of amp simulators over the past 15 years, some younger recordists these days may have never even tried miking an amp. If you fall into this category, I'd encourage you to give it a shot at least once, as it can be a really rewarding experience when done well.

Recording Procedure

The most basic method is to simply aim a mic (or mics) at your amp, plug it into your interface, arm the track(s), and set your levels. However, it's quite common to track guitars (regardless of recording method) with compression, as well. See Chapter 13 for details on this.

Single Microphone Techniques—Dynamic Mics

Perhaps the most common method of miking a guitar amplifier is that of close-miking with a dynamic mic, such as a Shure SM57 or SM7B, Sennheiser MD 421, or Electro-Voice RE20. While the MD 421 and EV RE20 are a bit out of our price range, the two Shure mics are attainable, with the SM57 coming in at just under $100 new and the SM7B scraping the affordable range at $349. (The incredible versatility of the SM7B makes it worth it, though, if you can swing it.)

Let's start with one of the most common of all: the Shure SM57. If you ask 15 different pro engineers how they mic a guitar cab, you'll probably get 15 different answers. But if you ask enough of them, you'll start to find a few methods that come up again and again. One common method is a few inches from the grill, on axis (directly perpendicular to the grill), and an inch or two to the side of the speaker cone. It's also common to lift the amp off the floor by placing it on a chair, stool, etc.

For this first recording, I'll be running through a VOX AC4C1 (see sidebar for details). The amp will be sitting on a small children's table about 20 inches off the floor and several feet away from the short wall of a room that measures roughly 13x25 feet (see picture). Since I'm going for a somewhat distorted tone here, I have the amp cranked a good bit (about 7 or 8). This is a completely dry recording, with no reverb or any other effects added. While we're at it, so you can hear the difference between the four different guitars I mentioned earlier, I'll record the same phrase with each guitar through the same exact amp/mic setup. I'm using the bridge pickup on each guitar.

VOX AC4C1 amp close-miked with a Shure SM57 dynamic microphone

13 **Peavey SC-2: VOX AC4C1 amp close-miked with SM57**

14 **Agile AL-2000 Gold Top w/ P90s: VOX AC4C1 amp close-miked with SM57**

15 **ESP LTD ST-203: VOX AC4C1 amp close-miked with SM57**

16 **Danelectro 59M NOS: VOX AC4C1 amp close-miked with SM57**

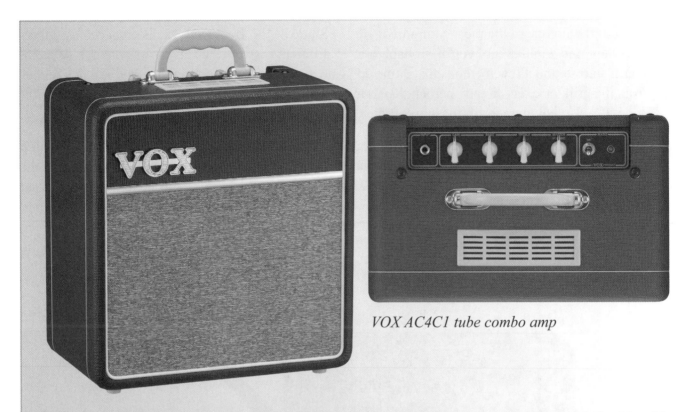

VOX AC4C1 tube combo amp

The VOX AC4C1 is an all-tube amp (two 12AX7 preamp tubes and one EL84 power tube) with a 10-inch Celestion speaker that puts out about four watts. It comes in a gorgeous, retro-looking blue vinyl and Tygon grill cloth combination that harks back to the style of the 1960s. Even for an amp sporting a 10-inch speaker, it's more compact than I was expecting, which makes it easy to stow when you need tone on the go. (Sorry—couldn't help the rhyme.)

The AC4C1 is much more than just a looker, though. It features a stripped-down set of controls, including gain, bass, treble, and master volume, and gets plenty loud for a four-watt amp. Assuming you don't need a sparkling clean sound, you can easily keep up with a drummer in rehearsals with this thing if need be. Of course, it will certainly do the sparkling, chimey VOX clean sound at moderate (read "still pretty loud") volumes. Cranking the gain produces some serious crunch, and the two-band EQ helps you dial in the right shade. VOX really hit it out of the park with this one!

Street price: $319.99

And now let's hear what happens when I simply pull the mic away from the amp about two feet. I'll use the Peavey SC-2 here, so compare this to the previous Peavey track. Not only does the tone drastically change, but you can really start to hear the room showing up on the recording. (This will be even more pronounced in headphones.)

VOX AC4C1 amp miked with a Shure SM57 dynamic microphone two feet away

 17 Peavey SC-2: VOX AC4C1 amp miked with SM57 two feet away

Role of the Room

By miking an amp closely (with a dynamic), you're minimizing the sound that the room will have on the recording. The *farther you move the mic* from the amp, the *more room you will hear* on the recording. This can be a good thing or bad thing, depending on how your room sounds. You'll also notice a difference in the sound, which is determined by where your amp is positioned in the room. This can be quite pronounced even when close-miking, as we will hear demonstrated.

If you'd like to further minimize the room on the recording, or you need to isolate the guitar track from sound leaking from other instruments (if recording several people at once, for instance), you can surround the amp with baffles or use a prefabricated device, such as the CAD Acousti-Shield AS16.

Compare this with the initial Peavey track.

 18 Peavey SC-2 with CAD AS16

CAD Acousti-Shield AS16
Copyright CAD Audio, used with permission.

Let's move back to the close-mic position but use a Shure SM7B dynamic mic instead of the SM57 to hear the difference. I'll use the Agile AL-2000 here, so compare this to the previous Agile track.

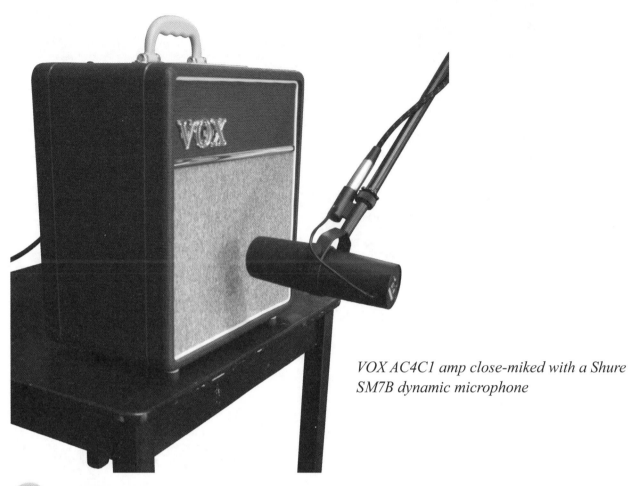

VOX AC4C1 amp close-miked with a Shure SM7B dynamic microphone

19 Agile AL-2000 Gold Top w/ P90s: VOX AC4C1 amp close-miked with SM7B

It should be becoming apparent that there are many variables in the sound of a miked amplifier. There's no better teacher than experience, so the more you experiment, the more you'll learn what sounds best for your particular needs. Every mic will sound slightly (or significantly) different, but if you're patient and willing to put in a little trial and error, you should be able to find a useable sound from just about any decent mic.

Other Variations on the Single Dynamic Mic

Aside from the method(s) I just demonstrated, there are several other common techniques for a single dynamic mic, including:

Off-axis: By varying the angle of the mic respective to the grill, you'll alter the tone. Generally speaking, on-axis will provide the brightest tone; the more off axis you move the mic, the darker and bassier the tone will become.

Different areas of the speaker: While the cone will produce the most biting, present tone, moving toward the edge of the speaker will result in a more muffled tone.

Varying distance from grill: I demonstrated the difference between two inches and two feet, but there's obviously a lot of leeway between those two. Six inches is a common distance, as well.

Experimentation is the key, and I can't stress that enough. It's well worth it to spend several hours one day (or several days) recording the same guitar riff with many different setups (on-axis mic, off-axis mic, varying distance, varying amp position in the room/on the floor/off the floor, different amps/guitars, etc.) so you can learn *your equipment*. There's no magical formula that works every time. There are conventions, which we're discussing, that usually get you pretty close (or right on), but tweaking a bit here and there is normally par for the course in turning a good guitar sound into a great one. The extra 10 or 20 minutes you may spend getting the sound right at the beginning of a session can save *hours* during the mixing process, when you're trying to fix something that wasn't right at the source.

Single Microphone Techniques—Ribbon Mics

Ribbon mics, such as a Royer R-121 or Beyerdynamic M 160, are also used frequently when recording guitar cabinets. Those models are a bit pricey, though, so we'll be using the excellent CAD D82 (see page 18 for details), which won't require you to donate your plasma in order to eat.

Ribbon mics are generally described as a bit warmer than dynamics or condensers, and they may take a little getting used to at first. But tracks recorded with them often tend to sit very well in a mix, which is always a welcome feature. Let's have a listen to the D82 on the VOX AC4C1 amp with a similar setup as before. (Note that this is a side-address mic, which is why it's faced the way it is.) I'll play the same phrase as before, and I'll use the ESP LTD ST-203, so compare this to the previous ESP track.

VOX AC4C1 amp close-miked with a CAD D82 ribbon microphone

 20 ESP LTD ST-203: VOX AC4C1 amp close-miked with CAD D82

Of course, aside from the guitar and microphone (and room, when it's present), the other huge variable is the amp, and every one will sound different. Let's take a listen to a different amp through the same microphone with the same setup to hear how this changes the sound. I'll be using an Orange Micro Terror through an Orange PPC 112 cabinet (see sidebar for details), which is a hybrid amp with a tube preamp and solid-state power amp section. This thing may be tiny, but it can get *loud* and it can seriously rock!

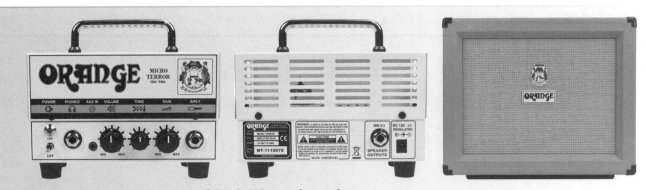

Orange Micro Terror amp and PPC 112 speaker cabinet

Copyright Orange, used with permission.

Orange Amplification made a big splash a few years back with their Tiny Terror head, which was an all-tube, 15-watt design (switchable to seven watts) in a lunchbox-sized portable package weighing only 12 pounds. They've shrunken things down even more with the Micro Terror, which is about the size of two effects pedals and weighs less than two pounds! The Micro Terror utilizes a hybrid design, with a tube preamp (12AX7) and solid-state preamp, and puts out 20 watts. Along with its volume, tone, and gain controls, it also features a headphone jack and a 1/8-inch aux-in jack for jamming along with an mp3 player or other device.

You simply will not believe how loud this thing can get for its size. It can power any 8-ohm cabinet, including up to a 4x12 model. I have it paired with Orange's beautiful PPC 112 cabinet, which features a 12-inch Celestion Vintage 30 speaker. The Micro Terror will clean up nicely when the volume is rolled down, but this thing is really just itching to rock out, in my opinion. It does an awesome job dishing out the midrangey grit for which Orange has become famous, and it'll go full-tilt, as well, if you really push it!

Street price: Micro Terror amp – $149, PPC 112 cabinet – $379

That's the great thing about these smaller amps: you can afford several different-sounding ones for what a big, high-wattage amp would run you, but you can still get big sounds out of them in the studio! And truth be told, any of the amps mentioned in this book would be loud enough even for decent-sized gigs if miked through the P.A. (which they normally are anyway). Neil Young's gigging amp (even for large venues) is a 1959 Fender Tweed Deluxe, which is a fairly low-wattage amp, so there you go!

Orange Micro Terror amp and PPC 112 cab close-miked with a CAD D82 ribbon microphone

21 ESP LTD ST-203: Orange Micro Terror amp close-miked with CAD D82

And now let's move the D82 mic out about six inches from the grill and about two inches to the side to hear how the sound changes.

 22 ESP LTD ST-203: Orange Micro Terror amp miked with CAD D82 six inches away

It's through repeated experimentation like this that you'll learn the proper mic placement for the sound you'd like to achieve. The very broad generalization is that you'll hear more treble the closer you get to the cone, but there are many other smaller variables that come into play, and the only way to familiarize yourself with them is by spending a little time and trying out lots of placements.

Single Microphone Techniques—Condenser Mics

Another option is the condenser mic, which will usually give a slightly more detailed sound in the treble end. When it comes to miking technique, it's not terribly different from that of a dynamic; however, people have a tendency to place a condenser a few inches farther back than a dynamic. Also, if you're recording very loud guitars, you'll probably want to engage the pad (attenuator) on the condenser mic—if it has one—to be sure no damage will come to the mic's delicate diaphragm mechanism.

Let's have a listen to the sound of the Orange Micro Terror amp close-miked with a Sterling ST55 LDC mic. I'll use the Agile AL-2000 for this track.

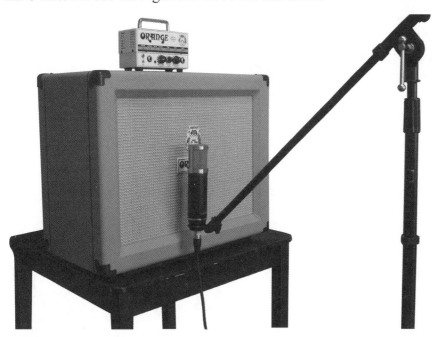

Orange Micro Terror amp and PPC 112 cab close-miked with a Sterling ST55 condenser microphone

 23 Agile AL-2000: Orange Micro Terror close-miked with Sterling ST55

And here's the same mic pulled out about two feet from the Orange amp, again using the Agile AL-2000. With a condenser mic, the room is even more apparent with this setting than when using a dynamic. This makes the condenser mic the obvious choice for when you're wanting to deliberately add an ambient "room" sound to the track.

 24 Agile AL-2000: Orange Micro Terror amp miked with Sterling ST55 two feet away

Dual Microphone Techniques

It's also very common to blend a dynamic mic with a condenser mic to form a composite sound. In this instance, you could record both signals to one track (pre-mixed), or you can record each mic to its own track and blend them at mixdown. If you have the resources, the second option will give you more flexibility. Both mics can be set close to the grill or one can be close and one far away to pick up more ambience. For example, let's combine a Shure SM57 (close-miked on the cone) with a Sterling ST55 about six inches behind it and a few inches to the side. In the audio track, you'll hear the riff played three times: once using only the SM57, once using only the ST55, and then once with both of them combined.

Orange Micro Terror amp and PPC 112 cab miked with a Shure SM57 (close) and a Sterling ST55 six inches back

 25 Orange Micro Terror amp with SM57 close and ST55 six inches away

And now let's do the same thing, but this time, we'll pull the ST55 about three feet back and one foot above the Shure mic. Notice the added ambience from the room.

Orange Micro Terror amp and PPC 112 cab miked with a Shure SM57 (close) and a Sterling ST55 three feet back

26 **Orange Micro Terror amp with SM57 close and ST55 three feet away**

On these tracks, I blended the dynamic and condenser mics about 50/50, but you can, of course, vary the mix as necessary. If you want more "bite" to the track, you might blend more of the dynamic. If you want more "body," you might add more of the condenser. Again, experiment to see what sounds best to you.

Effects Pedals

While some effects can be added during the mixdown (which we'll look at in Chapter 16), there are some that are more integral to the sound and are therefore generally added while recording. These tend to be effects through which the entire guitar signal travels. In other words, they generally won't have a "wet/dry" mix setting; your guitar goes in one side and it comes out the other side wholly effected. Effects that generally fall into this category include:

- Distortion/fuzz/overdrive
- Compression
- Octaver
- Phaser
- Wah
- Volume
- Tremolo
- Flanger

For these demonstrations, we'll check out the third, and final, amp that will be demonstrated in this book. It's another low-wattage tube amp by VHT called the Special 6 (see sidebar for details). However, you'll find that it sounds quite different from the VOX AC4C1. As this is another non-master volume amp, the only way to really get a good amount of distortion from the amp is to crank it up. While this sounds great, it's not always practical.

VHT Special 6 tube amp miked with a Shure SM7B

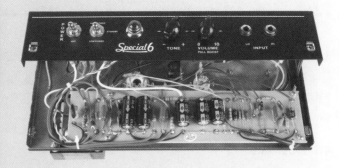

VHT Special 6 tube amp

VHT's Special 6 combo is a hand-wired, all-tube amp rated at six watts. It features a 10-inch VHT High-Sensitivity speaker and weighs 26 pounds. An eyelet-style component board houses the hand-wired components, making the Special 6 a modder's (one who modifies gear) dream. VHT encourages this, in fact. Two 12AX7s and one 6V6 comprise the tube layout.

Along with the barebones design of a volume and tone control, this amp packs a few not-so-obvious features that make it more than meets the eye in terms of features. One of them is a power mode that's switchable between full power (six watts) and approximately half power, the latter making it much easier to dial in some grit if needed without peeling the paint off the walls in your home studio. Another very nice feature is the footswitchable gain boost (also accessible by pulling up the volume knob). This is not one of those subtle, "is it really on" boosts. It adds a good bit of volume and some grit, as well, and would act perfectly as a lead boost at a gig. Also nice is the inclusion of three external speaker jacks: 4, 8, and 16 ohms.

The tone of the Special 6 is a little darker and throatier than the VOX AC4C1, for example, but it can still bite at you when cranked. The lack of a master volume means that you'll need to crank it in order to get some serious distortion, but the half-power mode (and boost) helps with that. I really enjoy the amp for meatier-type riffs, but it can handle cleaner things very well, too. With a pedal or two for added versatility, this amp would also make a killer live rig.

Street price: $249.99

This is where a *distortion pedal* can save the day. You can have your amp set at a respectable-yet-non-devastating volume and use a distortion pedal, such as an MXR Custom Badass '78 Distortion (see sidebar for details), to achieve your desired level of gain. In the track below, you'll hear it with the pedal bypassed (i.e., not in use), and then you'll hear the pedal kicked on: first set for a mild overdrive and then for a more fully distorted tone.

 27 MXR M78 Custom Badass '78 Distortion pedal

MXR M78 Custom Badass '78 Distortion, MXR M103 Blue Box, MXR M101 Phase 90,
MXR M102 Dyna Comp Copyright MXR, used with permission.

Among other things, MXR makes many of the most widely used effects pedals in the world of guitar, with their roster of users reading like a who's-who of guitar greats. Two such pedals are the M101 Phase 90 and M102 Dyna Comp, both of which have been heard in countless recordings over the years. The Phase 90 is dirt simple with only one speed knob, and that's all you need. The phasing just sounds excellent; that's all there is to it. It can go from lush to crazy and everywhere in between. If you've ever heard the early Van Halen albums, you've heard what this pedal can do. This is without a doubt my favorite phase pedal of all.

The Dyna Comp pedal has been a mainstay in country players' rigs for decades, as well as rock players. Its output knob allows you to match the volume of its bypassed state (or provide a boost if desired), while the sensitivity knob dials in the amount of compression. Extreme settings provide increased sustain without mega distortion, while more moderate settings result in the classic, squeezed sound with the percussive attack that's so ubiquitous in the country world.

The Custom Badass '78 distortion pedal is one of MXR's newer models, but it's definitely destined for greatness. It's designed to emulate the distorted—but not triple rectified—tones of the late 1970s, so it's great for more old-school, retro-style rock. The simple three-knob design (Output, Tone, and Distortion) is expanded by a Crunch button, which boosts the harmonic content of the distortion. What this translates to, in my experience, is an increase in creamy midrange character.

The Blue Box is one cool pedal. It's a fuzz pedal but with a very interesting twist: it also duplicates your signal two octaves lower and messes with it. What I really like about the pedal is its versatility and unpredictability. It has only two knobs: Output and Blend. With the blend knob all the way up, the pedal mostly just acts like a great-sounding fuzz pedal. But as you begin to turn the Blend knob counter-clockwise, the low octave begins to creep in. The farther counter-clockwise you go, the more glitchy and unpredictable the sound gets. It can create some mean-sounding riffs or ultra-thick solos. To hear a famous example of the latter, check out Led Zeppelin's "Fool in the Rain."

Street price: $80 each

A *compressor pedal* helps you even out the dynamics of your attacks, which helps the guitar sound more controlled and present. There are different types of compressors, based on the circuitry they use to achieve the effect, but the most common in the guitar world are *VCA* (voltage controlled amplifier) and *optical*. One of the most popular VCA compressors of all is the MXR Dyna Comp (see sidebar for details). These compressors are quite versatile and can be used to add a snappy, percussive quality to your playing (as heard in typical country guitar) or increase the sustain of your lead lines. In the following track, first it will be bypassed and then engaged.

 28 MXR M102 Dyna Comp pedal

An optical compressor is a very natural-sounding compressor. It's generally not used as much for an "effect" as it is a polishing tool. In fact, it's very hard to even notice it's being used unless you really squash (compress) the signal! For this demonstration, I'll use a Hotone Skyline Komp pedal (see sidebar for details): first bypassed and then engaged.

 29 Hotone Skyline Komp pedal

The Hotone Komp opto compressor is part of the company's Skyline series. These pedals are small and cute, but they're certainly not small in sound. The Komp pedal is an optical compressor, which means it's not as noticeable as an "effect" as, say, the MXR Dyna Comp, which is a VCA (voltage controlled amplifier) compressor. This is not to say that you won't be able to notice the Komp when you use it; you certainly will.

The pedal smooths out your dynamics and makes the guitar sound much more balanced and clear. It's one of those pedals you can set and leave on continuously, because it just makes your playing sound more professionally crafted. The three knobs—Volume, Tone, and Comp (which appears on the top of the pedal)—allow for a good bit of tweaking to get it sounding just the way you like it, while the Spark button produces an increased high-end response.

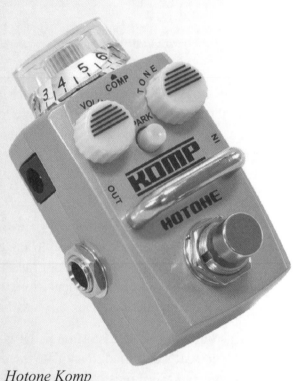

Hotone Komp
Copyright Hotone, used with permission.

The Komp is definitely not a muddy-sounding compressor pedal. If anything, it may ever-so-slightly reduce your bass response, which helps tighten up your sound a bit. The Tone knob allows you to tweak this if necessary. What's certain is that this pedal does what it does very well and without drawing a lot of attention to itself. Also be sure to check out Hotone's Nano Legacy Series guitar amp heads, which deliver killer tone for $99 in a 5-watt miniature package that can fit in the palm of your hand!

Street price: $80

Another common effect is the *phaser*, and one of the most common of all is the MXR Phase 90 pedal (see sidebar for details). This effect splits the signal into two and alters the phase of one. Sometimes this is variable, or sometimes it's fixed (as with the Phase 90). A "speed" or "rate" knob determines how fast the signals drift from being in phase and out of phase with each other. The result is a watery, wobbling tone that's great for livening up an arpeggio line, among many other things. Here's how the Phase 90 sounds. First it will be bypassed and then engaged.

 30 MXR M101 Phase 90 pedal

As with "character" guitars (such as the Danelectro), it's also great to have a few character pedals that are capable of creating some wacky sounds. The MXR M103 Blue Box (see sidebar on page 127 for details) is such a pedal. It's a combination fuzz/octave pedal that doubles your signal two octaves lower and fuzzes it up. As you'll hear on the track, it can go from simply a great-sounding fuzz pedal to a thick two-octave fuzz to a crazy, glitchy, ultra-cool noise maker. After being bypassed, you'll hear it with the Blend knob set at about 10:00. This will blend the fuzz with a good bit of glitchy octave chaos.

 31 MXR M103 Blue Box pedal

No pedal board would be complete without a wah, and the Morley Classic Wah (see sidebar for details) is a great-sounding and very affordable option.

 32 Morley Classic Wah

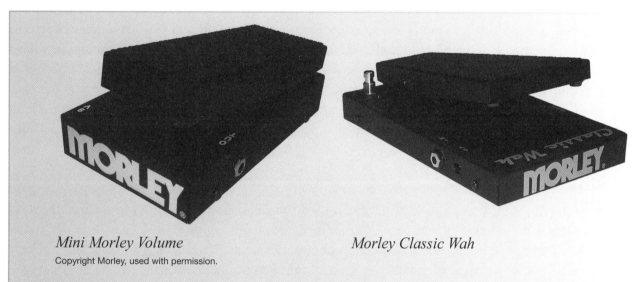

Mini Morley Volume
Copyright Morley, used with permission.

Morley Classic Wah

The Morley Classic Wah features an on/off switch and an LED indicator, so you don't have to guess whether the wah is active or not. You also don't have to worry about accidentally turning off the wah. Considering these two factors alone, it makes me wish that all wah pedal makers would employ these features. The tone of this pedal is very articulate, and the wah effect is not subtle in the least. You can get some extreme wah sounds when traversing the entire range. The more I played with the pedal, the more I enjoyed the wide range of tones available.

The Mini Morley pedal line aims to diminish the footprint, as it were, of pedals that generally take up a good deal of pedal board real estate—namely volume pedals. The Mini Morleys are built like a tank, powered by a 9 volt battery or AC adapter, and they feature optical circuitry, which means there are no pots inside that can get scratchy over time as is common in both wah and volume pedals.

The Mini Volume also features an LED to show power. If you're used to traditional volume pedals, this one will likely take a bit of getting used to. It will create smooth volume swells, but the smaller pedal size means that you'll need to practice with it for a few minutes first. After acclimating yourself to the compactness of the pedal's "throw," you'll be swelling like a pro.

Street price: Mini Morley Volume – $59.99, Morley Classic Wah – $72

A *volume pedal* is very handy for several reasons. It can act as a variable boost, a noise gate, or you can achieve those awesome swells. Check out the Mini Morley Volume (see sidebar for details) on this track. I'm adding a bit of delay on this one, which really helps accentuate the volume swells.

33 Mini Morley Volume

Another alternative to individual pedals is a *multi-effects device*, such as the DigiTech Element XP or DigiTech RP360XP (see sidebar on page 95 for details). These can be a great, cost-effective solution to owning multiple effects pedals. They can usually be programmed to store presets of various effects configurations that can be instantly recalled with the touch of a button. Let's hear the sound of the Element XP's tremolo and the RP360XP's flanger.

 34 DigiTech Element XP: Tremolo

 35 DigiTech RP360XP: Flanger

Recording Direct with an External Amp Modeling Device

One alternative to miking an amp is to use an external amp simulation device. The main benefit to doing this concerns the issue of volume. If you get the recording bug at 12:30 at night and just have to lay down that distorted riff, an amp simulator will allow you to do so with no sound at all, other than that bleeding from your headphones. Again, many purists will claim that a real amp is the only way to go, and there's no debating that a real amp sounds great. But amp simulators have come a long way since their introduction decades ago, and it's now entirely possible to get completely realistic-sounding tracks using them.

Recording Procedure

Plug your guitar into the amp modeler and run a cord from the modeler's output into a line input on your interface. Don't use the "guitar/bass" (high impedance) input on your interface, as this signal will already be coming in at line level. Arm the track and set the levels. If you plan on using stereo effects on the device, you'd run cords from both the left and right outputs into two channels on your interface. You'd then assign them to two tracks and pan those tracks left and right to achieve the stereo spread. **Note:** When using only one cable for a mono signal, the left output is normally the jack to use, but double-check this in your manual if necessary.

Amp modelers come in tabletop format, such as the Line 6 Pod series, rackmount format, and multi-effect pedal format (such as the DigiTech Element XP and RP360XP used in this book). Be aware that not all multi-effect pedals have built-in amp modelers—some just contain effects—so be sure to check this before purchasing one if going this route. There are also many modelers in full-fledged amp format, as well, such as the Line 6 Spider series, Peavey Vypyr series, and Roland Cube series. These amps all feature built-in effects and amp simulation, and you can run a line from their direct out jack into your interface when wanting to record direct. There's also almost always a way (often by plugging in a pair of headphones) to disable the speaker, as well. If you're wanting a great deal of versatility from your purchase—from gigging to recording—you might want to check out one of these.

These external amp modelers really shine when you want a quick, one-stop shop for a solid guitar tone. You can choose to print some of the onboard effects (such as reverb, delay, phaser, etc.), or you can record them totally dry and add effects on mixdown. Whatever sound you record will be printed on the track, so be sure you have the effects set correctly if you want to print them. Let's take a look at several different sounds from the DigiTech Element XP and RP360XP to get a glimpse at their versatility. All of the effects (if added) on these tracks come from the DigiTech units.

36 DigiTech Element XP: Clean Fender-style 2x12 tube amp with reverb

37 DigiTech Element XP: Slightly overdriven VOX-style 2x12 tube amp with reverb

38 DigiTech Element XP: Slightly overdriven Fender tweed-style 1x12 amp with tremolo and reverb

39 DigiTech Element XP: Overdriven Fender tweed-style 1x12 amp with analog-style delay

40 DigiTech RP360XP: Overdriven Fender tweed-style 4x10 amp with reverb

41 DigiTech RP360XP: Overdriven Marshall plexi-style 4x12 amp with wah and reverb

42 DigiTech RP360XP: Clean Roland JC120-style 2x12 amp with chorus and reverb

43 DigiTech RP360XP: Distorted Mesa/Boogie-style 4x12 amp with octaver and delay

44 DigiTech RP360XP: Overdriven Hiwatt-style 4x12 amp with rotary-speaker effect and reverb

As you can see, these little guys can pack quite a bit of tone into a very manageable size. Again, though, if you record with an effect on, that effect will be printed to the track and cannot be removed, so be sure you have the tone you want before you commit!

Recording Direct with a Plugin

Another common way to record electric guitars direct is with software—i.e., an amp modeling plugin. This affords the most versatility of all, because you can record the guitar part with the amp sound you want, but you don't have to print the effect while you record it. If you decide later that there's too much distortion, for example, you can change the tone completely. Of course, if necessary to free up computer resources, you can render the track, which will create a duplicate track but with that amp effect (and any others you may have on there) printed. This allows you to mute the original track, which means that the plugin won't be using any CPU power. This action is reversible, though, and your original track will still remain, should you need to change the sound again.

There are many great-sounding affordable amp modeling plugins on the market, including IK Multimedia's AmpliTube 3, Line 6's Pod Farm 2.5, Native Instruments' Guitar Rig Pro, and Peavey ReValver MK III.V, among others. They all feature fairly similar capabilities, but their user interfaces and functionality differ, as well as their sounds. For the recordings in this book, I used AmpliTube 3 from IK Multimedia (see sidebar for details).

Recording Procedure

Plug your guitar into your interface's dedicated guitar/bass (high impedance) input if it has one. If you don't have one, you'll need to run through a DI box, such as the Radial StageBug SB-1, to bring your guitar's signal up to line level. Then run a cable from the DI box into the interface. Assign the input to a track, arm it, and check your guitar's level. Open the effects window for that track to select your amp modeling plugin. Once you have the desired amp model selected, check your levels once more before recording. Consult your software's manual for the finer details of tone-shaping. This method allows you to monitor (listen to) the amp modeling effect while you record, but it won't print the effect to the track. If you later decide you don't like the amp model (or effects) you've used, you can change it.

There is a way to print the amp model effect to the track if you'd prefer to do that, and that has to do with an *input effect* (or *insert effect*). You'll have to consult your DAW's manual to see exactly what terminology is used for this, but basically it places the effect directly after the input, *before* the recorder, so what you hear is what's going to tape (hard drive). In Reaper, for example, once you arm a track for recording, you'll see a button appear in the track control panel called "input FX." By clicking this button, you'll open the input effect window, and any effect you add here will be printed to the track as you record. In other words, it cannot be removed from the track.

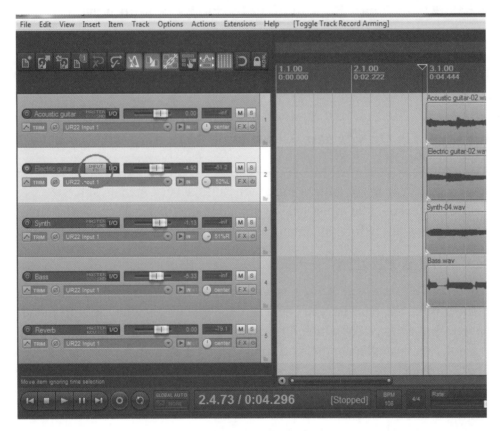

The Reaper "Input FX" button appears once you arm a track, enabling you to add an effect that will be recorded as part of the track.

This method (input or insert effects) is not commonly used for amp modeling plugins, because most people prefer the ability to change the effect if necessary, but you may find it useful for tracking with compression (see Chapter 13) if you don't have any outboard compressors. **Note:** Reaper allows for customization in many ways, one of which is the use of "themes," allowing you to change the look and layout of just about everything (drastically if you wish). In the theme I normally use, the input FX button is always visible (although it doesn't *say* "input FX" on it), but in Reaper's default theme (seen above), it's only visible when the track is armed.

IK Multimedia has been on the cutting edge of computer recording and music production for more than 15 years now, and their software and hardware solutions have become a mainstay for countless musicians. Their guitar amp simulation software, AmpliTube, has become one of the most popular amp simulators on the market, and the latest version of the plugin, AmpliTube 3, puts more power in the hands of guitarists and bassists than ever before.

IK Multimedia AmpliTube 3
Copyright IK Multimedia, used with permission.

AmpliTube 3 comes loaded with a boatload of models with which to create your own stellar guitar tones, including 51 pedal effects, 31 amplifiers, 46 speaker cabinets, 15 mics, 17 rack effects, and more. This alone is more than the typical recordist would ever need, and the tweakability is truly mind-blowing. Not only do you have complete control over the amps' and effects' typical features (volume, EQ, gain, etc.), but you can also match just about any preamp with any speaker cabinet configuration. When you select an amp, the standard cab is selected by default, so you'll already be in good hands. But should you choose to change things up, you're free to do so. You can also select from various mic models for the cabinet—two are included on each cabinet—and you can move them independently both side to side and/or near and far for further flexibility. There are also stereo room mics that can be added in various degrees as desired for ambience. With so much to try out at first, it took me a while to discover the usefulness of the mic selection and placement features, but now that I have, I use them extensively to refine tones as needed to sit in the mix better.

As if all this weren't enough, if you really want to customize your rig, you can do so à la carte with the Custom Shop. This allows you to purchase additional amp, cabinet, or effect models that specifically mimic the gear from such manufacturers as Fender, Orange, Soldano, Ampeg, Fulltone, Dr. Z, Gallien-Krueger, and more. Alternatively, you can purchase a branded version of AmpliTube, such as AmpliTube Fender or AmpliTube Orange, for a discounted price, which will only come with models specific to that brand, but you'll still be able to continuously add to your rig with any model (regardless of brand) through the Custom Shop. The prices in the Custom Shop range from about $5 to $15 for pedal or rack effects, $15 to $20 for amps, $5 for cabinets, and $5 for mics.

If you just want to get your feet wet to see if AmpliTube is for you, you can download the AmpliTube Custom Shop for free to get started. This is not a demo or crippled version of the program! It contains 24 pieces of gear (a chromatic tuner, nine stomp effects, four amps, five cabinets, three mics, and two rack effects) that you can use to your heart's content. You can then add collections or individual amp, cab, effect, or mic models as you'd like through the Custom Shop to flesh out your rig. A word of caution: The Custom Shop can be like a candy store for adults—don't say I didn't warn you!

All of these features wouldn't mean much if AmpliTube didn't sound amazing. I've recorded hundreds of guitar tracks with the program since I first got AmpliTube 2 back in 2007 or so, and I'm always getting compliments on the tones. It's a lifesaver when you've got young ones sleeping but still need to get some tracking done at night, and the flexibility is just second to none. It has run like a champ the entire time, and I've never had problems with crashes or glitches. You just can't go wrong with AmpliTube!

Street price: $199.99

It's truly amazing how detailed you can get with these amp simulation programs. For example, in AmpliTube 3, you can not only choose which type of speaker cabinet you'd like to pair with the amp, but you can also choose between several different mic models (dynamic, condenser, and ribbon), use one or two on the cabinet (and choose the balance between the two), move those mics' location along the cabinet, add ambience from additional room mics, change the room size, and more.

IK Multimedia's AmpliTube 3 lets you completely customize your speaker cabinet configuration, including mic choice(s) and location, room type, and more.

So let's take a listen to some of the amp models and effects within AmpliTube 3. All of the effects (reverb, delay, etc.) heard here will also come from AmpliTube 3. I'll use various guitars for these, so check the Recording Index (page 272) if you'd like to see which one was used. In the first track, you'll hear the direct guitar sound by itself first and then the same exact phrase but with the amp effect enabled. This is to demonstrate that the effect is not printed on the track (until you want to do that).

45 IK Multimedia AmpliTube 3: Fender '65 Twin Reverb clean with reverb

46 IK Multimedia AmpliTube 3: Fender '59 Bassman overdriven with room ambience

47 IK Multimedia AmpliTube 3: Fender '57 Deluxe distorted with spring reverb

48 IK Multimedia AmpliTube 3: Orange Rockerverb 50 MK II distorted with tremolo

49 IK Multimedia AmpliTube 3: Orange AD30 slightly overdriven with analog delay

50 IK Multimedia AmpliTube 3: Dr. Z Z Wreck overdriven with phaser and reverb

51 IK Multimedia AmpliTube 3: British Tube 30TB clean with reverb

52 IK Multimedia AmpliTube 3: British Tube Lead 1 distorted with rotary effect

53 IK Multimedia AmpliTube 3: Solid State Clean with reverb and chorus

54 IK Multimedia AmpliTube 3: Modern Hi Gain distorted with reverb

ACOUSTIC GUITARS

Whether it's in a folk song as the sole accompaniment to the vocal or a more elaborate production in which it serves as a background texture, the acoustic guitar has been a mainstay in the recording world since the beginning. As an instrument, it's an invaluable addition to anyone's studio. That said, it helps to know how to record it!

Basic Acoustic Guitar Types

Let's check out a few of the basic acoustic categories so we can get a sense of which ones are generally used for a particular sound.

Dreadnought

This is the most common type of acoustic and is probably what most people think of when they hear the words "acoustic guitar." The Martin D-28 is one of the most famous guitars in this category. Of course, they're quite expensive, as well, usually going for well over $2K. It's possible to get a very nice-sounding dreadnought in the under-$500 range, though, and the Breedlove Pursuit Dreadnought (see sidebar for details), which is the model I've used for the recordings in this book, is one such instrument. A dreadnought guitar can be used for just about anything, although they're probably strummed slightly more than fingerpicked.

Breedlove Pursuit Dreadnought
Copyright Breedlove, used with permission.

Breedlove makes a wide range of instruments ranging from extreme high-end guitars costing nearly $6,000 to quality beginner models that start at around the $300 mark. The Pursuit Dreadnought, from their Pursuit series, is described as a "step up" model, but I think that's being a bit conservative. The quality of the Pursuit Dreadnought is palpable upon first inspection, and that's only confirmed once you take it for a spin. It features a single cutaway design sporting a solid sitka spruce top, mahogany neck/back/ sides, and a rosewood fretboard. Tortoise binding and chrome tuners complete the attractive picture.

Included onboard is a Fishman ISYS+ pickup system with a top bout-mounted control panel including a digital tuner readout, volume/ bass/treble knobs, and a phase button. Aside from the standard 1/4-inch output jack, there's also a USB output for quick connection to a computer for recording whenever inspiration strikes.

The tone of the Pursuit Dreadnought is well-rounded, with a defined bass and pleasant treble. To my ear, it sounds somewhat in-between a Gibson and a Martin. It produces a very even sound whether you're fingerpicking or strumming, which makes recording with it a straightforward, painless process. Although the Fishman pickup sounds nice, I always prefer to mic the guitar when recording if I have the time, but the direct signal can work surprisingly well with a bit of EQ treatment. I've also combined the direct and miked signals at times for a bit of variety with great success. Breedlove may consider this a "step up" model, but for many, I believe they'd be content to stay put on this step for a good while.

Street price: $499 (with gig bag)

Folk Style

A folk style guitar (sometimes called "OM" for "orchestra model") is a smaller body shape with more pronounced bouts in the body. Its sound is generally a bit more focused than a dreadnought, but it still sounds great in many styles. Fingerpicking is common on these guitars, although they can sound great when strummed, as well. For the recordings in this book, I used an Alvarez RF26 OM model (see sidebar for details).

Alvarez RF26 OM
Copyright Alvarez, used with permission.

The Alvarez RF26 is part of the company's Regent series, which is marketed as entry-level with the aim of keeping beginner students motivated. The RF26 is an orchestra/folk model, which means its body is smaller and generally not as deep as that of a dreadnought. Folk-style guitars generally don't possess the big, booming sound of a dreadnought, but their sound is usually very well-balanced, which makes them ideal for fingerpicking. The RF26 features a laminate spruce top, mahogany sides/back/neck, rosewood fretboard and bridge, ivory binding, and chrome tuners. It's an attractive guitar with a unique-looking back-turned bridge and teardrop-shaped pickguard.

As to be expected, the RF26 excels in the fingerpicking category with a full, well-rounded tone. When strumming the guitar, I get a nice, crisp sound by using a thinner pick, and I like to use a medium pick for single-note melodies or arpeggios, which results in a pleasing but present tone. The guitar is light and very comfortable, which makes it great for travel. And speaking of travel, the included gig bag is nothing short of luxurious! I haven't tried any of the other models from Alvarez's Regent series, but the RF26 has certainly placed them on my radar.

Street price: $199.99 (with gig bag)

Jumbo

A jumbo is just that—big. It looks sort of like a puffed-up folk-style guitar. They generally have a nice scooped sound with booming lows and sweet highs and sound great when strummed along with a band. The Gibson J-185 is a famous instrument in this category. There are also super jumbos, which, as you may have guessed, are a bit bigger than jumbos. I didn't have access to a jumbo at the time of this book, so unfortunately, I wasn't able to record one. But rest assured, you've no doubt heard them on many recordings.

12-String

If you've never owned a 12-string guitar, you're missing out. They can really add that certain something when you need it on a recording. 12-strings actually come in other body variations, but for this book I used an Ibanez PF1512 model (see sidebar on the next page for details), which is a dreadnought. On a 12-string guitar, strings 6–3 are each paired with a thinner string one octave higher, while strings 2–1 are paired with unison strings. Each pair of strings is called a *course*. They can take some getting used to, as you have to be pretty precise with your fretting because of the cramped space between the extra strings, but it's worth the effort!

Ibanez PF1512 12-string
Copyright Ibanez, used with permission.

The PF1512 is Ibanez's most affordable 12-string acoustic, sneaking in at just under $200 (street price). It features a laminate spruce top, mahogany back/sides/neck, rosewood fretboard and bridge, chrome tuners, a high-gloss finish, and an attractive yet unadorned black and white rosette. Ivory binding on the neck and body complete the package nicely. The back and sides aren't quite as dark as most guitars I see, but it's a very attractive shade indeed.

Upon first handling the PF1512, I was quite shocked at the low price tag. Not only was the setup from the factory very near spot on, the playability and tone of the guitar were inspiring. It holds its tuning very well, which is often the Achilles' heel of a 12-string, and it shimmers like a champ when strumming chords. Single-note lines on the low strings sound round and powerful and can really help to thicken up a melody or two at the right place. I generally prefer to use 12-string guitars as a color or texture—rather than the main accompaniment instrument—and the PF1512 fits that bill to a tee, although it certainly produces a full enough tone to stand alone.

Street price: $199.99

Other Styles

There are smaller shapes than the folk, which are sometimes designated by an increasing number of 0s, as is the case with Martin guitars: 0, 00, 000, etc. The more 0s, the smaller the body shape. As you might expect, the amount of bass response usually decreases along with the size of the guitar, but that doesn't mean they aren't well-balanced instruments in and of themselves.

An honorable mention is certainly the nylon-string (classical) guitar, which can be heard on some pop recordings at times. Eric Clapton's "Tears in Heaven" is a good example of this. I didn't have access to a nylon-string at the time of this writing, so I wasn't able to feature one on the recordings. However, if you're interested in one, there are several fine, affordable instruments available, including the Ibanez GA5TCE, the Yamaha CG102, and the Alvarez RC26HCE, all of which are under $250 (but they don't sound like it!).

Now that we're familiar with the basic types of acoustics, let's get to the business of recording them. There are three different methods we'll discuss:

- Miking the guitar

- Recording direct (if your guitar has a pickup)

- Blending a mic with a direct signal

Miking the Guitar

Probably the most commonly used method in pro studios is that of miking the acoustic guitar. It tends to produce the most natural sound of all and is therefore the favorite of many, myself included. It's not that the other methods don't have their place (as we'll see), but when time is not a factor, nothing sounds like a well-miked acoustic, in my humble opinion.

Recording Procedure

Condenser microphones are the standard for acoustic guitars (although there are certainly some dynamics, such as the Shure SM7B, that can sound very nice, as well), and both LDCs and SDCs are used frequently. Simply set up the mic(s) and plug it into your interface. Arm the track, set the level, and you're good to go. Since you're using a microphone, you'll need to wear headphones if you're recording in your control room—otherwise, you could get feedback from the monitors or, at the least, the sound from the monitors will bleed into the mic, possibly creating some unwanted/unnatural ambience.

Single Microphone Techniques

The type of mic you use when it's the sole source depends on the type of sound you want. Generally speaking, an LDC will tend to produce a fuller-bodied sound with more bottom end. As such, they're typically used when the guitar needs to take up a lot of sonic space, such as when it's the sole accompaniment in a song. An SDC mic will generally produce a bit less bass and will tend to slightly accentuate the highs, which makes them an excellent choice when using the acoustic as a texture within a full-band context. Again, though, these are broad generalizations and should not be taken as a rule of any sort; they're simply places from which to begin experimenting.

When using one mic, one common method is to place it about a foot away and aim it at roughly the neck/body joint. The closer you move the mic toward the soundhole, the more bass you'll generally hear. Don't be afraid to try out several different locations when looking for the sweet spot; it'll usually be slightly different for every guitar.

Alvarez RF26 OM acoustic guitar miked with a CAD GXL1200BP aimed at the neck/body joint

For this track, I'm using a CAD GXL1200BP, which is an end-address SDC (see sidebar on for details). Notice how it's slightly off axis, but it's still aimed at the neck-body joint.

 55 SDC (CAD GXL1200BP) aimed at neck/body joint

CAD GXL1200BP small diaphragm condenser microphone
Copyright CAD Audio, used with permission.

The CAD GXL1200BP is a small diaphragm condenser microphone with a cardioid pattern and end-address design (as is the case with most SDC mics). Affordably priced and well within the grasp of the home-studio owner, this is a great mic to own, as it will earn its keep in myriad ways. The black chrome finish gives it a classy look, too.

I really like the sound of this mic on acoustic guitars. It's got a pleasing, airy quality to the high end that can help add a nice sheen—particularly on more textural acoustic parts. But the lower end sounds strong, as well, and it did a very nice job when miking a piano, too. Other applications on which I've gotten great results include a guitar cabinet, auxiliary percussion (tambourine, shaker, and bongos), and mandolin. At such an affordable price, they're an excellent candidate for a stereo pair (drum overheads, stereo piano, etc.), too!

Street price: $59.95

To illustrate the effect of mic placement, let's hear the same thing but with the mic moved: first it will be aimed about two inches closer to the soundhole and then about two inches further up the neck. Compare both of these with the previous SDC track.

 56 SDC (CAD GXL1200BP) aimed more toward soundhole

 57 SDC (CAD GXL1200BP) aimed more toward neck

And now let's hear the same thing but with another SDC: the Sterling Audio ST31.

 58 SDC (Sterling Audio ST31) aimed at neck/body joint

 59 SDC (Sterling Audio ST31) aimed more toward soundhole

 60 SDC (Sterling Audio ST31) aimed more toward neck

As you can hear, though the differences may be subtle at times, they're clearly there. It definitely pays off to spend an extra few minutes trying to get the sound right from the beginning. (We'll talk more about that in Chapter 16.)

To compare, let's hear the sound of the Shure SM7B, which is a dynamic mic, aimed at the neck/body joint.

Alvarez RF26 OM acoustic guitar miked with a Shure SM7B dynamic mic aimed at neck/body joint

 61 Dynamic (Shure SM7B) aimed at neck/body joint

It's a different sound, but it's a very useable one in the right circumstances.

Don't Forget to "Pick" the Right Pick!

The difference the plectrum's thickness makes, on acoustic guitar especially, can be quite profound and should not be overlooked. Generally speaking, thinner picks usually sound nicer and a bit more jangly when strumming than thicker ones do. If you're wanting the acoustic guitar to function in that way—a bit lighter and jangly sounding—then I'd definitely recommend a thinner pick. Thicker picks are nice if you want a beefier, more rattling tone from the acoustic.

To hear the difference, check out this example, which features the same strumming pattern played twice: first with a thicker pick (1 mm) and then again with a thinner one (.6 mm).

 62 Acoustic guitar strumming pattern with thick and thin picks

A LDC mic will often sound nice when positioned slightly behind the bridge, about a foot away from the body. This will generally produce a bigger sound, so you'll want to make sure it's not taking up too much room in the mix if there are other instruments in the same basic frequency range. Let's hear the CAD GXL3000BP in this position on the Alvarez to hear the change in tone.

Alvarez RF26 OM acoustic guitar miked with a CAD GXL3000BP LDC mic aimed behind the bridge (note that most LDCs are side-address mics, which is why the side of it is pointing toward the guitar)

The CAD GXL3000BP is the LDC companion to the GXL1200BP. It features the same attractive black chrome finish, which is especially striking on the larger body. It features a one-inch dual-diaphragm, gold-sputtered capsule and multiple polar patterns: cardioid, figure eight, and omnidirectional—a rarity in microphones of this price class. A hi-pass filter (set at 100 Hz) and a 10 dB pad complete the onboard features.

Because of the multiple polar patterns, this mic can really come in handy on numerous occasions. Not only is it a great-sounding lead vocal mic in cardioid operation, but you can set it to figure-eight for dual vocals—when you want that super-locked Simon & Garfunkel harmony thing—or put it in omni mode for several settings. These could include an intimate acoustic circle or, if you've got a nice-sounding space, room ambience for any moderate-to-loud sources (electric guitars, drums, etc.). Any way you slice it, the GXL3000BP is sure to be one of the most useful mics in your locker.

Street price: $121.95

CAD GXL3000BP large diaphragm condenser microphone

🔊 **63** LDC (CAD GXL3000BP) aimed slightly behind bridge

That was with the mic set to cardioid mode. Since the GXL3000BP is a multi-pattern mic, let's have a listen to the same thing with the different patterns to hear how it affects the sound.

🔊 **64** LDC (CAD GXL3000BP) aimed slightly behind bridge: Figure-eight pattern

🔊 **65** LDC (CAD GXL3000BP) aimed slightly behind bridge: Omnidirectional pattern

As you can hear, you'll pick up a lot more room ambience in the other two modes. If you have a nice-sounding room, you can choose to include it in the track if you're going for a very natural sound.

So now let's hear these techniques on the Breedlove dreadnought guitar with some different mics.

🔊 **66** SDC (CAD GXL1200BP) aimed at neck/body joint

🔊 **67** SDC (Sterling Audio ST31) aimed at neck/body joint

🔊 **68** LDC (CAD GXL 3000BP) aimed slightly behind bridge

🔊 **69** LDC (Sterling Audio ST55) aimed slightly behind bridge

🔊 **70** Dynamic (Shure SM7B) aimed at neck/body joint

🔊 **71** Dynamic (Shure SM7B) aimed slightly behind bridge

And here's the same set of mics and positions on the Ibanez PF1512 12-string:

🔊 **72** SDC (CAD GXL1200BP) aimed at neck/body joint

🔊 **73** SDC (Sterling Audio ST31) aimed at neck/body joint

🔊 **74** LDC (CAD GXL3000BP) aimed slightly behind bridge

🔊 **75** LDC (Sterling Audio ST55) aimed slightly behind bridge

🔊 **76** Dynamic (Shure SM7B) aimed at neck/body joint

🔊 **77** Dynamic (Shure SM7B) aimed slightly behind bridge

Dual Microphone Techniques

It's also common to combine the two mic approaches—the neck/body joint and behind the bridge—to form one composite sound with the characteristics of both. This is especially common in solo guitar recordings, where you want the guitar to fill up as much sonic space as possible. Ideally, you'll assign each mic to its own track so that you'll have complete control over the blend, EQ, etc. of each during mixdown. It's common to pan the mics left and right, especially for solo guitar recordings.

Ibanez PF1512 miked with both a Sterling Audio ST55 (LDC) and a ST31 (SDC)

Let's hear how this technique sounds with various setups. For each of the following tracks, you'll first hear the SDC mic, then the LDC mic, and then both blended together. I usually find with this technique that I want to pull the SDC slightly farther away from the soundhole than when using the SDC alone. Otherwise, the sound can sometimes get a bit too boomy. But experiment to see what sounds best for your setup.

78 Dreadnought: Sterling Audio ST31 and ST55

79 Dreadnought: CAD GXL1200BP and GXL3000BP

80 Folk: Sterling Audio ST31 and ST55

81 Folk: CAD GXL1200BP and GXL3000BP

82 12-string: Sterling Audio ST31 and ST55

83 12-string: CAD GXL1200BP and GXL3000BP

Phase Concerns

Anytime you use two microphones to record the same source, you run the risk of having "out of phase" problems. This phenomenon results when the sound waves reach the microphones in such a way that, when the wave on mic A is at its crest, the wave on mic B is at its trough. When this occurs, many frequencies will cancel out each other, and the result is usually a thinner, weaker-sounding tone. (Note that rarely are two signals totally in phase or totally out of phase. Rather, they're always some portion thereof.)

If you suspect that you have phase issues, try hitting the phase switch on one of the signals. This could be located on your mic preamp/interface, your DAW's track control panel, or other locations within the signal path. There are usually several spots to invert the phase. By doing this, you're flipping the signal 180 degrees so that, if the signals were more out of phase, they would then become more in phase. Phasing problems are easier to hear than to discuss, so check out this track. The mics are positioned in such a way as to emphasize the out-of-phase sound, which you'll hear at the beginning. Halfway through the track, I'll invert the phase on one of the channels, thereby placing the signals more in phase.

Phase invert button on Reaper's track control panel

 84 Dreadnought: Sterling Audio ST31 and ST55 – phase demonstration

Recording Direct

If your guitar is equipped with a pickup system, you have the option of plugging in and recording direct. This is generally a more hassle-free way of recording, because you won't have to spend time setting up a mic (and possibly clearing a space to do so, depending on how much space you have). And if you don't own a mic, it will be your only option! This generally won't sound quite as full or natural as a microphone (unless you have a *very* nice onboard electronics system, in which case it will likely blend a pickup with a small microphone), but it has its place and can be made to fit in nicely when used appropriately.

Recording Procedure

If your guitar has only a passive pickup, then you'll need to run through a direct box or preamp of some sort to get the level up to a useable one. This can be something like an LR Baggs Para preamp ($169), which has a three-band EQ with parametric mid-range, or a full-fledged acoustic effects processor, such as the Boss AD-8, which models the sounds of different body types and includes onboard reverb. If using the external preamp route, plug your acoustic into the preamp and then run out of the preamp into a line-in jack on your interface. If you have no external preamp, you can try running into your interface's guitar/bass (high impedance) input if it has one, as that will be better than nothing.

If your guitar has an onboard preamp, you should be able to run straight into a line-in jack on the interface. Once you're in the interface, check your level, assign the input to a track, arm it, and you're ready to go.

The Breedlove Pursuit Dreadnought actually has two options for recording direct: a standard 1/4-inch output jack or a USB jack. So you can either run from the standard jack into your interface or just plug a USB cable into your computer.

The Breedlove Pursuit Dreadnought features a USB jack in addition to the standard 1/4-inch jack.

Let's listen to the sound of the Breedlove's direct sound plugged directly into the interface. I've added a bit of reverb for some ambience.

 85 Direct acoustic (strumming) with reverb

 86 Direct acoustic (fingerpicking) with reverb

You won't have mic placement to worry about, but you'll most likely want to tweak the EQ—either on the guitar's preamp or in your DAW—to achieve the best tonal balance for the recording. What the guitar sounds like in the room doesn't matter in this case; it's only what ends up on the recording that matters. This may mean using settings that are radically different from those you use when playing live with the same guitar, for example. Be prepared to experiment.

Blending a Mic with a Direct Signal

One other option is to blend a mic (or mics) with a direct signal to form a composite tone. This is essentially done by just combining the two previous methods and using them simultaneously.

Recording Procedure

Plug a cable from your guitar's output jack (or run through an external preamp first if necessary) into channel 1 of your interface, and run a mic to channel 2. Assign each one to a separate track, arm them, set levels, and go!

Let's check out the sound of the Breedlove Pursuit with a mic and the Fishman pickup blended.

 87 Dreadnought: Sterling Audio ST31 (aimed at neck/body joint) and direct signal blended

 88 Dreadnought: Sterling Audio ST55 (aimed slightly behind bridge) and direct signal blended

 89 Dreadnought: CAD GXL1200BP (aimed at neck/body joint) and direct signal blended

 90 Dreadnought: CAD GXL3000BP (aimed slightly behind bridge) and direct signal blended

As you can hear, this results in a unique character. You get the very detailed sound of the pickup with the fullness and rounder tone of the mic. Again, you'll want to experiment with the percentage of the blend, the EQ of the direct signal, and the placement of the mic in order to find the sweet spot that suits your particular recording.

CHAPTER 9

RECORDING BASS GUITAR

In any style of music, the bass acts as the foundation. It's the lowest-pitched instrument on just about any recording, so it serves as the harmonic anchor for the song. Therefore, the sound of the bass is of critical importance. If it's too thin, the recording will lack body; if it's too boomy, the recording will sound muddy and unclear. In this chapter, we'll take a look at how to get that bottom end happening.

Remember to Tune Up!

Since the bass is often one of the first pitched instruments to get recorded—and the one atop which all the remaining instruments will sit—it's *vitally important* that it's in tune! Again, if you can use the same tuner for all your stringed instruments, this will usually yield the best results.

"BASSIC" BASS GUITAR TYPES

(Sorry…you can't pass up a pun like that.) Just as with guitars, there are several archetypal bass instruments that have laid the foundation for probably 95 percent of pop music since the beginning. Let's take a look at the key players.

Fender Precision Style

Probably the most famous bass in history, the Fender Precision (P-bass) was the first solidbody electric bass (introduced in 1951) and has likely appeared on more recordings than any other. It's used in rock, blues, funk, country—you name it. It features one split single-coil pickup, a volume knob, and a tone knob. Aside from the Fender Squire series, you can find great-sounding, affordable P-bass-style instruments from Peavey and other manufacturers. In the truly affordable category, it's hard to imagine a better bang for the buck than an SX Ursa 1 (see sidebar for details), which is the P-bass-style bass I used for this book.

SX Ursa 1 RN 3TS

SX, distributed exclusively by Rondo Music (www.rondomusic.com), has been steadily developing a reputation as one of the best Fender-style alternatives on the market. While that's impressive, what's more impressive is the price of these instruments. You simply won't believe it. The craftsmanship of these basses is just unreal considering the price. The wood and finish is beautiful, the frets are smooth (as are the fret tips), the neck is straight, and the electronics are solid. I've not had one issue with the bass in the three years that I've owned it.

As is obvious, the SX Ursa is a copy of a Fender P-bass. It's got a solid basswood body, a maple neck and rosewood fretboard (also available with a maple fretboard), a standard split-type single-coil pickup, chrome hardware, and an adjustable (at the headstock) truss rod. The sunburst is beautiful on this instrument. It even comes with a gig bag and an instructional DVD.

The bass was set up well from the factory; I only made a few minor tweaks, and it was ready to go. I assumed (from the price) that I was going to need to replace the pickup with something more high-end—and it would still be a great deal—but three years later, I've yet to do so. It feels, plays, sounds, and looks great. And with the price…geez…what more could you want?

Street price: $115 (with gig bag)

Fender Jazz Bass Style

The other most popular bass design in the world is also made by Fender—the Jazz bass—and was introduced in 1960 (though it was first known as the Deluxe Bass). Like the P-bass, it's also used in many styles, and many bass players don't consider their collection complete until they own at least one of each. The "J-bass" features two single-coil pickups—one near the P-bass pickup position and one nearer the bridge—with independent volume knobs for each pickup and a shared tone knob. You can blend the two pickups in any configuration to achieve a wide range of tones. Unfortunately, I didn't have access to a J-bass-style bass while writing this book, but if you're looking for an instrument in this style, you won't have to look far. There are probably more J-bass-style instruments on the market than any other. Check out models from Fender Squire, Ibanez, and ESP LTD, among others, for fine, affordable alternatives.

Music Man StingRay Style

Introduced in 1976 and designed by Leo Fender (yes, *that* Fender again!), Tom Walker, and Sterling Ball, the Music Man StingRay was the first mass-produced electric bass with active electronics. This basically means an onboard preamp (powered by a 9-volt battery) was included that resulted in a higher output with more lows and highs. The StingRay generally features a single humbucking pickup, volume control, and a three-band EQ (bass, mid, and treble knobs), making it an extremely versatile instrument. Sterling by Music Man (Music Man's affordable line) offers the S.U.B. Ray4 (see sidebar for details), which I used in this book.

Sterling by Music Man S.U.B. Ray4
Copyright Sterling by Music Man, used with permission.

Music Man's StingRay bass has become one of several key instruments that most pro bassists own at one time or another during their career. Its sound has graced the recordings of countless bands such as Queen, Red Hot Chili Peppers, AC/DC, Tony Levin (Peter Gabriel, King Crimson), Aerosmith, and Radiohead. They're not cheap instruments, however—starting around $1,500—and have therefore remained out of reach for most players on a tight budget.

Enter the Sterling by Music Man S.U.B. Ray4. These instruments capture much of the StingRay's essence and instill it into a truly affordable bass. Features include an active two-band preamp (powered by a 9-volt battery) with controls for volume, bass, and treble, an active humbucking pickup, a solid hardwood body, a six-bolt neck joint, easy-access truss rod adjustment, maple neck with rosewood fretboard, medium jumbo frets, and chrome hardware. It's available in several attractive finishes to suit your style.

The build quality on these basses is super impressive, and the sound is equally so. With the active two-band EQ, you can achieve a large range of tones—from dark and wooly to bright and aggressive and everywhere in between—allowing you to cover all the bases. The solid, punchy tone you expect from a StingRay is also present in the Ray4, and that's great news for budget-minded bassists. Thanks be to Sterling by Music Man for a job well done!

Street price: $299.99

Other Styles

Honorable mentions include the Rickenbacker 4001 series, popularized by players such as Chris Squire (Yes) and Geddy Lee (Rush), and the Gibson "EB" series, most famously played by Jack Bruce (Cream). And, of course, the upright bass (or double bass) dominates the world of jazz.

As I mentioned in the guitar chapter, it's also nice to have a "character bass" that doesn't fit neatly into any one category when you want to give your recordings something extra. One example of this also happens to be one of the most iconic instruments in history: the Höfner "violin bass"—a.k.a. the "Beatle bass." This is a hollowbody bass that has a sound all its own. While the original versions of this bass cost well over $2K, Höfner released an affordable version of it called the Ignition Violin Bass (see sidebar for details), which is the other bass I used in this book.

Höfner Ignition Series Violin Vintage Bass

As the instrument of choice for one of the most famous bassists in music history—Sir Paul McCartney—the image and sound of the Höfner "violin" bass has been burned into the minds of billions throughout the decades. Until recently, however, owning one of these iconic instruments meant shelling out thousands of dollars. Granted, they're stunning instruments, but if you're not made of money, it's hard to justify that kind of investment.

Höfner's Ignition series changes all that by introducing truly affordable versions of this unique bass. The attention to detail is very impressive on these instruments, and the finish is lovely. The bass features a spruce top, flame maple back and sides, a set maple neck with rosewood fretboard, a rosewood bridge, a trapeze nickel tailpiece, a pearloid plastic pickguard, and attractive white binding on the body's front and back. It's a looker for sure. As for the electronics, it features two Höfner Ignition Staple Nickel pickups, each with their own volume control and independent on/off switches, and a shared switch for a Rhythm/Solo setting (Solo mode providing a slight boost).

The first thing you're bound to notice upon picking one up is that it's light—extremely light. Even knowing it's a hollowbody didn't quite prepare me for this. But as soon as I plugged it in and played it, that fact just became icing on the cake, because it sounds awesome. It's warm, wooly, and full—just like McCartney's bass tone. It sounds beautiful when played fingerstyle, but as soon as you pull out the pick, a smile is bound to pop up as you veer into Beatles territory. It's far from a one-trick pony, however, and it has found its way onto many of my tracks—especially ones where I'm wanting a vintage vibe.

Street price: $299.99

We'll look at three different methods for recording bass guitar in this chapter:

- Recording direct
- Miking a bass amp
- Combining a miked amp with a direct signal

To Pick or Not to Pick

Although fingerstyle is more common on bass, don't forget about the pick! On certain songs, it can be just what the doctor ordered. The list of famous pick players is not exactly a short one and includes none other than Sir Paul McCartney, Chris Squire (Yes), studio legend Carol Kaye, and (on occasion) John Paul Jones (Led Zeppelin). You'll generally want a plectrum on the thicker side for bass guitar, as the thinner ones won't be able to stand up to the resistance of the thicker strings.

Aside from some EQ differences (i.e., if you want to enhance the sound of the pick attack), there's nothing terribly different about recording one or the other, although the levels may be different depending on the player, so be sure to double-check the levels if switching from one to the other. I'll make use of both techniques for the recordings in this book (although most of them will be played fingerstyle).

RECORDING DIRECT

Recording a bass guitar direct is probably the most commonly used method of all. It usually produces a full, present, and predictable tone with little fuss, which is always a good thing. There are several ways to do this, so let's examine some of the most common. Tracking bass with some compression is even more common than with guitar—it's actually the norm—as it helps to even out the attacks and can provide a bit of punch as well. See Chapter 13 for more on this.

Plugging Straight In or Using a Direct Box

One option is to simply plug the bass straight into the guitar/bass input of your interface or use a direct box if your interface doesn't have one. It's as simple as it gets.

Recording Procedure

Plug your bass into the guitar/bass (high impedance) input of your interface, set the levels, arm the track, and go. If your interface doesn't have a dedicated instrument input…

Plug your bass into a direct box, such as the Radial Stagebug DI, and run a cable from the DI box into your interface. Set the levels, arm the track, and go. Regardless of the recording method used, it's very common to track bass with compression, as well. See Chapter 13 for details on this.

Let's take a listen to these different basses using the straight-in method.

 91 **SX Ursa: straight into UR22 instrument input**

 92 **S.U.B. Ray4: straight into UR22 instrument input**

 93 **Höfner Ignition Violin Bass: straight into UR22 instrument input**

Depending on the bass, you may find that you'll want to EQ the signal a bit to achieve the tone you want, so don't be afraid to experiment with that.

Using the Direct Output Jack on Your Bass Amp

Another common method for running direct is to simply run a line from your amp's direct output if it has one. Depending on the signal path, this allows you to possibly make use of the amp's EQ on the way in for fine-tuning the tone. (Sometimes the direct out is pre-EQ, and sometimes it's post-EQ. Consult your amp's manual.) This is the method we used when we recorded our first song in Chapter 7.

Recording Procedure

Plug your bass into the amp and run a cable from the direct output jack into a line input on your interface. Set the levels, assign/arm the track, and go.

Let's hear what these basses sound like running through three different amps' direct out. Along with the Gallien-Krueger MB112-II we used in Chapter 7, we'll be using a Kustom KXB100 (see sidebar on the following page for details) and an Ampeg Micro-CL. For each recording, the EQ on the bass amps will be set relatively flat (all knobs around 12 o'clock) for consistency, but in practice, you'd most likely tailor these to suit your needs. If your direct out is pre-EQ, then this obviously won't matter. (On the Kustom KXB100 and Ampeg Micro-CL, it's post-EQ, and on the Gallien-Krueger MB112-II, it's switchable between pre- and post-EQ.)

Kustom KXB100 bass amp
Copyright Kustom, used with permission.

The Kustom KXB100 is a combo bass amp rated at 100 watts with a 15-inch Kustom speaker. It features classy retro-styled looks and a front panel with a four-band EQ: Bass, Lo-Mid, Hi-Mid, and Treble. Gain and Master knobs (with a Clip LED) allow you to dial in a wide range of tones, from clean to gritty, at different volumes. Two input jacks—0 dB and -6 dB—allow use with active or passive instruments, and a 1/8-inch auxiliary input and headphone jack allow you to practice along with an mp3 player through the loudspeaker or quietly with phones.

On the rear panel, there's a 1/4-inch external speaker jack that's wired in series with the internal speaker. This means that the internal speaker won't be defeated when you're running an external one; consequently, there's no minimum impedance load for the external speaker jack. An effects loop is provided for additional tone shaping via external EQ or signal processors. The Effects Send jack can also be used as a preamp out jack, while the Effects Return jack can be used as a power amp in. A balanced XLR line-out jack is paired with its own Direct Out Volume knob for connecting the amp directly to a mixer or interface. The signal from this jack is taken after the EQ section and effects loop but before the Master volume knob on the front. Finally, a ground lift switch removes the ground connection on the line-out jack, which can help to eliminate hum (if necessary) when running direct out.

The KXB100 is capable of achieving a nice variety of bass tones to cover a wide range of styles. It has good presence if you're after it, but it can really warm up, too, and simulate a tube-like sound if you're looking for a vintage Motown-style sound, for example. At 53 pounds, it's not exactly light, but it's a lot easier to transport than a stack, so it could easily double as a gigging amp. It'll more than handle small- to medium-sized rooms, and if you play anywhere larger, you have the option of running a D.I. line to the soundman, as well. It sounds like a much more expensive amp than its price tag would suggest, and it's built like a tank. There's just not much to dislike about it.

Street price: $249.99

 94 SX Ursa: direct out of the GK MB112-II

 95 S.U.B. Ray4: direct out of the GK MB112-II

 96 Höfner Ignition Violin Bass: direct out of the GK MB112-II

 97 SX Ursa: direct out of the Kustom KXB100

 98 S.U.B. Ray4: direct out of the Kustom KXB100

 99 Höfner Ignition Violin Bass: direct out of the Kustom KXB100

 100 SX Ursa: direct out of the Ampeg Micro-CL

🔊 101 S.U.B. Ray4: direct out of the Ampeg Micro-CL

🔊 102 Höfner Ignition Violin Bass: direct out of the Ampeg Micro-CL

Using an Amp Modeler (External or Plugin)

If you need to gig as a bassist or even rehearse, owning a bass amp makes a lot of sense. But if you only plan on recording bass, and you're wanting a bit more versatility than the straight-in method, an amp modeler is the perfect ticket. It can also be the perfect ticket even if you own an amp, of course, as bass amps are generally not back-friendly. If you store your amp in a room other than where you'll be recording, you may not want to move it every time you record.

Just as with guitar, you'll find both hardware (external) and software (plugin) versions of bass amp modelers, and both can offer excellent results. Check out the Zoom B3 and DigiTech BP90 or BP355 for great-sounding, affordable hardware versions. For our purposes, I'll demonstrate some of the bass amp models within IK Multimedia's AmpliTube 3.

Recording Procedure

Plug your bass into the guitar/bass input on your interface, or run through a DI box first if your interface doesn't have one. Set the levels, assign and arm the track. Open the track's effects window, add the plugin, and select the amp model (and effects if desired). Check your level within the plugin, and you're ready to go.

If using an external amp modeler, the process will be the same as with using the direct out on an amp (you'll just be using the amp modeling unit in place of the amp).

Let's hear what these basses sound like through some different amp models within AmpliTube 3.

🔊 103 SX Ursa: AmpliTube 3 – Ampeg B15-R

🔊 104 S.U.B. Ray4: AmpliTube 3 – Ampeg B15-R

🔊 105 Höfner Ignition Violin Bass: AmpliTube 3 – Ampeg B15-R

🔊 106 SX Ursa: AmpliTube 3 – Fender Bassman 300

🔊 107 S.U.B. Ray4: AmpliTube 3 – Fender Bassman 300

🔊 108 Höfner Ignition Violin Bass: AmpliTube 3 – Fender Bassman 300

🔊 109 SX Ursa: AmpliTube 3 – Orange AD 200

🔊 110 S.U.B. Ray4: AmpliTube 3 – Orange AD 200

🔊 111 Höfner Ignition Violin Bass: AmpliTube 3 – Orange AD 200

It's certainly nice to have a whole arsenal of sounds at your fingertips when you're searching for just the right tone on a song. In this way, amp modelers really are nice to have around. And don't forget that you can usually manipulate the speaker cabinet (and mics placed on them) with most amp modelers as well, including AmpliTube 3, for more tonal versatility.

MIKING A BASS AMP

Miking the bass amp is definitely not as common in home studios, and it's not difficult to guess why. Bass amps are loud, and bass frequencies carry (and carry). Still, if you have the opportunity to do so, I'd highly recommend trying it out, as it may be exactly the sound you're looking for. When miking an amp, you generally won't get the transient definition—i.e., the sound of your finger (or pick) striking the string—you do with a direct recording, but that's not always a bad thing. Sometimes you'll want a rounder, less-pointed tone, and in those times, a miked amp will get you on the right track. That's not to say you can't get definition from an amp, but it's not inherently built-in the way it is with a direct recording. (By the same token, you can certainly achieve a rounder, less-defined tone when recording direct, as well.)

Generally speaking, dynamic mics are usually the most common, but that doesn't mean you shouldn't try an LDC or a ribbon mic, as they can often produce excellent results.

Recording Procedure

Plug your bass into your amp and run a cable from the mic to your interface. Check your levels and assign/arm the track.

Dynamic Mics

Though ambience is common in guitar, keyboard, and drum tracks (at times), it's not often a part of a bass track. Therefore, you generally want to avoid recording bass in a big, "live" room with lots of reflective surfaces. If you have some gobos (see Appendix for how to make your own), you can place several around the amp to cut down on the reflections that will reach it. Some people prefer to raise the speaker cabinet off the floor (as shown in Chapter 8) and place a bunch of pillows or heavy blankets on the floor in front of the cabinet to cut down on early reflections.

Most people will use a close-mic technique similar to that on guitar amps—i.e., a few inches off the grill and positioned somewhere between the cone and edge of the speaker. If your cabinet has more than one speaker, you should compare the sound of each with the mic, as they may very well sound different. It should also be mentioned that you normally don't need to crank the bass amp to performance levels in order to achieve a good tone. If your wife or girlfriend screams at you to turn it down, it's probably too loud. But if she asks you nicely to turn it down, that's probably a good starting point.

Again, these are just suggestions for a starting point. Feel free to try different mic placements to see what you come up with. One other thing that will play a role in the sound of a miked amp is the speaker size. The three amps I'm using in this book run the gamut in terms of size: the Kustom KXB100 has one 15-inch speaker, the Gallien-Krueger MB112-II has one 12-inch speaker, and the Ampeg Micro-CL (see sidebar on the following page for details) has two 10-inch speakers. Let's listen to the sound of a Shure SM7B dynamic mic placed at two different spots (close and one foot away) on our three different amp cabinets. I'll use the SX Ursa for each of these tracks.

112 GK MB112-II close-miked with Shure SM7B

113 Kustom KXB100 close-miked with Shure SM7B

114 Ampeg Micro-CL close-miked with Shure SM7B

Ampeg Micro-CL bass amp close-miked with a Shure SM7B dynamic microphone. Normally I would enclose the mic with another baffle, but it's been left out to show the mic position.

115 GK MB112-II miked with Shure SM7B one foot away

116 Kustom KXB100 miked with Shure SM7B one foot away

117 Ampeg Micro-CL miked with Shure SM7B one foot away

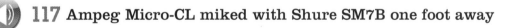

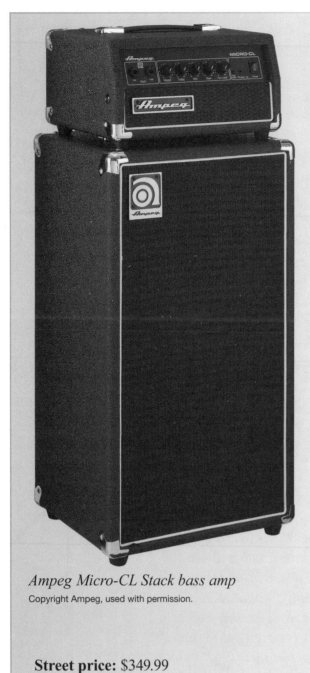

Ampeg Micro-CL Stack bass amp
Copyright Ampeg, used with permission.

Street price: $349.99

The Ampeg Micro-CL is one deceptive little guy. From the looks of it, you would not expect the amount of power it puts out. It's rated at 100 watts, is all solid state, and drives a 2x10 cabinet at 8 ohms. It's a fantastic-looking rig that's guaranteed to turn a few heads and likely surprise many when they hear what it can do. On the front panel, you have 0 dB and -15 dB input jacks for handling active or passive instruments, a Master volume knob, and Treble, Mid, and Bass EQ knobs. There's also an Aux Level knob for controlling the level of your mp3 player, CD player, or other device that's plugged into the 1/8-inch Aux Input jack. A 1/8-inch Phones jack defeats the speaker output, allowing you to practice quietly using only the head.

Speaking of the head, it weighs a mere 14 pounds, while the cabinet clocks in at 33 pounds. On the rear panel, you have the 8-ohm speaker jack, an effects loop with 1/4-inch Send and Return jacks, and a 1/4-inch line-out jack for running a direct signal. The line-out signal is post-EQ and shares the same Master volume as the front panel.

The Micro-CL is meant to be a scaling down of Ampeg's classic SVT-CL stack. I don't know how they did it with such a small package, but the sound actually is very reminiscent of its big brother. It's full, powerful, and solid through and through. It sounds like a loud 100 watts to me, and it's easy to keep up with drummers in rehearsals and up to medium gigs. And at this size, you can take the thing anywhere. That's good news for bassists who don't like to be too far away from killer bass tone.

Condenser and Ribbon Mics

As mentioned earlier, there's no reason not to experiment with condensers or ribbon mics on a bass amp. You could end up with just the sound you're looking for. If you have your amp turned up loud, you may want to engage the pad (if available) on your condenser mic. For moderate volumes, though, it won't be necessary. Let's have a listen to two different condenser mics on these amps: the Sterling Audio ST55 and an MXL 9000 (see sidebar for details), which is a tube condenser mic. We'll place the mics about six inches off the grill, aimed between the cone and edge of the speaker. I'll use the S.U.B. Ray4 bass for each of these tracks.

The MXL 9000 is a large diaphragm tube condenser mic with a cardioid pattern. It uses a 12AT7 tube and is powered by its own external power supply (included), so you don't need to have phantom power in order to use the mic. Its frequency response is 30 Hz to 20 kHz, and it includes a shock mount, a 7-pin power cable (which connects the mic to the power supply), and an XLR mic cable (runs from the power supply to the preamp/interface/etc.). The mic itself is cased in an attractive silver-finished metal shell that's quite classy-looking.

MXL 9000 tube condenser microphone
Copyright MXL, used with permission.

The buzzword encircling tube mics is generally "warmth," and the 9000 certainly delivers in this area. It's got a smooth, rounded quality that gives a pleasant tone to vocals and instruments alike. The high end is a tad understated but still clear and airy, and the bass response is firm and full. The mic shines on vocals for sure, but it also sounds brilliant on acoustic guitars, guitar amps, and other stringed acoustic instruments like mandolin and ukulele. If you can swing only $200 for a condenser mic, the 9000 would certainly be a fine choice. If you can swing a bit more, then by pairing this mic with a non-tube condenser, you'd have quite a nice option for a bit of variety when necessary.

Street price: $199.95

Kustom KXB100 bass amp miked with an MXL 9000 tube condenser microphone

🔊 **118** GK MB112-II miked with MXL 9000

🔊 **119** Kustom KXB100 miked with MXL 9000

🔊 **120** Ampeg Micro-CL miked with MXL 9000

🔊 **121** GK MB112-II miked with Sterling Audio ST55

🔊 **122** Kustom KXB100 miked with Sterling Audio ST55

🔊 **123** Ampeg Micro-CL miked with Sterling Audio ST55

Now let's check out a ribbon mic, the CAD D82, on the cabinets. We'll use a close-miking approach with this mic similar to what we did with the dynamic mic. I'll play the Höfner Ignition Violin bass for these tracks.

Gallien-Krueger MB112-II close-miked with CAD D82 ribbon microphone

🔊 **124** GK MB112-II close-miked with CAD D82

🔊 **125** Kustom KXB100 close-miked with CAD D82

🔊 **126** Ampeg Micro-CL close-miked with CAD D82

Of course, you could always blend two different mics—a dynamic and a condenser, for example—to see what you come up with. If you like the definition that one mic provides but don't like its low end very much, you could pair it with a mic that has a better-sounding low end. Then you could EQ the offending lows out of the first mic and EQ the mids and highs out of the second mic if necessary. You could come up with a well-rounded composite tone.

Combining a Miked Amp with a Direct Signal

This is actually quite a common method in professional studios, and it can be put to good use in home studios, as well. This can allow you to capture the definition and clarity provided by a DI signal while still retaining the warmth and power of an amp. Of course, you should ideally record each signal to its own track if possible, as you'll then be able to blend each to taste—not to mention EQ or process them independently if necessary.

Recording Procedure

First, you'll need to split your bass signal so that you can send it to two different places. For this, you can usually just use a DI box, such as the Radial StageBug SB-1. A typical DI box will generally have two 1/4-inch jacks—one is an input and the other a "thru"—and one XLR output. You plug your bass into one of the 1/4-inch jacks—it usually doesn't matter which one—and run a cable from the other 1/4-inch jack to your amp. Then you run an XLR cable from the XLR jack to your interface.

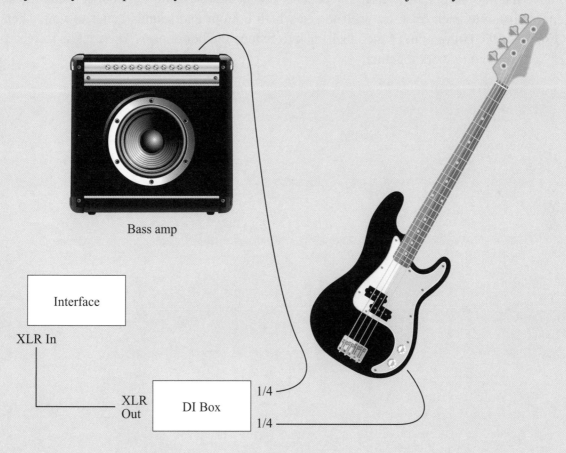

Bass amp

Interface

XLR In

XLR Out   DI Box   1/4

1/4

From here, simply follow the previous directions for each half of the signal (miking an amp and recording direct)

Let's hear this idea in action. We'll mic the bass amps with the Shure SM7B dynamic mic a few inches off the grill, and we'll run straight into the interface with the direct signal. For each of these tracks, you'll first hear the direct signal, then the amp signal, and then the combination of the two.

127 Hofner Ignition: GK MB112-II combined with direct signal

128 Hofner Ignition: Kustom KXB100 combined with direct signal

129 Hofner Ignition: Ampeg Micro-CL combined with direct signal

130 S.U.B. Ray4: GK MB112-II combined with direct signal

131 S.U.B. Ray4: Kustom KXB100 combined with direct signal

132 S.U.B. Ray4: Ampeg Micro-CL combined with direct signal

As you can hear, this approach can really produce a well-rounded tone. It's important to remember that, when using this approach, you want the tones to complement each other. It'll be counterproductive if you try to make each one sound like a full, complete tone on its own. You want one signal to provide what the other is lacking and vice versa. So if your direct tone has lots of highs in it, you may want to move the mic farther away from the cone. If things are sounding too boomy when the signals are blended, listen to each track by itself to see which bottom end sounds better to you. Then you can EQ some of the bottom out of the other track to reduce the boominess. The trick is to remember that they're supposed to work together.

CHAPTER 10

RECORDING KEYBOARDS AND OTHER VIRTUAL INSTRUMENTS

Keyboards and MIDI instruments are the secret weapons of the home recordist. With the explosion of virtual instrument technology, we're now able to flesh out our songs with convincing approximations of everything from vintage electric pianos and analog synths to tubas, pizzicato strings, and suitcase organs. In this chapter, we'll talk about the myriad options available and how to employ them. We'll also look at tips for increasing the realism of virtual instruments and some other fun tricks, as well.

THE SOURCE: MIDI KEYBOARD CONTROLLER OR KEYBOARD WITH BUILT-IN SOUNDS

The first thing we need to record keyboards is…a keyboard. Seems obvious, yes? Sure, but as with most things in today's recording world, there are two main options: a *keyboard with built-in sounds* and a *MIDI keyboard controller*, which is used to control sounds from another source (software or hardware). This distinction is also a bit deceptive, because they're not entirely exclusive. For example, most keyboards with built-in sounds—with the exception of some early analog synths—can always also be used as a MIDI controller. So, if you have a keyboard synthesizer, workstation, or digital piano of some type—even some fairly cheap Casio keyboards, for example—you can probably use that as a MIDI controller. Just check to see if you have either a MIDI out jack or a USB jack. The MIDI out jack is proof positive, and a USB jack is a pretty sure thing.

Some MIDI controllers (with no built-in sounds at all) can get extremely fancy, offering all kinds of onboard control options, including sample pads (for triggering certain sounds) and knobs and sliders that can all be assigned to various parameters for very expressive performance capability. I'd suggest that, at minimum, your controller—whether it's a synthesizer or MIDI controller only—have at least a pitch wheel and a mod (modulation) wheel, as these are incredibly useful in a variety of situations. A sustain jack (into which you can plug a *sustain pedal*) is also an incredibly useful addition to a controller, as it allows you to simulate the sustain pedal on a piano or electric piano—quite an inextricable part of their sound.

When dealing with virtual instruments (MIDI instruments), just about every part of the performance can be edited after the track has been recorded, including the instrument (sound or *patch*) itself and those aspects pertaining to the notes: pitch, duration, timing, and velocity (loudness), among many others (see Chapter 15 for more on this). If you're recording the built-in sounds of a keyboard to a track, however, you're not dealing with MIDI; you're dealing with audio. This is along the lines of what we talked about in Chapter 8 with regard to recording a miked amp signal versus recording a D.I. guitar signal and adding an amp simulator via plugin. In the first example, you're stuck with the amp sound you recorded; in the latter, you can change it as many times as you'd like until you find the right one.

RECORDING THE BUILT-IN SOUNDS FROM A KEYBOARD

Let's start with this method, because it's the least complicated. All you need is a keyboard with some onboard sounds that you like and a 1/4-inch instrument cable.

Recording Procedure

Run a cable from your keyboard to your interface. If you're recording a mono patch, you'll usually use the left output jack. If recording a stereo patch, run two cables—one each from the L and R jack—to two inputs on your interface. Check your levels and assign/arm the track(s). (Pan the two left and right if recording in stereo.)

That's all there is to it. It's pretty much the same procedure as recording a bass or a guitar direct. The thing to remember is that you're "printing" the sound (and any effects you may have added to it) to the track. This means you can't change it later the way you can when using softsynths (virtual instruments). Also, since it's audio and not MIDI, you don't have the ability to alter the notes, timing, etc. after the fact. This means you've got to get the performance right from the source. (You can still edit the audio file, of course, if you choose, which we'll look at in Chapter 15.) If you've got a board with some great sounds, though, and you can play the part well, it's a quick and easy way to lay down a track.

RECORDING WITH A MIDI CONTROLLER

This method is becoming more and more popular all the time. You obtain a MIDI keyboard controller, which is sort of like the typing keyboard on your desktop computer. By itself, it does nothing. But if you plug it into the computer and use the right software, all of a sudden, the buttons can produce letters in all shapes, sizes, and colors. So it is with a MIDI keyboard controller. You just need to connect it to a sound source. There are two ways to do this: with *external sound modules/synths* (hardware) or with *virtual instrument plugins* (software).

External Sound Modules/Synths

Going this route is very similar to using a keyboard with built-in sounds. The only difference here is that we've split that machine into two separate parts: the keyboard and the sound module. In the 1990s, rackmount sound modules became very popular, and you could control several with one MIDI controller (or more if you preferred). These aren't quite as common these days, but since then, analog synths have made a big comeback. Analog synthesis produces sound in a different way than digital does, and many people prefer the sound. Many analog synths don't have built-in keyboards; they only have knobs, buttons, and other ways to manipulate sound. In order to play melodies on them in a conventional way, you need to use a MIDI controller. (Many very old analog synths predate MIDI, but those aren't the ones we're discussing here.)

We discussed this idea briefly in Chapter 7, in which we recorded a track using a MIDI controller and a Korg Volca Keys analog synth (see page 99). Again, just as with the previous keyboard method, this is an audio track and is therefore fixed (i.e., the individual elements of the performance can't be tweaked). Even though we're using a MIDI cable, we're not *recording* the MIDI. The MIDI controller is controlling the sound module, and we're recording the sound module.

Recording Procedure

Run a MIDI cable from the MIDI OUT jack of your controller to the MIDI IN jack of the external sound module/synth. Then run an instrument cable from your sound module/synth to an input on your interface. Assign and arm the track and check levels.

Using Virtual Instruments

When using virtual instruments for the first time, you'll likely feel like a child who's walked into an ear candy store. You can just about play *anything* with your little MIDI controller. Pianos, organs, electric pianos? Of course. But how about congas, flute, cello, sitar, toy piano, theramin, slap bass, or tympani? No problem! If you want to simulate it, chances are someone has synthesized/modeled/sampled it. There are even tons of freeware virtual instruments out there, many of which are quite decent. Of course, you usually get what you pay for, and generally speaking, the more you spend on a program, the higher quality the sounds will be—to a point. The good news for home recordists on a budget is that there are many affordable virtual instruments that sound fabulous, and we'll take a look at a few here. As mentioned earlier in the book, Mac and PC use different formats for their plugins, so you'll need to confirm that your platform is supported before you make a purchase. Then you'll need to be sure you download the correct one (if you're downloading the program instead of receiving a boxed copy).

Recording Procedure

Run a MIDI cable from the MIDI OUT jack of your controller to the MIDI IN jack of your interface or USB MIDI adapter. Create a track, select "MIDI" for the input, and open the effects window. (**Note:** In some DAW programs, you may have to enable your MIDI controller after plugging it in for the first time. This is true for Reaper, but consult your DAW manual on this.)

Selecting a virtual instrument for a MIDI track in Reaper

Assign and arm the track and check levels.

After recording the track, you'll most likely notice that it doesn't look like normal audio tracks. Instead, the media window will (usually) show little rectangular blocks instead of a waveform. This indicates that it's a MIDI track and not an audio one.

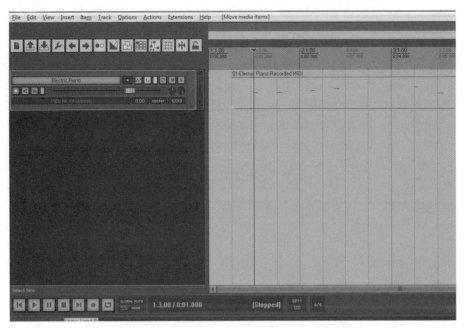

A MIDI track recorded in Reaper looks different than an audio track.

If you were to disable your effects on that track now, you'd hear nothing from the track when you played it back. This is because, again, MIDI data is not audio. It's simply instructions telling the sound generator (virtual instrument) what to do. Note that many virtual instruments also include built-in effects that are often used with the instrument. Depending on the instrument, this could include reverb, delay, chorus, phaser, tremolo, amp/cabinet simulation, overdrive, etc. Of course, you don't have to use those effects if you don't like them. You usually have control over which effects you add and the amount (not to mention other parameters). So, if you'd prefer to add reverb from a separate dedicated reverb plug, you can certainly do that instead.

Let's look at some different types of virtual instruments that are available to the budget-minded home recordist. The recording procedure for all of these is the same as described on the previous page.

Keyboard Sounds

One of the most obvious is the piano. For affordable instruments in this category, check out Toontrack's EZ Keys Grand Piano or XLN Audio's Addictive Keys Studio Grand. Organs are another common virtual instrument, and Arturia's VOX Continental V is a killer combo organ model, while UVI's Retro Organs contains some killer Hammond-style organ sounds; both are around the $100 mark. One of the most frequently used virtual instruments is the electric piano (Rhodes, Wurlitzer, etc.). With the vintage instruments becoming increasingly rare and therefore expensive, the software versions are a practical alternative. Lounge Lizard Session by Applied Acoustics Systems (see sidebar on the next page for details) is an excellent example of a brilliant-sounding and affordable electric piano instrument.

Applied Acoustics Systems Lounge Lizard Session and Ultra Analog Session

Applied Acoustic Systems specializes in modeling software and produces some of the finest-sounding virtual instruments around. Among others, these include analog synths, string synths, electric pianos, percussion, and guitars. In addition to their professional line, they offer a Session Series at a more affordable price. Included in this series are Lounge Lizard Session, Ultra Analog Session, and Strum Acoustic Session. In this book I make use of the first two. The Session Series uses the same sound engine as their professional line, but the features have been streamlined a bit.

Lounge Lizard Session is a leaner version of Lounge Lizard EP-4, which is a killer emulation of an electric piano. With Lounge Lizard Session, you get 16 programs based on classic electric pianos, such as the Rhodes and Wurlitzer, and a slew of other tone-shaping features. Besides having control over virtual Hammer, Fork, and Pickup variables, you can also choose between emulations of five different signal paths—which model a speaker cabinet, microphone, preamp, and recorder—for a different character, or select "None" for the direct sound of the electric piano alone. Then there's the effects section, which consists of a compressor, four-band EQ, chorus, phaser, and reverb. There's also, of course, a tremolo effect with Rate and Depth knobs, the latter of which can be controlled via the modulation wheel on your MIDI controller.

Ultra Analog Session is an analog-modeling synthesizer with 20 engine configurations covering all the essential synth tones, including basses, leads, brasses, pads, and strings. In the effects section, you have chorus, vibrato, delay, flanger, and reverb, and each comes with three parameters for specific settings. In the engine section, you have access to global controls, such as tuning, glide, and monophonic/polyphonic settings, as well as a select set of parameters for the oscillator, filter, and amp. Much of the intricate sound-shaping has been done for you with the 20 programs, but these features allow more tweaking to make the sounds truly your own. These parameters are fully automatable as well, which means you can map them to a MIDI controller so you have hands-on access to them in real time.

The sound quality of these instruments is simply stellar. I defy anyone to distinguish between Lounge Lizard Session and a real Rhodes in a blind listening test, and Ultra Analog is filled to the brim with fat basses, lush pads, and stinging leads. These two categories of virtual instruments—electric piano and analog synths—are some of the most commonly heard of all and, along with drums, are just about essential for anyone wanting a well-rounded library. And, especially considering the price, I can't imagine you're going to find better quality than Applied Acoustics Systems' Session Series.

Street price: $99 each

Let's take a listen to this instrument. All effects on these tracks come from the Lounge Lizard plugin.

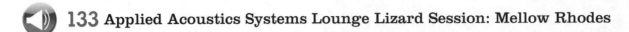 **133** Applied Acoustics Systems Lounge Lizard Session: **Mellow Rhodes**

134 Applied Acoustics Systems Lounge Lizard Session: **Rhodes with gentle growl and tremolo**

135 Applied Acoustics Systems Lounge Lizard Session: **Rhodes with phaser**

136 Applied Acoustics Systems Lounge Lizard Session: **Wurlitzer dry**

137 Applied Acoustics Systems Lounge Lizard Session: **Wurlitzer with growl and tremolo**

138 Applied Acoustics Systems Lounge Lizard Session: **Wurlitzer with growl and reverb**

Synthesizer Sounds

As mentioned earlier, analog synth sounds have made quite a comeback as of late, and that means there are tons of virtual analog synth-modeling instruments—not to mention plenty of digital synths, as well. This is another area of constant debate, in which you'll hear one side claim that a true analog synth will always sound better than a softsynth. But the simple truth is that, whereas a vintage analog synth can easily run you $2K or more, you can spend less than one tenth of that for a virtual instrument that's capable of fooling just about anyone in a blind listening test.

Monophonic or Polyphonic?

You may have heard this term before and not known what it meant. This simply refers to the ability of a synthesizer to play more than one note simultaneously. If it can only play one note at a time, it's a *monophonic* synth. This is common in some older Moog synths that are meant for lead or bass sounds. A synth that can play more than one note is *polyphonic*. This is common in synths that emulate string sounds, for example.

It's not an all-or-nothing thing, however. Some polyphonic synths have three-note polyphony, some have eight, etc. Not all polyphonic synths can play the same amount of notes simultaneously. This information will be stated on the spec sheet of the synth. So, if you're looking to purchase a virtual synth instrument (or a real hardware synth), be sure to consider this factor so you make sure you get what you need. Most virtual synths will adhere to the polyphony specs of the hardware synth after which they're modeled (if applicable).

Check out IK Multimedia's Sonik Synth 2, Arturia's Analog Laboratory, or Applied Acoustics Systems' Ultra Analog Session (see sidebar on page 165 for details) to hear some awesome-sounding affordable virtual synth instruments.

🔊 139 Applied Acoustics Systems Ultra Analog Session: Fat bass

🔊 140 Applied Acoustics Systems Ultra Analog Session: Monophonic lead

🔊 141 Applied Acoustics Systems Ultra Analog Session: Analog brass pad

🔊 142 Applied Acoustics Systems Ultra Analog Session: Warm pad

Bundle Up!

Many times, companies will sell several products together as a bundle at a hefty discount, so think before you buy. For example, if you're looking for piano, electric piano, and organ sounds, take a look around to see if you can find a bundle that includes all three for a discounted price. The discount can be significant, too. For example, if a company offers several different instruments for $80 each, you may find a bundle of three for $150, resulting in a savings of $90!

Orchestral, Big Band, and World Music Sounds

Extremely popular in the film-scoring and pop worlds, orchestral/world/big band sounds are another biggie. Let's face it: hiring an orchestra to play your music can be a tad pricey. There are numerous virtual instruments of these types available that are budget-friendly and still sound great. Garritan's Personal Orchestra, Jazz & Big Band 3, and World Instruments (see sidebar on the following page for details) are great examples of such collections. Let's have a listen to some of the sounds from these instruments (all sounds and effects come from the virtual instruments).

🔊 143 Garritan Personal Orchestra: String section

🔊 144 Garritan Personal Orchestra: Winds

🔊 145 Garritan Personal Orchestra: Brass

🔊 146 Garritan World Instruments: Indian ensemble

🔊 147 Garritan World Instruments: Scottish bagpipes

🔊 148 Garritan World Instruments: Native American Flute

🔊 149 Garritan Jazz & Big Band 3: Clarinets

🔊 150 Garritan Jazz & Big Band 3: Saxophones

🔊 151 Garritan Jazz & Big Band 3: Piano, bass, and drums trio

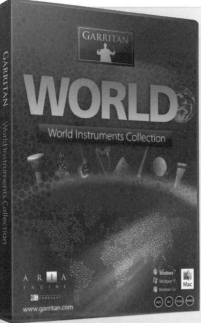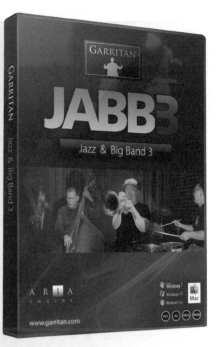

Garritan Personal Orchestra 4, World Instruments, and Jazz & Big Band 3
Copyright Garritan, used with permission

Years ago, the idea of having your music recorded by a professional orchestra was all but a pipe dream for most. It either required world-class composition/arrangement chops—likely paired with a good bit of luck—or a very deep pocketbook. Today, things have changed considerably. While it's still very difficult to have your music performed by a real orchestra, we have the next best thing. Virtual orchestral instruments have come such a long way these days that it's no longer unusual to hear them in a professional film score, among other things. Many TV show and video game scores use virtual instruments exclusively.

Garritan has long been a top manufacturer in this regard, and with the Garritan Personal Orchestra, you get an entire sampled orchestra at your fingertips awaiting your command. There are over 200 instrument choices, many of which are equipped with numerous expressive features for the most delicate touches of realism. There are even several different solo violins, for example, each one sampled from a different player (first chair, second chair, etc.) of the orchestra. From booming tympani drums and powerful brass to lush strings and delicate winds, the sound quality is stunning.

With Jazz & Big Band 3, you have access to a full, swingin' ensemble that includes everything jazz: saxes, trumpets, trombones, clarinets, flutes, keyboards (organs, acoustic and electric pianos), guitars, basses (electric and upright), drums, and percussion (auxiliary and tuned). There are over 60 instruments in all, and you have extensive control over many of them with regards to added realism.

Garritan World takes you all over the globe, collecting over 350 instruments from six continents and laying them on your lap. String, wind, percussion, and more instruments from countless countries and regions allow you boundless creativity in your compositions and arrangements. It would take you hours to simply play through all these samples—much less actually use them in a recording—so you can bet that you won't be running out of ideas anytime soon.

All of these libraries are powered with the included Aria Player. The main problem I've always had with sample players is their complex layout. Many of them are filled to the brim with countless buttons, knobs, menus, etc. and are quite intimidating to the first-time user. This is not the case with Aria Player. It's a powerful sample player that's easily the most user-friendly I've ever seen. It's laid out like a virtual mixing console, allowing you to load up solo instruments, small ensembles, or larger groups easily. Each one is easily assignable to a separate MIDI channel and has its own fader, pan knob, effect send (for adding reverb), and access to numerous sound-sculpting parameters, allowing you to tweak the instrument to perfection.

Whether you're just looking to dress up your pop recordings with some orchestral or ethnic touches, compose a full symphony, or arrange a standard for big band, you can't go wrong with these collections from Garritan.

Street price: $129 each

Options and More Options

Chances are, if you acquire a few virtual instrument collections, you'll end up with several versions of one instrument. This is because there's considerable overlap in many collections. For example, if you buy Lounge Lizard Session from AAS and also purchase Garritan's Jazz & Big Band 3, you'll end up with extra electric pianos because JBB3 includes a few, as well. Rather than seeing this as a waste of money, it's best to view it as simply an added bonus of more flexibility; it allows you to get that much more specific with the type of sound you need for a certain song or project.

You'll no doubt develop a group of favorite plugs that you find useful more often than others, and you can group those in your DAW to make them more easily accessible among the full list of plugins. It's not unusual to have a hundred plugin programs or more on your system, so rather than having to scan through them each time when looking for your favorites, it's well worth it to spend a little time learning your DAW's method for organizing your plugs. Reaper, for example, allows you to do this in at least two ways:

- **Creating subfolders within your effects window into which certain plugs can be placed for quick access:** For example, you may create separate folders for "electric pianos," "organs," "drums," etc.

- **Creating and saving effects "chains" that allow you to quickly recall an entire series of plugins at one time:** You may have a "Concert hall piano" chain, for example, that features a piano plugin, an EQ plugin, and a reverb plugin.

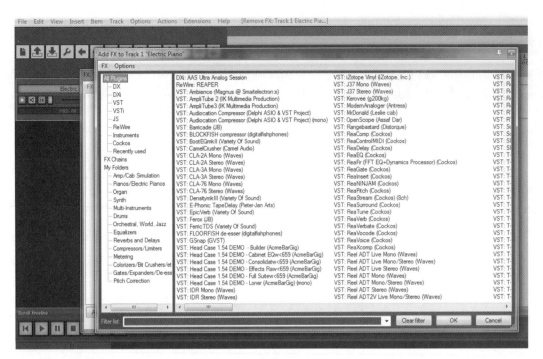

Reaper allows you to create subfolders that help you organize your plugins more easily.

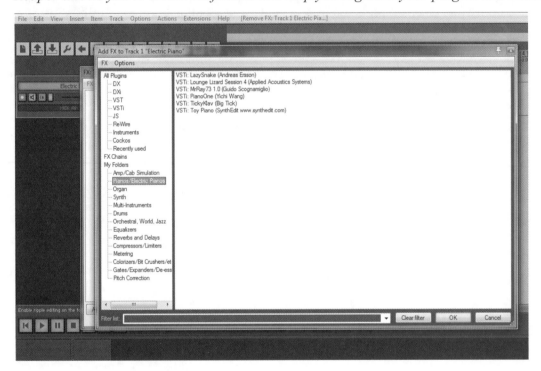

Complete Collections

There are also plenty of complete collections or "workstations" that include instruments from almost all genres. These may not be as comprehensive in every area as a specialized collection may be, but they're great for gathering a huge selection of the most commonly used sounds into one place. These can range in price from around $200 for IK Multimedia's Total Workstation XL or $250 for Steinberg's HALion Sonic 2 Software Synthesizer to $500 for Native Instruments' Komplete 10. If you're often needing to cover a wide variety of styles, this may be the way to go. Generally, the more you spend, the more sounds and flexibility you get, but do your research and read reviews to find which will suit you best if you're going this route.

Tips for Added Realism

If you're trying to use a virtual instrument as a convincing stand-in for a real one, there are a few things to keep in mind that will help sell the illusion. Of course, there are no rules in music, and there's nothing that says you *can't* use a virtual instrument in an unconventional way. But if you're going for realism, then the following list is important.

- **Observe the range of the instrument:** In other words, don't use a flute sound to play a bass line. Many virtual instruments (especially the more expensive ones) will take care of this for you by default (i.e., they won't make a sound below the flute's playable range), but not all of them will, so be mindful of this.

- **Don't play things that are impossible on an instrument:** If you're playing with an acoustic piano sound, for example, you don't want to use the pitch bend wheel. Again, this will often be handled for you with many plugs (in which case, the pitch wheel will simply have no effect on the piano patch), but that's not always the case.

- **Keep in mind physical limitations:** Wind instruments—such as woodwinds, brass, and reeds— require breathing; therefore, don't hold their notes eternally. You can even try breathing along as you play to try to get a sense of whether you may be stretching the limits. Also, don't play two notes on a monophonic instrument (such as most wind instruments). Most plugins will have separate patches for solo instruments ("solo sax") and instrument ensembles ("sax section"), so use the one appropriate for your needs.

- **If applicable, try miking an amp:** Some instruments, such as electric pianos or organs, are normally heard through an amplifier of some sort. And while many plugs of this type do feature built-in amp/cabinet simulation, there's nothing that says you can't try sending the signal out through a guitar or bass amp and miking that up. This is especially true if you have a nice-sounding room that you've been using for ambience on other tracks in the song. If your interface has more than two outputs, you can assign the output of the virtual instrument track to one of those outputs (instead of the default stereo pair—normally 1 and 2). Consult your DAW manual on how to do this. Then run a cable from that output to the amplifier. Make sure to start with the volume very low and raise it slowly until you have a good sound. Then mic up the amp and record that sound using the same procedure explained in Chapters 8 or 9. You can try this approach on just about anything, but it tends to work best on those instruments that are normally amplified, such as electric pianos, organs, and synths.

- **Read the manual:** Be sure to at least thoroughly look through the manual for the virtual instrument you're using. There are often many more options than just playing a note at different volumes and durations. If it's a wind instrument, there will likely be options to add breathiness to the tone, the sound of an inhalation of breath (before the phrase), legato playing (where the notes are connected instead of each one starting with a separate attack), vibrato adjustment, and other variations that enhance the realism of a particular instrument. The software programmers went to great lengths to include these touches, so you might as well take advantage of them!

As an example of how these various ideas can add up to a big difference, let's listen to an example of an alto sax solo. The first performance will not take any of these subtleties into account—I'll just play the notes without thinking about anything else. The second performance is basically the same phrase, but listen to the added realism you can provide by simply reading the manual and implementing some of the software's specific features.

 152 Garritan Jazz & Big Band 3: alto sax solo with no inflection

 153 Garritan Jazz & Big Band 3: alto sax solo with inflection

CHAPTER 11
DRUM SAMPLES AND LOOPS

If there's one area in which the budget-minded home recordist has lucked out lately, it's in the drum department. Recording good drum sounds is notoriously difficult. Not only does the kit need to sound good and be tuned well (which isn't quite as easy as tuning a guitar), but the room also plays a big role in the sound. If you don't have a good-sounding room, then your best option is to deaden the room as much as possible and then add things like ambience and reverb electronically via effects. This isn't to say, of course, that you shouldn't ever try to record a drumset at home. If you so desire, you should by all means give it a shot. You'll no doubt learn a good bit during the process. But whereas the home recordist can achieve truly pro-sounding guitar, bass, keyboard, and vocal tracks on a regular basis with experience, it's much rarer to hear pro-sounding drum tracks come out of a modest home studio. Of course, if it's for an indie project, then it might suit the music just fine, but for most types of music, live drums will generally suffer the most in the home studio.

So what's the good news? The good news is that we don't really have to record live drums anymore. Virtual drums have gotten so good at this point that it's not only possible for you to fool people into thinking they're real drums; it's been happening for years! The list of hits recorded with drum machines/samples/loops grows continually. And I'm not even talking about in the 1980s, when the sound of synthesized instruments was the fad. Everyone knows that plenty of drum machines were used then. I'm talking about "fake drums" that sound 100% like real drums.

There are basically three overarching categories when it comes to electronic drums: external drum machines, drum loops/samples, and virtual drum plugins.

EXTERNAL DRUM MACHINES

The *external drum machine* was the tool of choice throughout most of the 1980s, and it's continued to be used to some extent today. It was a common companion in a home studio when someone wanted to produce a demo of a song, for example. But until recently, the sounds of these boxes were generally recognizable as being produced by a machine if you listened closely enough (and sometimes you didn't have to listen closely at all). One commonly used machine for demo work was the Alesis SR16. (See page 70 for more on earlier external drum machines.) Boss also makes a mean drum machine.

Most drum machines nowadays come with only stereo L/R output jacks, although there are exceptions to this rule. With only stereo outs, you must make all drumkit mixing decisions within the box. This includes the level of the individual drums, panning, and tuning (if available). If the machine does have extra outputs, you can usually send some drums (the kick and snare are common) to their own output, which allows you to process them individually, apart from the rest of the kit. You could add a different amount of compression on the snare than the kick, for example, or you could EQ them separately. So that's a nice feature that allows a bit more control.

Recording Procedure: Stereo Outputs Only

Run a cable from the left output of the drum machine to input channel 1 on your interface. Run a cable from the right output of the drum machine to channel 2 on your interface. Assign and arm the tracks, pan them hard left and right (if you want to maintain the stereo image of your drums) and check levels by playing a few patterns.

Recording Procedure: Multiple Outputs

(**Note:** You'll need more than two inputs on your interface to make use of this feature.) Run cables from the main L/R outputs of the drum machine to inputs 1 and 2 on your interface. Assign/arm the tracks and pan these tracks hard left and right (if you want to retain the stereo image of your drums). Run cables from any other outputs of the drum machine (which will carry the signal of individual drums) to free inputs on your interface. Assign and arm the track(s) and check the levels.

The drum machine will normally allow you to select from various drum kit sounds and then use factory patterns, alter the pre-made patterns, or compose your own from scratch. You can then assemble those patterns into a song, which can be stored in the drum machine's memory. (Many machines nowadays allow you to transfer your songs to a computer via USB, as well.) Consult your drum machine's manual on how to do this.

Once you have the song fully assembled in your drum machine, you can record it into your DAW. Another option, assuming the drum machine has MIDI jacks (which most do nowadays), is to sync the drum machine with your DAW via MIDI. In this way, you won't have to record it; the drum machine would simply "chase" the DAW song and begin playing at the appropriate spot whenever you press play. However, this method is not recommended if you only have an interface with two inputs, as you'll need to have the drum machine patched into those inputs in order to hear it. The MIDI sync method is very useful when your tracks are limited (as they are with tape machines), because it allows you to save tracks.

SAMPLES AND LOOPS

In the late 1980s, *samples* and *loops* began to take hold in a big way, and they really took off in the 1990s. You could use a sampler to "sample" (or record) a brief one- or two-bar drum beat, or even just single drum hits. These could be looped (in the case of the drum beats) end-to-end to run the course of an entire song or triggered via MIDI controllers (in the case of single drum hits) to play realistic-sounding drums. Drum loops and samples are still very much in use today in various ways. Often times, samples of single drum hits may be snuck in behind real drums to fortify them if they don't sound full enough on their own. This practice is fairly common with the kick drum, for example. If you don't have quite the smack on the kick that you'd like (or enough thud), for example, you can find a kick sample that you like and mix it with yours—or simply replace yours altogether.

There are all kinds of loop software available. Some only contain short stereo files of recorded drum loops; in other words, it's just a collection of audio files. It's not unusual for there to be individual drum hits, as well, which allows you more flexibility. For example, you could use two-bar loops for the majority of your song and then you could use individual kick and cymbal hits for the final note of the song. And then there are other loop programs that are more like beat-making factories. They contain many loops and hits (often from many other instruments besides drums, as well) like the library packages, but they also allow you to manipulate the tempo and tuning for more versatility. You can literally piece together a track with a paint-by-numbers approach without even knowing how to play an instrument. You have a good bit of creativity as far as how you assemble things, but you're still dealing with pre-recorded beats or phrases. Check out titles by The Loop Loft and Big Fish for excellent-sounding, affordable loop packages.

There really is no recording procedure for using samples and loops because you're not really *recording* anything. You're simply importing them into your project to assemble a drum track piece by piece. You can usually just grab an audio file and drag it into your DAW project. Or you can position the cursor where you want it and import the file into the selected track. If you use the drag-and-drop method, and you're using a click track in your song, make sure you have the "snap to grid" setting engaged so that the loop will align perfectly with the beat you want.

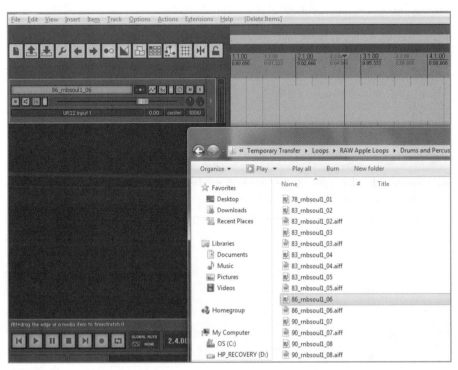

Pulling a drum loop into a Reaper project.

 154 Two-bar drum loop

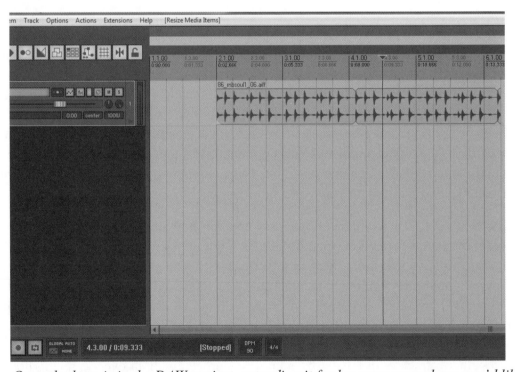

Once the loop is in the DAW project, extending it for however many bars you'd like is an easy matter.

 155 Two-bar drum loop extended for several bars

Time-Stretching

Although all loops were originally recorded at a specific tempo, they can often be *time-stretched* a good bit faster or slower and still be useable. Many times a loop will have its original tempo as part of the file name, and this will give you a good idea of whether or not it's likely to work for your song. If your song is at 90 bpm and the loop says 96 bpm, then it can easily be time-stretched and still be usable.

In Reaper, this is done by pressing the ALT key while clicking and dragging the end of the item. Consult your DAW's manual as necessary. If the tempo of a loop is faster than your song, it's going to be too short to align with the grid when you import it. Therefore, you just time-stretch it (make sure to have the "snap to grid" setting on) until it aligns. After that, you can copy it or loop it as necessary.

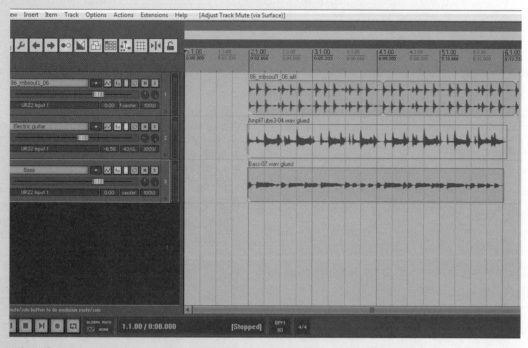

This drum loop has a tempo of 86 bpm, but the song's tempo is 90 bpm. Therefore, it sounds too slow.

 156 **Drum loop is too slow for song's tempo**

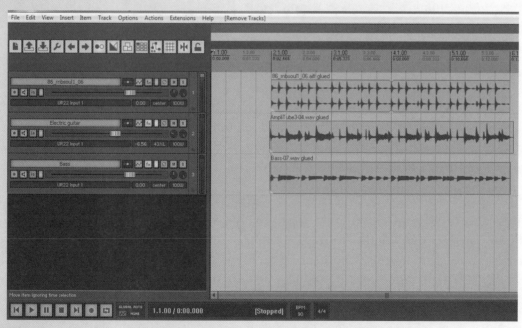

The drum loop has been time-stretched to fit the tempo of the song.

 157 **Drum loop has been time-stretched to fit the song's tempo**

VIRTUAL DRUM PLUGINS

Virtual drum software is generally geared toward letting you create a 100% completely customized drum track from scratch. These are collections of professionally recorded drumsets, playable via MIDI controllers, with each drum individually controllable in many ways. You can usually mix the kit however you'd like (i.e. make the snare louder, pan it to the right, etc.) and apply your own effects to the individual drums if you prefer (reverb, compression, etc.). These plugins have completely revolutionized home recording, as they allow you to, from the comfort of your mixing chair, program a completely convincing drum track that undoubtedly rivals the pro studio. Toontrack's Superior Drummer 2.0 and EZdrummer 2 (see sidebar for details) are brilliant in this category, the latter being my favorite bang-for-the-buck in the world of home recording. Other popular virtual drum software includes those from XLN Audio (Addictive Drums line), Steven Slate Drums, and Sonic Reality.

Toontrack's EZdrummer 2 has revolutionized the way I work with virtual drums. Never before have I encountered a program that makes it easier to create amazing-sounding drum tracks quickly and painlessly. It strikes the perfect balance of simplicity and complexity, giving you everything you need and nothing superfluous. Yes, there are more complex virtual drum instruments out there (Toontrack's own Superior Drummer is one of them), and if you really need to get absolutely surgical with every element of the track, then perhaps those are for you. But if you're like the rest of us who want great-sounding drums with the ability to tweak a whole lot (just not every nook and cranny), then you should look at EZdrummer 2. The interface is divided into four different main tabs: Drums, Browser, Search, and Mixer. Let's take a quick tour of each to show how EZdrummer 2 works.

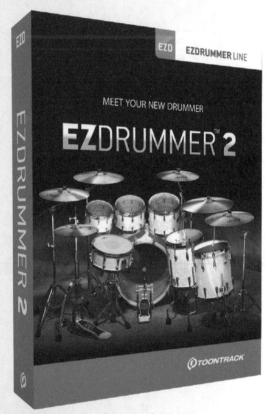

Toontrack EZdrummer 2

- **Drums:** This is the screen that allows you to select and customize your drumkit. First of all, you get two amazing-sounding drum setups—modern and vintage—each with a dozen or more presets to cover a vast array of styles. There are several choices for each part of a kit—the Modern kit, for example, has 13 choices for snare, nine choices for kick, etc.—each one based off a real-world drum or cymbal from the likes of DW, Ludwig, Yamaha, Slingerland, and others. You can set the tuning of each drum separately, and you can even mix and match any drum from either the Modern or Vintage setup to create your own custom, savable kits.

- **Browser:** This screen allows you to browse the extensive collection of grooves and fills for creating entire drum tracks quickly. Aside from countless one- and two-bar patterns (not to mention fills of varying beat lengths) in myriad tempos and styles, there are also section-long patterns for Intro, Verse, Pre Chorus, Chorus, Bridge, Ending, etc., allowing you to piece together a coherent track with minimum effort. It's as easy as dragging a pattern from the EZdrummer 2 window into the track within your DAW.

- **Search:** When you have a more specific idea of what you need, this screen lets you narrow it down by organizing patterns into various categories, such as Genre, Type, Play Style, and Power Hand (i.e., which hand is dominant in the pattern). There's also a "Tap to Find" feature that allows you to tap rhythms on a certain drum to find patterns that match. For example, you could tap a rhythm on just the kick drum, the kick and snare, just the snare, just the hi-hat, etc., and then see all the patterns that match it or come close by varying percentages.

- **Mixer:** The Mixer page allows control over each drum mic's level, panning, solo/mute, and effect functions in an intuitive manner. You can also specify each instrument's output channel, which will correspond to a specific track in your DAW. If you don't need to get too intricate with processing individual drums, you can just have the entire kit output to one stereo track. If you do want to treat individual channels with your own compression/reverb settings, etc., you can do that by sending each of them to their own output (up to 16) or grouping them to several outputs.

One other feature of EZdrummer 2 is the Song Creator, which allows you to build up a song within the program itself by dragging patterns to a timeline and moving, copying, and pasting them as necessary. This means you can treat EZdrummer 2 as a complete drum machine while in standalone mode without the need for a DAW. Of course, you can also create and record your drum parts from scratch, assembling them within Song Creator or your DAW.

With EZdrummer 2, the possibilities may not be *as endless* as with some programs, but they're certainly ample enough for many people, including myself. Toontrack has realized that sometimes endless possibilities can feel paralyzing to some—or are simply not necessary to others—so they've created a program that, while it allows you plenty of wiggle room, it also makes that wiggling extremely easy. And that's the best of both worlds to me.

Street price: $149

I've used EZdrummer 2 for nearly all the drum tracks in this book (the few exceptions are noted), so I'll be using it to demonstrate the process.

Recording Procedure

Run a MIDI cable from the MIDI out jack of your controller to the MIDI in jack of your interface or USB MIDI adapter. Create a track, select "MIDI" for the input, and open the effects window. (**Note:** In some DAW programs, you may have to enable your MIDI controller after plugging it in for the first time. This is true for Reaper, but consult your DAW manual on this.)

As stated earlier, while you can certainly program drums with a MIDI keyboard, you may find it much more intuitive with a MIDI drum controller. This can be as elaborate as a full electronic drumset or as basic as a MIDI drum controller with four different assignable pads. I programmed the parts in this book using the Multipad by KAT Percussion and the optional KT-HC1 Hi-Hat Controller Pedal and KT-KP1 Kick Pad Compact Kick Trigger (see page 45 for details). It doesn't make the drums *sound* different—it's still just MIDI instructions being sent to the virtual drum instrument—but it can certainly make it easier to achieve a "drummer feel" (even if you're not a drummer).

Assign and arm the track and check levels.

Stereo Out or Multi-Channel

Another option EZdrummer 2 has (as well as some other programs) is the ability to choose whether you want the instrument to output a *stereo channel* only or use *multiple outputs*. This is somewhat similar to the stereo versus multiple outputs I mentioned earlier when discussing external drum machines.

In the stereo channel option, the drum track simply acts like a stereo track in your DAW, and you raise the level of the entire kit with one fader. You can still make mix adjustments to the kit within the EZdrummer 2 plugin, but you won't be able to assign a separate reverb plugin of your own to only the snare, for example (although you can do this within the plugin, as EZdrummer 2 contains effects of its own). Any separate effect (reverb, compression, etc.) you add to the drum track would be added to the entire drum kit.

EZdrummer 2 in stereo mode: all mix adjustments to the kit must be made inside the plugin.

With *multiple outputs*, EZdrummer 2 will feed each drum to its own track, allowing you to control each drum with as much control as you have over any other track in your song. You can route them to an effects bus and add an insert effect (such as compression), just as you can with your vocals and guitars. This can be slightly more complicated at first, depending on your DAW, so you may need to consult the manual to make sure you fully understand the routing.

EZdrummer 2 in multiple output mode: each drum can be adjusted from the DAW mixer just like any other track.

After you've got the plugin set up in your DAW, you're ready to get started.

Step 1: Choose Your Kit

Most virtual drum plugins will come with several drum kits from which to choose—you can often create and save your own custom kits by mixing available sounds, as well—so the first step is to choose which kit you want to use for your recording. I'm going to use EZdrummer 2's Vintage Rock kit for this demonstration.

Selecting the kit within EZdrummer 2

 158 EZdrummer 2: Vintage Rock kit sounds

Step 2: Decide Whether You Want to Start from Scratch or Use Patterns

Many virtual drum plugins will contain built-in patterns, intros, outros, and fills that you can use to create your drum track if you prefer. Or you can simply use them as placeholders that you'll later replace and/or alter, after you finish tracking the rest of the song. Some prefer to finalize the drum track first, while others prefer to simply lay down a basic beat and track the instruments on top of that, coming back to create the "real" drum track afterward. The latter option is particularly common when you've got an idea that you want to lay down quickly.

Using Patterns

EZdrummer 2 makes it incredibly easy to find a suitable pattern for your song, thanks to its smart search feature. You can search for patterns based on rhythm by tapping parts on a specific instrument. For example, if you want to find patterns in which the kick drum plays on beat 1, beat 2.5, and beat 3, then you simply tap that rhythm on the kick drum. *Presto!* It will show you all the patterns available that contain that rhythm on the kick. You can do the same with a snare rhythm, hi-hat rhythm, etc.

Searching for a pattern in EZdrummer 2 based on the kick rhythm

 159 **EZdrummer 2: Pattern selected**

After you find the pattern you like, you can simply drag and drop it into your DAW program, just as with the audio loop. And just as with audio loops, you can extend the MIDI pattern as long as you'd like by dragging it out. However, if you decide that you want to alter a hit in measure 10, for example, because you're moving to the chorus, realize that this alteration will show up in all iterations of that loop so far. In other words, if it's a two-bar loop that starts on measure 1, and you've extended it by pulling it out to measure 10, then the alteration you made in measure 10 will also show up in measures 2, 4, 6, and 8.

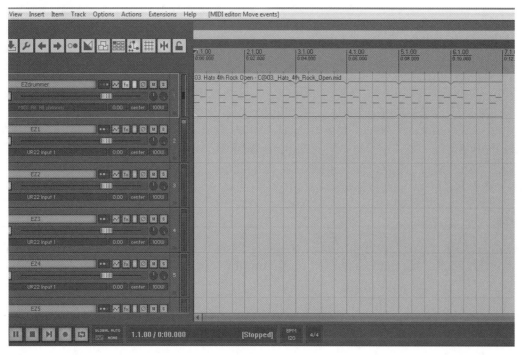

When dealing with an extended loop, one alteration will show up in every repetition of the loop.

160 EZdrummer 2: Looped pattern altered

There's an easy way around this, however, and that's by using the copy-and-paste function. If you copy the two-bar loop of measures 1 and 2 and paste it to measures 3 and 4, then the pattern in measures 3–4 will not be affected by changes to the one in measures 1–2 because they're two separate items. (Alternatively, you could simply drag the pattern in again from EZdrummer 2.)

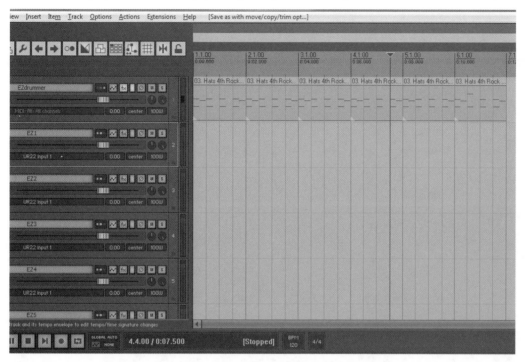

If you want to alter one pattern without altering the previous one, use the copy-and-paste function.

 161 EZdrummer 2: One altered pattern does not affect separate items

So in summary:

- If the pattern is extended and looped continuously, then any change made will show up at each recurring spot in the looped pattern.

- If it's a collection of individual patterns (not extended into a loop), then any change made to a pattern will not affect any others.

Recording Your Own Track from Scratch

If you're dealing with a very specific type of song that doesn't conform to a standard feel or beat, then you'll most likely need to create your own drum track from scratch. Again, you can use a MIDI keyboard or MIDI drum controller to record the parts. You should have your MIDI controller set up, and you'll need to have the drum track armed in order to hear it.

If using a MIDI keyboard, first take a moment to learn which keys correspond to which drum. The drum program will normally provide a MIDI map that provides this information, so it's a good idea to print it out for quick reference. If you're using a MIDI drum controller with a limited number of pads (such as four), then you'll need to decide which drums you'll want to control first and assign the pads to the appropriate notes. For example, you may typically start with a kick, snare, hi-hat, and cymbal. Consult your drum pad's manual to see how to assign the pads to specific MIDI notes.

You can then begin recording your track. It will probably be necessary to record the drum track in stages, depending on the complexity of it. For example, depending on your coordination level and setup, you may just want to record the kick and snare first or the kick, snare, and hi-hat if you can swing it. You can specify in your DAW whether you want a MIDI track recording to replace an existing one or overdub onto it. This way, you can record the kick and snare on the first pass, for example, and then come back and overdub the hi-hat.

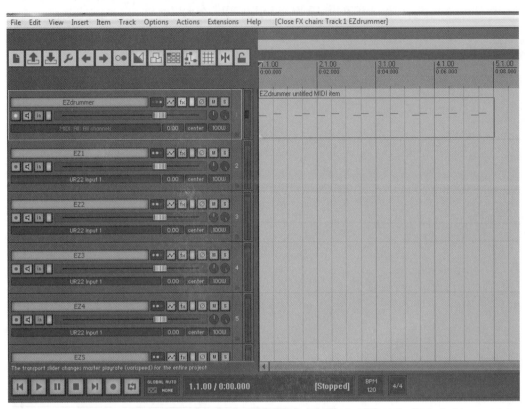

The kick and snare have been recorded in the first pass.

 162 EZdrummer 2: Kick and snare recorded

On a second pass, the hi-hat part has been added using the "overdub" setting.

163 EZdrummer 2: Hi-hat part added to kick and snare

Typically, you may record a two- or four-bar pattern and then copy and paste it if applicable. If you have a full drumset controller, though, and you have the chops for it—or if you're just really handy with the MIDI keyboard—feel free to play through the entire track if you'd like. You can always leave holes where you'd like the fills to go, or you can just play through and then come back and add the fills after the fact by switching to the "replace" mode instead of "overdub." If you have a four-bar pattern recorded and you want to add a fill in measure 4, just start recording from measure 3 to give yourself some runway and join in at the appropriate spot in measure 4. Most DAWs are set up so that a MIDI track won't start recording (and therefore won't start replacing the old track) until a note is played. This setting can be adjusted to your preferred behavior, so consult your DAW manual.

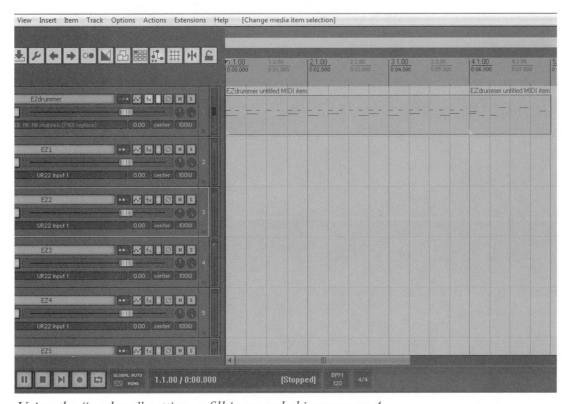

Using the "replace" setting, a fill is recorded in measure 4.

 164 EZdrummer 2: Four-bar pattern with fill in measure 4

It's also common to use a combination of both approaches. You may start with some pre-made patterns that work well with your song, adjusting them slightly via manual editing (see Chapter 15 for more on this) and/or re-recording fills and sections as necessary.

Step 3: Edit (If Necessary)

After you've recorded the entire drum track, it's a good idea to listen to it in its entirety to make sure nothing sticks out. For example, you may realize that the crash cymbal is much too loud or quiet or that a kick or tom is on the wrong beat during a fill. You should also check to make sure that you don't have any extra measures anywhere, which can happen on occasion if you're doing a lot of copying and pasting. So it's a good idea to listen through it twice: once to concentrate on the performance of the drums and once while running through the song in your head (or while playing along on guitar or keys) to check the length. Of course, even if you later discover that the length isn't correct, it's a simple measure to correct it, but it's nice if you don't have to worry whether or not the drums are playing the right beat when you're recording the other instruments.

Alternative Song-building

Some virtual drum programs, including EZdrummer 2, have song-building features inside them, allowing you to assemble your patterns and record your fills without leaving the comfort of the plugin. You may find this easier than dragging and dropping between two windows constantly. In EZdrummer 2, this is called "Song Creator." It's a powerful, intuitive tool that makes assembling a song quite an easy task.

EZdrummer 2's Song Creator feature allows you, should you choose,
to assemble the entire song within the plugin.

Once you have the entire song built, you can then drag the whole thing (or only parts if you prefer) into your DAW.

Quantization

This "editing" step is also the point where I'd recommend adding quantization to the drum track. I like to save it until the end like this because it allows you to be a bit more objective when it comes to the timing. When you *quantize* a MIDI performance, you correct rhythmic imperfections by moving the notes to the closest specified rhythm. If you choose to quantize to the nearest 16th note, for example, it will move every note forward or backward to the nearest 16th note in the measure.

If you set the quantization factor to 100%, it's going to make every note metronomically perfect, which will sound like a machine. If that's the sound you're going for, then that's the ticket. But if you're going for a natural sound, you're not going to want to do that. But you don't just have to choose between "too" human (i.e., downright sloppy) and machine-like. You can choose the specific quantization percentage. If you choose 75%, for example, it'll only move each note 75% of the distance to the nearest rhythm point. This can be a great way for you to retain a human feel while still correcting any grossly mistimed performances. I'd suggest experimenting with the percentage to see what sounds best to you; it may be 50%, 75%, 85%, etc. It will likely depend on the feel and tempo of the song, as well.

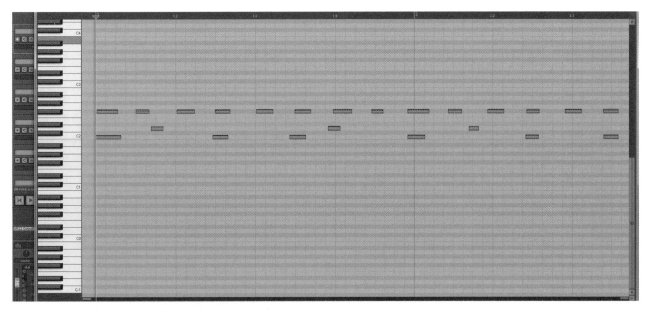

A drum performance before any quantization

As you can hear, this beat is a little on the sloppy side.

 165 EZdrummer 2: A recorded drum groove without any quantization

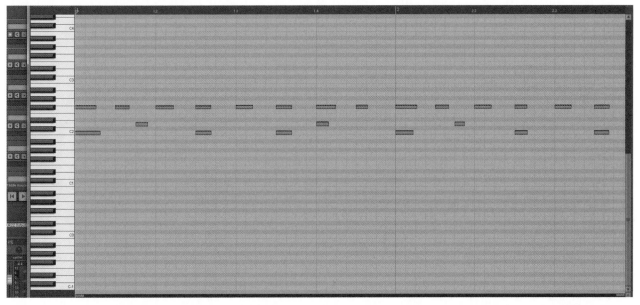

The same drum performance after 100% quantization to the nearest 16th note. Notice how each note now perfectly aligns with the grid.

Now it sounds totally mechanical.

 166 EZdrummer 2: Previous drum groove quantized with 100% setting

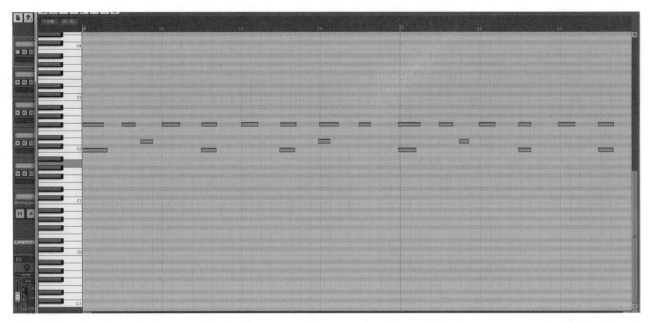

The same drum performance after 75% quantization: each note is pulled closer to the grid but not all the way.

This is a nice compromise. It sounds in time now, but it still sounds human.

 167 **EZdrummer 2: Previous drum groove quantized with 75% setting**

It should be mentioned that the quantization will usually only affect the currently selected MIDI item (pattern, fill, etc.). So if you have 20 items or so in your total drum track and you want to quantize the whole thing to the same setting, then you should glue them together first so that they become one item. In Reaper, this is accomplished by selecting all of the items, right-clicking, and then selecting "glue items."

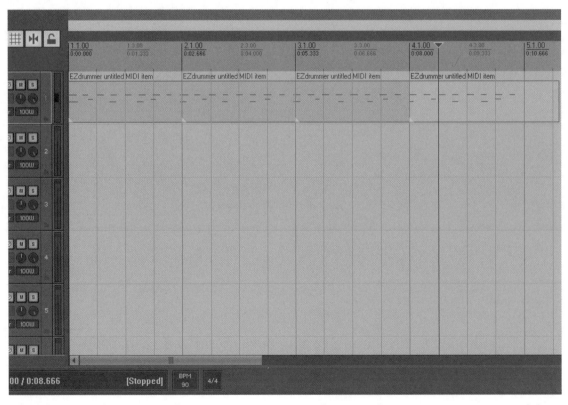

This drum track consists of many separate items. If you apply quantization to one of them, it won't affect the rest.

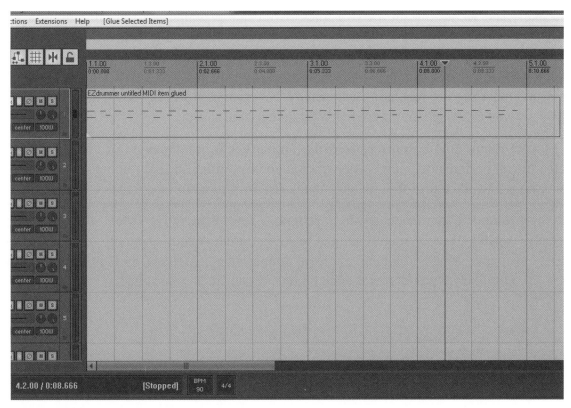

After gluing the items together, they become one. Now you can quantize the whole track at once.

TIPS FOR REALISTIC DRUM TRACKS

If you're going for the robotic 1980s drum machine sound, then that's pretty easy to get. But just as with other MIDI instruments, there are many things to keep in mind when programming a drum track if you want it to sound totally convincing.

- **Don't program impossible parts:** A drummer only has four limbs, so don't play five drums/cymbals at once. Also, don't program impossibly fast parts.

- **Don't over-quantize:** The more human feel you can retain in your track, the better. If you're finding that you're having to quantize a recorded part severely (more than 85%, for instance) for it to sound acceptable, then you should probably re-record it and get a cleaner take.

- **Listen to real drum tracks and notice the subtleties:** Spend a good amount of time listening closely (with headphones) to recordings that feature drum parts you like. What happens to the kick or hi-hat when they play a fill? What happens when they come back in after a fill? They often (though not always) end a fill or begin a new section with a cymbal hit. If you keep an eighth-note pattern on the hat going through a complicated tom fill, it's most likely not going to sound realistic. Though the difference may be subtle to the untrained ear, a drummer would spot it right away.

- **Try to use a MIDI drum controller if at all possible:** Playing with sticks in your hand really does help you mimic the feel better. Even a four-pad controller is preferable to pecking it out on a keyboard.

- **Try adding some "live room sound" to the drum track:** This is an interesting trick that can sometimes add to the realism of a track. If you have at least a decent-sounding recording room, try setting up your speakers in it and adding a pair of stereo condenser mics 5–10 feet away (experiment with the distance to see what sounds best) as room mics. Play the drum tracks through the speakers and record it with the two mics. While it's playing back, sit on a stool near the speakers and flail around like a real drummer. You can even add a subtle grunt now and then. After you're done, try mixing that stereo room mic track in with the drums lightly while minimizing the room mics of the virtual drum plugin to see what it sounds like. If you have a song in which your room sound plays a great deal into some of the other instruments in the song, it can really make the drums sound as though they were recorded in the same space.

- **Don't forget flams, double stops, rolls, drags, and other subtle touches:** Drummers will mix it up often in real performances, especially when it comes to fills, so listen to the way they do this on recordings and add a few of these techniques into your programmed tracks.

- **Read the Manual:** Drum machines, loop programs, and (especially) virtual drum instruments are usually capable of much more than just making a drum sound. There are often all kinds of subtleties available, including tuning, alternate drums/cymbals, effects, and alternate drum hits/ strokes, but you likely won't discover them all unless you crack the manual.

CHAPTER 12

RECORDING VOCALS

Compared to other instruments, recording vocals can seem deceptively simple on the surface. After all, you just sing into the mic, right? That's certainly true. However, considering the fact that the vocals are usually the centerpiece of the song (if it contains vocals), they usually need to be handled with care in order to make them as effective as possible. In this chapter, we'll look at the most common methods of doing so, the equipment of choice, and tips on getting the best performances out of the vocalist (whether it's you or someone else).

Don't Delay!

Since the vocals are usually the most important element in a song, most people end up recording them last. This makes sense, because a fleshed-out, great-sounding track can be inspirational to sing along to. However, it's always a good idea to record a scratch vocal track early on in the process. This doesn't need to be perfect at all; it can simply be a one-take wonder. The idea is just to get the basic idea down. Why? You can spend a great deal of time layering on the ear candy and creating the perfect backing track, only to discover later on that one (or more) of the parts totally conflicts with the lead vocal. (Ask me how I know this!)

One other thing: Even though it's meant to be a scratch vocal, it's not a bad idea to set up a good-sounding vocal chain when you record it (if it's not too much trouble), just in case in ends up sounding really good! Several hit songs contain the original scratch vocal (which was recorded pressure-free) in the final version.

THE RECORDING SPACE

Although printing (recording) ambience as part of the track may be common in other instruments such as guitar and piano, lead vocals are usually recorded in a dry environment so that they have clarity and presence. Any ambience, such as reverb or delay, is usually applied electronically via effects after the fact. The reason for this is two-fold: it prevents you from adding too much ambience to the track (which cannot be undone if it's recorded with it), and it allows you to have total control over any ambience applied to it (the type, how much, etc.). In other words, if you record your vocals in a very "wet" room (with lots of reflections), such as a garage or a large tiled bathroom, then you're stuck with the sound of that room on the vocal track. While in some instances this could be exactly what you're looking for on a track, many times it won't be. This is why the "vocal booth"—a fairly small room that's acoustically "dead" (for the most part)—is so common.

Of course, most home studios don't have the benefit of a custom-built vocal booth. However, there are several alternatives that are leagues better than an untreated bedroom. For example, a carpeted closet filled with lots of hanging clothes can make a pretty decent vocal booth. If you can add an absorptive panel or acoustic foam on the inside of the door, that's even better. I've gotten great results using just such a setup.

There are also several products available that can serve as temporary vocal booths. These range in price from around $100 to thousands of dollars. The Primacoustic VoxGuard Microphone Isolation Panel (see sidebar on the following page for details) is one such product. We'll look at its effectiveness with some upcoming examples.

Primacoustic's VoxGuard is designed to easily mount on a standard microphone stand for the purpose of cutting down unwanted room reflections when recording vocals. It measures 18 inches wide, 15 inches tall, and extends 7.5 inches deep. The shell is made from ABS plastic, which means it's durable yet lightweight—a nice feature considering the fact that you'll usually have a delicate microphone mounted to the same stand and don't want to see it come crashing down. It's lined with one-inch high-density open-cell acoustic foam in an attractive charcoal color.

Installation is a quick, easy process that took around two minutes the first time I did it and around 30 seconds each time after. You simply remove the mic clip from your stand (if there is one) and place the VoxGuard base onto the end. Secure this with a thumb screw (provided), which also acts as a new microphone mount. Screw your microphone mount onto this mount, and you're good to go. The only issue I encountered was when dealing with larger condenser mics, such as the MXL CR89. A large mic often means a large shockmount, and that particular one wouldn't easily screw on because the VoxGuard was getting in the way—even with the shockmount pointed vertically. However, the foam on the VoxGuard is obviously pliable, and the screen is made of plastic, so you're able to make accommodations if necessary. Therefore, I was able to get it on without too much trouble.

The VoxGuard certainly does its job of taming the reflections in an untreated room. It doesn't make an *incredibly* drastic difference—it's not like singing in a professional vocal booth, obviously—but then again, it doesn't cost thousands of dollars, either. Considering its price and portability, it's certainly a worthy investment, and if you've not been using any type of treatment thus far, you'll no doubt notice an increased clarity and presence in your vocal tracks.

Street price: $99

Primacoustic VoxGuard
Microphone Isolation Panel

It's also possible to build your own portable vocal booths by using panels similar to those used for treating the control room, as discussed in Chapter 2. This can be done for a very reasonable amount—assuming you don't mind sacrificing a weekend to get it done—and you can achieve excellent results. You can find details on this type of project in the Appendix.

Understand that these types of solutions aren't going to result in the soundproof-type of booths you'll see in pro studios. Those rooms are very expensive to build. But fortunately, they're not necessary to achieve great results. It's not that it wouldn't be nice to have one; it's just that they're overkill for our needs. They're meant to provide lots of separation so that, if necessary, a vocalist can sing along with a band playing in the studio—without the drums and loud guitars bleeding into the vocal mic. That's not the norm in the case of a home studio, so we usually don't need such luxuries.

LARGE DIAPHRAGM CONDENSER MICROPHONES

By and large, the prototypical microphone used for vocals is the large diaphragm condenser. This is hardly a steadfast rule, however, as we'll soon see. Nevertheless, the classic image you usually see when someone is singing into a mic in a studio involves an LDC. It should be mentioned, however, that everyone's voice is completely unique, and therefore vocal microphone choices can be much less standardized than mics used for other instruments.

Of course, there are classic vocal mics, such as a Neumman U67, AKG C12, and others, but these cost thousands and therefore don't make many appearances in the home studio. Even so, for those whose mic closet does contain such coveted treasures, sometimes they simply don't sound the best for a certain voice. This is why, if at all possible, it's best to try a mic out in person with your voice (if you're going to be recording your vocals, that is) before you buy it. Sometimes this is not an option, and so you may just have to do your best by reading reviews or asking around. You can usually get general information about a mic this way, including whether it's a brighter or darker mic, etc.

When singing into a condenser microphone, you don't "eat the mic" the way you often do when singing live (usually with a dynamic mic). You'll generally be singing between six to 12 inches away from the mic and usually with a *pop filter* between you and the mic. This helps prevent plosive sounds—such as those created with "b" and "p" words—from disrupting the mic's diaphragm and creating brief "pops" in the vocal track.

The pop filter clamps onto the microphone stand and prevents air bursts from disrupting the mic's diaphragm.

Recording Procedure

Plug the mic into your interface or external preamp (which would then plug into your interface) and set the levels. (See important notes regarding the use of phantom power on page 90!) Assign/arm the tracks, and that's all there is to it! Recording vocals with compression on the way in is very popular, as well. See Chapter 13 for details on this.

Let's have a listen to some LDC mics within the affordable home studio range. We'll check out three different mics in this category, ranging in price from $120 to $350. The first is the CAD GXL3000BP (see sidebar on page 141 for details). This is the least expensive of the three, but it also features multiple patterns (cardioid, figure-eight, and omnidirectional), which makes it quite handy to have around.

While we're demoing the sound of this mic, we'll also demonstrate the effect of the Primacoustic VoxGuard, comparing the sound of a vocal recorded in a typical, untreated bedroom to one recorded in the same room with the VoxGuard.

🔊 **168** CAD GXL3000BP: Male vocal in bedroom

🔊 **169** CAD GXL3000BP: Female vocal in bedroom

🔊 **170** CAD GXL3000BP: Male vocal in bedroom with Primacoustic VoxGuard

🔊 **171** CAD GXL3000BP: Female vocal in bedroom with Primacoustic VoxGuard

As you can hear, even adding nothing but the VoxGuard makes a noticeable difference in the sound of the vocal. It's more present and sounds focused, which will definitely make a difference in the final mix.

Now let's hear the same phrases sung into the Sterling Audio ST55 microphone (see page 17 for details). The rest of the signal chain will be the same as with the CAD GXL3000BP; see the Recording Index for these details.

🔊 **172** Sterling Audio ST55: Male vocal

🔊 **173** Sterling Audio ST55: Female vocal

Proximity Effect

The *proximity effect* is the increase in bass frequency buildup that happens when you get closer to the microphone. The science behind why this happens is a bit complicated, but the effects are quite noticeable. Check out the following track to hear it in action.

🔊 **174** Sterling Audio ST55: Demonstrating proximity effect

For such a small action (moving a few inches in), the difference is more than subtle. On occasion, this can be used to good effect. If a person's voice is on the smaller-sounding end, it can add apparent weight to the vocal. It's also somewhat common to use a bit when the vocal is accompanied by a sole instrument, such as an acoustic guitar or piano, and can therefore take up more sonic space. But in a typical pop or rock song, it results in a bit of muddiness more often than not and should therefore be implemented cautiously.

The final mic in this category that we'll check out is the MXL CR89 (see sidebar on the following page for details). Here are the same phrases sung with this mic through the same signal chain:

 175 MXL CR89: Male vocal

 176 MXL CR89: Female vocal

The MXL CR89 is a large diaphragm condenser mic with a cardioid pattern. Based on the well-respected V89 from MXL, the CR89 is a stunning beauty with a matte black finish covering its brass body and black chrome grill and trim. At less than 2 pounds, the mic is a bit lighter than its size would suggest, but the build quality on the mic is quite impressive. It comes with a well-made aluminum case with ample foam lining, a heavy duty shockmount, and a cleaning cloth. The CR89's frequency response is 20 Hz to 20 kHz, and it features a 6-micron gold-sputtered diaphragm inside a tuned grill cavity. The microphone was named "Best in Show" by *ProSound Network* magazine at the 2013 NAMM show.

The best news is that the CR89 sounds even better than it looks, and it looks *really* nice. Warm, high-end sparkle, full-bodied, and rich are just some of the words that spring to mind when trying to define its character. It shines on vocals for sure, but it'll do a beautiful job with just about everything you throw at it. I've loved it on acoustic guitar, piano, electric guitar, mandolin, percussion, and more. It's become my go-to mic in my studio, and if it were stolen, I'd get my hands on another one as quickly as possible (after filing a police report, of course). How this microphone costs less than $1,000 is beyond me. But in this case, ignorance is bliss.

Street price: $349

MXL CR89 large diaphragm condenser microphone
Copyright MXL, used with permission.

As you can probably hear, the differences between different mics can range from extremely subtle to more noticeable, but all of the mics produce very useable sounds. Generally speaking, the more expensive you get, the more subtle the difference becomes. In other words, the difference between a $100 mic and a $1,000 mic is more noticeable than the difference between a $1,000 mic and a $2,000 mic.

Let's listen to these mics again with some phrases in different styles to see how they react. Again, the signal chains will be the same for each mic within a specific phrase.

🔊 **177** CAD GXL3000BP: Male vocal rock

🔊 **178** CAD GXL3000BP: Female vocal rock

🔊 **179** Sterling Audio ST55: Male vocal rock

🔊 **180** Sterling Audio ST55: Female vocal rock

🔊 **181** MXL CR89: Male vocal rock

🔊 **182** MXL CR89: Female vocal rock

🔊 **183** CAD GXL3000BP: Male vocal intimate

🔊 **184** CAD GXL3000BP: Female vocal intimate

🔊 **185** Sterling Audio ST55: Male vocal intimate

🔊 **186** Sterling Audio ST55: Female vocal intimate

🔊 **187** MXL CR89: Male vocal intimate

🔊 **188** MXL CR89: Female vocal intimate

Tube Microphones

While technically an LCD, the tube microphone works differently and therefore is often singled out. Many people refer to tube mics as adding a pleasing warmth to the signal, which is often welcome in the digital recording domain. Whether this sound works for you will be a matter of personal preference, and I'm including an example here to help you make a decision. The tube mic I'm using is an MXL 9000 (see sidebar on page 157 for details), and we'll hear a new set of rock and intimate phrases sung through it.

🔊 **189** MXL 9000: Male vocal rock

🔊 **190** MXL 9000: Female vocal rock

🔊 **191** MXL 9000: Male vocal intimate

🔊 **192** MXL 9000: Female vocal intimate

USB Microphones

Yet another classification within the LDC umbrella is the USB microphone. This is a mic with a USB jack that allows you to simply plug straight into the computer's USB port. In other words, you don't even need an audio interface to record with one. They're especially handy when you want to take a laptop on the road or something and don't want to have to lug around a bunch of gear.

The MXL Studio 24 USB is a USB-powered large diaphragm condenser mic designed for portability and ease of use. It features a cardioid pattern, 20Hz – 20 kHz response, and an attractive silver finish with a nickel grill cloth and trim. It's housed in a very nice, protective travel bag that includes pockets holding the mic, a tabletop mic stand and base, a cleaning cloth, the USB cable, and a software CD. There's a 1/8-inch headphone jack and gain dial built into the mic itself, making it a one-stop shop for the musician or podcaster on the move.

The software includes a GUI program with numerous features, including controls for input gain, phase reversal, an adjustable hi-pass filter, output, and headphone volume, as well as useful effects such as a noise gate and a four-knob leveler. You can save and recall presets quickly and easily for specific applications. The mic sets up on a desk and plugs into a laptop in no time at all (of course you can mount it on a full-sized mic stand, as well). It's ideal for travel when you only want to bring a laptop or a tablet (you'll need an adapter to use it with your tablet most likely, which is sold separately). It sounds clear and full with a well-rounded response and can certainly handle most situations.

Street price: $140

MXL Studio 24 USB large diaphragm condenser microphone
Copyright MXL, used with permission.

Let's listen to some more phrases sung into an MXL Studio 24 USB mic (see sidebar for details). Since we're plugging straight into the USB port on the computer, we obviously won't be running through the same signal chain.

🔊 **193 MXL Studio 24 USB: Male vocal rock**

🔊 **194 MXL Studio 24 USB: Female vocal rock**

🔊 **195 MXL Studio 24 USB: Male vocal intimate**

🔊 **196 MXL Studio 24 USB: Female vocal intimate**

DYNAMIC MICROPHONES

Though condenser mics get the lion's share of vocal duties in the studio, dynamic mics are no slouches either. Generally speaking, dynamic mics are often employed in louder, more rock-oriented vocal tracks, but there are many exceptions to this. Thom Yorke, of Radiohead, prefers an Electro-Voice RE20 dynamic mic for nearly all of his vocals, simply because it works well with his voice. Another very common dynamic vocal mic in the studio is the Shure SM7B, which is used by Sheryl Crow and Wilco's Jeff Tweedy, among many others. Oh, and you may have heard of a little album by Michael Jackson called *Thriller*? Yep—the King of Pop recorded his vocals with the SM7B.

Let's hear the same rock and intimate phrases through the Shure SM7B. We'll be singing much closer to the mic on this track than with an LDC, which is generally in keeping with dynamic mic technique.

🔊 **197** Shure SM7B: Male vocal rock

🔊 **198** Shure SM7B: Female vocal rock

🔊 **199** Shure SM7B: Male vocal intimate

🔊 **200** Shure SM7B: Female vocal intimate

TIPS FOR BETTER VOCAL TRACKS

Recording vocals can be a very rewarding or very frustrating experience, depending on a number of factors. But there are several things that can help make the process go as smoothly as possible. Let's take a look at some.

- **Choose a quiet time:** Since you're most likely not going to have a soundproof vocal booth, you need to make sure that the neighbor's dog isn't going to be barking a duet with you. Of course, this is a concern anytime you use a mic, but it's much more of an issue with an LDC recording vocals than with a dynamic recording loud guitars or bass, for instance.

- **Have a lyric sheet in place:** Even if the singer knows the song cold, it can't hurt, and it usually makes communication smoother if you're recording someone else and want to discuss a certain line.

- **Make sure nothing is jingling, crinkling, or rattling on the singer:** Leave loud jewelry out of the vocal booth.

- **Give the vocalist exactly what they want in their headphone mix:** Everybody is different in this regard. Some people like their vocal loud and proud; others want it barely audible in the phones. Some like to hear a lot of drums or bass, or they want reverb/delay on their vocals. Make sure what they're hearing inspires them to perform their best!

- **Try to learn their preferred method of working:** Some singers like to only sing entire takes of the song, while others don't mind punching in line-by-line if necessary. Again, it should be up to the singer to decide which they want to do (at least at first).

- **Try to be positive and specific with any comments or criticism:** Rather than saying, "That sucks; let's go again," try to give them something they can use. Instead, you could say something like, "Okay, it's getting better, but I know you've still got a better take in you. Concentrate on really keeping those higher notes in tune."

- **Set the mood:** If it's a slow, intimate vocal, maybe try turning the lights down and lighting some candles or firing up the lava lamps. It might be more difficult for someone to get in the right mindset with a 100-watt bulb glaring at them from above.

- **Be mindful of fatigue:** If you can tell their voice is starting to go, don't push it (unless they're wanting a strained, tired sound for effect). This can only lead to increased vocal strain that could possibly result in an extended recovery time.

Remember: the vocals are usually the focal point of the song, so no expense should be spared (effort-wise) in getting them to sound their absolute best. Try to have fun with them and keep everyone in good spirits. Some people can get very self-conscious about their voice, so be mindful of that and try to find ways to inspire them to do their best.

CHAPTER 13
EFFECTS AND PROCESSING

Aside from good miking techniques and quality virtual instruments, there are plenty of other sound-shaping tools along the path from first track to finished mix in the form of effects and other processing. While some of these are more utilitarian in nature and others more decorative, they all play a vital role in the composite sound of the recording. In this chapter, we're going to look at the most common tools in this regard and learn a bit about what makes them tick. Note that many people choose to begin the processing stage after the editing stage; there are cases made for both methods, and you'll most likely find a way that makes sense to you.

EQUALIZATION (EQ)

One of the primary and most useful tools is the *equalizer*, or *EQ*. This is a device that basically allows you to boost or cut (i.e., raise in volume or lower in volume) a specific frequency or group of frequencies, thereby changing the character of an instrument's sound. If a vocal sounds too boomy or muddy, for example, you may cut some of the low frequencies with EQ. If the cymbals are too harsh, you can cut some of the highs or upper-mids to tame it, etc.

In the days of all analog gear, there were several different types of outboard EQs you could use, or you could simply use the ones normally included in each channel strip of the mixer. Nowadays, most people use plugins for EQ in the home studio, as they offer great flexibility. An EQ plug will generally have several different "bands," or selectable groups of frequencies, that will each fall within a different type of EQ. The most common are as follows:

- **Sweepable:** A *sweepable* band usually involves two knobs—one to select the center frequency (in Hz) and one to select the amount of boost or cut (in dB). The bandwidth (i.e., the range of frequencies affected above and below the center frequency) is set and cannot be changed.

- **Parametric:** The *parametric* EQ band is like a sweepable, but it adds another knob called the "Q." This knob adjusts the bandwidth, allowing you to focus on a very narrow or broad range of frequencies surrounding the center frequency. The higher the Q setting, the narrower the frequency range.

- **High Pass Filter:** A *high pass filter* allows all frequencies above a certain point to pass through unaffected while cutting all those below it. The slope at which the lower frequencies fall off below the frequency point is sometimes preset or sometimes adjustable with a Q setting. So, though it seems counterintuitive, a high pass filter normally affects the bass frequencies.

- **Low Pass Filter:** The opposite of the high pass filter, the *low pass filter* allows frequencies below a certain point to pass through. Therefore, a low pass filter normally affects treble frequencies.

- **Shelving:** *Shelving* (high and low) is similar to the high/low pass filter, but there are noticeable differences. First of all, the high/low pass filters are only designed for cutting, not boosting. A shelving EQ will allow you to select a cutoff frequency, just like a filter, but it will also allow you to specify a boost or cut in dB. For example, if you select a frequency of 12kHz for a high-shelving EQ with a boost of 4 dB, then the frequencies around 12kHz will be boosted by a small amount, and the boost will gradually continue in strength up to 4 dB, eventually leveling off at that amount at a higher frequency. Therefore, contrary to the high/low pass filters, a high-shelving EQ really does affect treble frequencies, whereas a low-shelving EQ affects bass frequencies.

- **Graphic EQ:** Much more common in outboard form than in plugins, a *graphic EQ* consists of many bands (usually 10 to 30 or so), any of which can be boosted or cut by the desired amount. The frequency points and the bandwidth are both preset on a graphic EQ.

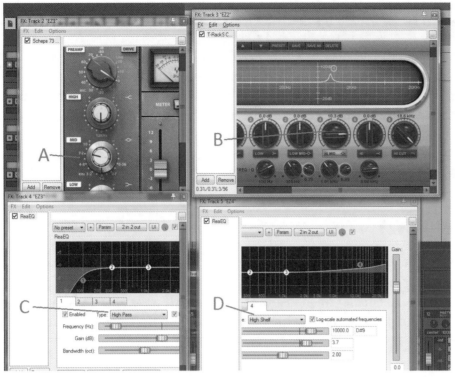

Different types of EQ frequency curves:
A) Sweepable at 1.6kHz (with preset bandwidth), B) Parametric at 1kHz (with a high Q setting),
C) High Pass Filter at 100Hz, D) High Shelving at 10kHz

Most DAWs will include at least one EQ plugin. The plugin will often include several bands—possibly anywhere from three to 10 or more—which can be assigned as one of the aforementioned types (excluding the graphic EQ, in which case, the plugin would contain a preset graphic EQ configuration). For example, the EQ that comes with Reaper, ReaEQ, allows you to add virtually as many frequency bands as you'd like, with the top and bottom ones switchable between high/low pass filters or shelves, and the middle ones defaulting to parametric bands.

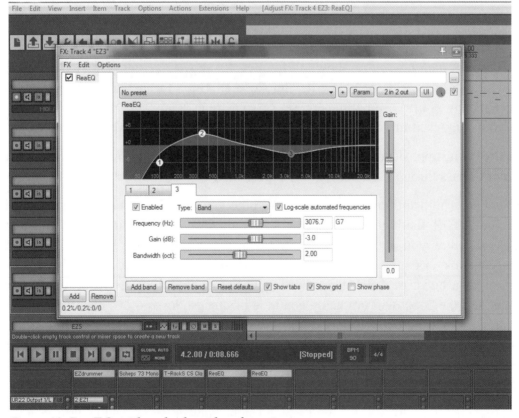

Reaper's ReaEQ with only three bands active

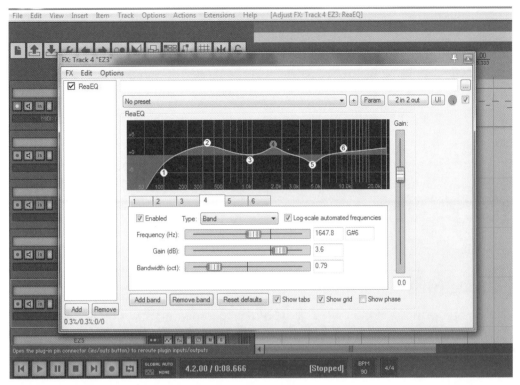

Reaper's ReaEQ with six bands active

Of course, if you'd like, you can also purchase more specialized EQs that model classic hardware EQs, such as the Neve 1073. The Scheps 73 by Waves (see sidebar for details) is such a plug. These are often designed to emulate their hardware companions down to the last detail—from the graphic interface to the way they may distort when pushed hard, etc. You'll find that, even though all EQs accomplish the same thing (boosting or cutting frequencies), many of them have their own unique sound. So you'll most likely find one or two that best suit your music and/or workflow and stick with them.

Waves Scheps 73 EQ plugin

The Waves Scheps 73 plugin was designed in cooperation with Andrew Scheps, a world-renowned mixing engineer who's worked with Adele, Red Hot Chili Peppers, Lana Del Ray, Metallica, and Black Sabbath, among others. The plug-in meticulously emulates a Neve 1073 EQ/preamp module in sound, appearance, and functionality. All of the controls are laid out and function just as those on the original hardware version, and there are even a few extras that Waves threw in as a bonus, including an added 10 kHz band from the Neve 1078 module.

The sound of this plugin is truly killer; it's one of those that seems to make just about anything you put through it sound better. To say it's a musical-sounding EQ is an understatement. You're able to get warm, saturated tones with rich harmonic distortion (the good kind of distortion!) that really help bring sterile-sounding tracks to life. It's what I call a "mojo" plugin, and mojo it certainly has!

Street price: $149

EQ Routing Procedure

You can apply EQ either by printing it (so that it's part of the recorded track) or by adding it after the track is recorded. Printing effects such as EQ was much more common in the days of analog, when processing power was more limited. These days, though, there's usually no need to print it unless you need to free up some CPU power or you just want to be done with it and move on (if you're really sure about the EQ settings!).

To print the effect, add the plugin to the input effects window. This will insure that the effect will be recorded with the signal.

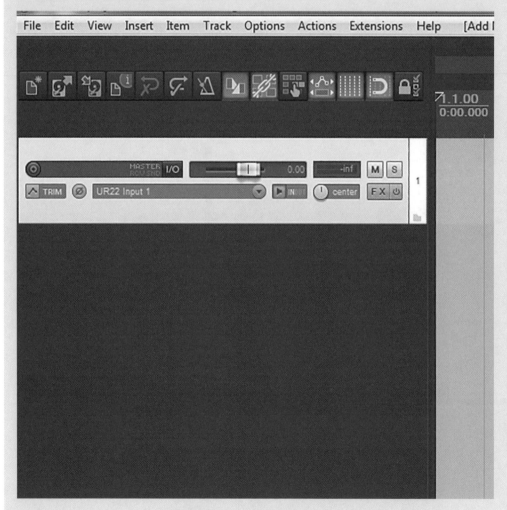

In some DAWs such as Reaper, the input FX option doesn't show up on a track until the track is armed for recording.

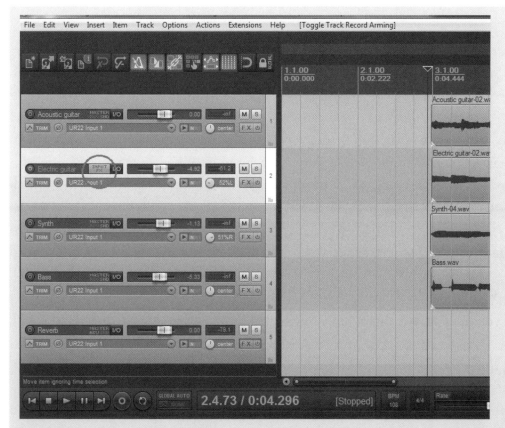

The Reaper "Input FX" button appears once you arm a track, enabling you to add an effect that will be recorded as part of the track.

To add the effect after the track is recorded, simply add the plugin to the track effects window.

To illustrate how EQs can sound different, let's hear the same set of boosts and cuts done with Reaper's ReaEQ and then with the Waves Scheps 73 EQ. For each track, you'll first hear the original track with the EQ bypassed (inactive) and then again with the EQ active.

201 Reaper ReaEQ: Acoustic guitar

202 Waves Scheps 73 EQ: Acoustic guitar

203 Reaper ReaEQ: Bass guitar

204 Waves Scheps 73 EQ: Bass guitar

205 Reaper ReaEQ: Snare drum

206 Waves Scheps 73 EQ: Snare drum

I'd recommend first trying out your DAW's included EQ plugin(s) and working with them to get the hang of basic EQ. After you feel comfortable with their functionality, if you'd like to purchase a specialized EQ, try demoing several to find one that fits your tastes and budget.

EQ Tips

Just as with most aspects of recording, there are no hard-and-fast rules with respect to EQ. There's no teacher like experience, and you really have to spend time twisting some knobs (or clicking and dragging some mice) to get a feel for what will sound best. That said, there are several tips that generally tend to produce good results.

- **Cutting is generally preferable to boosting:** There are plenty of exceptions to this rule, but more often than not, you'll probably find that cuts tend to sound more natural than boosts. If a vocal sounds a bit dark and lifeless, for example, try cutting some low mids before boosting some treble. You may find that it does the trick. Of course, it may end up sounding best with both.

- **Cut narrow bandwidths, boost broader ones:** Again, this is merely a guideline, but generally it'll sound better to cut a narrow range (higher Q settings) of frequencies and gently boost (lower Q setting or a shelving EQ) a broader range of frequencies.

- **Just because you have it, you don't have to use it:** If a track sounds fine with no EQ, all the better!

- **Boosts will make the track louder, but don't get tricked into thinking that's "better":** It's a physiological fact that louder tends to sound better to us. So don't equate a boost as better simply because it makes the track slightly louder. You need to evaluate the *sound* of the instrument—not just its volume.

- **It's always easier to get a great-sounding track at the beginning rather than fixing a poorly recorded track with tons of EQ:** The track that was recorded well from the start will usually sound more natural, and the extra few minutes you spent on mic placement or tone selection will pale in comparison to the time spent EQing it.

- **Sweep a boost through the frequencies to find an annoying frequency:** If there's a harshness on a guitar track, for example, set up a band with a narrow Q and a generous boost. Then sweep through the frequencies until you hear the annoying frequency really jump out at you. Once you've found it, you can apply the needed cut there.

- **Regularly bypass the EQ to make sure you're improving:** The longer you spend working on a track, the more fatigued your ears will become, and it will be harder to hear the effects of your tweaking. Bypassing the EQ can assure you that you are indeed making an improvement.

COMPRESSION

Much like equalization, compression deals with the relative volume of things, but it does so in a different way and includes time as a factor, as well. You can think of a compressor as an automatic volume control. It's like your own little personal minion that constantly rides the fader so you don't have to, turning down the really loud parts and bringing back up the quieter parts so that the whole track level is more consistent. They can affect a signal in other ways as well, because there's more going on that just that, and we can use their signal-shaping capabilities to great effect when shaping a sound.

On a typical compressor, there are usually several settings. Let's look at the basics.

Threshold

This is a volume level (in dB) that specifies at what point the compressor should take action. Any signal that doesn't breach this threshold (i.e., one that's below the threshold) will pass through the compressor without being affected at all.

Ratio

This setting, expressed by ratios such as 2:1 or 4:1 (read "two to one" and "four to one," respectively), tells the compressor how much to attenuate (turn down) the signal once it breaches the threshold. A setting of 2:1 indicates that, for every 2 dB that cross the threshold, only 1 dB will be able to pass. If 4 dB cross the threshold, only 2 dB will be allowed to pass. Said another way, the compressor would attenuate any signal over the threshold by 50%. In an 8:1 setting, the compressor would only allow 1 dB to pass through for every 8 dB that's over. So it will attenuate much more of the signal once it crosses the threshold. In other words, a 2:1 ratio will politely ask the signal to keep it down a bit, whereas an 8:1 ratio would just start swinging.

When the ratio is infinite—i.e., the signal is not allowed to breach the threshold at all—you have what's called *limiting*. This is commonly expressed as ∞:1. Limiting is commonly used on the master stereo track during the mixing and mastering processes to prevent any digital clipping. If you set a limiter at -0.1 dB, the signal will never breach the 0 dB clipping point.

Attack and Release

These controls tell the compressor how fast to start and stop what it's doing. With an attack time of 10 ms, for example, the compressor will wait 10 ms after the signal crosses the threshold before it clamps down and attenuates it (by the amount set in the ratio). The release control is the opposite. It specifies how long the compressor waits to let go of the signal after it falls back below the threshold. In other words, let's say you have an attack time of 10 ms and a release of 100 ms. The signal steps out of line, Mr. Cop Compressor waits 10 ms and then grabs the signal's neck and pushes him back toward the line. After the signal finally gets back in line completely, Mr. Cop Compressor holds onto the signal's neck for an additional 100 ms and finally lets go.

Output or Make-up Gain

Since a compressor only attenuates a signal, it makes sense that, if it's working at all, the average level of the signal is going to be lower than before. The output/make-up gain allows you to boost the entire level of the signal coming out of the compressor so that it still sounds as loud on average as it did before entering the compressor. It's just that now the softer parts are sounding louder, while the louder parts aren't sticking out as much.

Knee

This setting affects the threshold and, indirectly, the attack time. A "hard-knee" compressor is kind of the default. In other words, it does exactly what the instructions tell it to: it waits for the signal to cross the threshold and then applies the full amount of compression (ratio) as soon as the attack time is reached. It's like hanging a 50-pound weight around the neck of a runner as soon as he starts going above the speed limit (or 10 ms after if the attack time is set to 10 ms). The heavier the weight (higher the ratio), the more he'll slow down. A "soft knee" setting isn't so abrupt. It's like running alongside the runner as he approaches the speed limit and gradually slowing him down by adding weight bit by bit until he gets to the limit, at which point the full weight will be added.

A Picture Is Worth 1,000 Words

It's sometimes easier to visualize what a compressor does by looking at some graphs—just like in high school algebra class. Here we see two graphs depicting compression: hard-knee and soft-knee.

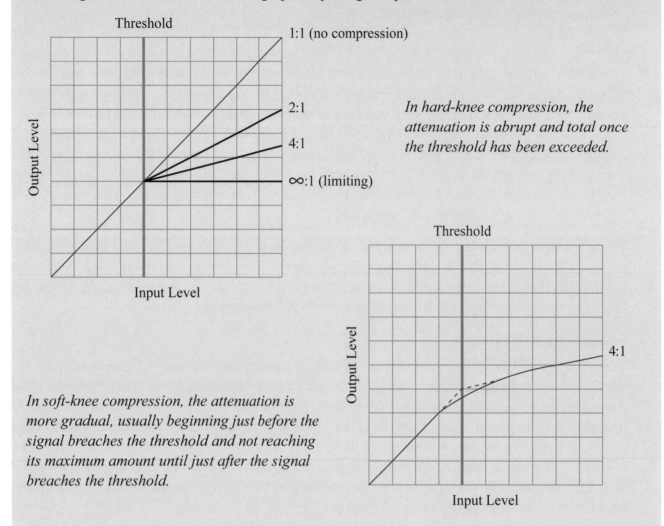

In hard-knee compression, the attenuation is abrupt and total once the threshold has been exceeded.

In soft-knee compression, the attenuation is more gradual, usually beginning just before the signal breaches the threshold and not reaching its maximum amount until just after the signal breaches the threshold.

With these graphs, it's easy to see where the terms "hard-knee" and "soft-knee" come from!

Bass and Guitar Compression

Compression is common on stringed instruments, and it's almost a given on the bass guitar. Let's take a look at some methods of employing it for these instruments.

Compression Routing Procedure

You can apply compression either by printing it (so that it's part of the recorded track) or by adding it after the track is recorded. Compression is probably the most common effect to be printed, and many people always track just about everything with a compressor—either for evening out levels or for creating a specific sound. The use of outboard compressors is popular in this regard, as are plugins.

To add compression after the fact with a plugin, simply add the plugin to the track's effects window. But let's look at some examples of routing scenarios for printing compression.

Guitar or bass straight in or with DI

If you're using an outboard compressor, you need to check whether or not it has a high-Z (high impedance) input or whether it only accepts line-level instruments. For example, the dbx 163X, a commonly used bass compressor in the home recording world (only available used nowadays), has a high-Z input on the front. So you can plug the bass directly into it and then run out and into a line input on your interface. However, a compressor such as the Art Pro VLA II, for example, is designed to accept line-level signals. So, in order to use it while tracking, you'd need to first run through a preamp with a DI input or at least an active DI box. You'd then go out of that, into the Pro VLA II, and then out of that and into a line input on your interface.

Direct out on guitar or bass amp

By using the amp's direct out, you can make use of any outboard compressor, because your signal will be at line level when it leaves the amp. Plug your instrument into the amp and run a cable from the direct out to the input of the outboard compressor. Connect the output of the compressor into a line input on your interface. Set levels, assign/arm track, and you're there.

Guitar or bass amp modeler plugin

To use an outboard compressor, the procedure will be the same as the straight-in method. Once you get from the compressor to a line input on your interface, then you assign/arm the track and add the plugin to the track's effects window. Remember to check the levels within the plugin, as well.

Miking an amp

To use an outboard compressor, you'll need to run through an external preamp, then to the compressor, and then to a *line input* on your interface (because the signal will already be amplified). Check your levels and assign/arm the track.

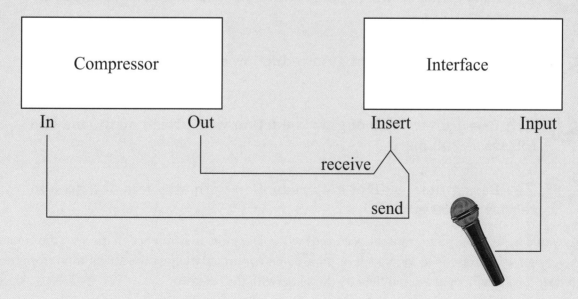

The exception to this is if your interface has insert jacks along with the inputs. An *insert* jack is like a send and receive loop contained within one TRS (tip-ring-sleeve) jack, so you can connect your compressor using the insert path. This is certainly not a feature on all interfaces, but it's a very useful one if you want to use the interface's onboard mic preamps and an outboard processor like a compressor or EQ.

Regarding the setting of the compressor, it's a safe bet to aim for around 4 dB of gain reduction on average, although some compressors (such as the dbx 163X) can still sound great even when peaking at around 10 dB. You can start with a short attack time between 5 to 20 ms and a moderate release time of around 100 ms or so. These numbers are just a rough guide, however, as every compressor is different. Generally speaking, the longer the attack time, the more of the transient you'll hear—i.e., the sound of the pick/fingers striking the string or the sound of a drumstick hitting the head of the drum—because the compressor won't clamp down on it. But when all is said and done, the most important thing is to simply use your ears. Experiment with the threshold, ratio, attack, and release times (if available) to find the sound that suits you best.

Let's have a listen to some various compressor settings and how they affect the sound of guitars and basses. For each track, you'll first hear the signal with the compression bypassed. Then you'll hear the same phrase played with compression.

207 Clean guitar: 3 dB of gain reduction with attack at 15 ms and release at 100 ms

208 Half-dirty guitar: 5 dB of gain reduction with attack at 20 ms and release at 60 ms

209 Distorted guitar: 3 dB of gain reduction with attack at 25 ms and release at 70 ms

210 Bass guitar: 3 dB of gain reduction with attack at 5 ms and release at 100 ms

211 Bass guitar: 3 dB of gain reduction with attack at 20 ms and release at 100 ms

212 Bass guitar: 3 dB of gain reduction with attack at 60 ms and release at 100 ms

213 Bass guitar: 6 dB of gain reduction with attack at 100 ms and release at 200 ms

214 Bass guitar: 6 dB of gain reduction with attack at 150 ms and release at 300 ms

As you can hear, the attack and release times will make quite a difference in the way the sound reacts. A very good exercise is to loop a riff or phrase and continually adjust the attack time from 0ms on up to hear the effect it creates, and then do the same with the release.

Vocal Compression

As with bass guitar, tracking vocals with compression is very common, as the decibel levels of a typical vocal track can be *all over the place*. In fact, it's sometimes necessary to track certain parts of a song with different level settings if the range gets too extreme. As with other instruments, the compression can come from an outboard piece of gear or a plugin, but the aim is the same: to tame the peaks of the track in order to make it more consistent throughout.

Compression Routing Procedure

To compress the signal after it's been recorded, simply add the plugin to the track's effect window and adjust the settings until you find the desired sound.

Printing the compressor effect is still fairly common for vocals, as well. If using an outboard compressor, plug the mic into your external preamp and send its output into the compressor. Run the output of the compressor to the input of your interface. Set the desired amount of compression and then set the levels on your DAW and assign/arm the track. Alternatively, your preamp may have an insert jack (common on mixers, for example) with which you could patch the compressor in, as well. In this case, the send cable would go to the compressor's input, and the return cable would go to the compressor's output. Or you may use a channel strip, such as the dbx 286s, in which case the compressor is built into the preamp.

However, since you don't have to worry about added tape hiss when recording digitally, you can leave a significant amount of headroom while recording the vocal—with the peaks remaining around -18 dB or so—to make sure you don't distort the signal, and then add all of your compression during mixdown. Still others do both of these, running through a compressor while tracking to help tame the peaks a bit and to make the level of the vocal that much easier to work with during the mixing process.

If using a plugin compressor, plug the mic into your interface or external preamp (which would then plug into your interface), set the levels, and assign and arm the track. Add the compressor plugin to your track's input effects window (this means the effect will be printed on the track) and set the desired amount of compression.

Typically, a good place to start is with a ratio between 2:1 and 4:1 with around 3 to 4 dB of gain reduction. The attack time is generally very quick (less than 10 ms), and the release is moderate to a little longer (between 250–300 ms, for example). Again, though, you should experiment to find what sounds best for each specific track. Let's have a listen to these types of settings on a few different vocal phrases to hear the effect (see Recording Index for signal-chain info). On each track, you'll first hear the uncompressed vocal, followed by the same phrase with the compression applied.

215 Male rock vocal with compression: 3 to 4 dB of gain reduction

216 Female rock vocal with compression: 3 to 4 dB of gain reduction

217 Male intimate vocal with compression: 3 to 4 dB of gain reduction

218 Female intimate vocal with compression: 3 to 4 dB of gain reduction

As you can hear, this is a subtle effect that just rounds out the edges a bit. The more gain reduction you use, the more drastic the effect will be. With gain reduction in the 15 to 20 dB range, for example, you'll really hear the compressor clamping down on the peaks, which can tend to sound unnatural in many cases.

🔊 **219** Male rock vocal with compression: 10 dB of gain reduction

🔊 **220** Female rock vocal with compression: 10 dB of gain reduction

🔊 **221** Male intimate vocal with compression: 10 dB of gain reduction

🔊 **222** Female intimate vocal with compression: 10 dB of gain reduction

It's definitely not so subtle anymore! On some very high-energy rock stuff, you may hear this type of compression being used, but if you're going for a natural, intimate sound, this type of setting is likely to stick out like a sore thumb.

Drum Compression

Even though we're not covering the subject of drum recording in this book, we can still certainly apply compression to our drum sounds. This is true of loops, entire stereo virtual drumkits (commonly referred to as a "drum bus"), or individual drums if you have them routed as such. Since the levels of drum samples are generally pretty well under control by default, the use of compression is generally done more for the effect they impart on the sound.

Compression Routing Procedure

To compress the signal of a loop or a stereo drum track, simply add the plugin to the track's effects window and adjust settings as desired.

If you want to compress an individual drum track in a virtual drum instrument, then you'll first need to set it up for multiple outputs. EZdrummer 2 gives you the choice of stereo routing or multiple outputs in which each virtual mic used on the kit will be sent to its own track in the DAW (see page 176 for more details). At that point, you can treat each one as its own separate instrument, adding whatever effects you'd like to the track's effects window.

Let's check out the sound we get from compressing various drum setups. For each track, you'll first hear the beat with the compression bypassed and then again with it active.

🔊 **223** Funky drum loop: 4 dB of gain reduction with attack at 10 ms and release at 100 ms

🔊 **224** Funky drum loop: 8 dB of gain reduction with attack at 30 ms and release at 150 ms

🔊 **225** Hard rock drum loop: 4 dB of gain reduction with attack at 10 ms and release at 100 ms

🔊 **226** Hard rock drum loop: 6 dB of gain reduction with attack at 20 ms and release at 70 ms

🔊 **227** EZdrummer 2 stereo drum bus - rock: 4 dB of gain reduction with attack at 10 ms and release at 100 ms

228 EZdrummer 2 stereo drum bus - rock: 10 dB of gain reduction with attack at 20 ms and release at 200 ms

229 EZdrummer 2 snare drum: 2 dB of gain reduction with attack at 10 ms and release at 100 ms

230 EZdrummer 2 snare drum: 4 dB of gain reduction with attack at 20 ms and release at 100 ms

231 EZdrummer 2 snare drum: 8 dB of gain reduction with attack at 30 ms and release at 600 ms

232 EZdrummer 2 kick drum: 2 dB of gain reduction with attack at 20 ms and release at 100 ms

233 EZdrummer 2 kick drum: 4 dB of gain reduction with attack at 30 ms and release at 100 ms

234 EZdrummer 2 kick drum: 8 dB of gain reduction with attack at 35 ms and release at 60 ms

It's very interesting to hear the sound of the drum(s) transformed with the simple twist of a few knobs. You can add extra punch and/or sustain with compression if you choose, or you can simply tame the peaks a bit and retain as natural a sound as possible.

Parallel Drum Compression

A very nifty trick that's frequently used on the drums is called *parallel compression*. This involves mixing two parallel signals: one uncompressed and one (usually very much) compressed. It's very common to compress the entire drum bus as a stereo set and then add that back in with the uncompressed individual drum tracks, for example. The routing for this can get a little tricky, but you'll get the hang of it.

What we want to do is set up our drum sounds with multiple outputs, as shown previously, so that we have independent control of each virtual drum mic. Then we want to create a stereo track called "Drum Bus" (or whatever you'd like to name it).

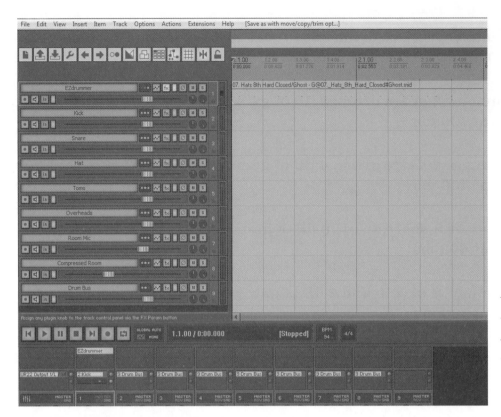

Each virtual drum mic has been routed from EZdrummer 2 to its own track, and a stereo "Drum Bus" track has been created.

Next, you'll want to open the Send window for each of the individual drum tracks and add a send to the Drum Bus track. Some DAWs, such as Reaper, will allow you to accomplish the same thing by opening the Send/Receive window for the Drum Bus track and adding *receives* from each individual drum track. It's the equivalent of tying a rope from the house to a tree or from a tree to the house.

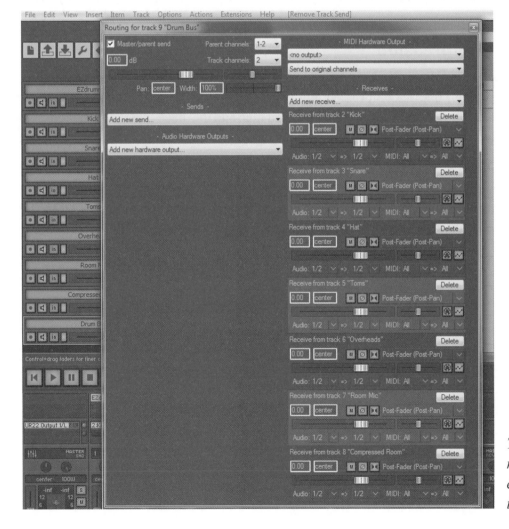

The Drum Bus track is receiving sends from each individual drum track

Attention: Forks in the Routing Road

When setting up these track sends, you want to make sure that the individual drum tracks are still going to the main mix, as well. In other words, the signal will be split: one part will go to the main mix, and the other—the amount determined by the send level—will head to the Drum Bus track. In Reaper, this is set with a tick box labeled "Master/Parent Send." If this box is not checked, then the signal will be sent to the Drum Bus track, but not the main mix. There are scenarios when you may want this, but this isn't one of those times. By default, in Reaper, this box is already checked.

By ticking this Master/Parent Send box, we're sending the track to two locations:
the main mix (Master/Parent) and the Drum Bus send.

Now that we've got the routing set up, we'll add the compressor plugin to the Drum Bus track. As mentioned earlier, it's common to really squash (compress a lot) the drum bus with this technique. Once you've achieved the desired sound, you can set the level of the compressed Drum Bus track in relation to the natural drums. Generally speaking, a little of the Drum Bus goes a pretty long way in this regard, but experiment and see what sounds good to you.

Let's hear this idea in action. First, here's a four-bar drum pattern with no compression:

 235 EZdrummer 2 pattern with no compression

And now we'll sneak in the parallel compressed track underneath it.

 236 **EZdrummer 2 pattern with parallel compression**

As you can hear, it's a nice trick. It combines punch and clarity with a natural, organic sound. It's a lot of fun to experiment with this idea in varying degrees. It can really bring an ordinary drum sound to life.

REVERB

The term "reverb" is short for *reverberation*, which describes the process of sound waves bouncing back and forth off of walls, floors, and ceilings. The difference between reverb and delay (or echo) is that, whereas delay consists of one or more distinct repeats of a signal, reverb consists of so many that they just end up blending into one continuous wash of sound. A canyon will generally produce a delay, whereas a large church will produce reverb.

Back in the early days of recording, they had to generate reverb by either recording in a large room or using other mechanical devices, such as plates (large sheets of metal that would vibrate in response to signals) or chambers. Nowadays, all of these physical types of reverbs are usually recreated digitally with one or more external processors or plugins. Most DAW programs will usually come with some reverb plugins, many of which can sound very nice. There are also many affordable, amazing-sounding reverb plugins that you can choose to add if you'd like. Waves offers numerous choices in this regard, including Renaissance Reverb and TrueVerb (see sidebar for details). If you're looking for an external unit, TC Electronic makes the M350 (see page 40 for details), which is an affordable multi-effects unit with some very nice-sounding reverbs.

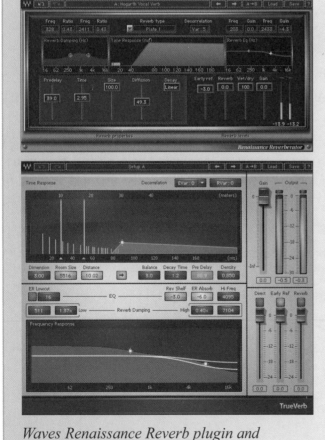

Waves Renaissance Reverb plugin and Waves TrueVerb plugin

The Waves Renaissance Reverb and TrueVerb plugins offer lush-sounding alternatives to any reverbs that may be included in your DAW software. You can never have too many great-sounding reverbs. Okay, maybe you can have too many, but it certainly helps to have several from which to choose. They'll all sound slightly different, and one may really shine on one song while another hits the mark on another song. This isn't to say that you can't make a great-sounding recording with only one reverb—you certainly can. But, just because you can live off PB&J your whole life, doesn't mean you have to.

TrueVerb features comprehensive control over numerous aspects of the effect, including early reflections, damping, density, room size, and many more in an attractive interface. Dozens of included presets allow you to quickly find something suitable and tweak from there, which can be an excellent alternative to starting from scratch when you're still learning how to use the plugin. Renaissance Reverb allows you to choose from 12 different reverb types and to customize them with numerous parameters for fine tuning. This is really nice for those who aren't well-versed in what different types of reverb (room, hall, plate, spring, etc.) sound like. However, you can certainly go deep enough to tailor the verbs to your liking once you decide to get more specific.

Both of these plugins sound lush and beautiful and would be worthy additions to anyone's effect arsenal. Reverb is one of the most commonly misunderstood effects, which is interesting considering it's the most commonly used effect of all. These plugins from Waves certainly provide you with the tools and parameters to grow as your understanding of reverb grows, as well, allowing you to color your music with the most stunning detail.

Street price: $149 each

Reverb is used to create a sense of space or depth in a recording. If you think about it, the way we record many instruments—i.e., by close-miking them—is not a very natural way to hear them. In other words, we rarely stick our ears right up to a guitar amp or a singer's mouth. We normally hear these instruments from a distance, which results in some added ambience. So a reverb effect can help to make things sound more natural. It can also be used as an effect of its own, where we're not necessarily going for a natural sound.

Generally speaking, the more reverb you add to something, the farther away it's going to sound. If you add no reverb at all to an instrument that was close-miked in a dead environment, it's going to sound very dry and forward. Sometimes this can be used to good effect, but it's generally not a very natural sound.

A Reverb for All Occasions

The main types of reverb most commonly found on a plugin or external effect are:

- **Hall:** This refers to a large concert hall. The reverb time (or decay) is generally quite long (up to three seconds or more), and these are especially useful for orchestral instruments.

- **Chamber:** A chamber usually refers to a rectangular, reflective room—usually made from concrete or wood—that was often used to generate reverbs in studios during the 1950s and 1960s. The reverb times are generally shorter than that of a hall—up to about two seconds or so.

- **Room:** This is fairly self-explanatory and suggests the sound of a room. This could be something as small as a bedroom or something as large as a ballroom. The reverb times generally fall within one second.

- **Plate:** The plate reverb was one of the first artificial methods of creating reverb. By suspending a metal plate and applying a signal to it via a surface-mounted transducer, the plate would vibrate. These vibrations were picked up by a contact microphone at another position on the plate. Due to their relative low cost and small size (when compared to building a chamber, for example), they were used extensively from the 1960s to the 1980s until digital reverbs became commonplace.

- **Spring:** This is the type of reverb commonly found in guitar amps today. Similar to a plate, a signal vibrates a set of springs to create the effect.

Parameters

A typical reverb may have various settings, which can help you tailor the sound of the effect to your needs. These can include:

- **Pre-delay:** This is the amount of time—usually expressed in milliseconds—that the effect will wait before applying reverb to a signal. This is commonly used when adding reverb to a vocal, as it allows a bit of clarity before the reverb begins.

- **Size:** This refers to the physical dimension of the space being emulated. As expected, larger sizes tend to have longer delay times.

- **Decay Time:** This represents the amount of time before the reverb has completely diffused. This is often linked to the Size parameter in some plugins.

- **Early Reflections:** This sets the level of the first reflections coming back from the imaginary space. Higher settings generally work better on more sustained sounds, such as synth pads or strings, as opposed to, say, percussion.

- **Damping:** This setting simulates the phenomenon that occurs when, say, a concert hall fills up with people: the reverb loses high frequencies. The more damping you add, the less bright the reverb will sound.

- **EQ (high or low):** You can often EQ the signal going into your reverb with settings such as this. For example, you can try reducing the highs—from around 5kHz or so—if your reverb sounds a little metallic or shrill. Conversely, reducing the low end going into the reverb can help it from sounding too muddy, especially when used on things like a kick drum.

- **Mix:** This sets the ratio of dry to wet (effected) signal that leaves the reverb unit. If you're using the reverb in a send, you'll generally set this to 100% wet and adjust the send level of the instruments to set the desired balance. If you're using the reverb as an insert effect—i.e., the complete signal is passing through the unit before moving on—then you'll use the Mix control on the reverb to set the dry/effect balance.

- **Level:** This determines the overall output of the reverb effect.

If your plugin or external unit comes with presets, they will most likely set these types of parameters in typical fashion for you. Therefore, a great way to become familiar with these settings is to start with a preset and then begin to tweak one parameter at a time, noting what it does to the sound.

Let's have a listen to hear how some various reverbs sound. For each example, you'll first hear the signal dry and then again with the reverb added.

237 Waves Renaissance Reverb: Acoustic guitar with hall reverb

238 Waves Renaissance Reverb: Acoustic guitar with plate reverb

239 Waves Renaissance Reverb: Electric guitar with room reverb

240 Waves Renaissance Reverb: Electric guitar with spring reverb

241 TC Electronic M350: Percussion with plate reverb

242 TC Electronic M350: Drum overheads with room reverb

243 TC Electronic M350: Strings with chamber reverb

 244 TC Electronic M350: Piano with hall reverb

Again, don't be afraid to turn (or drag with the mouse) some knobs to hear what they do! Experimentation can be an excellent teacher. You'll not only learn what generally sounds best (and why), but you'll most likely stumble upon some unique sounds of your own.

DELAY

Delay is another word for echo, and both refer to a distinct repeat (or set of repeats) of a signal. Like reverb, delay adds a sense of distance to an instrument. It's commonly applied to vocals, guitars, and synths, among other things.

Parameters

Just as with reverb, a typical delay unit or plugin will have several user-adjusted settings you can tweak. Most commonly, this will include:

- **Delay Time:** This specifies the length of time, usually in milliseconds, before the first delay is heard, as well as any repeats that follow.

- **Feedback:** This determines how many repeats will be heard. They'll generally get quieter with each one.

- **LPF/Damping:** Some delays feature a low pass filter or damping, which allows you to decrease the high frequencies on the repeats. This is characteristic of old analog or tape-based delay systems, and many plugins offer settings (or are entirely dedicated) to help emulate this.

- **Rate/Depth:** Some delays offer *modulation*, which allows you to create a chorused effect along with the delays. The depth setting determines how far the pitch will vary, and the rate determines how quickly it will do so in a cycle.

- **Mix:** As with reverb, this sets the dry/wet balance of the effect. Typically set it at 100% when using the delay in a send and adjust to taste when using as an insert effect.

- **Level:** This determines the level of the delayed signal (but doesn't affect your dry signal).

Delayed Gratification

There are several categories of delay, including slapback, timed, stereo/mono, and ping pong.

Slapback Delay: This refers to a short delay time—generally between 20 and 80 ms—with only one repeat (low feedback setting) and volume comparable to the dry signal. You've heard it in countless rockabilly songs, such as "Mystery Train," and John Lennon made extensive use of it in the 1970s on songs like "Instant Karma," as did many others.

Timed Delay: This refers to a delay time that aligns rhythmically with the tempo of the song in some way. Common values include eighth note, quarter note, dotted eighth note, or quarter-note triplet. U2's The Edge often uses this trick—especially the dotted eighth note—in his guitar parts, but you'll hear it on vocals quite a bit, as well. The Pink Floyd song "Us and Them" has a classic example of a quarter-note delay on the vocals.

Mono Delay: A mono delay refers to one in which only one delayed signal is present. Most analog delay guitar pedals (and digital ones that emulate them) are like this.

Stereo/Ping-Pong Delay: With a stereo delay, the repeats can be made to bounce back and forth between the left and right side of the stereo field.

Here are a few different delay settings as applied to electric guitar. You'll hear the same phrase first played with no delay and then again with the delay added.

🔊 **245** AmpliTube 3: slapback delay

🔊 **246** AmpliTube 3: ping-pong delay

🔊 **247** DigiTech Element XP: timed delay (dotted eighth note)

🔊 **248** DigiTech Element XP: timed delay (eighth note)

MODULATION EFFECTS

In this category, we'll include effects that include some sort of modulation. This can pertain to pitch, volume, or frequency. Sometimes delay is included in this category, as they often contain the ability to modulate pitch, as well (though not all delays do). These effects are generally the more noticeable ones and can usually be singled out even by non-guitarists (or non-musicians) as an "effect."

Tremolo

Tremolo is a modulation of volume and is commonly built into guitar amplifiers—the instrument on which it's most commonly used. (It's actually mislabeled as "vibrato" on old Fender amplifiers. Humorously, Fender also misnamed the vibrato bars on their Stratocasters as "tremolo" bars.) The effect, which constitutes a continuous rising and dipping of volume, was very common in ballads of the 1950s, such as "All I Have to Do Is Dream," by the Everly Brothers, or psychedelic rock of the 1960s, such as "Crimson and Clover," by Tommy James & The Shondells. It's never gone out of style, however, and can be heard throughout the years on countless hits. Another very common use of tremolo is on a Rhodes-style electric piano.

The two parameters for tremolo are usually *rate* and *depth*, which control how fast the volume-changing cycle occurs and how low the volume dips, respectively. Here's how the effect sounds in various settings. You'll hear the same phrases first played with no effect and then again with the tremolo added.

🔊 **249** AmpliTube 3: Gentle tremolo on clean electric guitar

🔊 **250** AmpliTube 3: Time-based tremolo (rate set to eighth note) on half-dirty electric guitar

🔊 **251** DigiTech RP360XP: Moderate tremolo on distorted electric guitar

🔊 **252** DigiTech RP360XP: Stuttering tremolo (very high depth setting) on distorted electric guitar

253 Lounge Lizard Session: Smooth tremolo on Rhodes electric piano

 254 Lounge Lizard Session: Moderate tremolo on half-dirty Wurlitzer electric piano

Vibrato

Whereas tremolo steadily modulates the volume of a signal, vibrato does the same with pitch. It takes the entire signal and gradually (or quickly) detunes it and retunes it over and over. It's most commonly heard on guitars (Jimi Hendrix used it often) and organ (Hammond organs are often played through a Leslie rotating speaker cabinet, which produces the vibrato effect—guitarists use Leslie cabinets in this regard, as well).

The two parameters are normally *rate* and *depth*, as with tremolo, only here the depth refers to pitch instead of volume. Let's check it out with a few examples. First you'll hear the unaffected phrase and then again with the vibrato.

 255 AmpliTube 3: Moderate vibrato on clean electric guitar

 256 DigiTech RP360XP: Moderate vibrato on half-dirty electric guitar

 257 J&BB3: Slight vibrato on Hammond organ

 258 J&BB3: Heavy vibrato on Hammond organ

Chorus

The chorus effect modulates pitch over time. It does this by splitting the signal in two and then delaying and detuning/retuning one of the signals while the other (dry) signal stays constant. The result is somewhat reminiscent of a "chorus" singing. This effect was all over the 1980s on guitar and keyboards and is used a bit more sparingly today. It's also heard on bass guitar at times, as well.

The parameters of a chorus effect usually include *rate* (how fast one pitch-changing cycle completes), *depth* (how far the signal is detuned), and *level* (the volume of the modulated signal). Some choruses also include *pre-delay* (or sometimes labeled just *delay*—the amount of time the modulated signal is delayed from the original) and *feedback* (sends the chorused signal back through the effect for an exaggerated effect).

Let's check out how it sounds on various instruments and settings. You'll first hear each phrase dry and then again with the chorus effect.

 259 AmpliTube 3: Slight chorus on clean electric guitar

 260 AmpliTube 3: Moderate chorus on bass guitar

 261 DigiTech RP360XP: Watery chorus (high depth setting) on clean electric guitar

 262 DigiTech RP360XP: Thick chorus on half-dirty electric guitar

 **263** Breedlove Pursuit: Moderate chorus on acoustic guitar

 **264** Lounge Lizard Session: Light chorus on Rhodes electric piano

 **265** Analog Session: Moderate chorus on brass synth patch

Flanging

A flange effect is basically created by splitting the signal in two and delaying the second one by a gradually increasing and decreasing time period. This produces comb filtering as the phase of the two signals shifts throughout the cycle. The result, in its most drastic form, is usually heard as a swooshing, "jet plane"-type of sound that's quite recognizable. A flange effect is actually capable of much more, however. Though it's common on guitar—Van Halen's "Unchained" features a very prominent use— it's also been used over the years on drums, vocals, keys, and sometimes an entire mix, as well.

The parameters on a flanger usually include *rate* (sometimes labeled *speed*, it determines the rate of the cycle), *depth* (sometimes labeled *width*, it determines the depth of the delay spread), *delay time* (determines when the delay cycle begins after the original signal), and *regeneration* (or *feedback*, which again feeds the effected signal back into itself for more intense effects).

Here are a few examples to demonstrate what this effect can do. You'll hear the examples first dry and then with the flange effect.

 **266** AmpliTube 3: Heavy flanging on distorted electric guitar

267 AmpliTube 3: Slight flanging on clean electric guitar

268 EZdrummer 2: Heavy flanging applied to drum pattern

269 Moderate flange applied to entire mix of guitar, bass, and drums

Phasing

The phasing effect is similar to that of flanging, but it's less uniform. Whereas flanging delays the entire signal to achieve its effect, phasing works by filtering the signal and delay-shifting different frequencies by different amounts. The result is an uneven, lopsided swooshing sound as compared to a flanger. It was very common in the 1970s on guitar (check out Pink Floyd's "Have a Cigar" for a perfect example) and keys and is still used today a good bit.

Simplistic phasers feature *rate* (or *speed*) as the only parameter, but others also sometimes include *resonance* and/or *depth* for more control over the effect, as well. Let's check it out on a few sources to hear what it sounds like.

270 AmpliTube 3: Moderate phasing on clean electric guitar

271 AmpliTube 3: Heavy phasing on half-dirty electric guitar

272 Lounge Lizard Session: Light phasing on Rhodes electric piano

273 Moderate phasing on background vocals

WAH WAH AND ENVELOPE FILTER

The wah wah and envelope filter effects work by sweeping through the frequency spectrum and emphasizing a certain frequency. In the case of the wah-wah pedal, you're controlling the frequency that's being boosted via the pedal's position. When you sweep from a low-boosted frequency (pedal up) to a high one (pedal down) while playing a note, you get the typical "wah wah" sound (think "Voodoo Chile" by Hendrix). An envelope filter achieves similar effects automatically by responding to the strength of the input signal (the solo to "What I Am," by Edie Brickell & New Bohemians, is a prime example). Both are most commonly heard on guitar and keyboard, although you'll hear them on bass at times, as well.

Let's check out a few examples to hear these effects in action. First you'll hear the phrases dry and then again with the effect.

274 Morley Classic Wah: Clean electric guitar with wah

275 Morley Classic Wah: Distorted electric guitar solo with wah

276 DigiTech RP360XP: Clean electric guitar with envelope filter

277 Lounge Lizard Session: Rhodes electric piano with envelope filter

While there are other effects available, this chapter certainly represents a collection of some of the most commonly used in the world of recording. As always, feel free to experiment however you like. If putting a drum bus through a tremolo effect sounds great to you, by all means go for it! You're limited only by your imagination.

CHAPTER 14
MOBILE DEVICES – TODAY'S PORTABLE STUDIO

Tascam released the first "Portastudio," the 144, back in 1979 with a price tag of around $1,000. This was a cassette-based four-track recorder with two-band shelving EQ (bass and treble), one cue mix, one auxiliary (effect) send, and the ability to record two tracks at a time. It did record at twice the normal tape speed, however, which helped the fidelity, and it allowed for 15% pitch control in either direction, which was nice if your song wasn't exactly recorded at A440 but you needed to record an instrument that wasn't quickly tunable (such as a piano). As mentioned earlier in the book, Bruce Springsteen famously recorded his sixth studio album, *Nebraska*, on this machine in 1982. Oh, and it measured 18 by 15 inches and weighed 20 pounds.

Fast forward to today, and you have portable studios that fit into the palm of your hand with more flexibility and processing options for a fraction of the price. There are still several dedicated portable studios on the market, such as Tascam's DP-006 6-track studio ($100 street price), Tascam's DP-008EX 8-track studio ($150 street price), and Boss' Micro BR-80 8-track recorder ($249 street price), and they're all capable of great-sounding recordings on the go. But ever since smartphones and tablets took over the planet, the portable recording trend has been moving toward them steadily. It's now to the point where you can achieve phenomenal results if you play to the platform's strengths.

Pros and Cons of a Smartphone/Tablet Studio

Considering that most people already own a usable device, a smartphone or tablet-based studio could be the biggest bang-for-buck studio of all. Of course, they're not for everybody or every situation. Here are some of the positives and negatives of these setups that you should consider when debating whether or not you'd like to go this route.

Pros

- You probably already own a suitable device.

- The software apps are very inexpensive, relatively speaking, when compared to home computer setups, with usable DAW programs ranging anywhere from $0 to about $30 on the top end.

- Since you are used to carrying this device around, it's even that much more portable.

- It's fun to feel as though you're getting some serious use out of the thing beyond email and texts.

Cons

- You generally won't have the flexibility of a home-based setup. For example, Apple's GarageBand app won't allow you (at this time) to create a dynamic mix. In other words, settings such as pan, volume, and effects can be set differently for each instrument, but when you mix the song down, they'll remain that way through the song's entirety and can't be adjusted mid-song.

- You may have other limitations, such as maximum track count, effects, etc.

- Your interface options may be limited, depending on your chosen platform. Apple has the upper hand here, with numerous dedicated accessories made for smartphone/tablet recording.

- The screen will obviously be smaller than your full-size monitor, and parameters adjustments may be a bit more cumbersome, as well.

A Word on Platforms

At the moment, there are basically two routes you can go when it comes to the mobile platform: Apple iOS or something else (such as Android or Windows). This is because Apple is currently the only company with dedicated hardware interfaces specifically built for mobile devices, such as their iPod Touch, iPhone, or iPad. Things haven't yet been standardized for Android or Windows, and therefore it's a bit more prickly when it comes to functionality on these devices. Things are beginning to change, however (see below), so don't throw out your Android phone yet!

Recently, Android phones added the ability to use USB interfaces (the same ones that plug into your home computer) as a means of getting high-quality signals into your device. However, the device has to support USB host mode (not all do), and even then, it can sometimes be a little buggy, depending on the device/interface combination. It's not a completely standardized system yet, but several main hurdles have been cleared, and it shouldn't be too long before they get it completely smoothed out.

iOS ACCESSORIES

Apple got the head start in the mobile recording world, and thus there are numerous devices on the market for this purpose, including interfaces, microphones, mixers, keyboards/controllers, and more. IK Multimedia leads the charge here (see sidebar for details), with interfaces dedicated to microphones, MIDI, guitar/bass, or all three combined, not to mention guitar pedals, stands, clips, and accessories. But other manufacturers, such as Alesis, Apogee, Line 6, Mackie, and Yamaha, all produce similar products, as well.

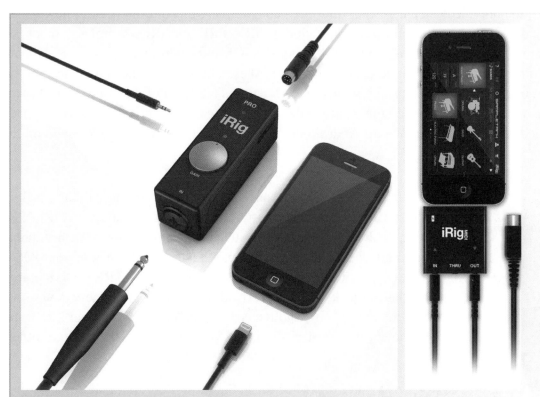

iRig PRO audio and MIDI interface for iOS and iRig MIDI interface for iOS
Copyright IK Multimedia, used with permission.

IK Multimedia's line of iOS devices allows you the freedom to travel with a professional studio like never before. An iPad or iPhone (or iPod Touch), an IK Multimedia accessory, a mic and/or instrument, a pair of cables and some headphones, and you're good to go. And when I say "good to go," I mean it! The quality you can achieve on these things now is truly amazing.

With iRig MIDI, you plug the unit into the device's charging port. It has 1/8-inch MIDI in, out, and thru jacks that connect to your MIDI equipment (keyboard, drum machine, drum pad, etc.) via two included cables with one 1/8-inch end and one standard MIDI five-pin end. There's even a micro USB port (with cable included) so your iOS device can remain charged for longer recording sessions. LED arrows show MIDI in/out activity.

If you're planning on doing both MIDI and audio recording on your iOS device, then the iRig PRO has you covered. In one succinct package, you have an 1/8-inch MIDI in jack (with included 1/8-inch-to-standard MIDI cable), a combo 1/4-inch/XLR jack, and a port for connecting to your iOS device or computer (including three cable types—30-pin, Lightning cable, and USB—to cover all your configurations). You want more? How about the fact that it has switchable phantom power (with LED display), which is provided via a 9-volt battery, so you can record with your nice condenser mics, as well. A gain dial lets you adjust the input signal, and a peak LED indicates clipping. The build quality of the unit is excellent—it feels nice and sturdy—and the connectors all feel solid.

I tried out both units using my iPhone 4 and was up and running in no time flat with each. Both units also come with free apps, such as SampleTank Free and others, to get you started. For portability and functionality—not to mention ease of use—you really can't ask for more. Now you have no excuse for not recording any time inspiration strikes!

Street price: iRig PRO – $149.99, iRig MIDI – $69.99

ANDROID ACCESSORIES

At the moment, the only dedicated hardware interfaces compatible with Android (that I know of) are by IK Multimedia. They have several devices, including iRig PRE and iRig 2, among others (see sidebar), that are either cross-platform (compatible with both iOS and Android devices) or specifically designed for Android. I haven't had the opportunity to try these out with an Android device yet, but the reviews are extremely favorable, and it seems to work without a hitch. For the price ($39.99 each), you simply can't beat it! Note that all of these are audio-only devices, and at this time, no one appears to produce a dedicated MIDI interface for Android devices. However, there is a workaround on this (see below).

IK Multimedia is currently the only company on the market that's making interfaces specifically designed to work with an Android device. iRig PRE features an XLR mic jack with switchable phantom power, a headphone jack, and an attached cord that plugs into the headphone jack of your iOS or Android device. As long as your Android device uses a TRRS configuration for its headphone jack—which nearly all major brands do these days—then you'll be good to go. The iRig PRE comes with the iRig Recorder FREE app, a simple waveform recorder/editor, and VocaLive FREE, a live vocal effects processor.

The iRig 2 is a guitar interface for iOS and Android that features a 1/4-inch instrument input, an 1/8-inch headphone jack, a 1/4-inch amplifier output jack, and an attached cable to connect to the headphone jack of your portable device. An FX/Thru switch lets you choose between a processed signal (i.e., using an amp simulation app) or a clean, unprocessed signal that can run out the amp output to your amp. In this way, the iRig 2 could be used as a tuner or simply a recorder while your signal will pass through to your amp

iRig PRE audio interface for iOS and Android devices

untouched. As a bonus, iRig 2 comes with the AmpliTube FREE app, so you can start laying down some mean tracks right away.

The Android world may have gotten off to a slow start in the mobile audio interface department, but it's finally coming around. Until it becomes standard practice, we can thank IK Multimedia for leading the charge.

Street price: $39.99 each

Another possibility for Android users recently arrived via eXtream Software Development. The company developed an app known as USB Audio Recorder PRO, which enables you to use any USB interface with your Android device. There are a few catches:

- You need to buy an inexpensive USB OTG cable. These are easily found online for under $5 (including shipping).

- Although the setup works on many devices, there are some devices and/or interfaces known to not function. (The company provides a list of known tested devices/interfaces on their site and even offers a refund for the app if you discover that your setup is non-functioning.)

- You can only use the functionality with eXtream apps. Currently, this includes USB Audio Recorder PRO, which is a basic stereo (or mono) digital recorder, and Audio Evolution Mobile, which is a full-featured DAW that records audio and MIDI (see sidebar for details). Note, however, that some in-app purchases are required to use the full functionality of Audio Evolution Mobile.

Audio Evolution Mobile

Audio Evolution Mobile is a powerful DAW app for Android devices that records unlimited audio and MIDI tracks (dependent only on the speed of your device). You have full editing capabilities, the ability to import several audio file types (WAV, AIFF, FLAC, OGG/Vorbis) or MIDI files, and built-in effects such as chorus, compression, delay, reverb, EQ, flanger, noise gate, and tremolo. You can even add automation for almost any parameter (volume, panning, etc.) and add crossfades for creating dynamic mixes, which can be mastered to a stereo WAV, AIFF, or FLAC file.

Although the basic app sells for $7.85, there are a few additional in-app purchases you'll need to make to take full advantage of all its features. These include additional effects packages, MIDI functionality, and USB device input functionality. With all of these upgrades (none of which cost more than $6 or so), you'll be equipped to plug a USB-powered audio interface—such as the Steinberg UR22—into your Android device for recording microphone or instrument signals or MIDI data. Alternatively, you can record MIDI tracks with a USB-powered external MIDI controller by using only an OTG cable. I've done this with an Android phone, and it worked flawlessly. AEM comes with a 16-channel virtual MIDI instrument sound module based on the SoundFont format that sounds very good. To my knowledge, there's not currently a way to record the sound of another app on your device (a synth app, for example) within AEM. You can, however, do this via USB interface and an external synth.

AEM is a powerful app that allows for extensive recording and editing. The only thing it lacks when compared to iOS systems is the integration of third-party apps, but seeing as this seems to be an Android issue across the board, I can't dock them any points for this. The sound quality of the effects is very good, and the layout is well-designed even when using it on a phone as opposed to a tablet. For Android users, there's no reason to wait anymore. Grab AEM and start making some music!

Street price: $7.85

RECORDING APPS

There are numerous recording apps available for both platforms that run the gamut from a basic four-track recorder to a full-featured DAW. The good news is that the most expensive of these only reaches around $20 (although some do feature optional in-app purchases for more flexibility, etc.). Let's take a look at some of the more common.

iOS
- GarageBand (Apple)
- Music Studio (Alexander Gross)
- MultiTrack DAW (Harmonicdog)
- AmpliTube for iPad, $19.99 (IK Multimedia) (Though predominantly a guitar amp simulator, it can be upgraded via in-app purchase to include a Studio feature that allows for eight-track recording on iPad, four on iPhone)
- Auria (WaveMachine Labs)

Android
- Audio Evolution Mobile (eXtream Software)
- FL Studio Mobile (Image-Line)
- Recording Studio Pro (Glauco)
- J4T Multitrack Recorder (Jaytronix)
- FourTracks Pro (NomadicWhales.com)

Cross-Platform
- n-Track Studio Multitrack Recorder (n-Track Software)

This list only includes apps that act like multi-track recording programs, but there are also numerous apps that are geared toward other areas of music production, such as synths, beat makers/drum machines, etc. Again, most of these are very reasonably priced, and many are available in a free version so you can try them out first to see if you like them.

SUMMARY

If portability is your prime factor, you'd be doing yourself an injustice by not investing in a mobile device recording studio. It may take a bit of getting used to at first, and there may be a slight learning curve, as with any system, but once you're up and running, you can have a very powerful system on your hands capable of producing professional sounds just about anywhere you find yourself.

CHAPTER 15
EDITING

After you've recorded all your tracks, the final step before mixing is *editing*. This is a step that can vary greatly from person to person. Whereas some may not even choose to edit anything at all (a stereo live-in-the-studio recording, perhaps), others may spend the bulk of their time here, building the song up brick by brick. It's also a little nebulous because many people incorporate editing techniques during the tracking process and/or before the application of any effects processing. Still others, who work predominantly with samples and loops, forego tracking entirely and basically begin immediately at the editing stages.

Nevertheless, we're going to cover some common uses and techniques for editing that apply to the majority of recordists at one point or another. In this chapter, we'll generally assume that you've recorded a multi-track song and you still have a bit of tidying up, rearranging, tweaking, or fine-tuning remaining before you're ready to begin the mixdown process.

COMMON REASONS FOR EDITING

Before we get into specifics, let's look at a few of the most common reasons why you'd need to edit in the first place. As mentioned earlier, if you're going for an organic, natural-sounding recording that's as close to "being there" as possible, then none of this may apply to you. But the typical pop/rock recording will often involve one or more of these elements:

- **Song Arrangement:** This is one of the broadest editing strokes you can make. What if, after recording the song, you decide that you really want the chorus to repeat at the end of the song? Well, if you recorded to a click, it's usually a fairly simple procedure of copying and pasting. If you don't want the repeat to be verbatim, you have the option of re-tracking one or more elements (if possible and/or desirable) or using some other tricks to achieve a similar result, which we'll look at in a bit.

- **Timing Issues:** This is a very commonly used technique. If upon listening back, you discover that the bass is rushed on a few beats, and you'd rather not punch in or re-track the part, it's fairly simple to move a few notes forward or backward in time to align better with the beat. It's also possible to stretch or condense certain notes in order for them to fit within a certain time frame if they're too long or too short. The further you go with this type of thing, the more unnatural it will sound. But if you're within 10% to 20% of the original tempo (and much more is possible), for example, it won't leave any audible artifacts whatsoever.

- **"Comping" Takes:** *Comping* (short for "compiling") involves choosing different parts of several different takes for the same instrument and patching them together into one finished track. The most common application of this technique is usually vocals. Many people will record several (four, ten, twenty, or more) vocal takes of the whole song, or a difficult section, and then listen through each, deciding which phrase (or word) is the best from each.

- **Level Adjustments:** Just as with timing concerns, if a few notes of the guitar solo are sticking out like a sore thumb because they're way too loud and can't be tamed with a compressor without undesirable artifacts, it's easy to adjust the volume of those notes.

- **Getting Rid of Unwanted Notes:** A great deal of the editing process simply involves tidying up a bit. You may have a noisy amp that buzzes on a track. While the guitar is playing, the noise may not be noticeable, but it may be quite noticeable (especially through headphones) when the guitarist is not playing anything. There also may be some mistakes or goofing off at certain points. Any of these instances that you don't want in the recording are easily removed.

- **Pitch Correction:** Again, most commonly used for vocals, pitch correction has completely changed the recording industry, for better or worse. Performance was great, but that high note is just a little flat? No problem—just run it through Auto-Tune, and all is right. Although it's extremely common in the world of professional recording—definitely the norm rather than the exception—it's still a greatly debated topic in the world of home recording. Some people have a real ethical issue with it, while others see it as nothing more than a tool at their disposal.

Although this list could go on and on, most editing techniques will usually fall within one of these categories. It's important to realize—if you didn't already know—that just about all of these editing techniques are *non-destructive*. Among other things, this means that, regardless of what you do to a media item, the original file is still intact on your hard drive and can be accessed if necessary. This is the single biggest difference between digital editing and analog editing back in the day, which involved cutting and splicing tape.

Tools of the Trade

Regardless of which DAW program you choose, you'll no doubt be using many of the same editing tools and features, although they may have slightly different names. Much like a word processing program, these are usually fairly self-explanatory; in fact, if you can edit a word document, you'll find audio editing to be quite similar in some respects. Let's look at the most common tools in the editing shed:

Cut/Copy/Paste: These work just as in a word processor. You select a media item (audio or MIDI) and either cut it (leaving an empty space) or copy it, which allows you to paste it at some other point—within the same track, a different track, or even a different song for that matter if you have more than one project open.

Split/Divide: This simply refers to splitting one media item into two so that they can be worked on independently. For example, if you want to nudge a bass note a little forward because it was rushed, you can split the item just before and after the note so that it can be moved (dragged) without moving the rest of the take.

Glue/Join: The opposite of split or divide, the glue tool allows you to join together two separate media items so that they may be treated as one.

Move: Rather than cut and paste an item or items (or portion thereof), you can simply drag it to a new place. This accomplishes the same thing, save for the contents of your clipboard.

Zoom: This feature allows you to magnify one or more items in the media window—horizontally or vertically—when necessary for precise edits.

Select/Marquee/Lasso: These are simply different types of methods used for selecting media items, or sections of them, that you need to edit in some way. They're not unlike those found on a graphic image editor.

Time Stretch: This feature allows you to stretch a media item without changing its pitch (if desired). For example, if, after moving a poorly timed guitar note, there's a noticeable gap left, you can stretch the note a bit to entirely fill the space needed.

Snap/Grid Tool: This is a feature that allows media items to snap, horizontally (time-wise), to a grid that you establish—every quarter note or eighth note, for example.

Trim Tool: This allows you to shave off portions from the beginning or ending of a media item.

Fade Tool: This allows you to apply fade-ins or fade-outs to media items.

Depending on your particular DAW, these tools may have different names or may be executed in slightly different ways, so consult your manual as necessary.

Before beginning any edits, I recommend that you just listen through the song a few times without concentrating on any one particular thing. If something jumps out at you, make a note of it. Then, if you feel it's necessary, you can go back through with a fine-toothed comb and concentrate on each instrument. Different people have different thoughts and standards on this. Some want to retain as much "human" feel as possible, others want everything to sound perfect, and many lie somewhere in between. There's no right or wrong in this regard, so it's entirely up to you and your aesthetic.

Let's take a closer look at each editing procedure and see what's involved. These are in no particular order, but I usually start with the "big picture" jobs first. You'll quickly find out which order you prefer and what suits your workflow best.

EDITING THE ARRANGEMENT OF THE SONG

To me, this is the first editing step because it has the capacity to affect things by the greatest amount. It's a "big picture" decision. This procedure largely involves the move, copy, and paste tools. In the following example, we're going copy the intro of a song and insert it after the first A section to serve as an interlude. If you haven't already, this is a good time to place markers in your song, identifying the various sections, as this can make locating specific phrases quicker and easier.

Here's how our guitar riff looks and sounds originally. Notice that the B section immediately follows the A section.

 278 Original song form

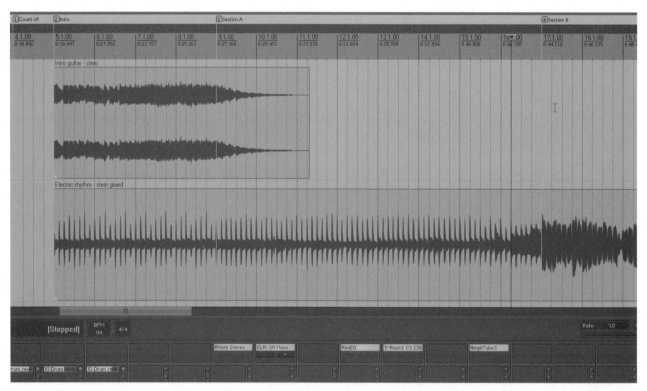

Originally, section B immediately followed section A.

The first thing we need to do, if it's not already done, is split the media item at the end of the A section. Again, if you recorded to a click, these types of operations are much easier. You'll want to have the "snap to grid" feature enabled at this point. It's not impossible if you didn't use a click, but it's usually a bit more time-consuming. (If you didn't use a click, "snap to grid" should be disabled.)

We'll select the media item after the split (the beginning of section B) and move it forward to allow room for the added section; in this case, four measures.

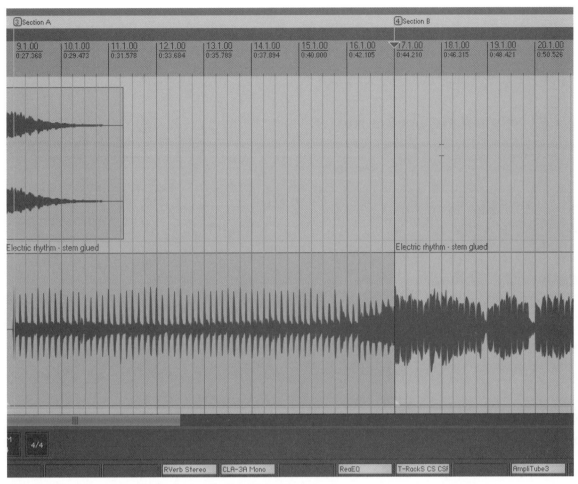

The media item is split at the end of section A.

The media item is moved forward four measures.

Next, we need to make sure the intro is sectioned off by splitting the item at its end if necessary. Then we simply select the four measures of the intro, copy them, and paste them in place. To paste them, move the cursor to the beginning of the space and use the paste command. **Note:** If you were doing this with multiple tracks, you want to make sure you have the first of those tracks selected when you go to paste them. In other words, if you copied tracks 1–4 from measures 3–6 and want to paste them at measure 12, be sure you have track 1 selected when you paste them at measure 12.

Here's how our new arrangement sounds and looks:

 279 New song form after edit

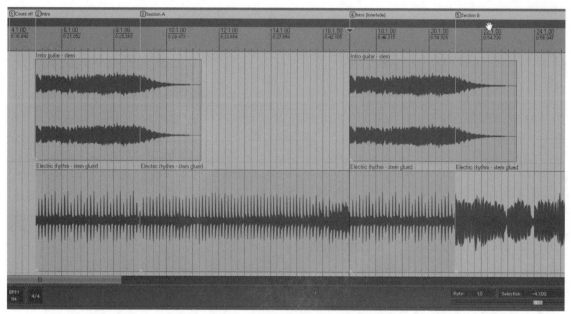

The four-measure intro has now been inserted as an interlude between sections A and B.

As an alternative to moving (dragging) the item in order to make room for the new section, you can also usually insert an empty space in the selected area. This has the benefit of keeping your markers aligned with the rest of the song, as they'll move forward with the added empty space.

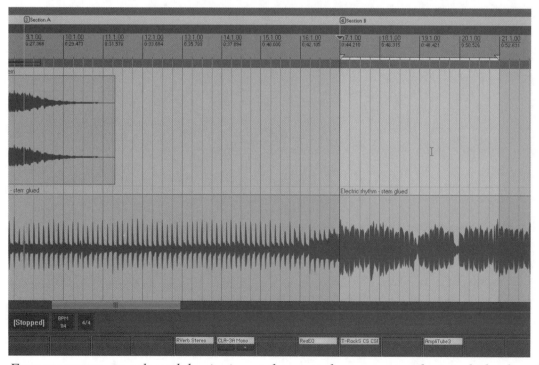

Four measures are selected, beginning at the spot where we want the interlude placed.

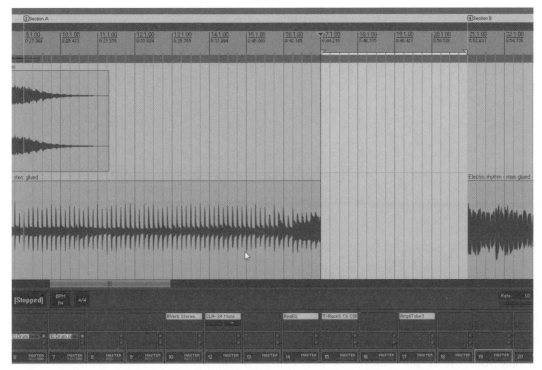

After using the "insert empty space" command, there's now room for the interlude. Notice that the section B marker has moved ahead, as well.

Depending on the situation, you'll find that one method may work better than the other. If any of the instruments aren't smoothly transitioning through the edit, you may need to tweak them individually at the edit point using the tools described in the topics that follow.

CLEANING UP NOISES AND MISCELLANEOUS THINGS

This is always a satisfying step—especially for the anal-retentive among us. You have the ability to make any part of a track that doesn't contain music absolutely silent. There are numerous ways to do this, but the method I normally use involves splitting items and deleting unwanted sections. For example, let's look at the beginning of a tune that involves several tracks: drums, bass, and two guitars.

The drums are virtual MIDI drums, so they aren't a problem. However, the bass track has a slight buzz that's audible, as does one of the guitars. The other guitarist has a case of "can't shut up"—all too common—and is noodling all over the place before the song starts.

 280 A noisy pre-song intro

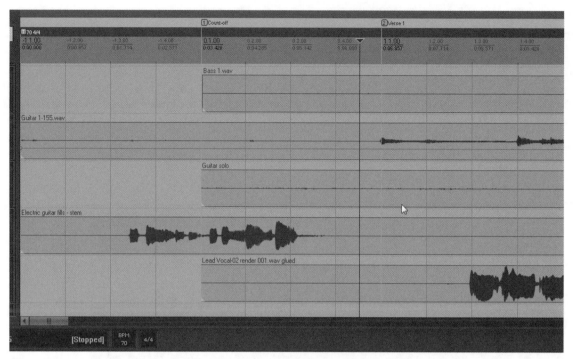

This song includes all kinds of unwanted noise before the downbeat.

No problem—these are all easy fixes. Simply split the item right before the first note starts, select the unwanted portion and delete!

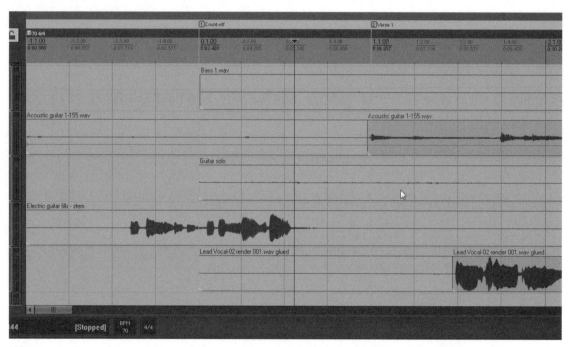

The items have been split and the unwanted portions have been selected.

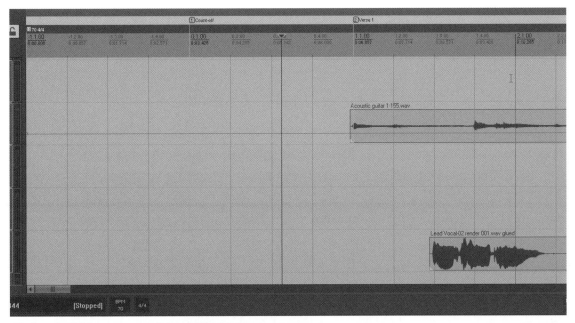

Delete! Ahhh...so satisfying! That's better.

 281 Clean intro with no noise before the downbeat

Of course, this isn't to say that you always have to clean up all (or any) of your tracks. If you're going for a loosey-goosey Rolling Stones vibe or something, you may want to leave some things a bit more natural. But it's nice to know how easy it is to tidy things up if you choose.

FIXING A TIMING ERROR

This is a common edit for times when someone just rushed or dragged a bit during a certain phrase. Let's check out an example in which the guitarist rushed a few chords during a riff. Here's the original phrase along with a drum pattern, which establishes the tempo.

 282 Guitar part is rushed on a few chords

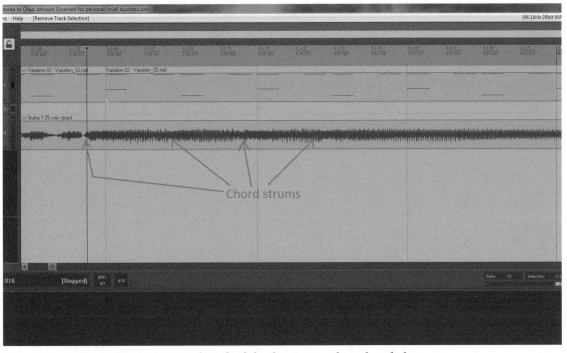

You can see how the guitar is ahead of the beat on a few chords here.

For this type of editing, we'll want to turn the snap setting off, because we'll need to have more precise placement capabilities. The first step is to split the item before and after each offending chord. If necessary, we can trim the ends of the media items to prevent overlapping. In Reaper, this is accomplished by placing the mouse pointer near the end of the item, at which point the pointer changes to an arrow. You can then click and drag to trim or extend the item. Consult your DAW's manual to see how this is done, if necessary.

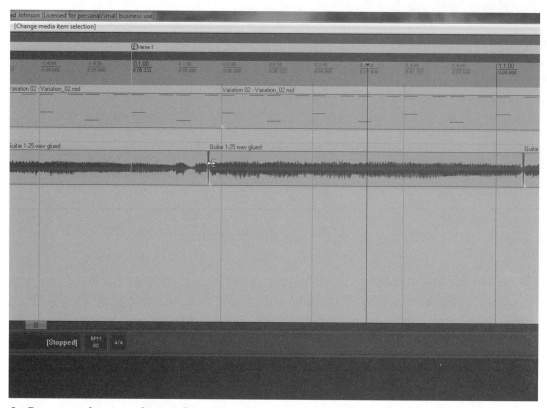

In Reaper, when you hover the mouse pointer at the end of a media item, the pointer changes to an arrow, indicating that trimming or extending the file is possible.

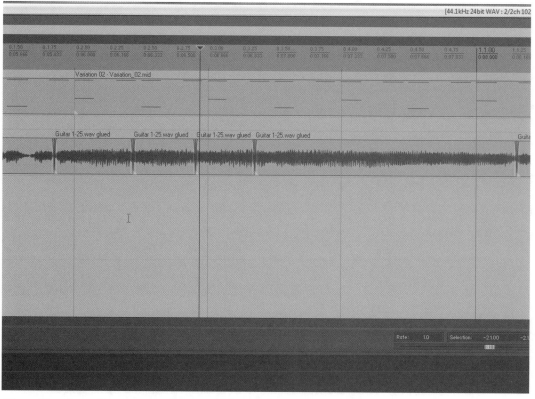

The offending chords are all moveable on their own now.

We can now move these individual chords and place them on the beat.

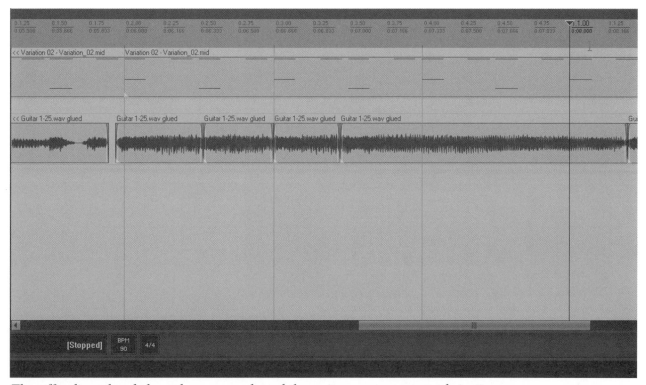

The offending chords have been moved, and the guitar part now sounds in time.

 283 Guitar part's timing is corrected

ADJUSTING THE LEVEL (VOLUME) OF A PHRASE OR NOTE

There are several ways to do this, and I employ different ones, depending on the situation. If it's just a few notes here and there, I'll usually split the items to single out the notes and then manually adjust them with the "item properties" feature. This may be called something else, depending on the DAW, but it's basically a way to look at all the significant info regarding the item.

For example, here's a phrase from a guitar solo in which two notes are just inappropriately loud and stick out a bit too much.

 284 Guitar phrase with a couple of notes that are too loud

So, after splitting the item to isolate those two notes, we can open the item properties window to get access to several things—among them is volume.

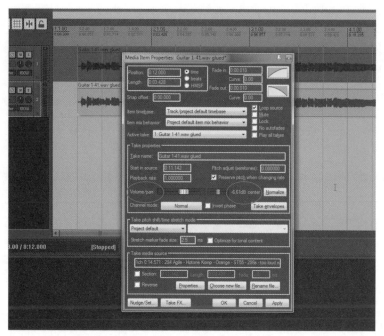

In Reaper, the item properties function allows you to view details about an item and make changes to it. Here, you can see that the volume for this item has been attenuated.

Now it sounds much smoother.

 285 Guitar phrase with loud notes attenuated

If the volume of an instrument is more erratic and would require extensive slicing and dicing to make it sound smooth (even with a compressor), then I may use some automation. You'll have to refer to your DAW's manual on how to do this, but most programs will allow you to record automation and/or draw it in manually.

Here's an example of how this type of automation curve looks on Reaper. Again, this can be accomplished by either playing the song (or a section of it) and "recording" the fader movement on the track, or you can begin with a straight volume envelope and draw in points by hand.

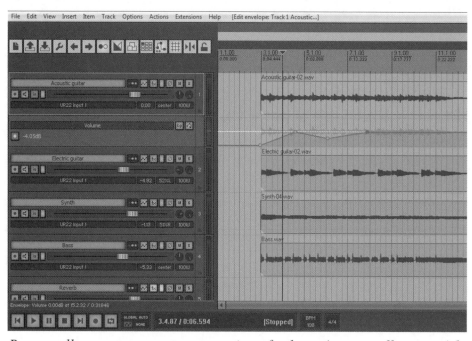

Reaper allows you to create automation of volume (or pan, effects, etc.) by recording fader movements or drawing in envelope curves by hand.

COMPING TAKES

"Comping" takes refers to the practice of cherry-picking the best parts of several performances of the same material and assembling them into one final performance. Again, there are several ways to do this, so you'll need to experiment to see which method works best. Part of it depends on how the performances were recorded. For this example, we'll use a vocal track.

Each Take Recorded to a Separate Track

If you recorded each take to a separate track, and you're not short at all on CPU power, then you could simply split the items to section off phrases as needed and mute or delete all but the saved take. For example, here we see two different vocal takes, each on their own track. We've sectioned off the phrases by splitting the items as necessary and then muted the unwanted portions.

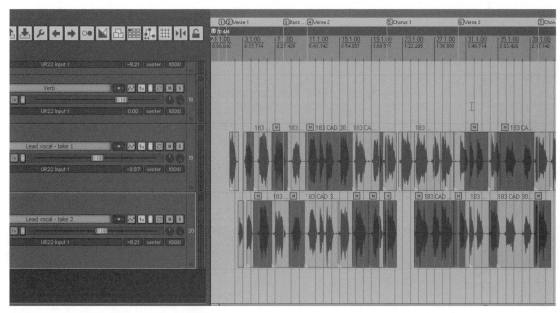

Two vocal takes, each on their own track, are sectioned off phrase by phrase and muted as necessary to leave one final take remaining.

Each Take Recorded on the Same Track

If you record each take on the same track, they will usually be stacked on top of each other. You can set your DAW up to handle this in different ways, but in this example, Reaper has been set to display each take in a separate lane.

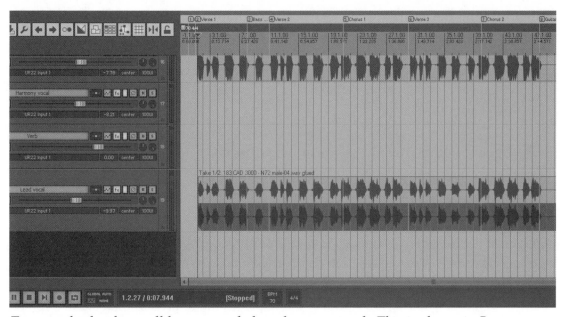

Two vocal takes have all been recorded on the same track. This is shown in Reaper as two stacked lanes.

From here, you can use basically the same idea, sectioning off the vocal into phrases and picking the best one. With this method, however, you only need to select the best take; the muting of the other two will be done in the process.

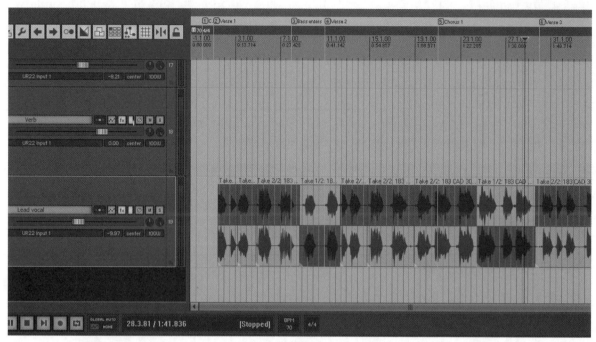

The phrases have been sectioned off and the winning take has been selected for each.

Comping Tips!

Listen through headphones: I prefer to listen to all edits through headphones because you'll usually hear details that may escape you with speakers, but this is especially true of vocals when it comes to comping. Of particular concern are breath noises. It's very easy to accidentally slice a breath in half or chop one off when comping takes, resulting in a very unnatural (and generally unpleasant) sound.

Split the item after the breath: This may seem a bit counterintuitive, but I've found that you're actually less likely to create a bad inhale edit if you split the item after the inhale and just before the singing begins. People aren't always terribly consistent as to when they'll start their inhalation before a phrase, but they'll usually leave a fraction of a second between the end of the breath and the beginning of the singing. And that's usually a great place to make the edit.

Be sure to listen through the entire section or track when you're done: You can get tunnel vision and lose sight of the big picture when comping takes, so it's important to make sure that the final take you've created sounds consistent and uniform throughout.

So you know what to listen for, here's an example of a bad comp in which the breath has been cut in half, causing a choppy, disjointed sound.

 286 Bad vocal comp (breath is chopped in half)

PITCH CORRECTION

This is certainly most commonly used on vocals, and it's really changed the way in which vocals are recorded. No longer is it necessary to have both the feel *and* the pitch be there on a vocal take. A note (or a few notes) can be a bit flat or sharp in an otherwise great phrase, and that's good enough, as the software can fix it for you. Again, this has been commonplace among professional studios for years now, and it's resulted in different-sounding music. It's rare that you hear vocals on the radio that sound as natural or loose as, say, the Rolling Stones, Bruce Springsteen, or Led Zeppelin. For better or worse, it's the way of the world—especially when it comes to major-label, radio-ready pop, rock, and country.

As may be evident by the subtext, I'm not a real proponent of using pitch correction. I certainly don't hold anything against anyone who does; it's just not my style. However, I know that most people do use it, and therefore it needs to be mentioned here. There are basically two different methods of pitch correction you can use. One involves a software plugin of some sort, such as Auto-Tune (by Antares) or Melodyne (by Celemony); nearly all DAWs nowadays have their version of such a program included. The other way is similar to the manual level-adjusting method previously mentioned under "Adjusting the Level (Volume) of a Phrase or Note."

Manual Method

If a vocal take is generally on pitch, with the exception of only a few notes here and there, you may choose to use the manual method, leaving the majority of the take completely untouched. This is accomplished by using the item properties feature again, just as we did when adjusting the volume (without automation). As an example, here's a vocal phrase that's mostly on pitch, with the exception of one note that's a bit flat.

 287 **Vocal phrase with one flat note**

By sectioning off that one note, we can open the item properties window and manually raise the pitch by whatever amount needed.

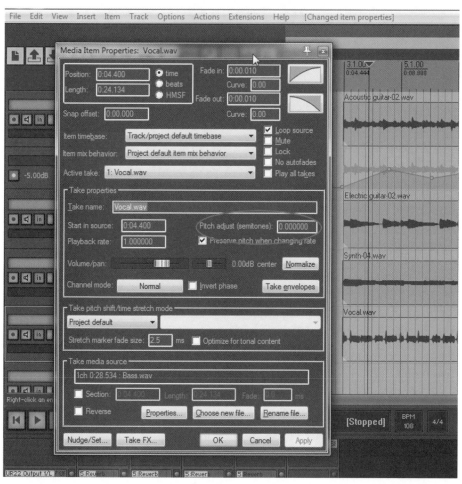

In Reaper, the item properties window allows you to manually adjust the pitch of an item by any amount.

And here's what it sounds like after the outpatient surgery:

 288 **Vocal phrase with the flat note tuned**

Software Method

If the vocal has numerous pitch problems, or if you're going for that ultra-clean, perfectly in-tune vocal, you'll save yourself lots of time by using software. Depending on the particular software you use, the exact process will differ, but most of them are generally capable of several core concepts. These include setting the key of the song and having the program automatically adjust the notes to the nearest "in key" note. Much like quantizing in the MIDI world, the distance the notes are moved, speed, and other factors can also be specified.

Let's have a listen to a vocal with several tuning problems throughout.

 289 **Vocal phrase with numerous tuning problems**

I'll be using Melodyne here, so you'll need to consult your software's manual if necessary to accomplish the same thing. You can see the phrase here as analyzed by Melodyne, graphically illustrating some of the tuning issues.

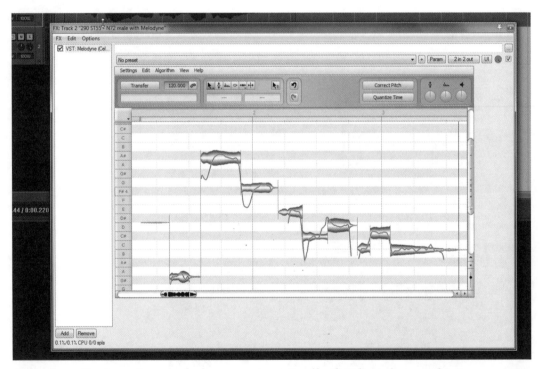

Melodyne displays the vocal phrase, automatically dividing the vocal into separate notes and displaying the pitch for each.

By specifying the key of the song and instructing the program to correct the pitch by the desired amount, the vocal is transformed instantly into a new take.

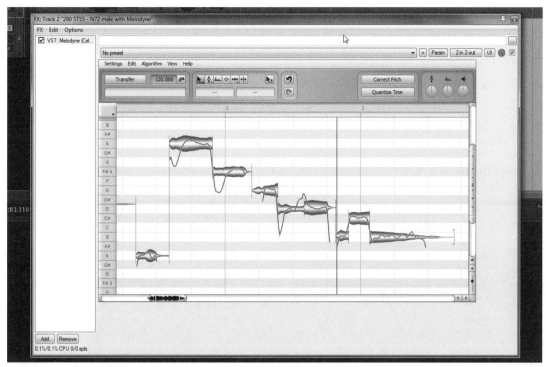

The pitches have been corrected by the specified amount.

And here's the result:

 290 **Vocal phrase after tuning with Melodyne**

It should be mentioned that programs such as Melodyne and Auto-Tune often contain many more features than pitch correction. You can usually adjust the timing/duration of notes, as well, in many cases making them one-stop track editors in their own right.

MIDI EDITING

As we talked about briefly in Chapter 11 on drums, we have pretty much complete editing control over a MIDI recording, even after it's been recorded. Quantizing is only a small part of what we can do. Among other things, we can control:

- Pitches (or the octave or key of the notes)

- Duration

- Volume, a.k.a. velocity (individually and/or by drawing/recording volume curves)

- Rhythmic timing (individually and/or via quantization)

- Adding or subtracting notes

- MIDI channel

- The instrument (sound) itself

- Copying and pasting of notes

- Looping phrases or patterns

- Add/change MIDI control change messages—i.e., pitch bend, modulation, etc.

And this list is hardly comprehensive. We'll demonstrate some of the most commonly employed MIDI editing tools here. It's beyond the scope of this book to fully cover the possibilities afforded by MIDI, but there are many other books and websites dedicated to the topic if you'd like to go deeper.

For this example, we're going to look at a keyboard phrase and various things we can do to it after it's been recorded. It was originally recorded with a Rhodes keyboard sound using Lounge Lizard Session and is in the key of C minor.

 291 Lounge Lizard Session: Rhodes keyboard phrase in C minor

And here's how the phrase looks in Reaper's MIDI editor using the piano-roll view:

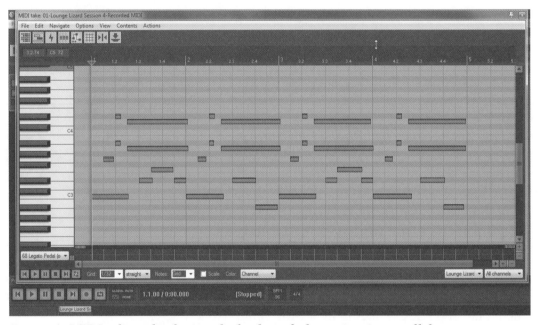

Reaper's MIDI editor displaying the keyboard phrase in piano-roll format.

First, let's just change a few of the bass notes. It's as easy as clicking and dragging them.

To move a note (or notes) in Reaper's MIDI editor, you simply click and drag them.

292 Lounge Lizard Session: Rhodes keyboard phrase in C minor with bass notes changed

Now let's say we want to make the phrase more dynamic by having a few notes really pop out. It's already recorded at a good level as is, so we're going to do this by actually lowering the volume of all but the notes we want to be loud. By right-clicking and dragging in Reaper's MIDI editor (in Windows), we're able to group-select as many notes as we want. If we selected too many or not enough, we can use control-click to add a note to the selection or remove one from it. You may need to consult your manual to see if this is done differently in your DAW.

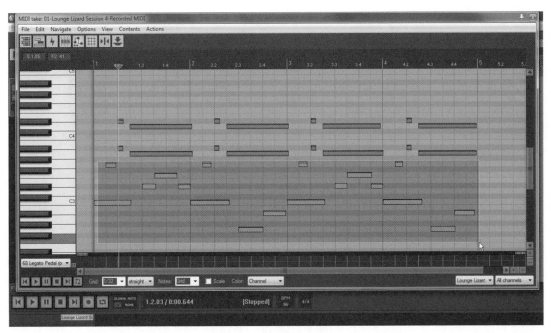

We use right-click and drag to select several notes at a time.

In Reaper, the volume (by default) of each note is displayed by a horizontal line through the note. When we hover the mouse pointer on that line, the pointer changes to vertical arrows, indicating that we can alter the velocity by clicking and dragging up or down. Since we have several notes selected, the velocity (selectable between 0 and 127) will change for all the selected notes relative to their individual values. Again, this may be done differently in your DAW. Let's bring the volume down on the selected notes a good bit.

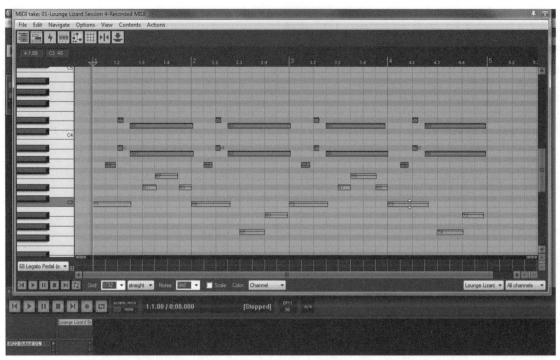

The velocity of all but the notes we want to stand out have been lowered.

 293 Lounge Lizard Session: Rhodes keyboard phrase in C minor with most notes lowered in volume

Now let's say we want to add a grace note to one of the higher notes. In Reaper, you can simply click and drag on an empty spot to draw in a note. By default, the velocity of this note will be the same as the last note you had selected. But you can easily and quickly change that right after you draw it.

And let's say we also want to thin out the phrase so it's not so busy. We just group-select the notes we want to get rid of and hit the DELETE key.

In Reaper, adding a note is as simple as clicking and dragging in an empty spot. To remove a note, just select it and hit DELETE.

294 Lounge Lizard Session: Rhodes keyboard phrase in C minor with some notes deleted and a grace note added

Finally, let's say we want to go with a different virtual instrument altogether. No problem—we just open the effects window, delete the Lounge Lizard Session plugin, and add the new one. Here, we've replaced it with the Rhodes sound from Garritan's Jazz & Big Band 3.

 295 Garritan J&BB3: Rhodes keyboard phrase with new virtual instrument

Again, you can go much deeper than this with MIDI, but for the casual user, you may not need to. If you're running a fully electronic studio, however, you'll most likely want to educate yourself more thoroughly on the MIDI subject overall.

CHAPTER 16
THE MIXING PROCESS

Once you have all the tracks recorded and have made any necessary edits, it's time to mix the song down to a two-track stereo file that can be listened to anywhere: on your stereo, computer, mp3 player, in your car, etc. Until you do this, you'd have to bring up your DAW project any time you wanted to hear the song. When we mix the song, we make all the final decisions with regard to track volume, panning, effects, and equalization, and then solidify those decisions into a stereo recording. The subject of mixing is incredibly vast and could easily fill (and has filled) books on its own, so we won't be able to cover every minute aspect here. Rather, we'll take a broad-stroke approach and look at the key concepts that are involved. I'd suggest further reading on the subject once you have the basic idea down.

As with most aspects of the recording process, there is no one way to mix. In fact, if you ask a dozen pro mixing engineers how they do it, you're likely to get as many different answers. Some start with the drums and work out from that, adding piece by piece until they get to the vocals. Others start with the lead vocal and get that to sound as good as possible, adding in everything else around it. Some like to pull up all the faders right from the start and tweak from them. Some mix very quickly, while others like to spend several days (or more) on one song. Therefore, it's not my intent to tell you how to mix a song. But I'll mention some common concepts that are usually considered in the process and discuss some different ways of accomplishing common goals.

A Slight Digression

It should be mentioned that, depending on the arrangement of the instruments, a song can be made more difficult or easier to mix. For example, if you have four separate guitar riffs, and they're all taking place in the same low register of the instrument, it's going to be more difficult for each to be clearly heard than if you had only one low guitar riff and one higher one. By the same token, multiple ethereal synth pads will be harder to distinguish from one another if they're all taking place in the treble region. In contrast, a song in which each track is occupying its own sonic space can almost seem to mix itself, comparatively speaking.

In this regard, you may find that you need to delete some parts altogether, or at least remove them from a certain section, if they're doing more harm than good. A mix can be like its own performance this way, and it's a very subjective thing. Remember that you can make as many mixes as you like, so feel free to experiment at first, trying different things to hear the result.

Let's look at some basic mixing concepts and discuss them in detail.

MAKING EACH INSTRUMENT HEARD OR GIVING EACH INSTRUMENT ITS OWN "SPACE"

One common goal in mixing is for each instrument to be heard clearly (unless you're going for a specific effect), and this usually gets more difficult with every track you add. There are several tools at our disposal that can help, and we'll discuss them here.

Panning

This is one of the most obvious tools we have for keeping instruments out of each other's way. If you have two instruments that are playing similar parts with similar sounds, for example, one easy way to give them their own space is to pan them to opposite sides of the spectrum. Here's an example in which two guitars are both playing in the lower-to-mid register. The track will begin with both of them panned down the center; then they'll be moved out to the sides—around 3:00 and 9:00.

296 Panning of two similar guitar parts for separation

Equalization

EQ is generally one of the underused techniques for creating space in a mix. Most people employ the panning technique because it's relatively easy; you just turn a knob and something drastic happens right away. EQ requires a little more study and effort, but, for me, it's actually the more important and effective tool.

For example, if you have two different instruments that both contain a lot of content in the same frequency spectrum, they're going to have a tendency to mask each other a bit, which will obscure their clarity. A common culprit here is rhythm guitar and bass. Although a bass guitar is tuned an octave lower than a guitar, each instrument still contains a good amount of content in the lower-mid-range area, which can end up resulting in a muddy sound.

As an example, let's listen to a phrase of bass and rhythm guitar.

 297 Bass and rhythm guitar

You may have noticed that there wasn't a lot of clarity between the two instruments. Let's take a look at a spectral analysis of both tracks using a spectral analyzer plugin. This is a free program called SPAN by VOXengo.

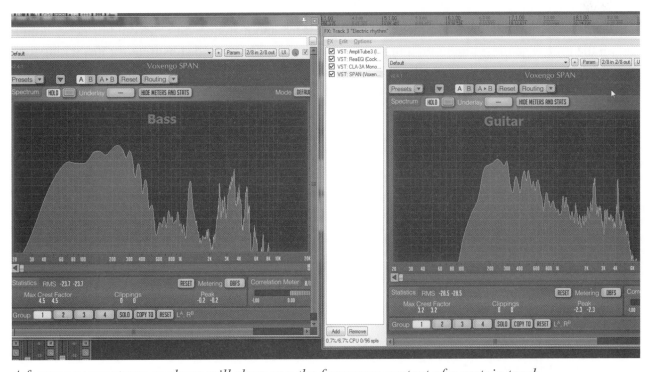

A frequency spectrum analyzer will show you the frequency content of a certain track.

You can see that there's a good deal of content on both instruments in similar frequency ranges. If there weren't a bass guitar, then the guitars could possibly use some of that low end. But since we have a bass in the mix, it just tends to muddy up things a bit. Listen to what happens when we simply add a hi-pass filter on the guitar at around 200Hz.

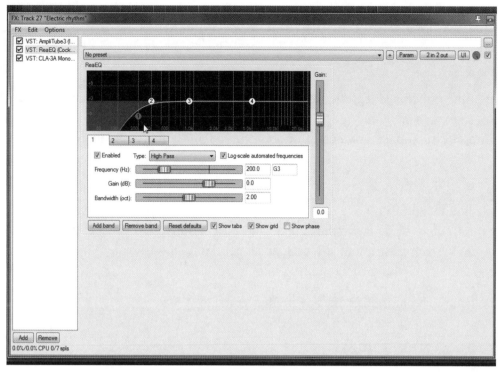

By simply adding a hi-pass (or low-cut) filter on the guitar, we can get rid of much of the muddiness between the instruments.

 298 **Bass and rhythm guitar with hi-pass filter on guitar**

While spectrum analyzers are nice tools to help learn about frequencies, I wouldn't depend on them all the time. The most important thing is to use your ears. There is no substitute for just taking the time and experimenting with EQ to learn what it does and how it affects the sound of one instrument, a group of instruments, or the entire mix.

Mixing in Mono

While we're on the subject of EQ, let's talk about the idea of *mixing in mono*. Some people like to begin their mix by using no panning at all; everything is panned straight up the middle—effectively mixing in mono. Why would you do this? Well, think about it this way: if you can get the instruments to sound distinct and clear with everything in mono, imagine how much more spacious it will sound when you pan things out to the side!

As an example, we'll take a look at a song with the following instrumentation:

- Drums
- Bass
- Acoustic guitar
- Synth
- Electric guitar
- Lead vocal

Here's what it sounds like with all the faders up in a rough level mix. There has been no reverb or any other effect added.

 299 **First rough, dry mix in mono**

As you can hear, things aren't quite as distinct as we'd like them to be. Again, we could immediately pan some instruments and achieve some separation, but that could also hide some deeper frequency-masking issues that we may have. Mixing in mono at first is a good way to force you to separate the instruments via EQ.

So let's go through and add some hi-pass filters to the guitars to help get them out of the way of the bass a bit to start off with. We'll set them between 150 and 200 Hz. Here's the result after doing that:

 300 **Rough, dry mix with hi-pass filters added to guitars**

Now let's concentrate on the kick/bass drum relationship. Generally speaking, a close-miked kick drum (or sample of one) will generally benefit from a hi-pass filter placed at around 40 dB or so, as anything below that will typically produce undesirable results. The same usually applies to the bass guitar; sometimes I'll even move this up to around 50 dB, depending on the source sound.

With those basic moves out of the way, I'll usually solo the bass track and begin to sweep the lower frequencies (usually from around 100 Hz up to around 350 Hz) to find the frequency that really defines the bass' character. This will be different for each track, so you'll have to use your ears. Set up a parametric band with a fairly low Q setting and a moderate boost (4 to 6 dB or so) and slowly sweep through the frequencies to identify the key bass frequency. This is often found between 100 and 320 Hz or so, but again, every track is different.

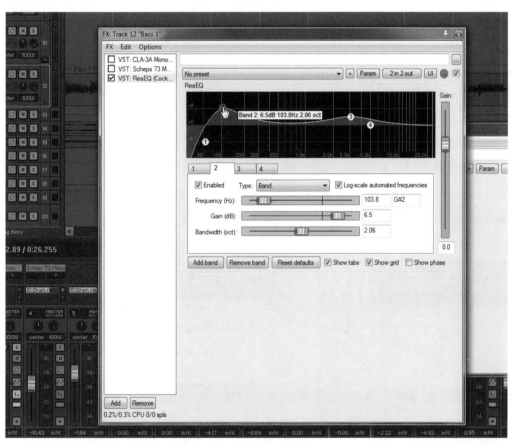

Sweeping the bass frequencies to find where the fundamental bass character frequency lies

In our instance, this ended up being about 115Hz. So I'll add a gentle boost there—around 3 dB max, usually. Now, I'll usually add a complimentary *cut* to the kick drum at that same frequency, as this will help make a little room for the bass. Next, I'll usually try to determine where the smack of the kick beater lies and apply a similar boost there and a complimentary cut on the bass at the same point. This is usually somewhere in the 1K to 3K range. And here's the result so far:

 301 **Rough, dry mix with filters, cuts, and boosts on bass and kick**

Now it's starting to get cleaned up a bit down there.

Mixing No-No 101

One thing that beginning mixers fall prey to—once they've begun to experiment with sound-shaping via EQ—is the temptation to get every instrument to sound great on its own by soloing it and EQing to perfection. With the obvious exception of solo piano and guitar pieces, the problem with this is that the instrument is not going to be heard by itself. It's going to be heard along with numerous others, each of which contain their own harmonic content. If you do this (get each instrument sounding as good as possible while soloing it), you'll likely have a great big mess when you put them all together.

The most important thing to consider is how the instrument sounds among all the others. In fact, if you took some of the best-sounding mixes and listened to the solo tracks, you may be a little surprised to hear that they don't quite sound the way you expected. They may be thinner, darker, or brighter than they sound within the confines of the whole mix. But if they sound good *in the mix*, the mixing engineer has done his job.

I'll usually continue this process for each group of instruments that share a similar frequency range. (Note that this may not be necessary, and there's no need to mess with it if they already sound distinct.) The electric guitar, for example, sits in a range that's similar to the synth line, so (if necessary) I'll do the same for those two: find the dominant, pleasant-sounding frequency for each, add a slight boost if needed, and add a complimentary cut on the other to make a little room.

The vocal tends to share the same range as the acoustic guitar, so I'll try to carve out a little space in the acoustic for the vocal to sit. This just takes practice. You normally don't have to make drastic cuts (although that can work if needed, or if the track was recorded in a less-than-ideal way); we're generally talking in the 2 to 4 dB range. But every mix is different, and so you'll just need to experiment to see what's needed.

Here's a look at the EQ settings for the acoustic guitar, electric guitar, synth, and lead vocal:

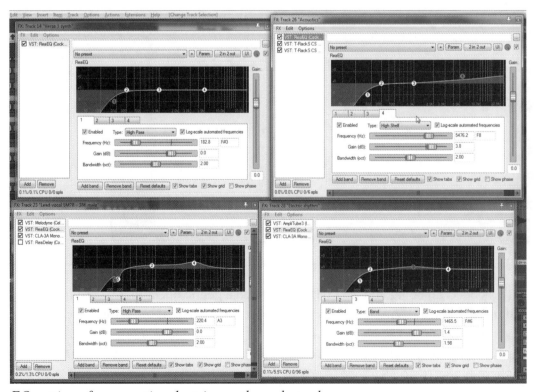

EQ settings for acoustic, electric, synth, and vocal

It's made quite a difference in the overall clarity of the mix, yet everything is still panned straight down the middle. I highly recommend trying out this approach, as it can only strengthen your EQ skills in my opinion, which will aid in all areas of the recording process. Of course, the other big factor in sound-shaping—besides effects like reverb, etc.—is compression (see following section). Aside from taming dynamics, they can impart a character all their own to the sound. I usually apply some type of compression to most instruments in the mix—some more drastic and some very subtle—and this is usually placed in the chain before the EQ, although this is not a hard-and-fast rule. Since the focus was purely on what EQ can do, up until this point in this mix, I'd had the compressors bypassed for each track, but now I'll engage them. In a real-world scenario, I would most likely apply my compression (usually only achieving around 3 or 4 dB of gain reduction) before EQ-ing.

And now let's listen to the result of all this work. Compare this to the first rough mix to hear the difference.

 302 Rough, dry mix with preliminary EQ and compression settings on all instruments

Standing on the Shoulders of the Pros: Referencing

One common practice when learning to mix is to reference your tracks against other pro recordings that are in a similar style. This isn't entirely fair, because your mix won't be professionally mastered like theirs will be, but it's good for getting a handle on overall colors. Ear fatigue can set in fairly quickly when listening to the same material over and over again, and referencing another recording can be a good reality check.

It's also advised that you take breaks periodically to keep your ears fresh. This can be every hour or two, or even as short as every 30 minutes, depending on your preference. Get up, stretch your legs, or walk around the block. Just be sure it's something non-musical so that your ears can reset.

COMPRESSION

We talked a good bit about compression in Chapter 13, and much of that applies here, as well. The main goal is to tame the peaks of an instrument, which will help it sound more consistent. If a rhythm instrument, for example, contains highly varying levels, it can draw attention to itself more than it should and start to distract from the lead instrument.

Here's an example in which a piano's comping sounds a bit too erratic, level-wise, and is therefore drawing attention away from the lead horns:

 303 Jazz combo with erratic piano comping

After applying some compression using a Waves CLA-3A plugin (see sidebar on the following page for details) with a gain reduction of about 6 to 8 dB, however, it sits much more naturally within the track.

 304 Jazz combo with piano compressed to even out peaks

It's a good idea to listen through the mix at the early stage, after you've done a rough adjustment of the faders, to hear if any one particular track is causing problems in this way, because the earlier you get it under control, the better (generally speaking), as it won't hinder your ability to make further judgments down the line.

Compression on the Master Bus

Another common practice—and one that is greatly debated—involves placing a compressor across the master output. In other words, you're compressing the entire mix. Proponents of this idea usually speak of a "gluing" effect, which helps make everything sound a bit more cohesive. I'd recommend that, if you're going to do this, you should add the compressor from the start. If you wait until you're completely done with your mix, then it could change the delicate balance of certain frequencies and effects you've worked so hard to create. Again, this is debated in certain circles, but, in my opinion, it makes sense to mix with the bus compression if you're going to do it at all.

Regardless of when you do it, most people go for a very subtle effect, with only 1 or 2 dB of gain reduction (3 dB at the most) occurring. The attack and release times will be dependent on the groove of the song, and which instrument is principally driving it, but longer times are generally the norm—say 100 to 600 ms for the attack and maybe 250 to 800ms for the release. Again, though, don't be afraid to experiment. I'd start with a low ratio, as well—around 1:2 would be a safe bet. Improper attack and release times can end up creating a "pumping" effect, in which the sound will duck down slightly after each kick drum hit, for example, and produce an unnatural feel. So you'll need to experiment with those suggested settings, if necessary, to tailor it for the particular song.

Waves CLA Classic Compressors bundle

Wave's CLA Compressors Bundle was created in close cooperation with mixing engineer extraordinaire Chris Lord-Alge, whose work is nearly impossible to avoid if you listen to the radio for more than 10 minutes. It's almost easier to name the artists with whom he hasn't worked than the ones he has. With this bundle, Waves sets you up with emulations of Chris' four go-to compressors: the Universal Audio 1176 in black- and blue-faced models, the Teletronix LA-2A, and the Universal Audio LA-3A.

You'll first notice that the graphic interfaces of these plugins are a beautiful thing to behold, faithfully recreating the vibe of the original hardware versions. You'll likely forget such novelties, though, when you hear how amazing these things sound. The CLA-3A features Gain and Peak Reduction knobs, a VU meter displaying input, output, or gain reduction, a compressor/limiter mode switch, and a sidechain frequency filter. The CLA-2A features similar controls, although the attack and release times differ from the CLA-3A in accordance with their hardware counterparts. And just like the hardware versions, the CLA-76 compressors give you input, output, attack, and release knobs, five buttons to select the ratio, three buttons to select the display (input, output, gain reduction), and a bypass button.

All of the plugins offer savable presets, of course, and each comes with several factory presets to get you started in the right direction. At $500, this is certainly stretching the limit of what's considered "budget gear," but it's pennies on the dollar when compared to the price of owning the hardware versions of these classics. This is, of course, not even considering the fact that you can run as many instances of these as your system can handle, whereas you'd have to cough up an additional two grand or so for another channel of the hardware versions. If you're made of money, feel free to do that. For the rest of us, there's the CLA bundle from Waves.

Street price: $500

Let's have a listen to a mix and compare the uncompressed mix bus sound to the compressed one. For this purpose, I'm using the CLA-76 plugin from Waves (see sidebar on page 252 for details), which emulates the famous UA 1176 compressor/limiter. This compressor, which has a very fast attack time of 1 ms down to 50 *micro seconds*, is a commonly used compressor for bus compression. So there's an exception right away to the guideline I mentioned about longer attack times. We'll compare this to the ReaComp plugin that comes with Reaper. For both tracks, you'll first hear the mix with no bus compression and then again with it engaged.

 305 **Waves CLA-76: Rough mix with compression of 1 to 2 dB of gain reduction on the mix bus**

 306 **Rea Comp: Rough mix with compression of 1 to 2 dB of gain reduction on the mix bus**

DYNAMIC ELEMENTS IN THE MIX

Another common idea often neglected by beginners is that of dynamic movement in the mix. Beginners will often "set and forget," leaving everything static throughout the entire song. While this can work well in more natural settings, it usually sounds more exciting to create some sense of motion in the mix when you're dealing with pop or rock styles. This can be a subtle thing. In fact, too much of it can tend to sound gimmicky and get old. But when tastefully done, it can add another dimension to a static mix.

There are a few different ways to do this. We can change the panning, level, or EQ of instruments. We can also add and remove effects or do the same with whole instruments themselves. Omission can often make a bigger statement than addition in this regard. So let's examine a few common techniques used to create a dynamic mix.

Adding or Removing Instruments Throughout the Song

This is a fairly simple concept, but many people forget about it. They're so happy with all these great sounds they've recorded, they want to include them through the whole song. This is a good way to lose your listener's interest, however, as they don't have any such attachments and are only listening in a linear fashion for interesting things to happen. This is not to say that you *always* have to switch things up; there are certainly plenty of hits that prove the contrary. But more often than not, it can help breathe some new life into a mix.

As an example, let's listen to one mix of a song in which the instrumentation remains the same pretty much through the whole song. In other words, everything that was recorded is being used throughout.

 307 **Mix 1 of song: every recorded part is included in its entirety**

And now let's check out a mix in which a few parts have been omitted at certain times to help keep things interesting.

 308 **Mix 2 of song: certain parts have been omitted to create more dynamics**

As you can hear, the song has a more dramatic flow now that there's some motion happening. Again, this is a personal preference, and no one way is more correct than the other. But, as for me, I tend to prefer the latter. It's something to keep in mind at least.

Adjusting Levels or Panning

Another method of creating movement in the mix is by varying the levels and/or panning of certain instruments throughout the song. There are some instruments—such as the kick, snare, bass, and lead vocal—that are customarily panned down the middle, and so they're not toyed with as much with regard to panning (although there are no rules). But the tracks that act more as "ear candy"—such as melodic fills and auxiliary percussion—are ripe for the picking in ideas like this.

Let's check out an example here of a song's intro containing drums, bass, rhythm guitar, synth, and a melodic guitar. In this first mix, everything will remain static.

 309 **Mix 1 of intro: each track remains static throughout**

And now let's have a little fun with the lead guitar during the intro. At the end of the intro, the lead guitar settles into position in the middle, but before that, it wanders about the stereo field, which helps to heighten the suspense a bit.

 310 **Mix 2 of intro: lead guitar is panned back and forth**

Another typical application of this kind of idea involves "riding the fader" of a fill instrument and bringing it up during the breaks between vocal lines. You could also even pan it to the middle if you really wanted it to take center stage. Here's an example of that kind of idea. This first mix of a song's verse is, again, static.

 311 **Mix 1 of verse: each track remains static**

And now let's bring up the level of the fill and pan it to the middle.

A Celebration of Automation

Nowadays, most of these types of moves—adjusting panning or levels during the mix—are handled via automation, which we talked a bit about in Chapter 15. Again, you'll need to consult your DAW's manual to see exactly how this is done in your system, but in Reaper, you can choose to make different "envelopes"—such as volume, panning, and effects send—visible for each track. Then you can draw in your own points to control those parameters, or you can record them in real time by moving the faders, pan knobs, etc. This automation is completely non-destructive, of course, and you can choose to bypass them, for quick comparison to the static version if you'd like, or delete/edit/redo them altogether.

For example, here's what the volume and pan envelopes look like for the fill instrument in the previous track.

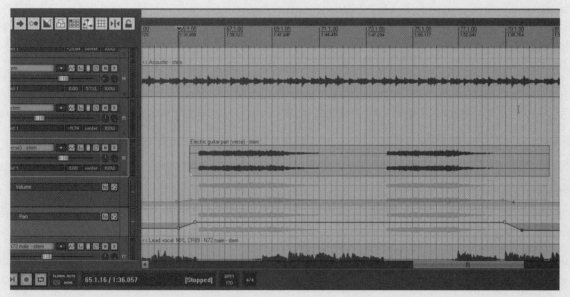

Here, the volume and pan envelopes are displayed.

USING EFFECTS

Effects are kind of like musical toys; they're very fun to play with. Often, they help us reconcile the unnatural method in which we record instruments (i.e., using close-mic techniques) by creating a more natural sound with reverb and ambience. They can also help you apply a unique sonic stamp to a song when used creatively.

We talked a good bit about effects in Chapter 13, so I won't retread a lot of ground in that respect. Instead, we'll just talk a bit about some strategies for applying them to a whole mix.

Reverb

Reverbs are often used to help create the illusion that all the instruments were recorded in the same space. This can refer to a more natural room-type sound, a very wet church cathedral, or anything in between. Generally speaking, the more reverb or delay you add to a track, the farther away it will appear to sound. So you can create a bit of depth in your mix by varying the amounts of reverb you use on different tracks.

Let's check out an example here. This first mix will be completely dry, with most of the instruments sounding very much "in your face."

 313 Mix 1: all instruments are completely dry

Now let's use a reverb plugin by Waves, TrueVerb (see sidebar on page 212 for details), to add different levels of the same reverb to each instrument. We'll do this by adding the plugin to its own track and then adding sends for each track to the reverb track (see Chapter 7 for more on this process).

 314 Mix 2: reverb has been added to each instrument in different amounts

How does it sound now? Do some instruments sound closer while others appear more distant? Again, this type of thing is a personal preference, so feel free to experiment with it. Also, listen closely to recordings you like and pay attention to the level of reverb (if any) that's being applied to different instruments. That said, here are some general conventions and/or suggestions when it comes to setting reverb levels:

- For a "natural" sound, add just enough reverb so that you can hear it clearly and then back it off a bit.

- For faster-paced songs, you'll generally want to use reverbs with shorter decay times so they don't obscure the beat. Conversely, ballads will generally sound nicer with longer decay times.

- When adding reverb to a vocal, using a bit of pre-delay can help provide clarity while still adding a bit of depth (see sidebar on the following page for more information on this).

- You don't have to use the same reverb for every instrument, although this is a nice way of making everything sound as though it was played together if you're going for a very natural sound.

- Adding reverb to low-pitched instruments, such as bass guitar or kick drum, can tend to produce a muddiness in the mix. For this reason, many engineers don't add any reverb at all (or very little) to such instruments.

Adding Pre-delay to Reverb

A dry vocal will often sound very unnatural and stick out like a sore thumb, so it's usually treated with reverb or delay. However, adding reverb to a vocal can sometimes make it less intelligible. Using a pre-delay will often help this quite a bit. Again, this is the amount of time that the reverb will wait to kick in. So you'll get a fraction of a second of dry vocal before the reverb begins. It's a common practice to time this setting to a rhythmic value of the song, such as a quarter note, eighth note, 16th note, etc. Generally, the faster the song's tempo, the longer the pre-delay can be.

A simple way of determining these values in milliseconds (which is used for the pre-delay time) is to divide 60,000 by the tempo of the song in beats per minute. This will give you the length of a quarter note. Let's say we have a song that's 120 bpm:

60,000 / 120 = 500 ms (quarter note)

From there, we just divide that number by 2 to get an eighth note, again for a 16th note, and so on.

250 ms (eighth note)

125 ms (16th note)

So let's hear the difference between a reverb with and without a pre-delay on the lead vocal.

🔊 **315** No pre-delay on lead vocal reverb

🔊 **316** 16th-note pre-delay on lead vocal reverb

🔊 **317** 32nd-note pre-delay on lead vocal reverb

It's a subtle thing, but you can hear that it does make a difference. I'd probably go with the 16th-note setting on this one, but it's a matter of personal preference.

Delay

Delay is another very common effect on vocals and other instruments. Assuming it's timed to some sort of logical rhythm with regard to the song, it can add depth, with less clutter than reverb. Common rhythm timings are eighth note, dotted eighth note, quarter note, and quarter-note triplet. The level of the delay and the feedback should generally be set fairly low, unless you're going for a specific effect.

Let's check out the same vocal as the previous one with delay (instead of reverb) on it.

🔊 **318** Eighth-note delay on lead vocal

🔊 **319** Dotted-eighth delay on lead vocal

🔊 **320** Quarter-note triplet on lead vocal

To determine the quarter-note triplet time, you can simply divide the quarter-note millisecond time by 3. That would give you an eighth-note triplet time. Double that, and you have a quarter-note triplet.

> 120 bpm
> 500 ms = quarter note
> 500 / 3 = 167 ms (eight-note triplet)
> 167 x 2 = 334 ms (quarter-note triplet)

Another common use for delay is a "stinger"—a delay placed on only one specific note of a vocal or instrument. For example, this may occur on the last note of a melody that coincides with the first beat of a new section. Quarter notes and eighth notes are popular rhythmic values for this type of thing. Here's an example of that kind of idea:

 321 Delay placed only on final note of phrase

Running Low on CPU? Rendering Is Your Friend!

All plugins eat up CPU resources. The more complex they are, the more RAM they use. If you have a good system, and/or depending on how many and what type of plugins you use, you may never find your CPU taxed at all. But if your CPU starts running in the 70% region or higher, you may start to experience glitches during playback. This can really be a nuisance and can make it very difficult to record new tracks.

If upgrading your system isn't an option, there is a workaround. You can *stem render* or *freeze* a track to help free up CPU resources. Basically, when you render a track, the program makes a copy of the track and prints all the effects to it. By default, the original track is generally muted. By muting this original track, any CPU resources normally being used by the effects are freed up. The downside is that, on the rendered version, you can't adjust the effects; you can only adjust the volume and panning, etc. Of course, you can always delete this rendered track, unmute the original track, make adjustments, and re-render it as necessary.

This guitar track has been rendered, leaving the original one muted and thereby freeing up CPU resources.

An alternative to this is freezing a track. It accomplishes basically the same thing (saving CPU power) by simply freezing the effects on the track so that they can't be altered until the track is unfrozen. So while frozen, only the volume, pan, etc., of the track can be adjusted—not the effects.

This guitar track has been frozen to free up CPU power, which is indicated by the shading and the lock symbol.

Another use for delay is doubling, which is similar to a slapback delay. You can set a short delay with a level near that of the dry signal and add some slight modulation to simulate a vocal double. Or you can find plugins, such as the Waves Abbey Road Studios Reel ADT (see sidebar on page 260 for details), that are specifically designed to do this. Although this is most commonly associated with vocals, it can sound great on many different sources. Check it out.

🔊 322 **Waves Abbey Road Studios Reel ADT on lead vocal**

🔊 323 **Waves Abbey Road Studios Reel ADT on electric guitar**

🔊 324 **Waves Abbey Road Studios Reel ADT on synth**

Modulation Effects

Aside from the common reverb and delay effects, anything else is up for grabs. For example, you could try running background vocals through a phaser or flanger and see what you get. Let's check that out!

🔊 325 **Background vocals processed with phaser**

🔊 326 **Background vocals processed with flanger**

Tape Saturation Emulation

Another common effect in digital systems is, ironically, analog tape simulation. It's kind of funny how you'll hear some people rant and rave about how crappy analog tape was/is compared to digital recording, but then they'll pay hundreds for top-of-the-line analog tape simulation plugins! These plugins are designed to give your recordings a bit of the warmth and non-linear artifacts that are par for the course with analog tape. Just as film colors images in a pleasant way, analog tape does the same for sound. In other words, whereas digital may be better at actually recreating what we hear, we tend to like the way analog colors it.

This effect is commonly used on the master bus and/or individual tracks—especially drums, guitars, and bass. I'm using the Waves Abbey Road Studios J37 plugin here (see sidebar for details) on drums and then a master bus. The effect can go from extremely subtle to dirty and grungy and everywhere in between. On each recording, you'll first hear the tracks without the effect and then again with it.

Waves Abbey Road Studios Reel ADT and Abbey Road Studios J37 plugin

If you're looking to add some vintage character to your digital recording, you have to check out Waves' Abbey Road Studios Reel ADT and Abbey Road Studios J37 plugins. Both were created in cooperation with Abbey Road Studios to emulate classic pieces of hardware that were integral in recording some of the most enduring albums of all time.

With the Abbey Road Studios J37 plugin, you get a meticulous emulation of the Studer J37 tape recorder. This machine was used on countless records in the 1960s but none perhaps more famous than the Beatles' *Sgt. Pepper's Lonely Hearts Club Band*. You get a number of adjustable parameters, including tape speed, bias, noise, saturation, wow and flutter, and three different oxide tape formulas for unique character. There's even an added tape delay feature with three different delay types and low-pass/hi-pass controls. If you can't afford a real ATR (analog tape recorder), or just don't want to bother with the hassle of maintenance, etc., then the Abbey Road Studios J37 will get you close enough so that no one will know the difference.

And if you really want to add that Beatles flair to your recordings, look no further than the Abbey Road Studios Reel ADT plugin. ADT (Automatic Double Tracking) was a technique created in the 1960s for use mainly on the Fab Four's work. You can create lush delay/chorus effects, tight doubling, and everything in between by way of the Varispeed control and separate volume and pan controls for the source and ADT signals. Drive controls also allow you to push the signal into saturation for added warmth and more if desired. If you're a Beatles fan, you won't be able to wipe the smile off your face after experimenting with this plugin for only a few minutes. But it's far from a one-trick pony, and you'll no doubt find uses for it in many more applications than "Tomorrow Never Knows" covers.

Street price: Abbey Road Studios Reel ADT – $200, Abbey Road Studios J37 – $249

On each of the following, you'll hear the track first unprocessed and then again with the J37 plugin engaged.

 **327** Waves Abbey Road Studios J37 Tape plugin on kick and snare drum

 **328** Waves Abbey Road Studios J37 Tape plugin on master bus – subtle

 **329** Waves Abbey Road Studios J37 Tape plugin on master bus – more pronounced

FINAL RENDERING

Once you've gotten your mix sounding just the way you want it, it's time to make the stereo two-track recording that will be playable on normal music players. This may be accomplished a few different ways, depending on your particular DAW, but in Reaper, it's called *rendering*. When you open the rendering window, you'll have numerous options, including where the file will be saved, the bit depth (use 16-bit if you plan to burn to CD, otherwise 24-bit is fine), file type, boundaries of the rendering (entire project, time selection, selected tracks only, etc.), stereo/mono, sample rate (44.1 kHz, etc.), and more. Until you learn more specifically about all the options, it's usually fine to just go with the default settings. Just make sure you take note of where the file will be saved so you know where to find it!

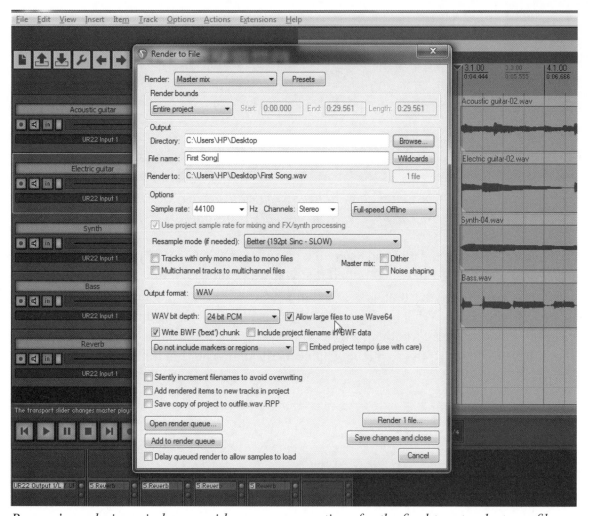

Reaper's rendering window provides numerous options for the final two-track stereo file.

Remember the Trails!

One thing to take note of when rendering the final mix is to make sure that none of the reverb trails at the end—or cymbal decays if you're using MIDI drums—are cut off. In some DAWs, the rendered file will end at the moment the last media item ends, regardless of whether or not the sound has completely decayed or not. So, if your last media item ends at 3:05, for example, the rendered file will be 3:05 long and no more. If the song ended with a guitar chord chop on the last hit, and the media item was trimmed immediately behind that, then the reverb trail on that guitar (if applicable) would be cut off before it had time to decay.

A simple workaround to this is to extend the length of one track (any one) sufficiently so that any and all reverb trails have a chance to die out. You can then split the media item right after the last note and mute the extension so that the last thing you'll hear is the dry final note and then the complete reverb tail after it.

Make sure the final track extends until after all the reverb trails have completely decayed.
You can mute the end of the track to make sure no miscellaneous noises pop up.

That's it! Now you can take the mix and listen to it on any system (car, MP3 player, home stereo, etc.) to hear how it sounds. You'll most likely find that you want to make a few revisions because you'll still be getting used to how your monitors sound in your control room. Again, ideally, the mixes will translate everywhere perfectly, but mixing in a bedroom isn't an ideal situation; it's a "make the best of what we have" situation. There's nothing wrong with making a few revisions, so don't feel that you've failed if you have to do so. Even pro mixing engineers make revisions at times.

To bring this all home, here are my final mixes of the four songs that you've heard in part thus far throughout this book.

🔊 330 "When You're Here"

🔊 331 "The Ballad of Fireflies"

🔊 332 "Traffic"

🔊 333 "Half-Finished Book"

A Quick Note on Mastering

The subject of mastering is well beyond the scope of this book and could easily fill one of its own. What is it? It's basically the process of taking a mixed song, or album of mixed songs, and preparing them for the final medium. This includes trivial tasks, such as possibly adding fades, cleaning up the front and back of each song if necessary, and placing the songs in the correct order. But it also includes the process of making the tracks sound like a cohesive unit and other audio sweetening in the form of EQ, compression, limiting, stereo enhancement, and other tools. A mastered song generally has more "punch" than a non-mastered one and will generally be considerably louder as well so that it will sound comparable to other professional tracks when played on the radio.

Mastering engineers normally work in very specialized rooms, with very specialized tools, and have specific experience in the field. It's very common for an artist to have an album professionally mastered even if they mixed it themselves. This can cost anywhere from a few hundred dollars for an album to several thousand or much more (for world-class engineers), but a ballpark figure would be somewhere around $100 or $200 per song. It's an art unto itself.

Having said that, all mastering engineers had to start somewhere, so there's no reason that you shouldn't mess around with it as practice if you care to. There are numerous "mastering suite" plugins available that feature common tools of the trade, including multi-band compressors, EQs, and limiters, so those would be a good place to start. There are many online tutorials on the subject as well which can help get your feet wet. Again, though, regardless of the fact that many people discuss mastering as if it's part of the dark arts curriculum at Hogwarts, it's not against the law to try your hand at it! It is possible to do more harm than good, so if you're serious about your music sounding as professional as possible, you'll probably want to have a pro handle it (if you can afford it) until you begin to get a good feel for it.

If you're on a shoestring budget, however, and you're dead set on doing it all yourself, my recommendation would be to read everything you can on the subject and start with small, subtle moves. In other words, ease into it by keeping your gain reduction on the multi-band compressors and limiters very low at first (for example), and keep the EQ adjustments slight as well. Once you begin to hear what they're doing, you can start to push things a bit more, always comparing it with the bypassed version to see if you're on the right track.

FINAL THOUGHTS

We've covered a lot of ground, and there's still plenty more ahead if you choose to explore it. Recording is a life-long hobby for many, and you never stop learning or improving. Everyone has a different approach to it—just as with playing instruments—and therefore the sonic possibilities are just about endless. Now that you have an idea of what's involved in the process, apply your newfound listening skills any time you can to expand your knowledge. Dissect your favorite recordings to see if you can identify types of reverb, guitars, and effects. How is space used? Does the mix change or remain the same throughout the song? Do some instruments sound nearer or farther than others?

This is a big book, so in closing, I'd just like to reiterate a few things that are paramount, in my opinion, and I don't want them falling by the wayside.

Experiment: There is no greater teacher than hands-on experimentation. Start with a preset on an effect and then tweak one parameter to see what it does. Put that one back where it was and then tweak another, etc. This is one of the best ways to learn how things work. And speaking of learning how things work…

Read the manual(!): Did I already say this? I just can't stress it enough. This applies to your DAW program, plugins, etc. I don't know how many times I've learned something *really* helpful after cracking the manual while looking for something completely unrelated. You can significantly increase your workflow by assigning command keys, shortcuts, and macros, but you most likely won't learn how to do these things if you don't read the manual.

Listen, listen, listen: And when I say listen, I mean listen *with your ears*—not your eyes. Ever since digital recording overtook analog, people have become more and more accustomed to "watching" music instead of listening to it. Many people will sit there for hours nudging and dragging every single note of every single instrument until it's all perfectly aligned without even once actually *listening* to the dang thing! As far as I'm concerned, I don't care what it looks like as long as it sounds good. For this reason, I made a computer monitor cover (actually from the box the monitor came in) that I'll slip over the screen when listening at times so I'm not tempted to look at the music. It really helps me focus on the most important thing: the sound.

There are no rules—only conventions: A lot of people like to tell you that you can't or shouldn't do certain things. Others will say that their method is superior for one reason or another. The simple fact is that there are no rules when it comes to music or recording. *Any* method you use for recording music is a viable one if it accomplishes what you want. Again, there are certainly conventions, as there are with any practice, but seriously: if it sounds good to you to pan the entire drumset hard left, then by all means do it! The Pan Police aren't going to bust down your door and haul you off. Remember that many concepts or techniques we take for granted as acceptable nowadays were once the crazy idiosyncrasies of rule-breakers and innovators. Among the list of such things are close-miking, guitar distortion, the cassette "Portastudio," and even multi-track recording itself.

It's been a joy to share this information with you, and I sincerely hope you've found it useful and inspiring. I'd love to hear any comments or questions you may have, and you can feel free to contact me at chadjohnsonguitar@hotmail.com. I wish you the best of luck in your recording adventures, and remember to experiment and have fun!

– Chad Johnson, 2015

APPENDIX

Welcome to the Appendix; stay a while! Here you'll find some fun, money-saving projects should you be so inclined to take them on. There's also an extensive Recording Index that details all the equipment used on every track in this book. Enjoy!

THE DIY CORNER

In the spirit of recording on a budget, I felt obligated to share some DIY ideas that can help you stretch your dollars and increase the quality of recordings at the same time. Some of these are weekend projects, while others may take a bit more time. None of them are terribly difficult, although they may require a few requisite skills—or at least a bit of practice obtaining those skills—before you can complete them.

1. Absorptive Sound Panels

These panels are the ones that you can hang in your control room at the reflective points (see Chapter 2 for details). The first one may take an hour or two, but once you get the hang of it, you can knock these out assembly-line-style in no time.

Materials Needed (for one panel):
- 2x4x8 boards (2)
- L brackets (8) and wood screws
- Burlap fabric – at least 2 ½ x 4 ½ feet
- Miscellaneous fabric (for back side) – at least 2 ½ x 4 ½ feet
- 2x4 sheet of mineral wool*
- Staple gun with staples (I use a $30 gun with 3/8-inch staples)
- Electric drill

*Mineral wool is usually available in sheets of 2x4 feet and in thicknesses of one, two, or four inches. For bass traps, I'd recommend a minimum of four inches. For all other reflective points, I'd recommend two inches.

1. Cut one 2x4 at the middle to create two pieces approximately four feet long (they will be slightly shorter than this because of the thickness of your saw blade).

2. Cut the other 2x4 into four equal lengths of approximately two feet each (again, they'll be slightly shorter than this).

3. Assemble a frame with two four-foot pieces and two two-foot pieces using the L brackets and screws (see illustration).

4. Cover the back side of the panel with your miscellaneous fabric by stapling it around the edges (I use old bed sheets a lot of times). Trim as necessary so there is no overlap hanging over the edges.

5. Stuff the mineral wool inside the frame. Cut the excess off and save it for later use.

6. Cover the front top and sides with the burlap, wrapping it around and stapling it to the back side.

Note: If you're making a two-inch panel, you can rip the 2x4x8 boards down their length to create 2x2x8 boards (approximately) for the frame and make twice as many.

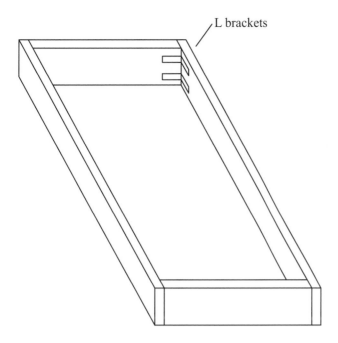

L brackets

These panels may not look fancy, but they're cheap, easy to make, and work well.

Alternative Method:

To make them a bit more attractive, do this:

1. After you build the frame, stain it with a stain of your choice.

2. Cover the back with fabric and then stuff the mineral wool inside.

3. Cover the front only with burlap, just as you did the back (with no material overlapping the edges of the frame).

4. Then rip some 1x4x8 boards down the middle to create some 1x2x8 boards. Stain these boards with the same stain used for the frame.

5. These 1x2 boards can then be attached to the front via screws (use a counter-sink bit) to form a border.

With just a little more effort, you can make the panels much more attractive by adding a front border and staining the wood.

2. Gobos

This is the quickest and easiest way I know to make gobos that work well and are easy to set up and tear down.

Materials needed (for one gobo):

See materials list for Absorptive Sound Panels and add:

- 2x6x8 board

1. Make a burlap covered panel, as shown in project #1.

2. Use the 2x6 boards and some long wood screws to create two feet to stand up gobo (see illustration).

3. If you desire a live side and dead side, you can add a thin reflective surface to one side of the panel, such as pegboard, etc. (If you do this, make sure to account for any extra thickness when building the feet from the 2x6 boards.)

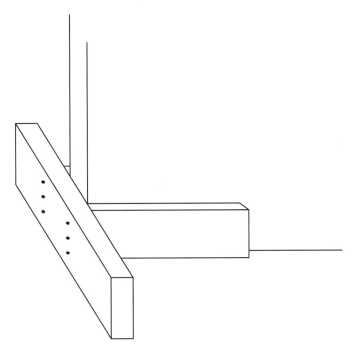

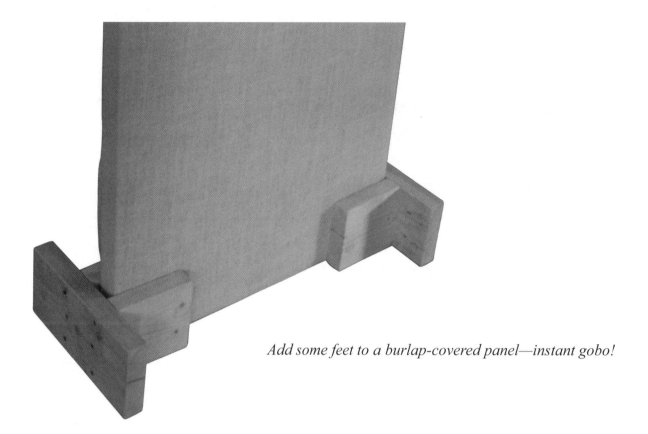

Add some feet to a burlap-covered panel—instant gobo!

3. Vocal Booth

There are several online articles regarding DIY vocal booths. Some are all-out rooms that are fixed installations, while others are nothing more than a few pieces of foam surrounding a microphone. This project is an idea I came up with after looking through various websites and deciding what I thought was a good compromise between cost and performance.

Materials needed (for one vocal booth):
- 2x4x8 boards (2)
- 1x4x8 boards (2)
- L brackets (12) and wood screws
- Medium-sized hinges (4-6)
- Burlap fabric – at least 2½ x 6½ feet
- Miscellaneous fabric (for back sides) – at least 2½ x 6½ feet (or 3 sheets that are at least 2½ x 2 feet)
- 2x4 sheets of two-inch-thick mineral wool
- Old pillowcases (2)
- Staple gun and staples
- Electric drill

1. Rip the two 2x4x8 boards down their length to create four 2x2x8 boards.

2. Using project #1 as a guide, build three square sound panels—using the stained wood and front border approach—that measure approximately 2x2 feet (in other words, just use one ripped 2x2x8 board to make one frame) and stuff them with the two-inch-thick mineral wool, cutting off the excess and saving it for later projects. You can use the 1x4x8 boards to make the front borders.

3. Attach panel A to panel B with two hinges on the front side (or three, if necessary) so that they will fold (almost face to face). Then attach panel C to panel B (the other side) the other way (see photo).

4. Add small hooks onto each end of their top boards.

5. Using 6 larger hooks that are screwed into the ceiling at the appropriate spots and a $10 chain (for hanging plants, etc.) with links that can be pried open and re-closed with pliers, you can simply "hang" the three sided booth from the ceiling.

Attach the two outer panels to the middle so that they fold in face-to-face.

For bonus points, place the booth beneath a panel mounted to the ceiling! (This applies to the stand-mounted booth, as well.)

With just a little careful measurement, some chain, and some screw-in hooks, you can easily hang an effective vocal booth anywhere.

4. Make Your Own Professional-Grade Mic Preamp

Mic preamps can get quite pricey when you start looking at the top-end ones, with numbers soaring into the thousands. But, if you're handy with a soldering iron and have a decent bit of experience with electronics, you can build your own fully professional-grade preamp for a fraction of the price. Numerous companies sell mic preamp kits that are based on classic designs. One such company is Seventh Circle Audio, which offers kits based on Neve, Jensen, and API preamps, among others.

For many of the recordings in this book, I made use of Seventh Circle Audio's N72 preamp, which is based on a Neve design. When purchasing a kit from SCA, you'll need to purchase a few things; at the very least, this includes the preamp module, a chassis, and a power supply. If you plan on making several of their preamp kits, then you'd likely want to purchase the CH02 chassis, which is a two-space design with space for eight preamp modules (of any combination) and includes a power supply.

If you want the most cost-effective way to purchase a single preamp module, however, the company offers its "OneShot Chassis," which includes a power supply and houses one preamp module. Although it's designed primarily for desktop use, it's also rackmoutable as a 1/4-space unit should you choose to do so. This is the configuration I used for this book, and I couldn't be happier with the quality. It's solid as a tank, extremely attractive, and, best of all, it sounds amazing.

The total price for the N72 module and OneShot Chassis comes out to be around $470, including shipping. (Depending on your location, shipping charges may vary.) When you consider the quality of sound you're getting—one channel of a purely professional-level preamp—that's more than a bargain! (By comparison, the cheapest Neve single-channel preamp available on the market today runs over $1,000.)

Disclaimer: Please Read!

These kits aren't paint-by-numbers! You'll need a good bit of soldering experience, a rudimentary understanding of electric components (such as resistors, capacitors, transformers, etc.), and the ability to basically read a schematic and parts layout. This should definitely not be your first electronics project! If you're interested in this and are new to electronics, you should definitely practice developing your soldering skills on something that involves a PCB (printed circtuit board)—such as a guitar effects pedal—and read up on some basic electronics concepts before taking it on. You should also know how to take measurements with a digital multimeter.

Having said that, it's certainly a doable project for those with the know-how and desire, and the folks at SCA have done everything in their power to make the process go as smoothly as possible. The kits include clear, detailed instructions with lots of close-up photos that guide you through the process step-by-step. There's also an active forum community on the website to help if you should have any issues, or you can email them directly to receive trouble-shooting help.

The kits are available at www.seventhcircleaudio.com.

Materials needed:

- Soldering iron (20- or 30-watt model) with fine tip
- Sponge (for cleaning soldering tip)
- Rosin-core (or "no clean") solder – .025-inch diameter works best
- Digital multimeter
- Needle-nose pliers
- Wire cutters
- Wire stripper
- Phillips screwdriver (#1)
- Precision (or jeweler's) straight-blade screwdriver
- Magnifying glass

Recommended (but not essential):

- Lead bender (for bending component leads)
- T-handle wrench
- 4-40 machine screw plug tap
- Molex crimp tool
- 1/4-inch and 5/16-inch nut drivers
- Oscilloscope
- Signal generator

Seventh Circle Audio OneShot Chassis

Seventh Circle Audio N72 preamp module fully assembled

RECORDING INDEX

In this section, you'll see exactly what gear was used on every track in this book. To avoid redundancy, there are a few items that we'll mention up front:

- Aside from Tracks 1–12, which were recorded onto the Tascam DP-24, every other track in the book was recorded into Reaper using the Steinberg UR22 interface.

- See the About the Audio section (page 9) for information on strings, picks, guitar cables, and mic cables. For any other patch cord needed (connecting an external preamp to the interface, for example), I used Hosa cables.

- Beginning with Track 18, all close-miked guitar amp tracks were recorded with the CAD Acousti-Shield AS16.

Track	Signal Chain
1	Breedlove Pursuit ➔ Sterling Audio ST31 ➔ dbx 286s
2	Agile AL-2000 ➔ Digitech Element XP
3	See Tracks 1 and 2
4	Korg Volca Keys ➔ direct
5	Höfner Ignition ➔ Gallien-Krueger MB112-II ➔ direct
6	See Track 1
7	See Tracks 1–5
8	See Tracks 1–5
9	See Tracks 1–5
10	See Tracks 1–5
11	See Tracks 1–5
12	See Tracks 1– 5
13	Peavey SC-2 ➔ VOX AC4C1 ➔ Shure SM57
14	Agile AL-2000 ➔ VOX AC4C1 ➔ Shure SM57

15	ESP LDT ST-203 → VOX AC4C1 → Shure SM57
16	Danelectro 59M NOS → VOX AC4C1 → Shure SM57
17	Peavey SC-2 → VOX AC4C1 → Shure SM57
18	Peavey SC-2 → VOX AC4C1 → Shure SM57 (with CAD Acousti-Shield AS16)
19	Agile AL-2000 → VOX AC4C1 → Shure SM7B
20	ESP LDT ST-203 → VOX AC4C1 → CAD D82
21	ESP LDT ST-203 → Orange Micro Terror → CAD D82
22	ESP LDT ST-203 → Orange Micro Terror → CAD D82
23	Agile AL-2000 → Hotone Komp → Orange Micro Terror → Sterling Audio ST55 → dbx 286s
24	Agile AL-2000 → Hotone Komp → Orange Micro Terror → Sterling Audio ST55 → dbx 286s
25	Danelectro 59M NOS → Hotone Komp → Orange Micro Terror → Sterling Audio ST55 (through dbx 286s) and Shure SM57
26	Danelectro 59M NOS → Hotone Komp → Orange Micro Terror → Sterling Audio ST55 (through dbx 286s) and Shure SM57
27	Peavey SC-2 → MXR Custom Badass '78 → VHT Special 6 → CAD D82 → dbx 386
28	Agile AL-2000 → MXR Dyna Comp → VHT Special 6 → CAD D82 → dbx 386
29	ESP LDT ST-203 → Hotone Komp → VHT Special 6 → CAD D82 → dbx 386
30	ESP LDT ST-203 → MXR Phase 90 → VHT Special 6 → dbx 386
31	Peavey SC-2 → MXR Blue Box → VHT Special 6 → CAD D82 → dbx 386
32	Danelectro 59M NOS → Morley Classic Wah → VHT Special 6 → CAD D82 → dbx 286s
33	Peavey SC-2 → MXR Dyna Comp → Morley Mini Volume → VHT Special 6 → CAD D82 → dbx 286s
34	Danelectro 59M NOS → Digitech Element XP → VHT Special 6 → CAD D82 → dbx 286s
35	Peavey SC-2 → Digitech RP360XP → VHT Special 6 → CAD D82 → dbx 286s
36	ESP LDT ST-203 → Digitech Element XP
37	ESP LDT ST-203 → Digitech Element XP
38	Danelectro 59M NOS → Digitech Element XP
39	Danelectro 59M NOS → Digitech Element XP
40	Agile AL-2000 → Digitech RP360XP
41	Agile AL-2000 → Digitech RP360XP
42	ESP LDT ST-203 → Digitech RP360XP
43	Peavey SC-2 → Digitech RP360XP
44	Peavey SC-2 → Digitech RP360XP
45	Agile AL-2000 → IK Multimedia AmpliTube 3
46	Agile AL-2000 → IK Multimedia AmpliTube 3
47	ESP LDT ST-203 → IK Multimedia AmpliTube 3
48	ESP LDT ST-203 → IK Multimedia AmpliTube 3
49	Danelectro 59M NOS → IK Multimedia AmpliTube 3
50	Danelectro 59M NOS → IK Multimedia AmpliTube 3
51	Peavey SC-2 → IK Multimedia AmpliTube 3
52	Peavey SC-2 → IK Multimedia AmpliTube 3

53	Agile AL-2000 → IK Multimedia AmpliTube 3
54	Peavey SC-2 → IK Multimedia AmpliTube 3
55	Alvarez RF26 OM → CAD GXL1200BP → Seventh Circle Audio N72
56	Alvarez RF26 OM → CAD GXL1200BP → Seventh Circle Audio N72
57	Alvarez RF26 OM → CAD GXL1200BP → Seventh Circle Audio N72
58	Alvarez RF26 OM → Sterling Audio ST31 → Seventh Circle Audio N72
59	Alvarez RF26 OM → Sterling Audio ST31 → Seventh Circle Audio N72
60	Alvarez RF26 OM → Sterling Audio ST31 → Seventh Circle Audio N72
61	Alvarez RF26 OM → Shure SM7B → Seventh Circle Audio N72
62	Alvarez RF26 OM → Shure SM7B → Seventh Circle Audio N72
63	Alvarez RF26 OM → CAD GXL3000BP → Seventh Circle Audio N72
64	Alvarez RF26 OM → CAD GXL3000BP → Seventh Circle Audio N72
65	Alvarez RF26 OM → CAD GXL3000BP → Seventh Circle Audio N72
66	Breedlove Pursuit → CAD GXL1200BP → dbx 386
67	Breedlove Pursuit → Sterling Audio ST31 → dbx 386
68	Breedlove Pursuit → CAD GXL3000BP → dbx 386
69	Breedlove Pursuit → Sterling Audio ST55 → dbx 386
70	Breedlove Pursuit → Shure SM7B → dbx 386
71	Breedlove Pursuit → Shure SM7B → dbx 386
72	Ibanez PF1512 → CAD GXL1200BP → Seventh Circle Audio N72
73	Ibanez PF1512 → Sterling Audio ST31 → Seventh Circle Audio N72
74	Ibanez PF1512 → CAD GXL3000BP → Seventh Circle Audio N72
75	Ibanez PF1512 → Sterling Audio ST55 → Seventh Circle Audio N72
76	Ibanez PF1512 → Shure SM7B → Seventh Circle Audio N72
77	Ibanez PF1512 → Shure SM7B → Seventh Circle Audio N72
78	Breedlove Pursuit → Sterling Audio ST55 (through Seventh Circle Audio N72) and Sterling Audio ST31 (through dbx 386)
79	Breedlove Pursuit → CAD GXL3000BP (through Seventh Circle Audio N72) and CAD GXL1200BP (through dbx 386)
80	Alvarez RF26 OM → Sterling Audio ST55 (through Seventh Circle Audio N72) and Sterling Audio ST31 (through dbx 286s)
81	Alvarez RF26 OM → CAD GXL3000BP (through Seventh Circle Audio N72) and CAD GXL1200BP (through dbx 286s)
82	Ibanez PF1512 → Sterling Audio ST55 (through Seventh Circle Audio N72) and Sterling Audio ST31 (through dbx 286s)
83	Ibanez PF1512 → CAD GXL3000BP (through Seventh Circle Audio N72) and CAD GXL1200BP (through dbx 286s)
84	Breedlove Pursuit → Sterling Audio ST55 (through Seventh Circle Audio N72) and Sterling Audio ST31 (through dbx 386)
85	Breedlove Pursuit → direct → Waves CLA-3A → Waves TrueVerb → IK Multimedia T-RackS Equalizer
86	Breedlove Pursuit → direct → Waves CLA-3A → Waves TrueVerb → IK Multimedia T-RackS Equalizer
87	Breedlove Pursuit → direct and Sterling Audio ST31 (through dbx 286s) → Waves TrueVerb → IK Multimedia T-RackS Equalizer

88	Breedlove Pursuit → direct and Sterling Audio ST55 (through dbx 286s) → Waves TrueVerb → IK Multimedia T-RackS Equalizer
89	Breedlove Pursuit → direct and CAD GXL1200BP (through dbx 286s) → Waves TrueVerb → IK Multimedia T-RackS Equalizer
90	Breedlove Pursuit → direct and CAD GXL3000BP (through dbx 286s) → Waves TrueVerb → IK Multimedia T-RackS Equalizer
91	SX Ursa 1 → direct → IK Multimedia T-RackS Classic Compressor (3dB GR)
92	Sterling by Music Man S.U.B. Ray4 → direct → IK Multimedia T-RackS Classic Compressor (3dB GR)
93	Höfner Ignition → direct → IK Multimedia T-RackS Classic Compressor (3dB GR)
94	SX Ursa 1 → Gallien-Krueger MB112-II → direct out → IK Multimedia T-RackS Classic Compressor (3dB GR)
95	Sterling by Music Man S.U.B. Ray4 → Gallien-Krueger MB112-II → direct out → IK Multimedia T-RackS Classic Compressor (3dB GR)
96	Höfner Ignition (w/ pick) → Gallien-Krueger MB112-II → direct out → IK Multimedia T-RackS Classic Compressor (3dB GR)
97	SX Ursa 1 → Kustom KXB100 → direct out → IK Multimedia T-RackS Classic Compressor (3dB GR)
98	Sterling by Music Man S.U.B. Ray4 → Kustom KXB100 → direct out → IK Multimedia T-RackS Classic Compressor (3dB GR)
99	Höfner Ignition → Kustom KXB100 → direct out → IK Multimedia T-RackS Classic Compressor (3dB GR)
100	SX Ursa 1 → Ampeg Micro-CL → direct out → IK Multimedia T-RackS Classic Compressor (3dB GR)
101	Sterling by Music Man S.U.B. Ray4 (w/ pick) → Ampeg Micro-CL → direct out → IK Multimedia T-RackS Classic Compressor (3dB GR)
102	Höfner Ignition (w/ pick) → Ampeg Micro-CL → direct out → IK Multimedia T-RackS Classic Compressor (3dB GR)
103	SX Ursa 1 → IK Multimedia AmpliTube 3 → IK Multimedia T-RackS Classic Compressor (3dB GR)
104	Sterling by Music Man S.U.B. Ray4 → IK Multimedia AmpliTube 3 → IK Multimedia T-RackS Classic Compressor (3dB GR)
105	Höfner Ignition → IK Multimedia AmpliTube 3 → IK Multimedia T-RackS Classic Compressor (3dB GR)
106	SX Ursa 1 → IK Multimedia AmpliTube 3 → IK Multimedia T-RackS Classic Compressor (3dB GR)
107	Sterling by Music Man S.U.B. Ray4 → IK Multimedia AmpliTube 3 → IK Multimedia T-RackS Classic Compressor (3dB GR)
108	Höfner Ignition → IK Multimedia AmpliTube 3 → IK Multimedia T-RackS Classic Compressor (3dB GR)
109	SX Ursa 1 → IK Multimedia AmpliTube 3 → IK Multimedia T-RackS Classic Compressor (3dB GR)
110	Sterling by Music Man S.U.B. Ray4 → IK Multimedia AmpliTube 3 → IK Multimedia T-RackS Classic Compressor (3dB GR)
111	Höfner Ignition (w/ pick & palm mute) → IK Multimedia AmpliTube 3 → IK Multimedia T-RackS Classic Compressor (3dB GR)
112	SX Ursa 1 → Gallien-Krueger MB112-II → Shure SM7B → dbx 386

113	SX Ursa 1 → Kustom KXB100 → Shure SM7B → dbx 386
114	SX Ursa 1 → Ampeg Micro-CL → Shure SM7B → dbx 386
115	SX Ursa 1 → Gallien-Krueger MB112-II → Shure SM7B → dbx 386
116	SX Ursa 1 → Kustom KXB100 → Shure SM7B → dbx 386
117	SX Ursa 1 → Ampeg Micro-CL → Shure SM7B → dbx 386
118	Sterling by Music Man S.U.B. Ray4 → Gallien-Krueger MB112-II → MXL 9000 → Seventh Circle Audio N72
119	Sterling by Music Man S.U.B. Ray4 → Kustom KXB100 → MXL 9000 → Seventh Circle Audio N72
120	Sterling by Music Man S.U.B. Ray4 → Ampeg Micro-CL → MXL 9000 → Seventh Circle Audio N72
121	Sterling by Music Man S.U.B. Ray4 → Gallien-Krueger MB112-II → Sterling Audio ST55 → Seventh Circle Audio N72
122	Sterling by Music Man S.U.B. Ray4 → Kustom KXB100 → Sterling Audio ST55 → Seventh Circle Audio N72
123	Sterling by Music Man S.U.B. Ray4 → Ampeg Micro-CL → Sterling Audio ST55 → Seventh Circle Audio N72
124	Höfner Ignition → Gallien-Krueger MB112-II → CAD D82 → Seventh Circle Audio N72
125	Höfner Ignition → Kustom KXB100 → CAD D82 → Seventh Circle Audio N72
126	Höfner Ignition → Ampeg Micro-CL → CAD D82 → Seventh Circle Audio N72
127	Höfner Ignition → Radial StageBug DI direct and Gallien-Krueger MB112-II → Shure SM7B → Seventh Circle Audio N72
128	Höfner Ignition → Radial StageBug DI direct and Kustom KXB100 → Shure SM7B → Seventh Circle Audio N72
129	Höfner Ignition → Radial StageBug DI direct and Ampeg Micro-CL → Shure SM7B → Seventh Circle Audio N72
130	Sterling by Music Man S.U.B. Ray4 → Radial StageBug DI direct and Gallien-Krueger MB112-II → Shure SM7B → Seventh Circle Audio N72
131	Sterling by Music Man S.U.B. Ray4 → Radial StageBug DI direct and Kustom KXB100 → Shure SM7B → Seventh Circle Audio N72
132	Sterling by Music Man S.U.B. Ray4 → Radial StageBug DI direct and Ampeg Micro-CL → Shure SM7B → Seventh Circle Audio N72
133	MIDI controller → AAS Lounge Lizard Session
134	MIDI controller → AAS Lounge Lizard Session
135	MIDI controller → AAS Lounge Lizard Session
136	MIDI controller → AAS Lounge Lizard Session
137	MIDI controller → AAS Lounge Lizard Session
138	MIDI controller → AAS Lounge Lizard Session
139	MIDI controller → AAS Ultra Analog Session
140	MIDI controller → AAS Ultra Analog Session
141	MIDI controller → AAS Ultra Analog Session
142	MIDI controller → AAS Ultra Analog Session
143	MIDI controller → Garritan Personal Orchestra 4
144	MIDI controller → Garritan Personal Orchestra 4
145	MIDI controller → Garritan Personal Orchestra 4

146	MIDI controller ➔ Garritan World Instruments
147	MIDI controller ➔ Garritan World Instruments
148	MIDI controller ➔ Garritan World Instruments
149	MIDI controller ➔ Garritan Jazz & Big Band 3
150	MIDI controller ➔ Garritan Jazz & Big Band 3
151	MIDI controller ➔ Garritan Jazz & Big Band 3
152	MIDI controller ➔ Garritan Jazz & Big Band 3
153	MIDI controller ➔ Garritan Jazz & Big Band 3
154	Pre-made drum loop (no recording)
155	Pre-made drum loop (no recording)
156	ESP LDT ST-203 ➔ MXR Dyna Comp ➔ IK Multimedia AmpliTube 3 SX Ursa 1 ➔ IK Multimedia AmpliTube 3 Toontrack EZdrummer 2
157	ESP LDT ST-203 ➔ MXR Dyna Comp ➔ IK Multimedia AmpliTube 3 SX Ursa 1 ➔ IK Multimedia AmpliTube 3 Toontrack EZdrummer 2
158	KAT Multipad ➔ Toontrack EZdrummer 2
159	KAT Multipad ➔ Toontrack EZdrummer 2
160	KAT Multipad ➔ Toontrack EZdrummer 2
161	KAT Multipad ➔ Toontrack EZdrummer 2
162	KAT Multipad ➔ Toontrack EZdrummer 2
163	KAT Multipad ➔ Toontrack EZdrummer 2
164	KAT Multipad ➔ Toontrack EZdrummer 2
165	KAT Multipad ➔ Toontrack EZdrummer 2
166	KAT Multipad ➔ Toontrack EZdrummer 2
167	KAT Multipad ➔ Toontrack EZdrummer 2
168	CAD GXL3000BP ➔ Seventh Circle Audio N72
169	CAD GXL3000BP ➔ Seventh Circle Audio N72
170	CAD GXL3000BP ➔ Seventh Circle Audio N72
171	CAD GXL3000BP ➔ Seventh Circle Audio N72
172	Sterling Audio ST55 ➔ Seventh Circle Audio N72
173	Sterling Audio ST55 ➔ Seventh Circle Audio N72
174	Sterling Audio ST55 ➔ Seventh Circle Audio N72
175	MXL CR89 ➔ Seventh Circle Audio N72
176	MXL CR89 ➔ Seventh Circle Audio N72
177	CAD GXL3000BP ➔ Seventh Circle Audio N72
178	CAD GXL3000BP ➔ Seventh Circle Audio N72
179	Sterling Audio ST55 ➔ Seventh Circle Audio N72
180	Sterling Audio ST55 ➔ Seventh Circle Audio N72
181	MXL CR89 ➔ Seventh Circle Audio N72
182	MXL CR89 ➔ Seventh Circle Audio N72
183	CAD GXL3000BP ➔ Seventh Circle Audio N72
184	CAD GXL3000BP ➔ Seventh Circle Audio N72
185	Sterling Audio ST55 ➔ Seventh Circle Audio N72
186	Sterling Audio ST55 ➔ Seventh Circle Audio N72

187	MXL CR89 → Seventh Circle Audio N72
188	MXL CR89 → Seventh Circle Audio N72
189	MXL 9000 → dbx 386
190	MXL 9000 → dbx 386
191	MXL 9000 → dbx 386
192	MXL 9000 → dbx 386
193	MXL Studio 24
194	MXL Studio 24
195	MXL Studio 24
196	MXL Studio 24
197	Shure SM7B → dbx 386
198	Shure SM7B → dbx 386
199	Shure SM7B → dbx 386
200	Shure SM7B → dbx 386
201	Alvarez RF26 OM → Sterling Audio ST31 → Seventh Circle Audio N72 → ReaEQ
202	Alvarez RF26 OM → Sterling Audio ST31 → Seventh Circle Audio N72 → Waves Scheps 73
203	Höfner Ignition → IK Multimedia AmpliTube 3 → ReaEQ
204	Höfner Ignition → IK Multimedia AmpliTube 3 → Waves Scheps 73
205	KAT Multipad → Toontrack EZdrummer 2 → ReaEQ
206	KAT Multipad → Toontrack EZdrummer 2 → Waves Scheps 73
207	Peavey SC-2 → VHT Special 6 → Shure SM7B → dbx 286s → IK Multimedia T-RackS Classic Compressor
208	Peavey SC-2 → MXR Custom Badass '78 → VHT Special 6 → Shure SM7B → dbx 286s → IK Multimedia T-RackS Classic Compressor
209	Peavey SC-2 → MXR Custom Badass '78 → VHT Special 6 → Shure SM7B → dbx 286s → IK Multimedia T-RackS Classic Compressor
210	Sterling by Music Man S.U.B. Ray4 → Kustom KXB100 → Sterling Audio ST55 → Seventh Circle Audio N72 → IK Multimedia T-RackS Classic Compressor
211	Sterling by Music Man S.U.B. Ray4 → Kustom KXB100 → Sterling Audio ST55 → Seventh Circle Audio N72 → IK Multimedia T-RackS Classic Compressor
212	Sterling by Music Man S.U.B. Ray4 → Kustom KXB100 → Sterling Audio ST55 → Seventh Circle Audio N72 → IK Multimedia T-RackS Classic Compressor
213	Sterling by Music Man S.U.B. Ray4 → Kustom KXB100 → Sterling Audio ST55 → Seventh Circle Audio N72 → IK Multimedia T-RackS Classic Compressor
214	Sterling by Music Man S.U.B. Ray4 → Kustom KXB100 → Sterling Audio ST55 → Seventh Circle Audio N72 → ReaComp
215	MXL CR89 → Seventh Circle Audio N72 → Waves CLA-2A
216	MXL CR89 → Seventh Circle Audio N72 → Waves CLA-2A
217	CAD GXL3000BP → Seventh Circle Audio N72 → Waves CLA-2A
218	CAD GXL3000BP → Seventh Circle Audio N72 → Waves CLA-2A
219	MXL CR89 → Seventh Circle Audio N72 → Waves CLA-2A
220	MXL CR89 → Seventh Circle Audio N72 → Waves CLA-2A
221	CAD GXL3000BP → Seventh Circle Audio N72 → Waves CLA-2A
222	CAD GXL3000BP → Seventh Circle Audio N72 → Waves CLA-2A

223	Drum loop → IK Multimedia T-RackS Classic Compressor
224	Drum loop → IK Multimedia T-RackS Classic Compressor
225	Drum loop → IK Multimedia T-RackS Classic Compressor
226	Drum loop → IK Multimedia T-RackS Classic Compressor
227	Toontrack EZdrummer 2 → ReaComp
228	Toontrack EZdrummer 2 → ReaComp
229	Drum loop → IK Multimedia T-RackS Classic Compressor
230	Drum loop → IK Multimedia T-RackS Classic Compressor
231	Drum loop → IK Multimedia T-RackS Classic Compressor
232	Drum loop → IK Multimedia T-RackS Classic Compressor
233	Drum loop → IK Multimedia T-RackS Classic Compressor
234	Drum loop → IK Multimedia T-RackS Classic Compressor
235	Toontrack EZdrummer 2
236	Toontrack EZdrummer 2 → IK Multimedia T-RackS Classic Compressor
237	Breedlove Pursuit → CAD GXL1200BP → dbx 386 → Waves Renaissance Reverb
238	Breedlove Pursuit → CAD GXL1200BP → dbx 386 → Waves Renaissance Reverb
239	Agile AL-2000 → Hotone Komp → Orange Micro Terror → Sterling Audio ST55 → dbx 286s
240	Agile AL-2000 → Hotone Komp → Orange Micro Terror → Sterling Audio ST55 → dbx 286s
241	Toontrack EZdrummer 2 → TC Electronic M350
242	Toontrack EZdrummer 2 → TC Electronic M350
243	Garritan Personal Orchestra 4 → TC Electronic M350
244	Garritan Personal Orchestra 4 → TC Electronic M350
245	Danelectro 59M NOS → IK Multimedia AmpliTube 3
246	Danelectro 59M NOS → IK Multimedia AmpliTube 3
247	Danelectro 59M NOS → Digitech Element XP → IK Mulitmedia T-RackS Classik Plate
248	Danelectro 59M NOS → Digitech Element XP → IK Mulitmedia T-RackS Classik Plate
249	Peavey SC-2 → IK Multimedia AmpliTube 3
250	Peavey SC-2 → IK Multimedia AmpliTube 3
251	Danelectro 59M NOS → Digitech RP360XP → IK Mulitmedia T-RackS Classik Plate
252	Danelectro 59M NOS → Digitech RP360XP → IK Mulitmedia T-RackS Classik Plate
253	MIDI controller → AAS Lounge Lizard Session
254	MIDI controller → AAS Lounge Lizard Session
255	Danelectro 59M NOS → IK Multimedia AmpliTube 3
256	Peavey SC-2 → Digitech RP360XP → IK Mulitmedia T-RackS Classik Plate
257	MIDI controller → Garritan Jazz & Big Band 3
258	MIDI controller → Garritan Jazz & Big Band 3
259	ESP LDT ST-203 → IK Multimedia AmpliTube 3
260	Sterling by Music Man S.U.B. Ray4 → IK Multimedia AmpliTube 3
261	ESP LDT ST-203 → Digitech RP360XP
262	ESP LDT ST-203 → Digitech RP360XP

263	Breedlove Pursuit → CAD GXL1200BP → dbx 386 → IK Mulitmedia T-RackS Classik Plate → IK Multimedia AmpliTube 3 (for chorus only)
264	MIDI controller → AAS Lounge Lizard Session → IK Multimedia AmpliTube 3 (for chorus only)
265	MIDI controller → AAS Ultra Analog Session
266	Peavey SC-2 → IK Multimedia AmpliTube 3
267	Peavey SC-2 → IK Multimedia AmpliTube 3
268	KAT Multipad → Toontrack EZdrummer 2 → Blue Cat's Flanger (freeware)
269	Blue Cat's Flanger
270	Peavey SC-2 → IK Multimedia AmpliTube 3
271	Peavey SC-2 → IK Multimedia AmpliTube 3
272	MIDI controller → AAS Lounge Lizard Session
273	MXL CR89 → Seventh Circle Audio N72 → IK Multimedia T-RackS Equalizer → Waves CLA-3A → MXR Phase 90 → IK Mulitmedia T-RackS Classik Plate
274	Danelectro 59M NOS → Morley Classic Wah → IK Multimedia AmpliTube 3
275	Peavey SC-2 → Morley Classic Wah → IK Multimedia AmpliTube 3
276	ESP LDT ST-203 → Digitech RP360XP
277	MIDI controller → AAS Lounge Lizard Session → IK Multimedia AmpliTube 3 (for envelope filter only)
278	See track 333
279	See track 333
280	See track 330
281	See track 330
282	Agile AL-2000 → MXR Dyna Comp → VOX AC4C1 → Shure SM7B Toontrack EZdrummer 2
283	Agile AL-2000 → MXR Dyna Comp → VOX AC4C1 → Shure SM7B Toontrack EZdrummer 2
284	Agile AL-2000 → Hotone Komp → MXR Custom Badass '78 → Orange Micro Terror → Sterling Audio ST55 → dbx 286s
285	Agile AL-2000 → Hotone Komp → MXR Custom Badass '78 → Orange Micro Terror → Sterling Audio ST55 → dbx 286s
286	MXL CR89 → Seventh Circle Audio N72 → Waves CLA-3A → IK Mulitmedia T-RackS Classik Plate
287	Sterling Audio ST55 → Seventh Circle Audio N72 → dbx163x compressor ($60 used) → IK Mulitmedia T-RackS Classik Plate
288	Sterling Audio ST55 → Seventh Circle Audio N72 → dbx163x compressor → IK Mulitmedia T-RackS Classik Plate
289	Sterling Audio ST55 → Seventh Circle Audio N72 → dbx163x compressor
290	Sterling Audio ST55 → Seventh Circle Audio N72 → dbx163x compressor → Celemony Melodyne
291	MIDI controller → AAS Lounge Lizard Session
292	MIDI controller → AAS Lounge Lizard Session
293	MIDI controller → AAS Lounge Lizard Session
294	MIDI controller → AAS Lounge Lizard Session
295	MIDI controller → Garritan Jazz & Big Band 3

296	ESP LDT ST-203 ➜ Hotone Komp ➜ VHT Special 6 ➜ CAD D82 ➜ dbx 386 Alvarez RF26 OM ➜ Sterling Audio ST55 (through Seventh Circle Audio N72) and Sterling Audio ST31 (through dbx 286s)
297	See Track 333
298	See Track 333
299	See Track 333
300	See Track 333
301	See Track 333
302	See Track 333
303	Garritan Jazz & Big Band 3
304	Garritan Jazz & Big Band 3 ➜ Waves CLA-3A
305	(See Track 333) ➜ Waves CLA-3A
306	(See Track 333) ➜ ReaComp
307	See Track 331
308	See Track 331
309	See Track 333
310	See Track 333
311	See Track 332
312	See Track 332
313	See Track 330
314	See Track 330
315	CAD GXL3000BP ➜ Seventh Circle Audio N72 ➜ IK Mulitmedia T-RackS Classik Plate
316	CAD GXL3000BP ➜ Seventh Circle Audio N72 ➜ IK Mulitmedia T-RackS Classik Plate
317	CAD GXL3000BP ➜ Seventh Circle Audio N72 ➜ IK Mulitmedia T-RackS Classik Plate
318	CAD GXL3000BP ➜ Seventh Circle Audio N72 ➜ IK Multimedia AmpliTube 3 (for delay only)
319	CAD GXL3000BP ➜ Seventh Circle Audio N72 ➜ IK Multimedia AmpliTube 3 (for delay only)
320	CAD GXL3000BP ➜ Seventh Circle Audio N72 ➜ IK Multimedia AmpliTube 3 (for delay only)
321	CAD GXL3000BP ➜ Seventh Circle Audio N72 ➜ IK Multimedia AmpliTube 3 (for delay only)
322	Sterling Audio ST55 ➜ Seventh Circle Audio N72 ➜ IK Mulitmedia T-RackS Classik Plate ➜ Waves Abbey Road Studios Reel ADT
323	ESP LDT ST-203 ➜ Hotone Komp ➜ VHT Special 6 ➜ CAD D82 ➜ dbx 386 ➜ Waves Abbey Road Studios Reel ADT
324	Korg Volca Keys ➜ direct ➜ IK Mulitmedia T-RackS Classik Plate
325	Sterling Audio ST55 ➜ Seventh Circle Audio N72 ➜ Waves TrueVerb ➜ MXR Phase 90
326	Sterling Audio ST55 ➜ Seventh Circle Audio N72 ➜ Waves TrueVerb ➜ Blue Cat's Flanger
327	Toontrack EZdrummer 2 ➜ Waves Abbey Road Studios J37
328	(See Track 331) ➜ Waves Abbey Road Studios J37

329   (See Track 331) → Waves Abbey Road Studios J37

330   "When You're Here"
             Drums: Toontrack EZdrummer 2: kick → Waves CLA-2A, snare → Waves Scheps 73 → Waves CLA-2A
             Bass: SX Ursa 1 → IK Multimedia AmpliTube 3 → Waves CLA-2A → IK Multimedia T-RackS Equalizer
             Acoustic guitar: Breedlove Pursuit → Shure SM7B → Seventh Circle Audio N72 → Waves CLA-3A → IK Multimedia T-RackS Equalizer → IK Multimedia T-RackS Classik Room
             Electric guitar (solo): Agile AL-2000 → Hotone Komp → Orange Micro Terror → Sterling Audio ST55 → dbx 286s → IK Multimedia T-RackS Classic Compressor → Waves Renaissance Reverb
             Electric guitar (clean fills): ESP LDT ST-203 → MXR Phase 90 → VHT Special 6 → Shure SM57 → dbx 386
             Electric guitar (chorus arpeggios): Peavey SC-2 → Hotone Komp → VHT Special 6 → Shure SM7B → dbx 286s → IK Multimedia T-RackS Classic Compressor → IK Mulitmedia T-RackS Classik Plate
             Rhodes: MIDI controller → AAS Lounge Lizard Session → IK Multimedia AmpliTube 3 (for amp modeling character) → ReaEQ → Waves CLA-3A
             Lead vocal: MXL CR89 → Seventh Circle Audio N72 → Waves CLA-2A → ReaEQ → IK Mulitmedia T-RackS Classik Plate
             Harmony vocal: MXL CR89 → Seventh Circle Audio N72 → Waves CLA-2A → ReaEQ → Waves Abbey Road Studios Reel ADT → IK Mulitmedia T-RackS Classik Plate

331   "The Ballad of Fireflies"
             Drums: Toontrack EZdrummer 2: kick → Waves CLA-3A, snare → Waves Scheps 73 → IK Multimedia T-RackS Classic Compressor
             Bass: Höfner Ignition (w/ pick) → Kustom KXB100 → Shure SM7B → dbx 386 → ReaEQ → Waves CLA-2A
             Acoustic guitar: Alvarez RF26 OM → CAD GXL1200BP → dbx 286s → ReaEQ → Waves CLA-3A → IK Multimedia T-RackS Classik Room
             Electric guitar (distorted): Peavey SC-2 → MXR Dyna Comp → VOX AC4C1 → MXL 9000 → dbx 286s → ReaEQ → Waves CLA-2A
             Electric guitar (clean): ESP LDT ST-203 → Hotone Komp → VHT Special 6 → CAD D82 → dbx 386 → ReaEQ → Waves CLA-2A → IK Mulitmedia T-RackS Classik Plate
             Electric guitar (vibrato): Danelectro 59M NOS → IK Multimedia AmpliTube 3
             Electric guitar (left solo): Danelectro 59M NOS → IK Multimedia AmpliTube 3 → Waves CLA-2A → ReaEQ → IK Mulitmedia T-RackS Classik Plate
             Electric guitar (right solo): Danelectro 59M NOS → IK Multimedia AmpliTube 3 → Waves CLA-2A → ReaEQ → IK Mulitmedia T-RackS Classik Plate
             Lead vocal: Sterling Audio ST55 → Seventh Circle Audio N72 → Waves Scheps 73 → ReaEQ → TC Electronic M350
             Harmony vocal: Sterling Audio ST55 → Seventh Circle Audio N72 → Waves Scheps 73 → ReaEQ → TC Electronic M350

332   "Traffic"
             Drums: Toontrack EZdrummer 2: kick → IK Multimedia T-RackS Classic Compressor, snare → Waves Scheps 73 → Waves CLA-76, overheads → Waves CLA-2A

Bass: Sterling by Music Man S.U.B. Ray4 → Ampeg Micro-CL → Waves CLA-2A → ReaEQ

Acoustic guitar: Alvarez RF26 OM → Sterling Audio ST31 → dbx 286s → Waves CLA-2A → ReaEQ → IK Mulitmedia T-RackS Classik Plate

Electric guitar (distorted riff): Danelectro 59M NOS → Hotone Komp → Orange Micro Terror → Sterling Audio ST55 (through dbx 286s) and Shure SM57 → Waves CLA-3A

Electric guitar (fills with echo): Peavey SC-2 → IK Multimedia AmpliTube 3 → ReaEQ

Electric guitar (solo): Agile AL-2000 → MXR Dyna Comp → VHT Special 6 → CAD D82 → dbx 386 → IK Multimedia T-RackS Classic Compressor → IK Mulitmedia T-RackS Classik Plate

Lead vocal: MXL CR89 → Seventh Circle Audio N72 → ReaEQ → Waves CLA-2A → IK Mulitmedia T-RackS Classik Plate

Harmony vocal: MXL CR89 → Seventh Circle Audio N72 → ReaEQ → Waves CLA-2A → IK Mulitmedia T-RackS Classik Plate

Harmony vocals (oohs): MXL 9000 → dbx 286s → IK Multimedia T-RackS Equalizer → Waves CLA-3A → Waves Abbey Road Studios Reel ADT → IK Mulitmedia T-RackS Classik Plate

333   "Half-Finished Book"

Drums: Toontrack EZdrummer 2: kick → Waves CLA-76, snare → Waves Scheps 73 → IK Multimedia T-RackS Classic Compressor

Bass: Sterling by Music Man S.U.B. Ray4 → Radial StageBug DI direct and Ampeg Micro-CL → Shure SM7B → Seventh Circle Audio N72 → Waves CLA-3A → Waves Scheps 73

Acoustic guitar: Breedlove Pursuit → Sterling Audio ST55 → Seventh Circle Audio N72 → ReaEQ → IK Multimedia T-RackS Classic Compressor → IK Mulitmedia T-RackS Classik Plate

12-string acoustic guitar: Ibanez PF1512 → Sterling Audio ST55 → Seventh Circle Audio N72 → ReaEQ → IK Multimedia T-RackS Classic Compressor → IK Mulitmedia T-RackS Classik Plate

Electric guitar (clean power chords): Agile AL-2000 → MXR Dyna Comp → VOX AC4C1 → CAD D82 → dbx 386 → ReaEQ → Waves CLA-3A

Electric guitar (intro with delay): Peavey SC-2 → IK Multimedia AmpliTube 3 → Waves CLA-76

Electric guitar (solos): Peavey SC-2 → MXR Blue Box → VHT Special 6 → CAD D82 → dbx 386 → IK Multimedia T-RackS Equalizer → IK Multimedia T-RackS Classik Room

Electric guitar (distorted tremolo): Agile AL-2000 → IK Multimedia AmpliTube 3

Synth (monophonic): Korg Volca Keys → direct → IK Mulitmedia T-RackS Classik Plate

Synth (intro): MIDI controller → AAS Ultra Analog Session → Waves CLA-2A → TC Electronic M350

Synth (verses): MIDI controller → AAS Ultra Analog Session → Waves CLA-2A → TC Electronic M350

Lead vocal: Shure SM7B → dbx 386 → ReaEQ → Waves CLA-3A → ReaDelay → Waves TrueVerb

Harmony vocal: MXL 9000 → dbx 386 → ReaEQ → Waves TrueVerb

How To...

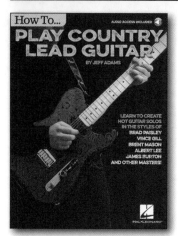

HOW TO PLAY COUNTRY LEAD GUITAR
INCLUDES TAB

by Jeff Adams

Here is a comprehensive stylistic breakdown of country guitar techniques from the past 50 years. Drawing inspiration from the timelessly innovative licks of Merle Travis, Chet Atkins, Albert Lee, Vince Gill, Brent Mason and Brad Paisley, the near 90 musical examples within these pages will hone your left and right hands with technical string-bending and rolling licks while sharpening your knowledge of the thought process behind creating your own licks, and why and when to play them.

00131103 Book/Online Audio $19.99

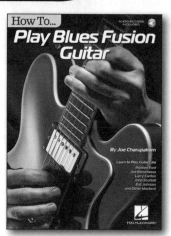

HOW TO PLAY BLUES-FUSION GUITAR
INCLUDES TAB

by Joe Charupakorn

Learn to play guitar like Robben Ford, Joe Bonamassa, Larry Carlton, John Scofield, Eric Johnson, and other blues/fusion masters! In *How to Play Blues/Fusion Guitar*, you'll study the key elements of style – what scales, chords, and arpeggios are most commonly used, and how to use them. Book includes access to audio online for download or streaming, with loads of demonstration tracks, plus play-along tracks for practicing!

00137813 Book/Online Audio $19.99

HOW TO READ MUSIC
by Mark Phillips

In learning to read music, we encounter basic symbols for pitch, duration, and timing. As we advance, we learn about dynamics, expression, timbre, and even special effects. *How to Read Music* will introduce you to the basics, then provide more advanced information. As a final reward for all your hard work, you'll get a chance to play excerpts from three classic piano pieces. Topics include: pitch • rhythm • meter • special words and symbols • plus classical piano pieces by Bach, Mozart, and Beethoven.

00137870 Book $9.99

HOW TO WRITE YOUR FIRST SONG
by Dave Walker

The hardest song you will ever write is your first. This book is designed to help you accomplish that goal. We're not going to jot down just any song, but one that you are proud of, one that gives you the confidence and the process required to write your second song, your third song, and on and on. Here you will find the basic musical knowledge you need and a process for putting that knowledge to work. Let's get started. Let's make *you* into a songwriter!

00138010 Book/Online Audio $16.99

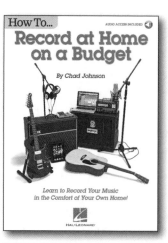

HOW TO RECORD AT HOME ON A BUDGET
by Chad Johnson

Whether it's simply a laptop with a camera microphone or a decked-out studio with tens of thousands of dollars in equipment, more people are recording their music at home now than at any other time in history. In *How to Record at Home on a Budget*, we'll look closely at all aspects involved in getting quality recordings from your modest home studio rig. The technological revolution has made high-grade production from home more attainable than ever, but the instruments won't record themselves. If you're willing to put in a bit of effort to learn the tools of the trade, great sounds await!

00131211 Book/Online Audio $19.99

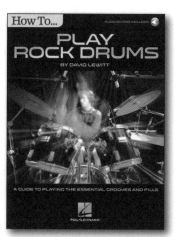

HOW TO PLAY ROCK DRUMS
by David Lewitt

In rock music, the drums steer the ship. In *How to Play Rock Drums*, you'll learn all the necessary skills and tools needed to fill this important role. Whether it's classic four-on-the-floor beats, funky rock, 12/8 beats, or just about anything else you're likely to encounter behind the kit when playing rock, this book has you covered. Designed for the beginner-to-intermediate player, this nuts-and-bolts method provides essential beats in numerous subgenres along with plenty of great ideas for fills – over 340 examples in all! With the included online audio access, you can hear every beat and fill demonstrated so you'll know exactly how they should sound.

00138541 Book/Online Audio $16.99

HAL•LEONARD®
CORPORATION

7777 W. BLUEMOUND RD. P.O. BOX 13819 MILWAUKEE, WI 53213

www.halleonard.com

The Entire Recording Process *Explained!*

The Hal Leonard Recording Method by Bill Gibson is the first professional multimedia recording method to take readers from the beginning of the signal path to the final master mix.

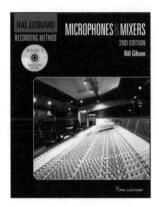

BOOK 1: MICROPHONES & MIXERS – 2ND EDITION
Revised and Updated

Topics include how professional microphones work, which to choose and why (plus accepted techniques for using them), understanding the signal path from mics to mixers and how to operate these critical tools to capture excellent recordings, and explanations of the most up-to-date tools and techniques involved in using dynamics and effects processors.

HL00333253   978-1-4584-0296-7
Book/DVD-ROM/Online Media.........$39.99

BOOK 2: INSTRUMENT & VOCAL RECORDING – 2ND EDITION
Revised and Updated

This edition addresses new equipment and software concerns that affect the way excellent recordings are made. You'll learn what you need to know about capturing the best vocal and instrument tracks possible, no matter what kind of studio you are working in or what kind of equipment is used.

HL00333250   978-1-4584-0292-9
Book/DVD-ROM/Online Media.........$39.99

BOOK 3: RECORDING SOFTWARE & PLUG-INS – 2ND EDITION
Revised and Updated

You'll need to know next how recording software programs work and how to choose and optimize your recording system. This book, DVD-ROM, and online media use detailed illustrations and screen shots, plus audio and video examples, to give you a comprehensive understanding of recording software and plug-ins.

HL00333437   978-1-4584-1651-3
Book/DVD-ROM/Online Media........$39.99

BOOK 4: SEQUENCING SAMPLES & LOOPS

Learn to create amazing music productions using the latest sequencing techniques with samples and pre-recorded loops. With detailed screen shots, illustrations, video and audio examples, and more on the accompanying DVD, you're on your way to rounding out your recording education.

HL00331776   978-1-4234-3051-3
Book/DVD $39.95

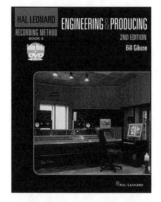

BOOK 5: ENGINEERING AND PRODUCING – 2ND EDITION
Revised and Updated

Learn how to engineer and produce like a pro, recording excellent tracks ready for the mix. This updated edition addresses newer concerns such as social media and making money in today's business climate.

HL00333700   978-1-4584-3692-4
Book/DVD-ROM/Online Media..... $39.99

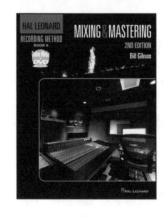

BOOK 6: MIXING & MASTERING – 2ND EDITION
Revised and Updated

This important second edition demonstrates techniques and procedures that result in a polished mix and powerful master recording, using current plug-ins, software, and hardware. You'll then learn how to prepare the mastered recording for CD replication, streaming, or download. Updated illustrations, photographs, and audio and video examples from the online media will reinforce your understanding of what you need to mix and master like the pros.

HL00333254   978-1-4584-0297-4
Book/DVD-ROM/Online Media..... $39.99

www.halleonardbooks.com